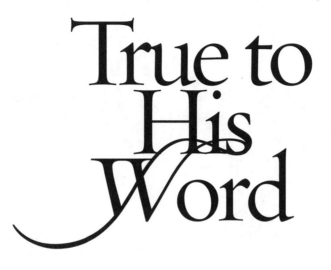

True to His Word

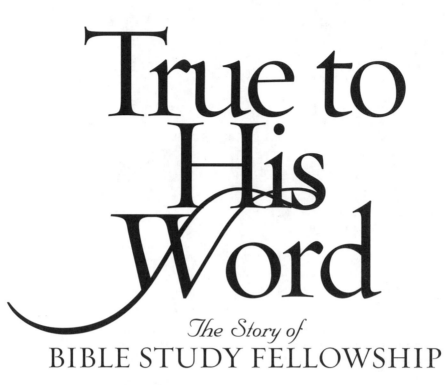

# True to His Word

*The Story of*

## BIBLE STUDY FELLOWSHIP

Gregg and Deborah Shaw Lewis

Biblica Publishing
We welcome your questions and comments.

USA     1820 Jet Stream Drive, Colorado Springs, CO 80921
www.authenticbooks.com

India    Logos Bhavan, Medchal Road, Jeedimetla Village, Secunderabad
500 055, A.P.


True to His Word
ISBN-13: 978-1-60657-089-0

12 11 10 / 6 5 4 3 2 1

Published in 2010 by Biblica Publishing

A catalog record for this book is available through the Library of Congress.

Printed in the United States of America

Some quotations in this book have been edited for brevity or clarity without using ellipses or brackets. The speaker's intent was retained as nearly as possible.

All photos courtesy of Bible Study Fellowship.

My word that goes out from my mouth . . .
  will not return to me empty,
but will accomplish what I desire
  and achieve the purpose for which I sent it.

—Isaiah 55:11, New International Version

# CONTENTS

# A TRIBUTE TO 50 YEARS

What a joyful privilege to pay tribute to Bible Study Fellowship International for the significant milestone of 50 years as a life-changing, life-enriching ministry! Truly our beloved BSF has been a fruitful vine that has extended to the uttermost parts of the globe, including my own personal world.

From my first introduction to Bible Study Fellowship, my spirit so resonated with its mission, message, and materials that I knew it was the answer to my heart's longing to draw nearer to God. BSF led me home . . . home to the heart of the Father and to the foot of the Cross and to the pages of my Bible where I was continuously met in a personal, powerful way by the Author.

One of the greatest blessings of my life was to be taught and trained by Miss A. Wetherell Johnson during my orientation in Oakland, California, in 1976. During the five years that I served under her, I became a Teaching Leader that fell in love with "Miss J." And while she expressed reservations about planting a class in the South that she pictured from *Gone with the Wind*; and although she also expressed doubt that I would make it through the pilot study because of my youth, ignorance, and lack of BSF exposure, I was privileged to serve as a TL of a thriving, capacity class in Raleigh, North Carolina, for twelve years. I was so hungry to receive all that God had for me, I actually never missed a class.

Nine other BSF classes in our city were spun off from my original class, including one of the first singles classes as well as a class in our state's maximum security women's prison. Today, those classes continue to operate with maximum capacity attendance (the class in the women's prison has changed its name to Shepherd's Heart and ministers weekly to approximately three hundred inmates). In addition, BSF has produced many "copies," so that more than seven thousand men and women are studying God's Word for themselves each week in our city. To God be the glory!

*I thank my God every time I remember you. In all my prayers for all of you, I always pray with joy . . . It is right for me to feel this way about all of you, since I have you in my heart . . .*

—Philippians 1:3–4,7 (NIV)

Anne Graham Lotz

# PREFACE

The thought of writing a history of Bible Study Fellowship was a daunting one.

In researching BSF's entire story thus far—its ministry developing over five decades, its reach extending across dozens of countries, its impact touching millions of souls, thousands of people providing loving labor, and fond recollections amassed from hundreds of interviews—we found more material than could possibly be contained in a single volume. We had a good idea of where and how we might begin the task, but the further we proceeded, the more challenging it became.

We knew that any organization's history, comprised solely of dates, numbers, and administrative details, could prove deadly dull. The only hope for making such a project come alive would be to tell Bible Study Fellowship's story through the voices, experiences, and lives of BSF people.

Over a fifty-year period, however, hundreds of individuals have played a notable role in BSF's history. Thousands could share vivid memories about leaders and organizational milestones. Literally millions might testify to BSF's influence in their lives or in the lives of friends, family, or fellow church members. Out of all these, finding the *right* voices to tell the BSF story *best* seemed a formidable challenge.

The national headquarters staff and Board of Directors provided us an initial list of people to interview. And every one of those people suggested others. Where do you begin looking for essential facts and other meaningful matter in such a mass of available material? When do you stop looking for details and documentation in thousands of pages of training materials, Board minutes, newsletters, and more? We prayed specifically for the Lord's guidance regarding our list of possible interviewees: for wisdom in who to contact and for help in reaching them. We also prayed for divine discernment when we walked into the organizational archives: which recording to listen to and which documents to read.

What we've ended up with is not so much an encyclopedic history, but a big family album containing a collection of clippings, assorted facts, verbal snapshots, and postcard-sized memories, all of it held in place with a narrative thread. In the pages that follow, you'll find three main categories of recollections.

### FROM THE DIRECTOR:

Quotes from BSF's first three Directors—Wetherell Johnson, Rosemary Jensen, and Jean Nystrand. (The newest Executive Director, Susie Rowan, takes her turn to speak in the Afterword.)

### IN OTHERS' WORDS:

Remembrances from secretaries and Board members, Teaching Leaders and Area Advisors, and many others who had some share in the Bible Study Fellowship story.

### IMPACT STORY:

Either first- or second-hand narratives of the powerful—and sometimes surprising—ways God has used BSF to reveal His glory and the beauty of His Word.

Even with all these glimpses into BSF's history, *True to His Word* offers an incomplete picture. But we pray that the hundreds of pieces making up this project will provide a lasting record of God's work in the lives of countless numbers of people around the world through one remarkable organization during its first fifty years. To God be the glory!

*Part 1*

# AN UNEXPECTED BEGINNING
# (1950–1959)

# Chapter 1

# AT LIFE'S CROSSROADS

Audrey Wetherell Johnson arrives in California

Audrey Wetherell Johnson paced the rolling deck of an ocean freighter as the North American coastline rose out of the blue-gray waters of the Pacific. At the age of forty-two, and now half a world away from the two countries she called home, England and China, this proper Englishwoman realized that a crucial crossroads lay ahead.

Wetherell Johnson in 1936

## Wetherell Johnson in China

As uncertain as the future seemed that June day in 1950, looking back was also unsettling.

As a youth, Wetherell had committed her life to serve the Lord in China. Feeling a great burden for Chinese Christians, she spent seventeen years—nearly all her adult life—as a missionary there. She thought she would stay in China until she died.

But that day on the freighter, knowing that the California coastline marked the end of her trans-Pacific voyage, she faced the reality that her work in China was over as well.

Arriving in America, she could not have foreseen how the years she lived and the lessons she learned in China would provide a foundation of faith upon which the rest of her life and legacy would be built. But almost thirty years after standing on the deck of that ship, Wetherell Johnson stood before an audience of thousands and gave a very different perspective on her years in the Far East.

### ⟶ FROM THE DIRECTOR
*Wetherell Johnson:*

I had a marvelous time in China. First of all, I went to Kiangsi and nearly died of bacillary dysentery. They couldn't get me to a doctor in time, but God got me through. Then I had another operation, which was considered serious and made me a convalescent for a very long time. Following that, they sent me to a place in China where the people had never seen a white woman before.

One day, I'd had it. I'd been there about two years. I thought, *Two years wasted.* Isn't it awful? Our superintendent was coming to see us, and here was I in a little kind of a hut. The walls were painted, and all I had were three tin-lined boxes that I covered with chintzes. That was my chair and table.

I knelt down by the little camp cot and I said, "Now, Lord, please, I've had it. Did You train me to do this sort of thing?" The superintendent was coming the next day and I was going to give a letter to that man saying, "Now, look, if I'm not transferred, it's either/or."

So, I put my pad on the bed, knelt down, and began to pray to the Lord. My eye caught a picture of a crown of thorns and the cross on a poster with a little text at the bottom, and do you know what I heard? I heard a little recording in my mind and it said, "Lord, I am willing, at whatever cost, that Thy death should be worked out in me, in order that Thy resurrection life of the Holy Spirit might bring fruit in somebody else." Awkward, isn't it?

And then another thing the Lord said to me is this: "I was in the sticks of Nazareth thirty years, the brightest man the world has ever known, and you're fussing over two years in the sticks?" I felt a little embarrassed. So, I didn't say a thing.

Within that week, one girl of about twenty-four came asking me how to be saved. Before I left, she had memorized the entire book of Matthew, and I heard her give it in Chinese.[1]

## Longhua Prison Camp

War with Japan had engulfed China during those days and threatened many Christian missionaries and their converts. Eventually, Wetherell, along with other missionaries, was arrested by the Japanese invaders and taken to Longhua Prison Camp, where the crowded facilities and the living conditions were indeed brutal.

### ⟶ FROM THE DIRECTOR
*Wetherell Johnson:*

In August 1942, a boiling hot day, we were allowed to take one single bed with bedding and one suitcase. We were herded onto a bus and taken to the concentration camp, to a room of fifty feet by one hundred, a former horses' stable, which they thought would be excellent for us. I thought we might be there for six weeks; we were there for nearly three years.

I never had a shower for three years. Rice was all we had. I used to be particular in the early days and take out the bugs. In the end, I decided I did need a little bit of meat, so down it went.[2]

Wetherell had entered the Japanese prison camp weighing 145 pounds; three years later, she weighed 106. When she was finally released from Longhua, she hoped for a joyous reunion with her Chinese students and friends. Instead, she was among the first released prisoners who were packed up and sent home.

She spent some months in England, speaking about her experiences in China, visiting friends and family, and regaining her health. Then, she returned to China in 1948 to join the work of China Bible Seminary.

Although no longer at war with Japan, China was at that time rocked by civil war, a conflict between communists and nationalists. Mao Tse-tung and his forces steadily gained the upper hand. Their *Communist Manifesto* demanded the removal of all "imperialist" influences, so the pressure on local churches to force out foreign missionaries became unbearable.

In December 1948, the faculty of the seminary began to pray about closing the school. Months later, when the decision to close was finally made, the school's buildings were given to a Chinese orphanage. It was then that, after much prayer, Miss Johnson believed that God was leading her to leave China.

"I left China in tears," Wetherell said, "yet knowing without a doubt that I had obeyed God."[3]

Years later, in writing her autobiography, Wetherell Johnson said: "At this time God reminded me of His great faithfulness, and that He is my Father. He was totally responsible in love for His own child. Somewhere there would be a future unexpected and more fulfilling than I could ask or think. My heart was filled with His peace."[4]

## God's Special Purpose

When Wetherell Johnson's ship docked in San Francisco, she was met by Dr. Jean Holt, in whose southern California home a prayer meeting had been held monthly for the work of China Bible Seminary. Dr. Holt invited Miss Johnson to stay in her home for a time and to speak to that prayer group.

At the June 1950 prayer meeting, Miss Alverda Hertzler, vice principal of a San Bernardino high school of three thousand students, listened intently as Miss Johnson recounted her work in China. Alverda had been praying about a closer walk with the Lord and for some new opportunity to serve Him.

Shortly after that first encounter in Dr. Holt's home, Miss Hertzler asked Miss Johnson to speak to a Bible class at her church and to stay overnight in her home. The following morning, as the two women washed dishes, Alverda told Wetherell that after her previous night's talk on the glory of God, she felt as if her life would never be the same.

Miss Johnson responded, "I believe God has brought us together for a special purpose."

Little did either of them know!

# Chapter 2

# NO SPOON-FEEDING

The formation of Wetherell Johnson's Bible study methods

W etherell Johnson's plans called for a brief stay in the United States, mainly to speak and raise funds for missions. She would then return to England, where she had been offered a teaching position in a missionary training school.

Dr. Holt, however, concerned about Miss Johnson's physical health, advised her to spend at least six more months in America. Dr. Holt arranged for Wetherell to spend that time residing at Alverda Hertzler's San Bernardino home in sunny southern California.

Nearly three decades later, Miss Hertzler recounted how God had worked to bring about their friendship, which led to a shared ministry.

### IN OTHERS' WORDS

*Alverda Hertzler:*

I had prayed for the China Bible Seminary in a prayer circle for a number of years. But it wasn't until 1950, when Miss Johnson was driven out of China because of the Communist invasion, that I met her. That summer, Miss Johnson and I went together, in the Lord's providence, to attend a spiritual retreat at "The

Firs" in Bellingham, Washington. There Miss Johnson began a study of Genesis with me. I really did not know the Word, and I had seen in her eyes something that I wanted.

That was the beginning of one of the most enriching friendships I've had in my life.[1]

Those six months stretched into two years. Miss Johnson took numerous speaking and short-term teaching engagements at churches, colleges, and retreats—wherever the Lord opened a door. Repeatedly, she saw evidence that God was using this extended time in America to touch many lives.

Miss Johnson wrote about that time: "These were two years of happy days, but I knew this was not to be my permanent work."[2]

## The Unwanted Bible Study

In San Bernardino, at the end of the summer of 1952, Miss Johnson spoke at a church. Following the service, some women who attended that meeting went to Miss Hertzler's home to ask Wetherell if she might lead them in a Bible study of Colossians.

### ⌒ FROM THE DIRECTOR
*Wetherell Johnson:*

These five dear fundamentalist ladies, who knew the Bible from beginning to end, said, "Would you teach us?"

I thought, *What have I come to?* There in San Bernardino was such an abundance of churches, while by contrast, in China there were millions of pagans who had not even heard His name. Now if these women had been pagan Americans, I would have been thrilled. But they were die-hard Christians. So I said, "I'll pray about your request."

And when I prayed, God said three things to me. The first thing was from Jeremiah 45: "Seekest thou great things for thyself? Seek them not." The second was "What is in thy hand? Use it." The third thing was "Be thou faithful in little things and I will give you great things."[3]

When the ladies returned for Miss Johnson's answer, she told them, "I won't spoon-feed you. I will give you two or three questions to help you in your study of the lesson. I would then like you to first share with all of us what God has given you from the passage, and then I will give you what He has given me."[4]

From the beginning, that was the format: each woman was to pray, asking the Lord to help her understand as she studied the Bible passage. She was to listen for what God had to say, with no help from commentaries or lessons. The class members would then meet for each to share what the Holy Spirit had taught, and finally they would listen to Wetherell Johnson's lecture on that week's passage.

The five women brought friends, and before long, the group had outgrown Miss Hertzler's home. They moved to the home of Mrs. Edna Voss, but the class soon outgrew that home as well.

The pastor of a nearby church invited the group to use his congregation's facilities, which included a nursery for children of the young women attending the class. Attendance jumped to thirty, then soon to seventy members.

During this time, when a woman in the class wanted to answer a question, she would raise her hand and then stand. Miss Johnson noticed that the same individuals were offering to answer most questions. She thought, *The others aren't reading the Word.* She remained determined *not* to spoon-feed the students. She considered what might be done for the ones who weren't reading the passage each week.

Miss Johnson invited seven women from the group to Miss Hertzler's home to pray with her for the Lord's direction in solving this problem. She described that day: "This was a morning of spiritual oneness never to be forgotten. The Lord made us aware of the power of the Holy Spirit. As we talked together the Lord also gave us a unique pattern of something God would later reveal as a key feature in the birth of a wide ministry He alone knew was to come."[5]

Because of that meeting, Miss Johnson divided the members of the Bible study into seven groups, according to their knowledge of the Bible. Each of the seven women at that prayer meeting would lead one of these groups.

They also agreed on one of the first BSF rules: unless a class member had a written answer to a question, she could not participate in the discussion of that question. Thus, women had to do their homework to be allowed to talk. "Then," Miss Johnson recalled years later, "the Word of God captured them! That's how the discussion groups came about." She added, "And that little policy that you don't answer unless you've written it down? What's it for? So you'll read the Bible."[6]

When Miss Johnson noticed women taking notes during her lectures, she decided to type a summary of each lesson so the women could listen without having to also write. Those prepared notes became the final step in the fourfold approach unique to Wetherell Johnson's Bible study:

1. Daily, study only the passage (no commentaries), asking the Holy Spirit to teach.

2. Share in a discussion group, listening to what others had learned.

3. Listen to a teaching of the same passage, taught by a Teaching Leader.

4. Review the passage by reading printed notes.

The Discussion Leaders quickly realized that they needed to meet together weekly to be trained by Miss Johnson. Those leaders' meetings became a meaningful time of fellowship, prayer, and personal growth.

Soon the women in each discussion group developed a bond with each other and with their leaders, leading to the first discussion class luncheons.

One day after a class at Miss Hertzler's home, Wetherell found some money left on the coffee table. She telephoned the women from that day's class to inquire who had misplaced the money. She was informed, "It is for you, for lesson paper and expenses. It comes from God, through us." Every week after that, someone set out a plate from Miss Hertzler's china cabinet for gifts to be left in it. When the class relocated to a church, an offering plate was placed where members could make anonymous contributions.

⟶ **FROM THE DIRECTOR**
*Wetherell Johnson:*

I want you to see that Bible Study Fellowship is founded on the Word of God. I want you to see that Bible Study Fellowship is founded on faith. We don't ask for money. We leave offering plates in the back. I don't know who gives and who doesn't. But God has given us the money to keep going.[7]

## A Little Something Called Bible Study Fellowship

The group meeting at the Voss home made another significant decision. The members discussed what to call their group. Someone proposed "Miss Johnson's Class," to which Wetherell responded with an adamant no! In the end, the group settled on a simple, straightforward name—the Bible Study Fellowship.

None of those women, not even Miss Wetherell Johnson, could have imagined how their little group would grow from "this small thing" in one southern California town into something God would use to affect millions of lives around the world.

Vergene Lewis was a Discussion Leader in that first BSF class.

⟶ **IN OTHERS' WORDS**
*Vergene Lewis:*

Miss Johnson was teaching her class in my home church in 1955 when a friend of mine invited me to come with her. I thought, *Oh no! I've heard missionaries before. I teach Sunday school and don't need a Bible study.* Besides, the class met on Thursday, and that was my housecleaning day.

Another friend invited me, but added, "And I would love to take you to lunch afterward." My daughter was a baby and I didn't get out to lunch much. So I went.

Miss Johnson was teaching on Hosea—this British lady with

the high-pitched voice. At first I thought, *What am I doing here?* Then all of a sudden, though the voice didn't change, I began to hear what she was saying. And these very personal applications were coming through from this Old Testament book that I had never read before.

I knew, I just knew, that my friend had told Miss Johnson all about me! I asked my friend at lunch, "Did you tell that teacher to say something to me?"

"No." My friend laughed. "That's just the way God works."

God is so good. In my heart I had known there must be more to the Christian life than to get saved, wait to go to heaven, and go to work in the church. I began to learn what that "more" was. I did that first week's questions in a couple of days. I was so excited, and that was just the beginning.

Soon about one hundred women were coming from different churches all over town. That was unusual. San Bernardino was not a big city, and most people had not seemed interested in spiritual things. But BSF was unique.

The first leaders' meeting that Miss Johnson invited me to was at Edna Voss's house. I was ten minutes late. When I walked into the leaders' meeting, Miss Johnson stopped everything, looked at me, and said, "Good morning, Mrs. Lewis." She didn't say anything else until later in the lesson, when she commented, "When you are late, you rob other people of their time, and it is rude." I could have died. I was twenty-eight years old at the time, the youngest in the group. But I was never late again![8]

# Chapter 3

# BIBLE STUDY FELLOWSHIP
# IN THE BAY AREA
Miss Johnson moves to Oakland

B illy Graham planned an evangelistic crusade for the Bay
Area of California in 1958. Just a year earlier, the Graham
Crusade in New York City had been a phenomenal success. The
opening-night crowd at Madison Square Garden on May 15 had
numbered eighteen thousand. So many thousands responded to
the nightly invitations that the organizers extended the crusade
through September 1. The people planning the Bay Area crusade
prayed that the Lord would grant them similar results, and they
prepared for His blessing.

Dr. Ernest Hastings, pastor of Melrose Baptist Church in
Oakland, co-chaired the follow-up committee for the Graham
Crusade in the Bay Area. One of his church members, Kay
Gudnason, had met Wetherell Johnson and Alverda Hertzler and
believed that Miss Johnson's method of Bible study could prove
an invaluable part of the local strategy for following up with new
converts in the wake of the Graham crusade.

More than twenty years later, Kay Gudnason recalled her
memories of that first encounter in 1957.

## ⌒⊃ IN OTHERS' WORDS

*Kay Gudnason:*

I was in our cabin at Mount Hermon, a Christian conference center when a mutual friend of ours, Lucy Sullivan, came to the door and said, "I want you to meet two terrific people that I'm going to be staying with." We made a date and had lunch with Miss Johnson and Miss Hertzler. Immediately our hearts were cemented together in a bond of love in the Lord.

What meant so much to me during those early days were the Bible study classes that Miss Johnson would have just for our little group. We would take blankets from her cabin to an open space across the street, spread them out under a great overhanging oak tree, and there in that hayfield, she would, morning by morning, lead us in Bible study. I had never heard Bible teaching like that, so personal and convicting it seemed to hit me right where I was. When it ended, I longed for further Bible teaching to that degree.

I thought, *Oh, maybe she could move to the Bay Area and have classes where I could attend.* I suggested that to my husband, Harold, and our pastor, Dr. Hastings.

The Lord was leading. So, Melrose Baptist Church was the founding church for launching Bible Study Fellowship in the Bay Area.

My husband and I had the marvelous privilege of having Miss Johnson live with us for three months. I always thought our living room furniture was particularly sacred, especially a huge red ottoman, where this first nucleus of Discussion Leaders were trained. She trained us and we poured out our hearts for the new work in prayer around that red ottoman. It has been a sacred place ever since.

In October 1958, she held the first class at Melrose Baptist Church, introduced by Dr. Hastings and with thirty-five women present. In the next weeks, class doubled and then tripled. Within a year, it was necessary to start a second class in Berkeley, California.

One thing that I remember was Miss Johnson at the close of each session. She would wave aloft a sheaf of notes and say, "Now, who will type up the notes for next week?" There was always a volunteer, usually Dorothy B. She'd run the notes off on the mimeograph machine. And so, we would go week by week.[1]

## An Invitation

While Kay Gudnason was one catalyst in Wetherell Johnson's migration to the Bay Area, two other individuals played key roles in that Bay Area Billy Graham crusade.

The first was Myrl Flood (now Glockner), who served the Graham team as director of counseling and follow-up for women. During a recent interview, she offered this background.

### ⌐◯ IN OTHERS' WORDS
*Myrl Glockner:*

I received a phone call one day from a woman wondering if she could have an appointment with me. She had an English accent. I had been told about this Bible study of five hundred women in San Bernardino. In those days, that was unheard of.

I met with Miss Johnson and she told me a minister in the Bay Area had contacted her and encouraged her to begin a new Bible study class in the Bay Area, believing that it might be one of the avenues for effective follow-up with the crusade converts. That request was why she had contacted me.

A prayer group of about thirty women meeting in Walnut Creek had asked me to speak to them. I thought that it would be a nice thing to introduce Miss J to them and that they might be the nucleus from which she could start her class.

As I found out later, Miss Johnson had just learned to drive, which explained the trip I then had with her across the Bay Bridge and out to Walnut Creek.

I didn't realize what Miss Johnson had in mind—that she

was looking for strong leadership. Miss Johnson was seeking a special kind of woman who could open many doors. She sat on the back row in a crowded house full of women as I spoke on the importance of the Word in our lives. These women had prayer, but they weren't in the Word, so I talked about their needing a two-way conversation with the Lord. Here I was speaking on the importance of the Word, with Miss Wetherell Johnson sitting on the back row. It was an interesting first encounter.[2]

Ernest Hastings was the third key person in bringing Wetherell Johnson and her Bible study to the Bay Area. He vividly remembers when Kay Gudnason approached him to say, "You know, there is a wonderful Bible teacher down in southern California who would be excellent for following up on the conversions from the Crusade."

As Dr. Hastings listened to his friend, he had no idea that those words were his introduction to someone and something that became a significant part of his life for the next fifty-plus years.

## ⌒⊝ IN OTHERS' WORDS

*Dr. Ernest Hastings:*

Soon after Kay told me about her, I flew south to meet Miss Johnson. I sat in on the class in San Bernardino; then I told her what we had in mind. She had several things going for her. Number one, she already had five different lesson series and it was terrific material. Secondly, she was an exceptional Bible teacher, really par excellence. And she had a way of using inductive Bible study that was a genius system.

When I saw what she was doing, I used every ounce of persuasive ability I had and said, "You ought to come to the Bay Area and help us follow up on the Billy Graham crusade." She eventually decided to come.

We started with eighteen people in the first class, if I remember right. The offering was thirty-seven dollars. The dream was to do the follow-up and have a few classes; but it grew so fast that it became apparent we had something more here.

That first class in the Bay Area was in my church, the Melrose Baptist Church in Oakland. From there, we began a second class at the First Presbyterian Church in Berkeley, and then we expanded to the Presbyterian church in Walnut Creek. People in those classes were telling other people, and things just kept growing.[3]

## Leaving but Not Disconnecting

Wetherell Johnson's decision to relocate to the Bay Area could not have been an easy one. The move would have far-reaching ramifications, not only for her life but also for the women she had been ministering to for years in southern California.

One Discussion Leader in that first class recalls how Miss Johnson informed the leaders that she was leaving.

### ◡ IN OTHERS' WORDS
*Vergene Lewis:*

In 1958, she had us for a closing luncheon at the Mission Inn in Riverside. About twenty ladies—Discussion Leaders and people involved in class leadership—were there. She had rented a room upstairs, where we prayed together. We had no clue she was leaving. Miss J taught us on John 21: "Feed my sheep." It was powerful!

When she got through, she told us, "I have something to tell you. I am going away. You are going to continue this work. If this is the Lord's work, it will continue. I am going to the Bay Area to help Billy Graham with some follow-up work and to see what God has for me there. I feel that this is God's leading." We knew it was permanent. That was settled by the time she had finished speaking.

Then Miss J said, "God has spoken to some of you to be teachers. Who has He spoken to?" Six people out of twenty raised their hands. I was one of them. I thought, *What have I done? I cannot do this!* But I genuinely felt God saying, "You need to be a part of this."

After a couple of days of wrestling with it, I went to see Miss J at Miss Hertzler's house, crying, "I can't do this! I know I said I would, but I just can't."

Miss J listened and let me talk. Then she said, "All right, my dear, you have to start somewhere. How would you like to be a Substitute Teaching Leader?"

"Oh yes," I answered, "that will work. I will be a substitute."

I ended up teaching almost every week as a substitute. That was my beginning. I still have one of those lessons I taught. Looking at it now, I see enough material to lecture for three hours; but at that time I had no idea how much I would need to teach forty-five minutes.

All five classes were held at the same location, in the same church. Each class met in a large room with a Discussion Leader. We had weekly training sessions, just as we had with Miss J. As leaders, we met at my house to teach each other that week's lesson. We would gather in the morning to pray, go over the lesson, and then eat a sack lunch. Following lunch, we trained until three in the afternoon.

Each of us was responsible for teaching the lesson to the others; then we critiqued each other. That was grueling. But it was our training and we learned. The pastor of that church became something like our Area Advisor. He came to some of our meetings and taught us homiletics.

Miss Johnson would send the lessons down from the Bay Area. We often prayed that the lessons would arrive in time for class. Sometimes we got them at the last minute and had to mimeograph them the morning of class.

Miss J didn't leave us orphans, though. She kept in touch and even invited us to the Bay Area, two at a time, just to see what they were doing there. We felt as if we were a part of what she was doing in the Bay Area.[4]

# Chapter 4

# IDEAL PARTNERS

Miss Hertzler joins Miss Johnson in Oakland

The phenomenal growth of the new Oakland class confirmed to Wetherell that her move to the Bay Area had been the Lord's leading. This was where her growing ministry needed to be centered.

Having lived for a couple of months as a guest of her gracious friends the Gudnasons, then house-sitting for a time in the home of a traveling widow, it dawned on Wetherell that she had spent her entire life living in other people's homes. She began asking the Lord if He might provide her a place of her own. Rental houses were prohibitively expensive, and apartments were too small for her to entertain guests or to hold training sessions for her Bible study leaders. So, she thought that perhaps she could purchase a small house with a double mortgage.

### ⌒ IN OTHERS' WORDS
*Kay Gudnason:*

Miss Johnson took my husband, Harold, to the bank with her to buy this house. We chuckle every time we think of the banker's questions:

"Well, what is your profession?"

"I teach the Bible."

"What is your salary?"

"Well, I don't have a salary."

"How do you live?"

"I live on faith."

"And you expect to buy a house on faith?"

"Yes."

And she did just that. Harold helped her a bit by cosigning, but he knew how her faith operated.

In that house on Laird Avenue, the first volunteers formed, and that started a pattern that has continued to this day. The devoted Teaching Leaders and Discussion Leaders would see needs in that first home and would rally their husbands to get in the act, to build cabinets and make bookcases and lay carpet, even give the carpet, and do plumbing and gardening work. The Lord just blessed.[1]

When Wetherell left the bank and excitedly called her friend Alverda to say she had just bought a house, her friend's amazed response was "With what?"

Years later, in her autobiography, Wetherell credited God's provision. "Never once did I need to call on Mr. Gudnason for financial help, and never once did I default as payments became due!"[2]

## The First Team

God was putting together the team that would launch this new ministry. First, and most crucially, He was working in the heart of Alverda Hertzler about being a part of it all.

### ◠◠◠ IN OTHERS' WORDS
*Alverda Hertzler:*

When the invitation came to Wetherell to start classes in the San Francisco Bay Area, I rejoiced with her. At the request of the high school Principal, I was still counseling gifted students periodically. One early morning six months later, during a quiet time, the Lord laid it on my heart that Miss Johnson's work was more important than counseling. Thus, in the Spring of 1959, I went to Oakland; a Board of Directors was formed, an application for non-profit status for the Bible Study Fellowship was filed with the IRS, and a year later, the organization was incorporated.[3]

In December 1979, Miss Johnson introduced Miss Hertzler to thousands of BSFers at the Oakland Coliseum by recounting the beginning of their partnership.

### ⟶ FROM THE DIRECTOR
*Wetherell Johnson:*

Alverda left her home in southern California, came to Oakland, and said, "Do you need me?"

I said, "Well, I could really do with you." At that time, I was struggling with everything, writing lesson notes, teaching, training leaders, and administering classes.

The first thing she said was "We'd better get incorporated, and then we'd better have a Board." She just took hold, and got people trained, and has taken hold of administrative work. I couldn't possibly have kept speaking and doing the administrative work. She has that gift; she can keep numbers in her mind, which is more than I can do.[4]

In February 1959, the month after the Lord called her to help in her friend's ministry, Alverda was cranking out copies of the organizational bylaws on an old mimeograph set up in the basement of Wetherell's little house.

The initial Board was composed of Harold Gudnason, Dr. Horton Voss, Rev. Robert Pietsch, Dr. Ernest Hastings, Alverda Hertzler, and Wetherell Johnson. At their first organizational meeting, the members unanimously elected Ernest, who had drafted both the bylaws and the organization's statement of faith, to serve as chair of the BSF Board—an office he would hold for the next twenty years.

### ⌒◯ IN OTHERS' WORDS
*Dr. Ernest Hastings:*

The growth of Bible Study Fellowship was based on God's blessing and leadership. It is the story of the hand of God moving in the decisions that were made. It is much more than the story of any one person. BSF and everything that has happened with this ministry came about because a group of Christian laypeople and ministers, three times a year, gave their time and energy to consider major decisions that were prayed over, worked through, and unanimously agreed upon.[5]

When Alverda Hertzler left her career in education, she lived for a time with Wetherell, until she located an apartment of her own not far from the house on Laird Avenue. There they began the ministry partnership that would last until the end of their lives.

People who knew the women well in those days still enjoy sharing inspiring, amusing, and revealing memories about Wetherell Johnson and Alverda Hertzler—what made them uniquely gifted individuals and at the same time a formidable team.

Betty Hunter was a secretary in the BSF headquarters in Oakland.

### ⌒◯ IN OTHERS' WORDS
*Betty Hunter:*

I first met Miss Johnson in 1958 while I was working in the office of Melrose Baptist church as Ernest Hastings's secretary. We always enjoyed talking with each other, but the thing that struck me was her hat. She wore gorgeous hats. They were going out of style, but Miss Johnson and I still wore hats. We believed in being ladies and enjoying it.

She and Miss Hertzler were total and complete opposites.

Miss Johnson was like a silver Mylar balloon that always has to be tied down. Her thoughts were always heaven bound, and she needed someone on the end of the string to hold her down to earth.

Miss Hertzler could do that. Miss Hertzler was totally earth connected. The Lord used their contrasts and strengths in a marvelous way. They had a great affection for each other, but they would fuss like sisters.

A few years later, they shared an upstairs/downstairs duplex in Oakland. I have been there when one stood at the top of the stairs and the other at the bottom, yelling back and forth to, and sometimes at, each other. They both were intense personalities, and that was the way they operated. But they were also the best of friends; it was truly a wonder to behold their relationship.

Because Miss Johnson was not closely connected to earth, she had no sense of time. She would phone you at any time in the twenty-four hours you came to her mind. If she wanted to ask you a question at 2 AM, she would phone you right then. That was occasionally a bit hard on people's other relationships.

Miss Hertzler kept things together and going. Without her, Miss Johnson would have had a difficult time accomplishing anything of lasting significance—BSF could never have worked or grown the way it did. On the other hand, there could never have been BSF without Miss Johnson, who provided the biblical and spiritual foundation for the entire organization.[6]

One Teaching Leader and Area Advisor for more than thirty years shared her own memories of the duo:

## ∽ IN OTHERS' WORDS

*Jan Myers:*

Miss Johnson and Miss Hertzler were such a pair! Miss Hertzler was a brilliant woman. She had been a dean and guidance counselor for gifted girls in San Bernardino schools and had a mind like a steel trap. She would project and anticipate and

plan. Miss Johnson sometimes had a hard time making decisions; Miss Hertzler did not. Miss Hertzler always put herself
in the background. She never pushed herself forward. Miss
Hertzler was just a dear woman who always felt privileged to
work with Miss Johnson.

They made a perfect pair. BSF couldn't have happened
without their unique combination of strengths—which were
perfectly suited for what God called them to do.[7]

From the beginning of her classes in the Bay Area, Wetherell
Johnson's new ministry required more help than her friend
Alverda alone could provide. In fact, even before Alverda joined
her in Oakland, Wetherell had begun building a faithful corps of
volunteers to provide leadership in her classes and to help in the
production of the necessary resources.

Pearl Hamilton, one of the first members of that Melrose
Baptist Church class, often accepted the challenge. She would
struggle to decipher Miss Johnson's handwritten notes, stay
up half the night typing them, and then run the typed notes by
the Laird Avenue house the next morning to be proofread. Miss
Johnson, invariably seeing things she wanted to say differently,
made cuts here and inserted new comments there, until the whole
thing had to be done over again.

The extra work never seemed to bother Wetherell. There
were always volunteers (and later employees) who gladly did
whatever needed to be done. Ruth Stagner began as one of those
volunteers; she then became the first full-time secretary for BSF.
She was ninety-four years old when she recalled the following:

### ⌒⌒ In Others' Words

*Ruth Stagner:*

I attended my first leaders' meeting in Miss Johnson's home
on Laird Avenue—to train leaders for the new class at Melrose
Baptist Church. The living room was full of women, fifteen or so,
when Miss Johnson asked, "Oh, perchance do we have anyone
here who can take shorthand?"

I had just resigned from a job as a secretary and did not want to ever see another shorthand notebook! I looked around and didn't see another hand. My conscience said, "You'd better be honest." So, I raised my hand.

"Oh, Mrs. Stagner!" Miss Johnson exclaimed. "You're an answer to prayer, dear."

How could I refuse that?

First, I would take notes at our leaders' sessions. Then I got involved in typing lesson notes. Miss J wrote all of her notes in longhand, and God gave me the gift of reading her writing.

You'd be surprised at the places I went to get those notes. Often Miss J wrote while at the beauty salon, under the hair dryer. I picked up notes there, and then went back to the office to type them. First, I typed a rough draft that had to go back to Miss J so she could add some, scratch some out, add something else. Then I checked to be sure the Scripture references were correct.

Like many other people, I was so excited about BSF that I would gladly do anything for Miss J. I guess I was in awe of her at first. She could make anything interesting.[8]

## Making It Work

That first Oakland class grew quickly. One woman who drove to Melrose Baptist from the suburbs wanted a similar class started in her Presbyterian church in Lafayette. When her pastor extended an official invitation, Wetherell launched a second class. The leaders for the Lafayette class joined the Melrose leaders for leadership training sessions on Monday mornings.

No sooner had that class gotten off to a great start than Wetherell received a warm invitation from Dr. Robert Munger of the First Presbyterian Church in Berkeley to begin a class there. She resisted for a time, believing her schedule was already too heavy. But Dr. Munger assigned his young associate, the Rev. Don Moomaw, to call Miss Johnson at regular intervals to talk about the possibility. Finally, convinced of the great potential in Berkeley, home of the University of California, she yielded to persuasion and accepted the invitation.

Soon after starting the Berkeley class, however, Wetherell realized it was impossible for her to teach three classes every week, conduct a weekly leaders' meeting, and write extensive lecture notes. So, she turned over the teaching of the Melrose class to Miss Hertzler for a short time—until Pearl Hamilton took over as Teaching Leader for the original Melrose class.

Before long, all three classes were flourishing, each with more than three hundred women attending. By then, a fourth class started in the area—in Castro Valley. The explosive growth in those new Bible Study Fellowship classes and the rapid spread from Oakland to other locations around the Bay Area confirmed again for Wetherell and Alverda that they were doing the Lord's work where He obviously wanted them to be.

Meanwhile, the southern California class, taught by the women left in charge of the original San Bernardino class, was experiencing a different kind of growth. Those Teaching Leaders, one by one, moved to different cities, carrying BSF with them: to Castro Valley, Redlands, and Los Angeles, respectively, with one woman remaining in San Bernardino to continue with that original group.

The ministry's growth presented logistical challenges in Wetherell Johnson's Laird Avenue house. BSF's single most crucial piece of equipment was a bulky old mimeograph, located in Miss Johnson's basement. The basement floor consisted of dirt and sand, luxuriously covered with the finest of wall-to-wall cardboard.

When the production process—printing, assembling, and shipping, not to mention storing all the supplies—outgrew Miss Johnson's cramped basement, a class member volunteered her son to run the press in the roomier basement of her home. But the humidity at that house, near the Bay, curled the lesson paper. That's when another class member, Ruth Spidell, who lived in a drier area, volunteered to locate the press in her basement.

For several years, the weekly notes for all the classes, and any other printed material BSF needed, were produced by mimeograph, and then collated by Alverda Hertzler and a small but committed army of volunteers recruited from various classes. Thousands, and soon tens of thousands, of pages of notes were "published" each week in those primitive conditions—literally cranked out on antiquated equipment never intended for such a workload.

The production crew often wondered if that week's deadline would be missed and the leaders would have no lesson notes or study questions to distribute. Many days, and sometimes nights, they gathered to pray over that increasingly tired and finicky mimeograph. Occasionally the workers produced the lessons only after what seemed to be divine intervention—when a hopelessly jammed or mysteriously stalled machine was prayed over and suddenly began working smoothly again.

Once when Miss Johnson joined Alverda and her helpers in the basement for a particularly desperate and long time of prayer and petition around the old mimeograph, she tapped her friend on the shoulder and whispered, "You keep praying, Alverda. I have to go and teach the class." Somehow, week after week, the lessons were printed.

Indeed there was a reassuringly clear sense of divine providence in every facet and at every level of Bible Study Fellowship—from the mind and heart of Wetherell Johnson and Alverda Hertzler to the growing number of class members and everyone in between. That was the point made by another headquarters secretary:

### ⁓ In Others' Words
*Jean Werum:*

Miss Johnson was still writing or revising lessons from week to week. She would start with one piece of paper and write something. When that was full, she'd get another piece of paper and put a piece of Scotch tape on it. These strips of paper would get longer and longer as she taped more pages together, until she'd bring this roll of stuff in and present it almost like the Torah. That's what I had to work with—from these long scrolls, I typed up the lesson notes.

I always made several carbon copies. Miss Hertzler got a

copy because she was the first editor; then we had a theologian evaluate and edit. Another person double-checked all the Bible references. We then had to meld all those copies to come up with the final version. Some weeks, in the early days, the lesson notes would be fourteen or fifteen printed pages long.[9]

Here, too, the paired strengths of Wetherell Johnson and Alverda Hertzler came into play as another indication of God's hand of provision for BSF. The Board recognized it in their interactions.

### ⌒ In Others' Words
*Dr. Ernest Hastings:*

Miss Johnson always reported to the Board on things such as growth and policy decisions. But in the Board meetings, Miss Hertzler took the everyday and long-term business aspect— discussing, recommending. From time to time, Miss Johnson would try to interrupt and say, "Now, Alverda . . ." And Alverda would come right back, "Now, Wetherell, I know what I'm talking about. I have investigated this." And she had. The woman was sharp. Wetherell was the Bible teacher—and a gifted one. But Alverda was a remarkable administrator, a thorough organizer, a detail person, a true planner.[10]

Perhaps the greatest evidences of God's blessing were the complementary skills Wetherell Johnson and Alverda Hertzler brought to BSF. Everyone who knew and worked with them realized that God put together these unique individuals, from the beginning, at the very heart of Bible Study Fellowship.

They may have sensed it, but they could not know how much was just around the corner for their fledgling organization.

# Part 2

# Rapid Early Expansion
# (1960–1979)

# Chapter 5

# GOD'S PLAN FOR EXPANSION
The many ways Bible Study Fellowship classes grew and spread

A ll those personally involved during the early years of Bible Study Fellowship—from the Board, Miss Johnson and Miss Hertzler, the Teaching Leaders and other faithful volunteers, to committed class members who attended week after week—were quickly convinced that God's blessing had been bestowed on this organization and its ministry. The most obvious and persuasive evidence was BSF's remarkable numerical growth and the surprising geographical spread of its classes during its first decade.

The 1960s began with just 4 BSF groups. By 1970, there were 110 BSF classes in more than a dozen states and one beginning in Australia; a total of twenty thousand people attended weekly. Yet the organization's leadership claimed they never had a blueprint for such expansion.

### IN OTHERS' WORDS
*Dr. Ernest Hastings:*

Never at any point did the organization's leadership or staff ever look at a map of the country and make a decision that "We need to spread out and get better coverage, so it's probably time to think about starting a new class there in Arkansas or here in

Minnesota." What usually happened was that some woman in an existing Bible Study Fellowship class would have to move to some other city when her husband was transferred by his company. She'd soon miss her old BSF class and want to start a new class there. There was no pattern, no predetermined strategy. It just *happened*. Yet, every year the Board got encouraging reports telling where all the new classes were and how BSF had spread.[1]

The Berkeley class played a unique role in the spread of BSF to other parts of the country. In her autobiography, *Created for Commitment*, Miss Johnson acknowledged, "I could never have dreamed that God would use that Berkeley class as the first means of 'circumstantial expansion.' Some ladies who attended my Berkeley class were in the San Francisco Bay Area because their husbands were studying for their doctorates at the University of California, Berkeley. When the degrees were granted, these ladies who prepared to return East came to me in real distress. 'This personal study of the Scriptures has meant so much to me. I will miss not having the study.'"[2]

## How BSF Spread to Indiana and Arkansas

Mary Nell Schaap moved from Berkeley to Indiana when her husband graduated from the university. She recalled what happened.

### ◠◯ IN OTHERS' WORDS
*Mary Nell Schaap:*

When I got an invitation to a Bible study, I just knew I had to go! I could see later that it was the Lord prodding me. I went and it felt like home. I really needed BSF. The class was about 250 to 300 ladies—an impressive number for a Bible study at that time in Berkeley, California. At our last meeting that year, we all shared our testimonies. When I stood to talk, I started to cry and confessed, "I hate to go back home to Bloomington, Indiana, and be my old self."

Miss Johnson cornered me afterwards and asked, "Would you like to start a class in Indiana?" She was suggesting to me a new idea—to let someone far away teach by herself. She said I would have to be the one to teach the class. At first I said, "I can't do that." I had majored in Christian education for children, but to teach women was nothing I ever thought I could do. I entered this with fear and trembling.

In the fall of 1961, we started a class in Indiana with about fifteen people. By the end of the year, we had doubled. And it wasn't just "good church people"; it was people from our neighborhood. A couple of years after we started, I had several university faculty members attending my class, and I was feeling inadequate. When I let Miss Johnson know that in one of my letters, she wrote me back and said, "Honey, they may know their field, but they don't know the Scripture." That helped me. She was a wonderful encourager.

For my class in Indiana, I received my lessons by mail. I would get what they were teaching on the West Coast two weeks late. One Wednesday morning our lessons hadn't come, so I started the class and then I drove around until I found the mailman. He got the lessons off his truck just before I needed to hand them out.

Our class grew each year—until we had three or four hundred members. After about ten years in Bloomington, it became the "in" thing to do. Even the country club set and other prominent women in the city would all come to BSF. My husband was a vice chancellor by that time, and I remember having dinner at the home of the Indiana University president. Around the table were all these university administrators along with their spouses. And all but one of the women there had been involved in BSF. The other women all told her, "Oh, you need to get into BSF." To have that kind of witness at the university level was a real blessing.

Over the years, we had several other classes start out of ours. People came into our area for graduate school and they would move on. Or a young professor would move to another school.

For example, one of our class members moved to Madison, Wisconsin, and started that BSF class. Then she later moved to Vicksburg, Virginia, and started another BSF class there.

When Mrs. Oma Smucker's husband finished his graduate studies, she left her California class and wanted to get BSF started where they moved in northern Indiana. Miss Johnson told her, "You first need to attend Mrs. Schaap's class to observe and see how she teaches." Oma lived almost four hours away from me, but she did come to my class for a time before starting her own BSF class up in Goshen.

My husband eventually taught a BSF Men's Class. And I continued to teach for a total of twenty-six years.[3]

BSF continued to spread eastward. Another member of the Berkeley class told her sister in Arkansas all about what she was learning in BSF. Lib Wenger, who had been teaching a Bible study for some time, became so excited about her sister's report that she traveled to Oakland from Little Rock for training so that she could begin using the BSF materials and pattern of study with her class.

## How BSF Spread to Los Angeles

Including the classes in Indiana and Little Rock, plus a new one in Glendale, California, there were thirteen classes by the fall of 1962. Growing and expanding required hard work and adaptability on the part of everyone in the organization. That year Miss Johnson taught a training class every Monday for combined groups of Discussion Leaders and Children's Leaders from four classes. On Tuesday, Wednesday, and Thursday mornings, she taught classes of two to three hundred members. Some of them were committed Christians; others were nominal church members or even unchurched people who had never before considered studying the Bible.

And many of those first class members played significant roles in BSF's early growth.

## ∽ IN OTHERS' WORDS

*Vergene Lewis:*

A woman in our church came to me and said, "We have a missionary meeting that is so boring. How would you feel about doing a Bible study for us one night?" She had no idea of my connection with BSF.

I said, "Okay, but you'll have to do questions. If I give you some questions the week before, would you do them?"

We studied Colossians. Of ten ladies, nine had picked up lessons and four had done the homework. Not a bad percentage under the circumstances. When we finished our session, the room was quiet. Someone asked, "Could we do this again? Would you consider a weekly Bible study?"

I called Miss J to tell her, "I think God is opening the door here." She agreed that we could do a pilot class. But by then the policy was that you had to have forty people to have a class. Miss J sent her material and we did it. At the next to last meeting, we had thirty-five people, including me! I told two of the leaders, "We've got to have forty people!" They said, "Let's have a luncheon." We held a luncheon for the last lesson, and forty women showed up. The next year we had a class there in Anaheim.

And that class immediately began to grow. People were coming from all over Anaheim and beyond.

The second year I taught, one of the beach women came to me to say, "We need a class nearer our homes. We are driving so far and traffic is getting bad. We could invite more people if it were not so far away." I suggested she pray about it. She agreed, saying, "Obviously I am not the Teaching Leader, but I will pray about it." I recall my response: "God does wonderful, strange things with us sometimes."

In a couple of months, she called me back to say, "I am at the place where I believe God wants me to start the class. I still don't think I am supposed to teach the class, but I believe I should start it."

The class was scheduled to start in the fall. The Discussion Leaders and two hundred class members were signed up, right off the bat. Finally, this woman who had the burden agreed to teach it. She taught for four years before another woman, who became a Christian under her teaching, took over as a long-term Teaching Leader for that class.

The Lord took one woman's concern and willingness to be used to accomplish His will. That is just one of the ways BSF grew.[4]

## How BSF Spread to Minnesota

By 1964, there were twenty-three classes with a total of three thousand members representing seven hundred congregations. The following year, there were five thousand class members attending thirty-five classes—twelve in the Bay Area and twenty-three scattered in five states. And in 1966, BSF sent out six thousand lessons each week to members of forty-eight classes in eight states.

Myrl Glockner had been in charge of women's follow-up for the Billy Graham Crusade. Shortly after the crusade, she married and moved to Minnesota.

### ⌇ IN OTHERS' WORDS
*Myrl Glockner:*

In Minneapolis, I led this small Bible study group of four women. One of the women, Alice Parrish, was transferred to California and eventually became a Discussion Leader in Miss Johnson's Walnut Creek class.

She was so excited that she told me all about it. Then Alice got a group of women together, BSF leaders, in the summer months and began praying that I would feel led to bring BSF to Minneapolis.

I was resisting. Everything I heard about BSF impressed me. But I wanted to be a normal housewife and be comfortable. I knew BSF would be a costly commitment.

My husband was working with the Billy Graham Association and we went to Australia in 1967. Bob went over ahead of me. On my way later, I stopped in Alamo, California, to visit my friend Alice. She had a group of Discussion Leaders over so I could meet them. These were the women who had been praying that I would start a class.

We drank our coffee and were about to get on our knees to pray when the phone rang. The call was for me and I was relieved that I didn't have to pray with the women. I didn't want any more pressure to start BSF in Minneapolis.

One afternoon, after I joined my husband in Brisbane, I was on my knees, fulfilling my promise to pray about BSF, when the presence of the Lord came into the room so strongly I could have touched Him. It was a breaking moment. He broke my will. He shattered my defensiveness and drew me to Him in submission. It was such a powerful encounter with His holiness, one of the most powerful experiences I've had ever with the Lord. Then I began to dream dreams, thinking someday we could see five hundred women in the Word for themselves in Minneapolis.

When I came back from Australia, I applied to start and teach a BSF class, and Miss Johnson accepted me. I recruited my sister Grace to be my assistant Teaching Leader and my friend Shirley Horn for Class Administrator, and the three of us went to Oakland together for training.

We started a pilot class in April 1968, and the first year there were 185 women. By the third year, there were more than five hundred. Vergene Lewis, our Area Advisor, recommended we draw a geographical line, and everybody who lived east would go to the existing Ridgeview class, which Grace would teach. I started a new class on the west side of Edina. Both classes were over five hundred that first year. In the Edina class, enrollment went up to 834. We had seventy in the leaders' group and over two hundred in the Children's Program.

By the time Ruth Mitchell started a third class in Bloomington, she, too, had a capacity class. We had to keep splitting our classes. It wasn't long before we had twenty-one classes, and Miss Johnson gave us a guideline that classes needed to be at least ten miles apart. Those twenty-one classes included Men's, Young Adults', and Evening Women's Classes that all developed over a period of ten years or so.

BSF exploded in our area because people were hungry for God's Word. It certainly wasn't human effort. It was a work of the Spirit.[5]

## The Result of Obedience

The 1965–1966 class year saw five thousand members in thirty-five classes. By 1968, the number of classes had doubled to seventy, with eleven thousand members in twelve states. And nowhere was the growth more impressive than in the Bay Area, where the organization was founded. Classes continued to grow as more and more lives were changed.

Perhaps the incredible expansion of Bible Study Fellowship throughout the 1960s is best understood in light of a comment made by another Teaching Leader who was trained by Miss Johnson and who went on to teach for more than thirty years. She said, "I have heard people suggest that Miss Johnson never had a vision for BSF's growth. But I don't think I would say she didn't have a vision, because she had a vision for teaching God's Word to whoever came along. That was her vision. Maybe she didn't have a five-year plan. But she lived so in the moment with God that whatever He called her to at that moment was what she did."

That's what happened when those five ladies in San Bernardino asked Wetherell Johnson to teach them Colossians. She obeyed. And just as Jesus did when He took and blessed the young boy's meager lunch of loaves and fish, the Lord took the willingness to do "a small thing" and multiplied it to feed multitudes of people who were hungry to better understand His Word. And the ministry of Bible Study Fellowship continued to deepen and spread.

# Chapter 6

# THE YOUNGEST BSFERS
The beginning of the Children's Program

F rom the beginning of Bible Study Fellowship, a major stimulus for its growth has been the impact of the ministry not only on individual class members who commit to study and apply the Word of God in their lives but also on their families.

The first BSF class in San Bernardino moved from a home to a church setting for two main reasons. The first was space. The second was to offer child care for preschool children, allowing young mothers to attend. Subsequent classes in the Bay Area provided the same service.

As one longtime Teaching Leader pointed out, "Neither Miss Hertzler nor Miss Johnson, of course, was ever married; they never had children. So for them to see children's ministry as an important thing was very special."

Ernest Hastings remembers, "Alverda was the person most responsible for the Children's Program. She convinced the Board that we had to do something for the children of these women coming to Bible study. It started as child care. Then she thought, *Why are we doing just child care, when we could be teaching them?*"[1]

From there, it was just a step to get a Children's Program in place.

## Meeting a Need

While attending a conference at Mount Hermon, Wetherell and Alverda made the acquaintance of one of the speakers, Doreen Shaw, who had been in charge of eight hundred children in a displaced persons camp in Germany after World War II. Alverda discussed with Doreen the possibility of a Bible study program for small children. Immediately catching that vision and its potential, Doreen committed a month of her time that summer to compiling a manual to be used in creating the new program. She also wrote a one-year series of Bible lessons for children.

In September 1963, Doreen's friend and co-author Martie Johnson joined the BSF staff for a year to help implement the program. During that time, with Doreen's assistance, Martie wrote an additional two-year series of lessons so that three-, four-, and five-year-olds could have their own three-year cycle of weekly lessons.

Marcella Altmann, director of BSF's preschool ministry, said the following:

### ∽ IN OTHERS' WORDS
*Marcella Altmann:*

At the earliest years of BSF, we provided only basic child care in church nurseries using paid attendants. All children, newborns through kindergarten, were welcome.

A Bible storybook, published by the Lutheran Press, was selected, and then a teacher's manual was put together. The program included proper enrollment, nametags, the use of pre-school toys and group games, art materials, a rest time, snacks, and singing. All parts of the program were designed to set the stage for the Bible story.

Then Miss Hertzler and Miss Johnson decided to use volunteers from the BSF discussion classes, rather than paid church nursery workers, to teach the children. It was also determined that all the new Children's Leaders would be trained by a staff member. I was already a Discussion Leader, but I volunteered to be one of the first Children's Leaders. I loved the program and its focus on Bible stories. Children have needs, and I wanted them to know that, just as God helped David and Moses and Samuel, He loved each one of them and was always there to help them.

As BSF continued to grow, Miss Hertzler needed to spend more time with the class teachers and administrators. So, she asked me to join the staff part-time to assist Martie Johnson in visiting classes and training the Children's Leaders. Soon each class had a Children's Director, chosen by the Teaching Leader, who was responsible for all the needs of the Children's Program and nursery care in that class.

The decision was made to replace the original Bible story-book with a packet of pictures, created by artist Frances Hook, to be used in telling the Bible story.[2]

This new venture was called the Children's Christian Training Program, which clearly described both the process and the intent of the program. Mothers were thrilled because the children's classes lived up to the name. And the program's popularity only added to the appeal of BSF for class members.

As Bible Study Fellowship attendance skyrocketed, and as increasingly more children attended, Martie Johnson wrote a letter to parents for each Bible story in the program, adding notes on how to guide a child in social and spiritual development. The young mothers loved the letters.

### ⟳ Impact Story

*Marcella Altmann:*

One of my favorite anecdotes involved a little girl whose family had gotten a new goldfish that she insisted on naming it Hezekiah. That's what the Bible story had been about that week. The BSF influence starts in early, which was one reason I was thrilled to be in it.

In everything we did, we told the children about Jesus and how He loved them.

We got lots of feedback from the children. It was exciting to see and hear how children were absorbing what they learned at BSF. We realized these children were going to carry these positive feelings for God's Word and their love of the Lord through their entire life. We were making an imprint. We knew that.

Part of our training was to teach the mothers how to understand and talk to their children on their level. We put out a pamphlet every month, and we always included a child's story that showed how the children were really flowering. That was truly exciting.[3]

While there is no way to quantify the effect the new children's ministry had on the growth of BSF during those next few years, some numbers from the organization's early days are certainly telling. After just one year, there were seven hundred kids in the program. By 1965, there were fifteen hundred in the Children's Christian Training Program. From then on, the kids' numbers, like the total number of BSF class members, escalated faster than anyone could have imagined.

For a time, the youngest children—those under age three—remained in the church nurseries, cared for by paid attendants. But Miss Hertzler was convinced that BSF should do more. It disturbed her when people referred to "the terrible twos." She said, "They're the 'trainable twos.'" That's what prompted her to ask Martie Johnson to write a manual for an additional program to teach that age level. They first called the two-year-old program Two's Are So Smart.

Marcella Altmann, in 1972, explained the purpose for teaching this youngest age group.

### ⌒◯ In Others' Words
*Marcella Altmann:*

These youngsters will now be prepared for the Three-to-Five Year Old Program. The foundation of training children receive in these programs is not only a head start for their school life, but for the development of their spiritual life. Our Children's Program of the Bible Study Fellowship is designed to have children come to know God's love for them. It is our goal to begin to lay a foundation for the spiritual life and growth in the Lord and "to encourage parents to teach their children the things of God, His Person and His love, and all that is our Christian heritage."[4]

Janice Pinckney, Director of the Children's Program Division from 1985 until 2004, discussed the consistent teaching philosophy from early days of the children's work to more recent times.

### ⌒⊙ IN OTHERS' WORDS

*Janice Pinckney:*

The basic philosophy then was what we still do today: teach the Bible. Introduce the children to a Bible verse. Don't emphasize memorizing the Bible. Just show it to them. Let them hear it. And what we do in the classroom goes home and the moms do the follow-up and repetition.

Two hours is a brief time, alternating active and inactive time. We have a hymn time that is structured and corresponds to what is being taught. We sing pieces of music that contain biblical truth. Those are basic to what we do today—in the School Program that began in 1996 and what we still do in the preschool. The curriculum has been changed and revised, but it's all still the same philosophy.

Back then there was a three-year cycle for the three- to five-year-olds so that a child could be in for all three years and hear different stories each year. The curriculum for the two-year-olds remained the same every year.

Our hymn time is unique. We teach two-year-olds how to sing hymns such as "Holy, Holy, Holy," "Great Is Thy Faithfulness," and "Trust and Obey." We don't teach them repetitious things that might be easier. There's nothing wrong with choruses such as "Jesus Loves Me," but there is so much more that even the youngest children can learn.[5]

## Growing Pains

By 1970, there were seventy-seven hundred children on roll for BSF's Children's Program. Its popularity became a problem as the numbers overwhelmed some classes with limited facilities.

One early BSFer laughed as she remembered, "When I was a Teaching Leader in those early days, we'd ask those poor leaders, 'Do you want to be a Children's Leader? Do you have a trunk big enough to haul a playpen?'

"In the first years, the Children's Leaders didn't have the manuals that they have now. There was no area person to help them. I had seven hundred women in my class, and for a while we had nineteen babies in a crib room with six cribs."

Increasing reports of similar challenges led to one of the most difficult changes ever instituted by the BSF Children's Program: the decision to stop offering a nursery for children under two years of age. The problem of overcrowding in the nurseries was serious enough to be brought before the BSF Board on October 12, 1970. Policy decisions made at that meeting resulted in the following statement issued in the *BSF Newsletter* that fall:

> Many nurseries are so overcrowded that problem situations have sprung up. For the first time we are having complaints concerning our nurseries from host churches, especially where classes are so large or there are overcrowded infant and toddler rooms. After careful consideration of all the problems involved, for the welfare of the children, we are instituting two new policies regarding their care.[6]

A separate section of the newsletter informed class members that, beginning immediately, nurseries would not be offered for children under two and that children over two needed to be potty-trained in order to attend BSF with their mothers. And in the "prayer request" section of that newsletter, Miss Johnson wrote, "We are asking all day class members to pray concerning the new policy regarding the Children's Program, especially for young Mothers who may not immediately see a solution. Let us all pray with them, believing the Lord will provide some way they can work out their individual problems."[7]

Marion Mann, longtime Teaching Leader, recalled the following:

### ⌒ IN OTHERS' WORDS
*Marion Mann:*

At that point, I wasn't a Teaching Leader, but often volunteered in the nursery. People in the community heard that there was free babysitting and would bring their children and leave them, to go shopping. They didn't even leave diapers! I remember running downtown and buying diapers and bottles. The logistics were impossible, so the new policy of not providing child care for children under two made sense.[8]

## More and More Kids

This difficult policy change seemed to do little to slow the growth of BSF classes or the children's ministry itself, as evidenced by the following excerpts from the organization's official publication:

1972: "Sets of lesson notes for the adult classes will exceed the one million mark this class year and for our children an added million 'take home' lessons and songs."

1972: "In the Children's program average weekly attendance reached 9,000 in September."

1974: "The Children's program of BSF began this year with nearly 12,000 little children coming to hear stories from God's word. They are met each week by our 1,200 dedicated Children's Leaders who are well-trained and eager to lovingly teach these little ones the things of God."[9]

During this time, someone told a Teaching Leader that the Children's Program was "the best-kept secret in BSF."

The TL exclaimed, "We're not trying to keep it a secret!"

And it wasn't really a secret. Those who knew anything at all about BSF recognized and proclaimed its value. One TL even wanted to know, "Why can't I advertise it? If I told them that it was a thousand dollars a month, a lot of people would line up to enroll their children. It is such a fine Preschool Program."

But perhaps its greatest consequence was the wonderful way the children's ministry dovetailed with BSF's original goals. Many were the variations Teaching Leaders heard of one little boy who pleaded with his mother, "Do your questions this week so we can go to 'Bible-ship' class."

# Chapter 7

# ADDING BASS NOTES
# TO THE HARMONY
The beginning of Men's Classes

B ible Study Fellowship had a big impact on families through its Children's Program. Another family-related impact of BSF was on the husbands of class members. From those first classes in San Bernardino, Oakland, Lafayette, and Berkeley, most class members' husbands were intrigued by their wives' excitement over studying the Bible. Many others were impressed by the positive changes they witnessed in the women's lives. As a result, class members and their husbands asked Miss Johnson about the possibility of offering Bible Study Fellowship classes for men.

Wetherell Johnson began considering Evening Classes for married couples. By the beginning of 1960, she had decided to create a pilot class to see how BSF methods would work with men and women together.

One member of that pilot Couples' Class recalls:

### ⌒⌾ IN OTHERS' WORDS
*Dr. Bob Stevens:*

My wife, Shirley, and I had come to the Bay Area from Tucson, Arizona, in 1958, for me to do graduate work at Berkeley. We had both led Bible studies back home, but when Shirley became involved in Wetherell Johnson's day class for women at the Lafayette-Orinda Presbyterian church, she was awestruck by this learned British lady who taught the class. When Shirley told me Wetherell had announced she was going to start a trial class for couples, I quickly agreed to go.

The plan for this four-week pilot was to meet at a house in Lafayette, but the first night it was so crowded that we had to move to a church in Lafayette the following week. Miss Johnson taught 1 Thessalonians. That was my first face-to-face meeting with her. She was a great teacher—such insight to the Scripture! She drew out both the theological meaning and the application to our contemporary lives from her teaching on the apostle Paul's letter to Thessalonica. I hated to see that four-week class end.

We moved back to Tucson when I finished my graduate work that summer of 1960. But Shirley and I had both been so impressed by Miss Johnson's teaching that my wife started a Tucson BSF class for women in 1962, and I began an Evening Class for couples in 1965. Later we moved back to the Bay Area for me to go on staff with BSF.[1]

The response to that pilot class for couples in the spring of 1960 quickly convinced Wetherell Johnson of BSF's potential to minister to men as well as to women.

## Couples' Classes
Nearly a hundred people attended an introductory meeting held to gauge the interest in a Couples' Class the coming fall. The woman hosting the event at her house on that chilly June evening had to lend Miss Johnson a coat and move the meeting into the

yard so everyone could see and hear what she had to say.

So positive was their reaction to the idea of Couples' Classes that three Evening Classes began within a year. Wetherell Johnson herself launched the one in Lafayette. Dr. Richard Smith, a former medical missionary and a member of Melrose Baptist Church, taught a second class in his home in nearby San Lorenzo. In San Bernardino, Dr. Horton Voss, a Board member, taught the third Evening Couples' Class.

From the beginning, the Couples' Classes separated into discussion groups by gender, men leading men and women leading women. But Miss Johnson soon realized that Evening Classes for men only, instead of for couples, would enable Teaching Leaders to deal with specific male issues and practical life applications difficult to discuss with wives present. She began thinking that classes for men only might be a better idea.

In the meantime, the initial response to Couples' Classes was quite positive. And as the impact on marriages rippled outward through family, friends, neighbors, and fellow church members, the growth of Bible Study Fellowship gathered momentum.

Of course, including men in BSF created new challenges, as Miss Johnson herself explained in her autobiography.

### ⌒ FROM THE DIRECTOR
*Wetherell Johnson:*

> Men were inclined to dispense with some of the established procedures that we considered a key to the ministry. Some Discussion Leaders would allow members to express opinions on a passage even if they had not attempted to study or to write their summarized answers to questions ahead of time! I knew that such an attitude would ultimately erode the women's classes, where they were increasingly enjoying what they now called "the discipline." I brought this problem to the Board and felt supported by the reply of Dr. Ray Stedman: "You train women leaders; you will have to train the men also. If they wish to hold a Bible Study Fellowship class, they must follow the procedures."

Soon thereafter, I invited twenty-five potential men's class leaders in and near the Bay Area, who came to my home at 6:30 every Saturday morning. I prepared a light breakfast, and by 7:00, we were all on our knees in prayer.

I learned a great deal in the five years of meeting with the key men who became the leadership of what developed into the division of "men's work." Some men considered the questions in each week's study to be overly geared to the feminine temperament. After listening to examples, I learned increasingly to create questions that would fit both men and women. During those five years together, we developed a meaningful relationship. Gradually the men's evening classes followed the same basic patterns as in the women's classes.[2]

Despite the reluctance she felt as a woman exerting authority over men by teaching the Bible, Wetherell Johnson was persuaded to press ahead with plans for Couples' Classes and for including men in Bible Study Fellowship. She was convinced there was no greater need among contemporary Christians, male or female, than to regularly read and study the Word of God in order to apply His truth to their daily lives. Another compelling factor was the enthusiastic way so many men embraced their opportunity to share in BSF with their wives. And then, too, there were the changed lives.

One man, who eventually became a Teaching Leader in Texas, says God first had some work to do in his life.

### ↶∾ IMPACT STORY

*Larry Heppes:*

My wife, Mary, had been in Bible Study Fellowship for one year. And she completely changed—not that she hasn't always been a godly woman, but she quit nagging me. As a result of the difference I saw in Mary, I began to examine my life, which was going nowhere fast. At thirty-two years of age, I wasn't really a nice person.

I'll never forget going to a Campus Crusade for Christ event where Billy Graham was a guest. He didn't speak, but three hundred men just stood up and cheered when Billy walked in the room. Goose bumps went all over me because I knew he stood for everything I didn't. I could really see that, even before a dozen kids gave their testimonies.

Four or five months later, we had started attending this Bay Area church. Mary, who had been going to some membership classes, told me, "Our time to join the church is next Sunday. And we're going to give our testimonies to the Board of Elders that night."

I said, "Our testimony?"

She said, "What Jesus Christ means to you."

I knew Jesus about as well as I knew George Washington. Fortunately, I had a golf tournament scheduled in Sacramento that weekend, so I made sure I stayed late enough to miss the testimony time. Unbelievably, that was the only time in my life I ever won a golf tournament. I finally got home and Mary said, "Guess what? There were so many giving their testimonies that they had to hold us and one or two others for next Sunday!"

Good thing I wasn't killed during that week!

The pastor preached on Romans 1 that next Sunday morning. I went forward at the end of the service and gave my life to Christ. That night, when we joined the church, I had a testimony.

I started in Bible Study Fellowship that fall. I almost immediately got involved in leadership, which was silly because I couldn't find one end of the Bible from the other.

I loved Miss Johnson; she was my "mother in the Lord." My first Saturday morning at leaders' meeting, she greeted me by saying, "Oh yes, Larry, we've been praying about you for months!" I thought nobody knew about me!

We had a good chemistry between us. She really liked the men. She loved to kid with us and had such a great sense of humor. But, man, when she prayed, I felt like I was right there in the upper room![3]

## "The Men's Work"

Despite the encouraging growth of the organization and the rapport Wetherell Johnson had with the men in her weekly leaders' class, she never felt at ease being in charge of the ministry to men. According to one Teaching Leader, "She told us she always got up a couple hours before the men arrived at her house for their leaders' meeting. And she said she used the entire time for prayer."

The first BSF class for men

Periodically, when she broached the subject with Alverda Hertzler or some of the Board members, she would say, "Wouldn't it be great if we could find a man who could take over and lead the men's work?" Naturally, she looked for that man first among those who were already Teaching Leaders in a BSF Evening Class.

### ◦ In Others' Words

*Dr. Bob Stevens:*

In the spring of 1965, at the annual leaders' retreat at Arrowhead Springs, California, Miss Hertzler sat next to my wife during lunch. Alverda turned to Shirley and said, "Wouldn't it be great if your husband was on our staff?"

Two or three months later, Wetherell flew down to Tucson to invite me to come on staff. "We anticipate that the men's work is going to explode," she said. "If it does, we will need to train a lot of men, and I want a man to work with other men under my direction."

In 1966, I accepted the job. Wetherell called it "the men's work." But I thought of it as "the men's division." And that was how I came to be part of the headquarters staff in Oakland. One of the great privileges of my job was that every Friday afternoon I had an appointment with Wetherell Johnson. Just the two of us would sit in her home and talk about men's work and BSF in general. We would always end up on our knees together, side-by-side, praying for BSF and the work. She was an inspiring lady and was almost desperate to get people into the Word.

I admit I was somewhat intimidated by her at first, until I realized how warm she really was. She was not dictatorial with me at all. She had good suggestions and was deeply spiritual. My fondest memories of her were those times on our knees together. Listening to Wetherell Johnson pray, I could certainly tell she knew the One to whom she was praying.

While I was on staff with BSF, my office was in my home, so except for our Friday visits, I didn't interact with Wetherell much. I did hear her voice on the teaching tapes every week, and her insight into Scripture amazed me.

I taught three Bay Area Evening Classes a week. I took one existing Couples' Class in Richmond and another Evening Class down in Fremont. But by that time, Wetherell had decided not to begin any new Couples' Classes, that all-male classes would be more beneficial.

Another assignment Wetherell gave me was to write another pilot series of studies. She had written two but felt we needed a third. So, I wrote a six-week series on 1 John.

I also had many responsibilities when new men applicants came to Oakland for their Teaching Leader training. I'd pick them up at the airport on Friday evening and take them as a group to meet with Wetherell at her house. Then on Saturday, I spent more time with the men, together and individually. We would review and discuss the rules and regulations and procedures of the organization. And I would teach them some of the essentials of homiletics.

Occasionally Miss Johnson would ask me to speak to the entire group. I attended regional retreats where I would do workshops with the men Teaching Leaders.

During the time I was on staff full-time, Miss Johnson taught at Walnut Creek Presbyterian Church what was then the largest existing BSF class. Some 850 women attended. But what a lot of people probably never knew was that a few men convinced Miss Johnson to allow them to attend that Women's Day Class as well. I think Wetherell served as Discussion Leader for that group of guys before I came on. Then she assigned them to me.

Allowing men in that Women's Class was a true anomaly in BSF. I think she made the exception originally because these men appealed directly to her. She could see they genuinely desired to study the Scripture.[4]

When Bob Stevens joined the staff in 1967 to help Miss Johnson with "the men's work," there were twelve Couples' Classes in the United States with men teachers. By the time Bob left in 1970, BSF had twenty-four male Teaching Leaders, most teaching Couples' Classes. But there were a handful of new all-men classes as well. In the two years he was employed full-time for BSF, the men's work didn't explode as everyone had thought it could. It merely grew.

Bob and the Board agreed that in his third year he would work half time with BSF and half time with his church as an associate pastor. After that year, Bob Stevens left BSF to go back to teaching; he also started his own Bible study company.

### ∾ IMPACT STORY
*Dr. Bob Stevens:*

The company I founded after leaving BSF eventually had thirty-two different Bible study series, which were used by more than a thousand congregations over the next twenty-five years. I started my company and called it Church Bible Studies because I knew most churches are desperate for good Bible study material.

I tried to adapt my studies especially for churches. It is much like the BSF format, using Miss Johnson's four-prong approach because it was just brilliant. I don't know why no one had thought of it sooner.

In order for churches to start one of our classes, the teacher had to come to a seminar. So even our training paralleled the BSF type of training.

I know a number of other Bible studies spun off of BSF over the years, but I believe mine was the first. And I did so with Miss Johnson's blessing and encouragement. For that, and for the training I received from her, I will be eternally grateful. I also think that the Lord would need to credit anything I have done to Wetherell Johnson because she was an incredibly creative and special lady.[5]

It was one thing for Wetherell Johnson to conclude that offering men-only and women-only classes would be better than creating Couples' Classes. But implementing that conviction proved a slow and gradual process.

Even so, the 1970s began with some encouraging and notable developments in BSF's growing ministry to men. As had been the case with Women's Classes, the spread of Men's Classes came about in a variety of unplanned ways.

Here one of the class members recounts the beginnings of the first Men's Class in southern California.

### ∽ IN OTHERS' WORDS
*Rollin Mann:*

My wife, Marion, got involved in BSF in 1969. When she learned about an Evening Couples' Class, I joined. For two years, I was a Discussion Leader. Then our Teaching Leader resigned, another fellow was asked to take over, and he asked me to be his Administrator and Substitute TL. I taught about once a month for about eight years. When that second guy stepped down, I took over as Teaching Leader and did that for seventeen more years.

After my second year as a leader, we split the class. Miss Johnson wanted to phase out the Couples' Classes to have all Men's Classes and Women's Classes. So, when our Men's Class began, the women who had been going to our Couples' Class created an Evening Class of their own. But I think we were the only all-men's class in southern California for a long time.[6]

Myrl Glockner, Teaching Leader in Minneapolis, Minnesota, tells what happened there.

### ⟋⟍ IMPACT STORY
*Myrl Glockner:*

My husband, Bob, observed this incredible growth of our women's BSF classes around Minneapolis for a couple of years and wondered if the men could do what the women were doing and hold to these same guidelines. He thought it was worth a try. So, he was trained to be a Teaching Leader in 1970 and started a Men's Class. In two years, he had five hundred men in his class, and before long, there were three Men's Classes totaling over nine hundred men.[7]

The Men's Class in San Antonio, Texas, followed a very different pattern.

### ⟋⟍ IN OTHERS' WORDS
*Larry Heppes:*

A year after I joined a BSF class in the Bay Area, I had a big job opportunity, so we moved to San Antonio. One of my friends and I got together on our own to pray and to do some of the questions in my old BSF notes.

At that same time, I tried to talk another guy into starting a BSF class. He sent in a Teaching Leader application, but Miss Johnson never answered it. I called Lib Wenger, an Area Advisor, one day to ask, "Why doesn't Miss Johnson answer this guy?"

Lib said, "Because, Larry, Miss Johnson wants *you* to teach the class."

I talked with Miss Johnson and told her all the reasons why I would never make an adequate Teaching Leader. "Oh, Larry, don't worry about it," she said. "You'll have the notes. You'll be about forty minutes ahead of everybody else." She was a doll, that woman!

We held a pilot class one spring, and then that fall, we kicked off the class. We established our Men's Class before the

Women's Class opened—we were the only class ever to do that, I think. We started with about eighty guys, and then it dropped down into the sixties. But when the Women's Class got going a year or two later, our attendance started climbing again.

A quick story about Miss J: When I went out to California for training, my Substitute Teaching Leader and I came into a meeting maybe five minutes early. To our horror, when we walked through the door, we found the entire group on their knees, praying.

Suddenly Miss J looked up and grinned, "Fooled you!" The whole thing was a set-up—Miss J's practical joke on us![8]

With every passing year, it became clear to Wetherell Johnson that BSF's best hope for reaching men was through all-male classes. Other people in the organization were discovering that as well. While attending a regional retreat, one Teaching Leader who had started a successful Men's Class met another teacher of an all-men class in Seattle. Comparing notes with other male TLs, they learned that theirs were the only two classes growing. Many of the Couples' Classes were also struggling.

Wetherell Johnson continued to have a burden for BSF to attract and reach men. And despite any lingering concerns she had about assuming authority over men, a lot of her rapport with men was rooted in the respect she earned as a biblical scholar. She could hold her own with any theologian of the day. And, she exuded a genuine interest and concern for Christian men, quickly creating a bond of mutual affection and respect. She was thrilled to see Men's Classes become a growing and significant part of Bible Study Fellowship.

The TL of the first BSF class east of the Mississippi told how the men's work began in her neck of the woods:

꒰꒱ **IMPACT STORY**
*Mary Nell Schapp:*

I had been teaching the Bloomington (IN) Women's Class for ten or more years when my husband, Ward, got involved in BSF.

Our daughter had many friends who found the Lord through a local Young Life group. They asked me to do a Bible study for them, and when they would come over on Thursday afternoons, they always wanted me to pray for their parents.

They soon found a chance to say things such as, "Hey, Mom, why don't you go to Mrs. Schaap's Bible class?" In time, all those mothers came to BSF. One of them in particular, a surgeon's wife, committed her life to the Lord in an impressive way. She would even do her notes while on trips with her husband to medical meetings. That certainly thrilled the daughter—to see her mother come to the Lord and grow as a new Christian.

Several of those women then wanted me to start a couples' Bible study so they could get their husbands to come. Eventually those men became the core of the Men's Class after they had a real experience with the Lord through the teaching of that Couples' Class.

Two men went out to train to start the Men's Class in Bloomington. One, Charles Edwards, was an outstanding lawyer in town, and the other was my husband, a vice chancellor of Indiana University. Both men came back home smitten with Miss Johnson. My husband used to say, "She makes up for four men; she knows more than four men would know."

Our Men's Class attracted many professional people. Twenty doctors attended one year—and we're not a big town. One of those doctors loved the class so much that when he found out his nurses and secretary wanted to go to BSF, he closed his office on Wednesday morning so that his staff could come to my class.[9]

Charles Edwards's wife tells her side of that same class's story.

### ⟪ IMPACT STORY

*Carolyn Edwards:*

I was first dragged into BSF by a neighbor who was a Children's Leader in Mary Nell Schaap's Bloomington, Indiana, class. At that time in our family, we had a child with a serious injury, and I was terribly preoccupied with that. I was also busy with my own church, and we lived fifteen miles away from Bloomington. So, when my friend first invited me, I thought, *I don't have time to go to some Bible study with a bunch of little old ladies in tennis shoes.* That was my picture of it. That was about 1970.

Because she kept asking me, I finally decided to go with her, thinking that would shut her up and I would be done with this. But the first time I went, I was so taken with this woman who was standing up front talking, who seemed to know an awful lot about me. I could hardly believe it. I was mad at my friend because I figured that she had told her all about me. Yet, I could hardly wait to get back the next week to find out what else this lady knew.

Before the year was out, I had been asked into leadership and became a Discussion Leader for a number of years. Meantime, it soon became evident that we really needed a night class for women and a Men's Class. So, we started praying for that. We had one discussion group that really clung together and ended up meeting through the summer with our husbands. Before that summer ended, it was decided the husbands should lead the class.

Some of these men were doing well just to know that there was an Old Testament and a New Testament. But others were real scholars. Mary Nell Schaap's husband was in it, and he was a brilliant man, vice president of the university and quite a strong Christian. And some assumed that my husband Charles, who was a lawyer, should be a leader as well.

One day Charles came to me and said, "I've been praying about this, and I really think I should write to Miss Johnson about starting a class here."

My immediate reaction was "You don't have time!"

But Charles began corresponding with Miss Johnson and they wrote back and forth a number of times. In one letter, she told him she could see that he was a strong-willed man. He wrote her back, saying, "I can out-humble anyone you want to put up there."

I told him, "You can't send that to Miss Johnson!"

But he and Ward Schaap were invited out to California for training, and Miss Johnson chose my husband to be the Teaching Leader. He and Ward started the Men's Class here in Bloomington. Charles taught it for nineteen years, with Ward as his substitute and Class Administrator.[10]

## The Impact of Men's Classes

Wetherell Johnson acknowledged that, in the beginning, the changed lives of wives brought most men into BSF classes. But she prayed that wouldn't always be the case. And by the time she wrote *Created for Commitment,* she was able to say that it wasn't.

 **FROM THE DIRECTOR**
*Wetherell Johnson:*

Now men ask their men friends and business associates into a class. A businessman, accustomed to the majority of women in churches, is enthralled when he comes for the first time to a class of 300 men excited over Bible study—men from all walks of life. He feels there must be something to Bible study, for he knows how hard it is for a man who is occupied in business all week and who has family responsibilities to make time for solid Bible study. It is during testimony meetings at Discussion Leaders' retreats and Teaching Leaders' seminars that we truly see the demonstration of what God's power has wrought in the lives of men class members.[11]

One Californian shares the impact BSF had on him and on men in his class over the years.

## ∽ IN OTHERS' WORDS

*Norm McBride:*

My wife, Betty, started in BSF first, then she prayed me in. I joined a class and soon became a Discussion Leader, then Class Administrator, and finally a Teacher Leader. For my last fifteen years in BSF, I was TL for the Men's Class in Danville, California. The last year I taught, we had about 250 men and about 50 kids attending.

*Burson*

We had a class member named Darrell who was a strong Christian but also a "sixties guy," full beard and all that. When we asked him into leadership, he did not own even a sports coat to enable him to meet the dress standard for leaders. When he prayed about it, he said, "Lord, if You want me to be a BSF leader, You'll have to give me a suit." *Central Baptist in Alameda*

The following Sunday, at church, a lady came up to him and said, "Darrell, I have a suit that the Lord is telling me to give to you." Darrell came into leadership and was a great leader for us!

Tuesday night, I would bring the lecture. Then Wednesday, I'd read the notes and start reading the commentaries. Thursday, I'd listen to the tape, make notes on the tape, and start the lesson. Friday, I'd finish the lesson and prepare to train the guys for the leaders' meeting on Saturday morning. On Saturday, after the meeting, I worked on my Bible study for church on Sunday. Sunday afternoon, I'd start preparing my lecture and finish it on Monday. I'd leave it alone on Monday evening. Then I'd give the lecture on Tuesday, come home, and start the entire process over again for the next week.

You know, the members of our class represented between twenty-five and thirty different denominations and maybe a hundred different congregations, plus there were many guys who didn't go to church anywhere. And yet, incredible as it may seem, I don't think I ever once heard an argument at BSF, which goes to show you the unanimity that can come from studying the Bible together, especially if you are strictly studying the

Bible. I've been out of BSF a number of years, but we still get together, those of us who were friends in BSF, because those relationships we established are ongoing and eternal.[12]

Testimonies such as these heartened Wetherell Johnson. She described the joy she felt about including men in BSF this way: "To me it is like adding the quality of bass notes so necessary to music, harmonizing with the treble testimonies of the women. The men exhibit a total oneness in the fellowship, recognizing their fulfillment and leadership in both home and church."[13]

While "the men's work" of Bible Study Fellowship may not have exploded to the degree she had hoped, and never approached the total numbers for women, Miss Johnson obviously found great satisfaction in seeing the ongoing impact of her Bible study methods on countless men who discovered for themselves the power of God's Word in their lives.

As one San Francisco Bay Area class member explained:

### ⟳ IMPACT STORY
*Bill Knopsis:*

The most important thing is that BSF gets you into God's Word. You see Him. And that's where most Christians fall down. They go to church for forty years, and maybe they dust off their Bible on Sunday morning, or maybe they don't even take their Bible on Sunday morning.

If you don't read the Bible, how can you get to know the Lord? This is what Bible Study Fellowship teaches you: to get in the Word and really understand the Word.

It's truly amazing. When you first go through Matthew or John or whatever, you have questions to ask. Then the second time you go through, the same verse means something altogether different to you than it did the first time. Because as you grow, He shows and explains new things to you. But if you don't get in the Word, then you never know.[14]

# Chapter 8

# FROM FOOTHILL TO SKYMOUNT

Evidence of God's provision at headquarters

W hen Wetherell Johnson went to the bank in Oakland to arrange to purchase a home on Laird Avenue, she believed God would provide the means. The skeptical banker, however, found it hard to understand how she could be so confident that God would provide.

But He did. And her trust in Him grew even greater over the next twenty years as God's bountiful provision extended far beyond Miss Johnson's personal home: He also supplied the facilities and resources required for BSF to grow into an international ministry that affected hundreds of thousands of people.

This chapter covers only a few of the highlights in God's provision for BSF's headquarters during those years.

## The Headquarters on Foothill Boulevard

When Miss J moved to the Bay Area, her house on Laird Avenue served as BSF's only headquarters. Miss Johnson prepared and wrote her weekly lessons there. She taught forty to fifty class leaders there. The Board met there.

Volunteers typed on borrowed typewriters until 1960, when

*my Lst*
*area advisor*

someone donated an IBM typewriter to the organization. The
same year, classes raised money to purchase a table-model Ditto
Press, which was better suited for printing a thousand sets of
lesson notes and questions each week. The BSF printing and
production operation soon moved to Ruth Spidell's basement.

The need for space grew almost as fast as the classes. The
increasingly complex logistics required to operate the various
aspects of the growing ministry soon made it obvious that the
organization required a real headquarters.

Until this point, BSF's income had been sufficient to meet only
routine operating expenses. But by 1962, the donations collected
by the classes each week totaled more than was required for the
general operating budget. That provision prompted the Board to
direct Alverda Hertzler to look for property that would meet the
need and to report on that search at the next Board meeting.

### ⌒ FROM THE DIRECTOR
*Wetherell Johnson:*

> After three months of searching and answering classified ad-
> vertisements weekly, just three days before the regular meeting
> of our Board, only two houses seemed possible. We met with
> a close friend for a long session of urgent prayer. Then just two
> days before the Board meeting, Alverda saw a "For Sale" adver-
> tisement in the newspaper for a house on Foothill Boulevard, a
> convenient location. When she called, the owner replied, "That
> ad was not supposed to be in until next Saturday, but I will show
> you the house." It was the right one! The purchase of this house
> was a big leap of faith, but it was the Lord's timing.[1]

In the fall of 1962, Bible Study Fellowship opened its first
true headquarters in that house at 5133 Foothill Boulevard in
Oakland. The chair of the Board, Ernest Hastings, told Wetherell,
"This is a real venture of faith; there is no turning back now."

That house/office, conveniently located near Melrose Baptist
Church and not far from where Miss Johnson and Miss Hertzler
lived, quickly proved a great asset. It contained adequate room

for training classes; office space for Miss Johnson, Miss Hertzler, and their first full-time secretary, Ruth Stagner; plus a basement large enough to accommodate the volunteers who manned BSF's printing/assembly/shipping operation. A couple of bedrooms provided housing for Teaching Leader trainees from distant places who were invited to Oakland for their orientation.

Everyone considered the wonderful new accommodations another sign of God's blessing and provision in what was indeed, as Miss Johnson proclaimed, "the Lord's timing." Because BSF's ministry continued to grow.

The new headquarters soon housed the organization's first offset press, a photocopier, a collator, and a large paper cutter in a new and improved production department, all resources that figured to meet the demands of increasing production. The new press could churn out six thousand pages per hour.

That same year, the Lord also provided a new home that Miss Johnson and Miss Hertzler could share. The time had come when both women realized distinct advantages to living under the same roof. Sharing a home would be simpler than living in separate homes in different directions from the office.

### ⌒ FROM THE DIRECTOR
*Wetherell Johnson:*

In 1962, Alverda and I began our search for a house and hoped to find a home high in the Oakland hills. First, we found a reasonably priced lot, but regrettably, it had no view. I returned to my own little Laird Avenue home and prayed. God knew what a beautiful view meant to me, but I realized there were many of His people who also loved nature but lived without a view. Why should I insist upon His indulgence? At that, I gave my will to His, determined to be content (Heb. 13:5).

The next day we returned once more to see the lot minus the view, upon which we had by now almost made a final decision. I remarked to Alverda, "Let's go back by way of scenic Snake Road." As we did this, to our surprise, I saw a small vacant lot with an indescribable view of San Francisco Bay and a deep

ravine thickly wooded with a forest of trees. There we saw a tiny
sign, "For Sale by Owner." We made great haste to telephone
the owner and lost no time making our deposit payment! Psalm
37 had special meaning to us, "Delight thyself also in the Lord:
and He shall give thee the desires of thine heart."

The design of our home had to adapt to a steep downhill
slope and had to be built on two levels where Alverda would
occupy the upper floor and I the lower. A well-known engineer
designed the foundation. We later learned that his design of our
foundation, with provision for earthquakes, became a model for
student engineer examinations. God's provisions continued in
such surprising ways.[2]

When construction on their new home was completed in
January 1963, the ladies held a special housewarming and dedication, inviting fifty people who'd helped build or moved them into
the house. On that occasion, Dr. Ernest Hastings declared, "I see
this home as an extension of the office on Foothill Boulevard—it
is part of a ministry—a quiet and lovely place where you will
come closer to the heart of God and be able to interpret and teach
the Word, not to a few but to thousands." And in his dedicatory
prayer he told God the house was a "gift from Thy hand" to be
used at God's direction for His ministry.[3]

By 1964, the headquarters' basement had to be excavated and
extended to house an electric stapler, a new collator, and enough
storage for 200,000 lessons. In addition to the full-time roles of
Director and Administrator, BSF employed a full-time secretary
(now Jean Werum), three half-time people (one of whom was
Pearl Hamilton), and two part-time printers.

And the growth continued. By 1966, the ever-increasing
demand for materials prompted Alverda Hertzler to purchase
a larger, faster printing press and a collator that enabled the
production volunteers to keep up with the needs of the classes
and the output of the new press.

## ⌒ IN OTHERS' WORDS

*Dr. Ernest Hastings:*

In the beginning, it was a gigantic decision for the Board when we bought any new piece of equipment. We'd talk and then we'd pray, then we'd decide.

I remember Miss Hertzler walking in to the Board meetings, and she would start by saying, "I think if we purchase this new mimeograph machine, it will hold us for the foreseeable future." So, we did that.

But the classes were growing so fast, and we needed to produce so many materials, that soon no mimeograph could produce the volume of notes we needed. She did the necessary research, found the table-model Ditto press, and told us that she thought, "This will meet all of our needs for the foreseeable future."

We got that press, and within a year or so another request would be made with the assurance that "I am sure this larger press will take care of the foreseeable future." Eventually the Board began to tease Alverda by reminding her, "We think we've heard these promises about meeting our needs for the foreseeable future before."

While we did always need another bigger, more sophisticated press every year or so, inevitably there seemed to be enough money to purchase what we required. So, it was always an enjoyable experience, never a negative thing, having Miss Hertzler come in and talk about the growing needs of the printing situation. It was a concrete reminder of God's blessing and provision for the ministry's exciting and unforeseeable growth.[4]

## New People, New Equipment

Everyone who worked with Alverda Hertzler considered her one of the most significant provisions God had bestowed upon BSF. Yet, her growing workload concerned not only her but also everyone in the organization. The *BSF Newsletter* carried numerous appeals for someone with the skills required to ease her administrative load. That need became critical in the summer of 1967 when Miss Hertzler suffered a heart attack while attending a conference at Mount Hermon. Suddenly Miss Johnson and the BSF Board were forced to face the prospect of replacing her immediately and providing for the future of Bible Study Fellowship with another qualified Administrator.

What seemed a major organizational crisis became yet another opportunity for God to demonstrate both His sovereignty and His provision. Bill Gwinn, the director of Mount Hermon and a friend of Wetherell Johnson and BSF, had someone in mind.

The November 1967 *Bible Study Fellowship Newsletter* made the following announcement:

> As many of you already know, the Lord has given wonderful answers to prayer in sending to us Miss Marguerite Carter as our new Administrative Secretary in charge of our headquarters office. Miss Carter comes to our work with a wealth of experience from executive positions in commercial corporations as well as in Christian work. She was formerly Executive Secretary of Gospel Recordings. We are deeply grateful to the Lord for bringing her to our staff and pray that God will lead Miss Carter into that rich ministry which He has for her in Bible Study Fellowship. Miss Carter is renting a "chalet type" house conveniently located near Miss Johnson and Miss Hertzler. We had prayed that she might be near us since the coordination of the work would be facilitated and we have so enjoyed having her with us in our homes.[5]

The initial idea was that Marguerite Carter would replace Miss Hertzler if Alverda's health prevented her from returning to work. But Marguerite was hired and given the title of Executive Secretary to Miss Johnson.

Thankfully, Miss Hertzler returned to work sooner than anyone thought possible. But she gladly abdicated a significant part of her administrative responsibilities to the efficient and capable Miss Carter. There was more than enough work to keep both women busy.

According to one longtime BSF headquarters staff member who knew Marguerite Carter well, this addition to the staff had a big impact.

### ⌒◎ IN OTHERS' WORDS
*Anna Kingsbury:*

> Marguerite was an incredible presence—quite regal, aristo-cratic, Canadian. In the afternoon, she'd come down the hall and she'd say, "Tea? Tea?" And Jean Werum would say, "Yes." That teapot held just enough for two proper china cups of tea. So, Jean and Marguerite would have tea.
>
> Another Marguerite memory: Early on, when lessons needed to be shipped, we'd go to grocery stores and liquor stores and get their used boxes. We'd cover the liquor boxes with brown paper because they were not proper for Bible lessons. Then Marguerite came along with the idea that God's work deserves the best. So, we purchased, not just standard boxes, but *white* standard boxes. And the print had to be in block letters. Marguerite was a perfectionist.[6]

Divine provision continued to come not only in the form of much-needed personnel but also in additional new and necessary equipment. And as had been the case since incorporation, Alverda Hertzler played the crucial role in researching and acquiring the latest in production and printing technology.

The same edition of the *BSF Newsletter* (November 1967) that announced the hiring of Marguerite Carter also reported the following:

> Our new IBM Selectric Composer ordered last spring arrived in August. Miss Hertzler had seen this model demonstrated at the Printing Show in San Francisco. It is as convenient to use as a typewriter and produces "copy" for our printing equipment with the effect of professional printer's type. This newsletter, printed on this new composer, will give you an idea of how

readable and attractive is its "product." A number of
different type styles add to its versatility. Because of
the demand made for it upon its introduction to the
business world, it was predicted our machine could
not be delivered before September. However, God so
worked for us that it actually came a month early,
just in time to produce our new series on Life and
Letters of Paul and the new TL's Manual! We realized just how wonderful this was when we learned
our composer was one of the first 5 delivered in the
Bay Area.

Those of you who participated in the purchase of
the new A. B. Dick printing press last fall will be glad
to know that it has proved most valuable in keeping
up with our increased quotas of printing—operating
smoothly—and since it prints 2 sheets at a time it is
more economical than the former press. The large
Michael Miracle paper cutter (weighing nearly one
ton) posed some serious problems of installation
because of its size (and our available space). But we
tucked one end of it under the basement stairs! It is
completely automatic, operating on 3-phase electricity and cuts through reams of paper smoothly "in the
twinkling of an eye."

These purchases are being made with a long view
to our future "as well as our present" needs. Another
new addition is the equipment for putting plastic
binders on manuals and an Elliott Addressograph to
save time in addressing envelopes and parcels.

How grateful we are to God who has made possible
such modern instruments to facilitate the production
of our lessons and other materials. Those of you who
contributed to the project of the new printing press
purchased last year will be especially interested to
know that as its cost was covered by your gifts including several Memorial gifts, it became possible to
purchase the new IBM composer.

As a faith organization, it is our policy not to go

into debt for equipment, yet we constantly see God so wonderfully provide each month for our needs as He touches hearts to send the specially designated gifts, often very small, but always precious to Him and to us. Sometimes, individuals prefer to designate their gifts specifically for equipment to provide for future development and such gifts should be designated "for equipment."[7]

## Upper Skymount

The headquarters on Foothill Boulevard proved sufficient for seven years. But by 1968, the explosive growth of Bible Study Fellowship classes and the resulting increase in staff and production needs led Miss Johnson and Miss Hertzler to look for larger offices. A BSF brochure entitled *The Story of Skymount* spelled out a detailed account of the process:

### ◠ FROM THE DIRECTOR
*Wetherell Johnson:*

For many months, we had searched for a piece of land on which we could build a new Headquarters adequate for the rapidly expanding work of our organization. Again and again, we had set our hope upon a plot of land, only to find after much prayer it was not His choice for us. Then, while Miss Hertzler and I were away during the summer of 1968, Marguerite Carter wrote to us about a project of the Nahas Company of Oakland to develop an Office Park on some acres of land on Redwood Road, situated on the hill opposite their own offices. We would purchase the first plot in the proposed development, contingent upon its being commercially zoned. The price offered on this undeveloped land was more reasonable than any other property we had found.

After much prayer, our Board of Directors felt we should move ahead and trust God for His protection in the period of isolation during the completion of the Office Park development as well as for His wisdom and strength to plan and build the type of Headquarters necessary. Needless to say, it would have been a very long project.

Everything seemed to move along smoothly toward our goal. Only one obstacle remained—the approval of Oakland's Planning Commission for commercial zoning of the land for this Office Park. However, all indications led us to believe that the Nahas Company's application would be passed without hindrance, in view of the beauty of the projected plan. Then came the disappointment and seeming end of all our hope—Oakland's Planning Commission flatly turned down this petition for commercial zoning for the entire development. God never mocks His children. Therefore, we determined to "wait for Him" on tiptoes of expectancy to see what surprising and wonderful thing He would do for us. Although we completely trusted Him, there was one little nagging regret—namely that on the following Seminar day, when we were to open our first Teaching Leader's Seminar, we could not give them the good news of a completed transaction regarding the new property.

Then our loving Father indeed worked beyond anything we had asked or even dreamed! On the very day of the opening of the Seminar, the Nahas Company approached us with an offer to sell their own office building to us with its beautiful landscaped garden and unusually artistic offices. We would only need to build an addition for printing and shipping. We could move in comparatively soon, and this beautiful building, set in a glorious location, far surpassed anything we could have requested both for suitability and attractiveness!

Another step of faith lay before us. We needed to trust God to provide for the purchase of the existing building and the addition of a new printing and shipping wing. Although we had been laying aside reserve funds for this anticipated expansion of our work for several years, we did not have all that would be needed. However, as soon as our Bible Study Fellowship family realized what was ahead, spontaneous contributions began to come. Some gifts were memorial gifts; one or two gifts were of larger amounts than we have ever received during the ten years we have been incorporated. Many were gifts that represented real sacrifice! When we began to build, payments were needed at certain stages, but as each new stage for payment arrived, we found that God had provided sufficient money to cover that stage, until the whole was completed.

Much dedicated labor was also given. Miss Alverda Hertzler, Administrator, poured out energies and hours of time in negotiating for the purchase, in planning and supervising with the architect and builder during the entire project. Both the architect and builder, members of the Walnut Creek evening class, had a deep personal interest in the building.[8]

One member of the Walnut Creek class who was also the builder of that first Skymount production addition tells the story of his involvement with BSF.

### ◯ In Others' Words
*Bill Knopsis:*

My wife and I were going to a church in Martinez, California. We hadn't found the Lord yet at that time. I was Sunday school superintendent at our church and still going out and drinking and doing all that good stuff.

Our friend Jeanette started going to Bible Study Fellowship, and she got my wife to go. They were studying the Minor Prophets, and my wife spent all her time in the Bible. My wife found the Lord in the Minor Prophets. I got jealous that she was spending all her time in the Bible, so I got into it.

I was an alcoholic and had told my wife I was going to quit drinking probably four hundred times, give or take a few. One day I came home and my bags were packed, and my wife said, "That's it. You're out of here." So, I went upstairs and got down on my hands and knees, and I said, "If there's really a Lord, please take this booze away from me."

Well, a light came right through that bare wall. Not a word, nothing was said. Just a light. And I knew I would never take another drink. For forty years now, I could go sit in a bar and die there and never be tempted to take another drink. Isn't that great? That's the Lord.

So, that started it. We changed churches and found out that there's power in prayer and that the Lord is really alive and well. I walked into our new church and I felt the Holy Spirit, and I knew then that that's where I belonged.

My wife got me going to Bible Study Fellowship, and one night, about a year and a half later, my Teaching Leader stood up and said, "Bible Study Fellowship bought a building down on Redwood Road and they want to build an addition on it. Any of you guys who are contractors out there, and want to bid on this, call Ted Williams afterwards."

I saw Ted after the meeting, and he said, "Okay, Bill, come on down to my office in the morning and I'll give you a set of plans."

This was Tuesday night. The bid had to be in Thursday. I got down to his office in the morning and he was not there. There was this note and one set of plans hanging on the doors. One set. I took that set of plans and I prayed. "Lord," I said, "there's no way I can bid this. Lord, You need to give me a number."

God gave me the number $52,479—and I wrote it down. All these years later, I still remember that figure! Then I got my line-item cost breakdown, and I started running the numbers the best I could. I totaled it all up, and the number the Lord gave me was $10,000 more than what I came up with. So I said, "Okay, Lord, I'll go with your number." It came down to two guys bidding on it. Before we could get the job, we had to meet with the architect and Miss Hertzler. I went in the afternoon. We had a prayer time together. And I got the job. The Lord took care of everything, because evidently He wanted me to build it.

At the ground breaking ceremony, Miss Hertzler and Miss Johnson were there. We pulled that big rig in and cranked up that bit, and on the first revolution, *boom*! We hit the main line of water. It erupted about thirty feet in the air. I said, "Ladies, it's all right! The Lord is baptizing this job, and now we can go ahead and build it." We all laughed. If only I could have gotten a picture of Miss H and Miss J when that water shot up! What better way to start a project than with the Lord baptizing it?

We built on the storage to Skymount. All the racks had to hold the paper and had to be one-inch boards. We joined the buildings; we had a ramp there because of all the heavy paper and everything that they had to haul.

Miss Hertzler knew those plans better than I did. She was sweet, and we had a lot of fun. We built the job and it went well. We made money and they were tickled to death. It was a smooth job. I learned that when the Lord takes care of things, things go fine. They really do.[9]

*The Story of Skymount* brochure tells more about the new headquarters:

### ⟋ FROM THE DIRECTOR
*Wetherell Johnson:*

Several class members contributed materials as their participation. Dr. Stevens brought in volunteer teams of men to replant shrubs, paint areas of the existing building, and move office equipment and enormous amounts of lessons and other materials from the old Foothill Headquarters. Women volunteers cleaned and put away new lessons, helping in many ways.

Certain facts and features of this project may be of special interest: the 30,000 square feet of land will allow for possible future building. The original one-story building contains approximately 4,000 square feet of space in the offices. The new wing, which is also one-story and similar in design, has added 2,250 square feet. The cabinets provide storage for approximately 400,000 lessons as well as supplies of manuals, forms, tape recordings, and other materials. The tie-in of the new wing with the existing building is remarkable—just another evidence of God's working to make a most practical and attractive whole.

Paul closes Romans 11 with a paean of praise:
   "O the depth of the riches
   Both of the wisdom and knowledge of God!
   How unsearchable are His judgments,
   And His ways past finding out!
   For of Him, and through Him, and to Him,
   Are all things:
   To Whom be glory forever" (KJV).[10]

The new-building dedication took place at Skymount on September 11, 1969. That same year, BSF bought its first "orientation house," where staff members could live year-round and where Teaching Leaders could stay during their training week. Two other staff/orientation houses were acquired later, in 1971 and in 1974.

## Lower Skymount and the Production Facilities

When BSF moved into the Skymount headquarters in the fall

Lower Skymount

*Just down Skyline from where I live. Not quite 2 miles.*

of 1969, there were more than 100 classes and the membership approached twenty thousand. By 1971, with 131 classes and thirty thousand members, the Board finally hired a full-time professional printer, although BSF still depended heavily on volunteers to assemble and ship the lessons. The large number of employed staff required to train leaders and administer their classes, along with the production required to supply lessons for all those members, meant that headquarters was again bursting at the seams by 1972.

## ꝏ IN OTHERS' WORDS
*Marguerite Carter:*

At Skymount, one of the pleasures of every day work is in our circle of staff-team as we gather for prayer.

Class needs are what makes our office wheels go 'round. Last year's totals spiraled to quantities we measured by the ton, carried by freight lines into eighteen states and by cargo ship across the Atlantic and Pacific. This year, the increase of hundreds more means an almost constant pounding of our Tandem press and clicking of staples on "companion collators," piling up a wall of lessons every day that reflects Bible Study Fellowship, in the paper industry, as a Bay Area top consumer. Sets of lessons for adult classes will exceed the 1.25 million mark this class year and for our children an added half million "take home" lessons and songs. We praise God for the joy He gives each one at Skymount in these preparations. We, too, need your prayers applied to all our daily operations.[11]

In 1972, a building just below Skymount came up for sale. BSF bought that building and named it Lower Skymount. Miss Johnson, the growing training staff, and the administrative offices moved into those new offices. Miss Hertzler and her production folks then extended their domain into all the first building, which became known as Upper Skymount.

## ꝏ IN OTHERS' WORDS
*Alverda Hertzler:*

As we look back on the way the Lord has guided us this year, our hearts overflow with praise for the way He challenged us to step out in faith in acquiring the new building. It has indeed been an exciting spiritual adventure. To give one instance, a permit had to be secured from the City of Oakland to use the building for meetings of any sort. First, we were told a firewall would have to be installed in the large central room. An estimate showed this would be difficult, and a considerable expense. But as the

Lord worked, the escrow closing was delayed, and during this delay the city building code was changed, so we did not have to build a firewall after all.

The meeting of the Board of Directors on October 24 was characterized by rejoicing and praise. The Board members toured the new building, seeing the teaching staff offices and other facilities it provides. Following a luncheon there, their afternoon session continued in the new Conference Room. Then at 3:30 PM, all the members of the Staff and Bay Area Teaching Leaders assembled in the central room for the Dedication of the building as we joined in expressing deep gratitude to God for His provision for the needs of this expanding work![12]

As the years passed and BSF's ministry mushroomed, Alverda Hertlzer became an expert in printing and production. No one appreciated that expertise more than did her dearest friend and partner in ministry.

### ⌒ FROM THE DIRECTOR
*Wetherell Johnson:*

In 1969, when we moved to Skymount, Miss Hertzler planned the first printing addition. There we acquired a press that printed 50,000 pages per hour, and we hired our first printer. A second printing addition was built in 1973. By 1977, we had built a new building of 14,000 square feet on some adjacent land to Upper Skymount. Then Miss Hertzler purchased a huge press fed by 600-pound rolls of paper that ran off 65,000 double sheets of four pages each. How grateful I am God called Alverda Hertzler into the work. Although I had charge of the general direction and pattern of the work, the training of the Teaching Leaders, and the relationships with them, I could never have handled the other basic requirements of the work.[13]

One of BSF's long-time production staff confirmed Miss J's assessment with the following story about the addition of the new production building in 1977.

## ⁓◯ IN OTHERS' WORDS

*Anna Kingsbury:*

Miss Hertzler was the chief engineer for the project. She was well into her seventies, with her hard hat on, out there talking to the men. I love to tell this story about her, because it demonstrates Miss H and the Lord.

She was in charge and would pray about everything. But as the project went on, she was waking earlier and earlier—and then would have to retire earlier. She was wrestling with how to make everything work efficiently, especially how to move a very significant amount of materials from one room to another. One night, she prayed about it and then just went to bed. At 2 AM, she awakened, with a picture in her mind, of graded hardware rails that could transport huge pallets of lessons.

The next morning Miss H talked to Phil Seaton, the man who was handling the hardware and machinery for the project. She described to him what she had seen in her mind when she woke after having prayed and slept. Mr. Seaton immediately flipped through his catalogue, stopped, pointed to a picture, and said, "Do you mean like this?"

And there it was. She wasn't an engineer, so she didn't know how it worked or what it was called. God showed Miss H just what was needed. That whole concept that she dreamed about has been replicated in the new press at our current headquarters in San Antonio, along with her design for a collating room and a packing and shipping facility.

I used to tell that story to the people who were being trained to be Teaching Leaders. No one is ever fully equipped to do what God wants you to do, no matter how much training you get. But God is equipped, and He will provide the resources you need.[14]

## ⌒◇ IN OTHERS' WORDS

*Dr. Ernest Hastings:*

Every move, every change, every acquisition, every decision that we made was dictated by the realization that what we had was too small. The building was too small. The printing presses were too small. The printing area was too small. Evidently, God had bigger plans than we did. So, we'd have to take the next step up—in faith. And He kept on providing everything we needed.

However, in Oakland we had the printing press and production operation at Upper Skymount, with the main administrative offices down the road in Lower Skymount. Miss J and Miss H lived on Snake Road. The orientation houses where trainees came to stay were scattered around. You had to get in a car and drive to get from one part of our headquarters operation to another. So, it gradually became obvious that there could be some real benefits to having a unified campus.[15]

# Chapter 9

# A YOUTH MOVEMENT

Reaching out to young adults

It had hardly been a secret. But the rather low-key, after-the-fact announcement in the monthly organizational newsletter may have been the first time many class members heard the BSF leadership's exciting new plans.

⤳ **FROM THE DIRECTOR**
*Wetherell Johnson:*

Perhaps the most thrilling advance of Bible Study Fellowship has been in the establishment of our new Young Adult class. Although the work is still in the experimental stage at Oakland, there is every indication that God is pleased to transform lives of young adults through the study of God's Word and to fill them with an eager desire to be used by Him.

During the Spring, we tried to feel out the situation with a six-week Pilot class for young adults, ages 17 to 25. The first meeting in my home consisted of about 26 young people. We met in the new building, Lower Skymount, and concluded the six-week's series with a steady attendance of about 50. There were more men than women and about one third had no previous church contact.

The summer months represented an observation period for me. I was invited to speak at an International InterVarsity Christian Fellowship, which was held at their Mittersill Castle in Austria. This gave me a good opportunity to observe InterVarsity Christian Fellowship's present-day methods and to interact with present-day students. I was greatly encouraged by the students' responsiveness.

Following Mittersill, I also attended student sessions at L'Abri, with Francis and Edith Schaeffer, which further confirmed the Lord's leading regarding our present avenue of approach.

Today represents the third stage. At present, we have seventy to eighty young adults on Thursday nights from 7:15 to after 10:00 PM, who complete the study and give attention to the lecture, followed by a time of fellowship.

Gradually we are choosing our young adult leaders for training as Discussion Group Leaders. We also are preparing to give them further study through tapes and commentaries and personal counseling. Perhaps from this class, God may call out future Teaching Leaders.[1]

## The Schaeffers and the Start of "the Young Adult Work"

Naturally, the thought of Bible Study Fellowship classes for young adults originated long before the newsletter announcement. Some young adults around the country were already enrolled in classes. And for years, class members had bombarded Miss Johnson with inquiries about classes specifically for their youth and young adult children. These concerned parents longed for their kids to know early what they had come to learn much later in life—the power of God's Word to change lives.

Wetherell Johnson felt that the personal discipline and the theological depth required to participate in BSF classes were beyond the capabilities, or at least the interests, of most high school students. And, she wasn't sure how the BSF approach would appeal to college students and other single young adults. She realized that other fine organizations, such as Youth for Christ, Campus Crusade, InterVarsity, and Navigators, already focused on the younger generation. Yet, she said the pressure continued to provide what she referred to as BSF's "lay Bible school approach" for young people.

Anna Kingsbury, a member of the first Young Adult Class as well as a BSF headquarters staff member, offered a unique perspective on some of the factors which triggered the young adult ministry.

### ⌒⊘ IN OTHERS' WORDS
*Anna Kingsbury:*

When we began the young adult work, the headquarters was up in the Oakland hills—near the University of California, Berkeley. Kay Gudnason, who was so influential in Miss J's moving from San Bernardino to the Bay Area, knew anybody and everybody who was worth knowing in the Christian community, or at least it seemed so to me. She must have read the Schaeffers' book and given Miss J a copy of it.[2]

That book, according to Wetherell Johnson's recounting of the start of the young adult ministry, was Edith Schaeffer's *L'Abri*.

### ⌒ FROM THE DIRECTOR
*Wetherell Johnson:*

Mrs. Schaeffer's early experience as a missionary's child in China naturally caught my attention. Following this, I discovered that the story of the founding of L'Abri, near the time of the first classes of Bible Study Fellowship, was an absorbing history of God's miraculous leading. I took the unusual step (for me) of writing to Mrs. Schaeffer telling of my appreciation of her book and Dr. Francis Schaeffer's work. I received a gracious reply, giving me a cordial invitation to visit her and to learn more about the L'Abri work. Since I have deep roots in Switzerland as well as France, Alverda and I were planning to visit the continent again. We decided to accept Mrs. Schaeffer's kind invitation, little realizing at that time the enriching fellowship that would follow.[3]

The original plans for Miss Johnson and Miss Hertzler's trip to Europe had been delayed. Wetherell went to her doctor for a smallpox vaccination, required for travel to Europe, but found that she needed emergency radical surgery for breast cancer. The members of BSF not only flooded her with cards and letters but they also prayed for their leader. And in just over a month, she and Miss Hertzler boarded a plane for Switzerland.

### ⌒ FROM THE DIRECTOR
*Wetherell Johnson:*

> It so happened that Dr. Francis Schaeffer was away for some speaking engagements, but Alverda and I spent a delightful time with Mrs. Schaeffer. As we compared notes concerning the work for God we each had been given, in America and in Switzerland, Mrs. Schaeffer said, "I think the Lord has brought us together for a special purpose." This proved true far beyond our expectations.[4]

A few months later, when the Schaeffers came to America on an extended speaking tour, Miss Johnson and Miss Hertzler volunteered to arrange a week's vacation and retreat for them in Carmel. They met Dr. and Mrs. Schaeffer upon their arrival in San Francisco and enjoyed talking with them during the drive to Carmel. Miss Johnson later commented, "This was the beginning of one of the most precious friendships we have ever had."[5]

In 1971, Miss Johnson arranged for Francis Schaeffer to be the guest speaker at a Teaching Leader seminar. The more she learned about his student ministry, the more she thought about a young adult ministry for BSF. The Board encouraged her to pursue the concept.

For a variety of reasons, Wetherell hesitated to begin a trial class at a church. But about that time, the Lower Skymount building was placed on the market to sell. The first time she looked at it and saw the lounge area, kitchen, and large hall on the lower level, she thought, *Wouldn't this be an ideal place for a Young Adult Class?*

### ⌁ FROM THE DIRECTOR
*Wetherell Johnson:*

> Knowing that Dr. Schaeffer understood student needs better than anyone, I asked him if he could arrange a visit with us. He graciously came to help us with this important decision. When I asked him if he thought students would be interested and willing to give their precious time to such a serious study, I can see him now standing in the middle of that empty hall, appraising the situation. He said, "Wetherell, if the Board is willing, I urge you to go ahead. This would be a perfect setup for students, and I am convinced they would revel in the Bible study presented."[6]

Once Francis Schaeffer gave his blessing, in Wetherell Johnson's mind, the purchase of Lower Skymount and the BSF ministry for young adults were both done deals. Indeed, Anna Kingsbury remembers, "It had been through Miss J's connection with the Schaeffers that she decided she wanted to do in the student scene what she had done with adult Bible studies. So, Dr. Schaeffer came and chatted with her. Shortly thereafter, she called to ask if I would go to L'Abri with her. We were in Switzerland for about six weeks, and after we came back, we began that first young adult class."[7]

The six-week young adult pilot class in the spring of 1972 covered Paul's letter to the Ephesians. When the Young Adult Class officially began in September of that year, class members began their yearlong study of *The Life and Letters of Paul,* on schedule with the other Bay Area classes.

Years later, when writing her autobiography, Miss Johnson recalled that first Young Adult Class.

## ⌒⌒ FROM THE DIRECTOR
*Wetherell Johnson:*

Mrs. Pearl Hamilton and I, after a long time of discussion and prayer, began this new venture with young adults. The Reverend Mike Ladra was an early staff man who contributed much to its development.

The construction of this new program involved some adjustments in the class structure; we tried to enroll an equal number of girls and young men, although discussion groups temporarily separated them. After the lecture time was given, they assembled to ask questions and to give testimonies as to what God had given them. Class commenced at 7:30 PM, but no time limit was set for closing of the class. Afterwards, refreshments were served, which gave opportunities for men and women to become acquainted and for personal counseling.[8]

## ⌒⌒ IMPACT STORY
*Susy Harbick:*

Miss Johnson always wanted to be down on the floor with the young adults, and that was not an easy thing for her to do with her bad back.

I was the Class Administrator, and she would drive me nuts because she had no concept of time when she was lecturing. It was amazing that she could be still in her introduction, with five minutes to finish. Somehow, she would just go through her outline and finish.

Miss Johnson also used to have a personal evaluation time for us. She was very much into application and trying to motivate people to think beyond where they were—to give them a broader or very different view. In the Young Adult Class, she wanted young people who had never been married to have the opportunity to think of something beyond marriage, to go on and explore missions or Christian work, and to meet Christian mates. They could have Christian marriages, but the whole motivation was to get us out and get us working in the world.

She affected me with the challenge to be willing to go beyond where I was comfortable. I never would have gone to Africa, which I did in the early seventies, if I hadn't learned that from her. I might not have been willing to trust God enough to do any number of things I've done in life if not for her. That kind of trust in God was a whole new thing for me.[9]

## BSF with "Rap Time"

After Miss Johnson observed young people at L'Abri, Francis Schaeffer proposed that she not change her basic approach or even her study questions. She and the BSF leadership, however, understood that for their young adult venture to succeed, the basic BSF class structure would require some creative adaptation and concessions to the lifestyle and the natural interests of young people. Although she had phased out the Couples' Classes in favor of single-gender Evening Classes, Miss J recognized that a Bible study aimed at students and young single adults would have more appeal with the added opportunity to meet with like-minded members of the opposite sex. The discussion groups remained single gender, but the rest of the class session was coed.

An informal "rap time" immediately followed the lecture, a Young Adult Class distinctive. Having no set ending time was certainly different for a BSF class. With that format, the yearlong pilot class continued to succeed. It began meeting at headquarters in the fall of 1972. By the following spring, the *BSF Newsletter* reported the following:

> Our Young Adult Outreach is a continual joy and concern that we establish these classes on a firm basis. Although we accept new members over 18 years of age, the main interest is from ages 20 to 25, and under 30. They enjoy the lesson notes and complete

the questions as well as, and sometimes even better than, some classes of older persons. Our rap session has become a special time of warm fellowship and both generations (staff leaders and young people) are in process of learning each other's kind of spiritual songs![10]

Another member of that first Young Adult Class shares the following recollections:

### ⌒⊙ IN OTHERS' WORDS

Karen Dable: — *Later became Miss J's secretary & was a member of my discussion group.* —

*Karen married Greg Dabel — he "invented" Ps & Ts. — They both became TLs — they now live in Santa Rosa.*

I came to Skymount from San Francisco on the night of our Young Adult Class, by bus, and would arrive at class early and have to wait around. Miss Johnson always came early, and she took me in.

At first, that Young Adult Class was small, of course, maybe eighty members. There were more later. We used to give Miss Johnson a bad time. She would assign us to come up with a song of the week—something that was supposed to go with whatever we were learning. Miss Johnson always thought they were spiritual songs, but sometimes they weren't. One week we were studying the Flood, and we started singing "Somewhere Over the Rainbow."

Miss Johnson exclaimed, "Sing it, dears, sing it!" We had fun with her, we teased her a lot, but we were also respectful of her. You might say we had a kind of awe and reverence.[11]

In the *BSF Newsletter*, the Deputy Director reported on the special relationship between the aging British lady and the young Americans.

### ↶◠ IMPACT STORY

Pearl Hamilton:

The Teaching Leader Retreat, March 9–11, 1973 included the first group of Young Adult Leaders to attend a Bible Study Fellowship conference. Eight of these Young Adult Leaders represented the Skymount Young Adult class, which Miss Johnson is currently directing. They made a real contribution as they led the singing with their guitars at the Saturday evening family session. Their enthusiasm was manifest throughout the conference and was contagious.

One refreshing touch from the young leaders was when they spontaneously scribbled a message to Miss Johnson in block letters on binder paper, and each held up a letter. Then so all should see, they ran on stage and spelled it out.

It was, "W-E L-O-V-E Y-O-U"![12]

One member of that first Young Adult Class, and the mother of another class member, tell about the unique, lasting relationship several class members developed with Wetherell Johnson.

### ◠ IN OTHERS' WORDS

*Karen Dable:*

When I first started the BSF Young Adult Class, I was working as a young, inexperienced secretary in San Francisco. I had just graduated from college the year before. A month later, Wetherell Johnson asked me if I would come on staff. I said, "I'll pray about it." But I was thinking, *I can't believe it!*

She sent me to night school to learn stenography, so I was able to take shorthand. Marguerite Carter was her official secretary, but I had an office outside of Miss Johnson's, so I handled correspondence for her and did whatever else she needed me to do.

I loved her instantly. She was British. I would sometimes spontaneously hug her. Some of the older BSF women, as they saw me interact with her at retreats and different events, thought that was wonderful, that I could soften her.[13]

*~∞* IMPACT STORY *former TL of Concord Day Class*

*Skip Brey:*

I'm sure Miss J was like this with a lot of people, but when she got be your friend, she made you feel as if you were her individual friend. And yet, for a long time after we became friends, she continued to formally address me as Mrs. Brey. It wasn't until she'd had the young adult group for a while that she began calling me Skip like everyone else did. It was through the influence of the young adults that she became what she called "Americanized." She would say, "Americans do this."

The story came home from my daughter, who was in that class, that sometimes Wetherell Johnson actually sat on the desk and dangled her legs when she was giving her lectures to the young adults. Evidently, she got very, very informal with the kids. And yet she always said, "Young people need to be challenged, and they will pick up on a challenge if you give it to them." So, she didn't water things down for the young adults whatsoever; they worked hard.[14]

## Signs of Spiritual Growth

The new Young Adult Class at Skymount continued to grow in its second year, with an almost equal number of men and women attending. For many BSF staff, that measure of success alone was evidence of God's leading into "young adult work." But even more heartening for Miss Johnson was the spiritual growth she saw in the class leadership—they began the class as members, they ended as leaders and even staff members. The *BSF Newsletter* regularly hinted at headquarters' excitement over this new venture.

Fall 1974

- "The feature that is different from the regular classes is the Rap Sessions. After closing the lecture promptly, the young people stay in their seats and begin a rapid-fire of questions and comments directed to Staff Members, Miss Johnson, and Greg Dable who shares the lecturing responsibilities. The questions are more focused on their real doubts, curiosities, and concerns than before."

- "An outstanding fact of this evening class is that all our Discussion Leaders have their class socials at their homes and tell of rich intercommunication which demonstrates a significant growth in their lives."

Summer 1975

- "Our two Young Adult Classes are moving well. We have about 120 at Skymount; a new class, led by a Professor of Architecture at Fresno City College, has also reached that number. We have discovered that the present youth want solid answers now.

  "We find they prefer a person of experience so long as he or she 'speaks their language' even though their 'lifestyle' must be re-oriented to become Christ's 'lifestyle' and they recognize the absolute necessity of private personal study of the Bible, and appreciate the value of following the BSF format."

Christmas 1975

- "Ahead lies the promise of new developments in the Young Adult work. The first Young Adult Classes at Skymount and Fresno have proved that the new generation are eager and open to God's Word—ready for serious study."

- "A young pastor, who is a graduate of Princeton Seminary, is now assisting Miss Johnson in the areas of Young Adult and Men's classes."

Christmas 1976

- "This September several of our Skymount Young Adults began a new Young Adult class in Contra Costa under the direction of Miss Johnson, Pearl Hamilton, and Mike Ladra. Both classes are growing rapidly."[15]

Wetherell Johnson remained personally committed to the organization's young adult experiment. Just as she won the respect and affection of BSF's young members, they also won hers. To hear the stories recounted by some of the principals, the relationship between these California kids of the sixties and seventies and a formal English lady old enough to be their grandmother was something of a mutual love fest.

## ⌒ꙩ IN OTHERS' WORDS

*Karen Dable:*

She would have us to her home for evening meals. I would go over to help her prepare. We would take out her lovely china. She always bought Gino's Pizza Rolls, because someone had told her young people loved pizza, and I was forever in the kitchen putting these in the toaster oven.

We would sit out on her glassed-in deck at this long table. She had a spectacular view, with all three San Francisco Bay bridges visible out the windows. She would also make name cards for us and would write a special verse for each of us. Mine was John 15:16: "You did not choose me, but I chose you and appointed you to go and bear fruit—fruit that will last." All of my life God has continued to use that little place card that Miss Johnson gave me personally. I think that's amazing.

My husband was saved through Miss Johnson in that Young Adult Class. He went to U.C. Berkeley and was not a believer. The first night he walked in, he was wearing a checked shirt, coveralls, and a Calypso scarf, with hair hanging down and long muttonchop sideburns. Only three weeks after he started coming to the class, he accepted Christ. Eventually he was asked to come into leadership.

Our wedding was a total BSF wedding. Miss Johnson and Miss Hertzler were both there. Pearl Hamilton played the organ. She played through all our *Leaders' Hymnal*: "I Am His, He is Mine"; "Be Thou Our Vision."[16]

## ⤳ FROM THE DIRECTOR

*Wetherell Johnson:*

Marriages were so frequent that almost all of our leadership had to be changed each year, as this was an "unmarried class." It was delightful to see new homes founded upon a Biblical basis.

In order to stabilize and deepen theological knowledge in both students and staff, some summers Miss Hertzler and I would take a group to study for a month under Dr. Schaeffer at L'Abri. Those who could, paid their own expenses; otherwise, we helped with their travel. This was a delightful experience. I introduced them to mountain climbing and the ski lifts and was available for counseling. I don't know who enjoyed it most, they or Miss Hertzler and I. The theological training of Dr. Schaeffer led several to think in terms of full-time Christian work and seminary.[17]

## ⤳ IN OTHERS' WORDS

*Karen Dable:*

In Miss Johnson's summer vacations, she would go visit Dr. and Mrs. Schaeffer. She took me once to L'Abri. I was there for three weeks with her and Miss Hertzler. My friend Lynn Murphy and I were roommates.

One morning, Lynn and I were sleeping in, but Miss Johnson decided she wanted adventure in the mountains. She came to our chalet and threw little pebbles against the wooden shutters. We went to the window to see what the ruckus was, and there was Miss Johnson waving and saying, "Honeys, honeys, we're going on a ride. Hurry up!"

That woman loved the countryside! And she loved chair lifts. Once Lynn, Miss Johnson, Miss Hertzler, and I rode a chairlift up a mountainside over summertime greenery and flowers. Miss Hertzler was giggling; she had such a wonderful laugh! And Miss Johnson exclaimed, "Oh, Alverda, isn't this just wonderful!"

We came down, got back in the car, and headed on to wherever we were going.

This same woman was so intent on expanding our spiritual horizons that she also took us to the Congress at Lausanne, with Dr. Schaeffer, in 1974. Here was this incredibly impressive and sophisticated woman with such a deeply intense relationship with God, on the one hand. Then you also have this person who takes little-girlish delight in things like flowers and chair lifts. I saw in her this wonderful mixture—the depth of God and the awe of God as Creator and the joy of life. She was an adventurer who would try to do just about anything, which, to me, was God in her.

I'll have to admit that I did put her on a pedestal at first. I loved her and felt this real warmth toward her. Not as if she were my mother. Or even a grandmother. I just felt as if I could soak up God with this woman.

Fortunately, the Lord did not allow her to stay on my pedestal. I soon saw her human side, which was lovely as well and was what endeared her to me the most.

Miss Johnson would dictate to me, holding the copy of the letter she was answering. But she often wouldn't say the name of the person she was writing. She'd simply make up a name. "Dear Miss Diggiwhiskers"—she'd often use that one. She'd tell me what to say as I took the shorthand. When she reached a conclusion, she would tear up the original letter and toss it in the circular file, never telling me whom her response was for.

Because I was young and in awe of her, I wouldn't say anything.

When she would go home for lunch, I would slip into her office, get down on my hands and knees by the wastebasket, dig out the original letters, and figure out which response needed to go to which correspondent. Then I could type the letters and send them out. Finally, one day, after a couple of months of that, I thought, *I've got to tell her she needs to hand me those letters.* So, as she wrapped up her response, I worked up my courage, reached for the original letter, and said, "I'll take that, Miss Johnson." After that, she would always hand them to me.[18]

The young adult work was never so much about numbers as it was about the chance to enable young Christians to apply the Word of God to their everyday lives—for the rest of their lives. The effectiveness of BSF's young adult ministry was best illustrated in the lives of the three members of that first Skymount class quoted in this chapter. Anna Kingsbury, Susy Harbick, and Karen Dable not only attended but they also were invited into leadership for the class. All three then became part of the BSF headquarters staff, all three became Teaching Leaders, two taught BSF classes overseas, and all three were active in BSF for thirty or more years.

Members of the eleven Young Adult Classes meeting at that time were asked to comment on the value of their BSF experience. Some of those testimonies—evidence of the lasting impact of BSF—were recorded in the May 1990 *BSF Newsletter.*

- Members of classes have many of the same struggles and hurts as married couples; however, they do not necessarily have family or friends in the city as a support group. There is an atmosphere that this is a safe place to come, share, and grow. Young adults feel better about sharing their struggles relating to their singleness because of the mutual understanding.

- When the Minneapolis/Richfield class, now in its thirteenth year, started, it drew primarily from the young adult children of BSF members in other classes. As the class grew and matured through the years, class members began to reach out to their coworkers and friends, resulting in a more diversified and interesting class with a wide range of backgrounds, occupations, interests, and denominations.

- It fills a void left by bars, dating services, et cetera.

- It is a tremendous witnessing tool; since it is citywide, anyone can be invited. It's also unifying.

- Positive Peer Pressure.

- It brings me together with other single Christians who are also searching for life's answers through biblical teaching.

- It educates us about God's Word and better prepares us to share His Word with unbelievers.[19]

Clearly, Wetherell Johnson's vision for young adult Bible Study Fellowship lived on—as it does today in twenty-five classes.

# Chapter 10

# REPEATING THE PATTERN, PART I
## Training leaders

O ne of Bible Study Fellowship's most important distinctives, from the beginning, has been a commitment to training. Wetherell Johnson's determination not to "spoon-feed" those first five ladies who came to her in San Bernardino grew out of her understanding of their deepest spiritual needs and her subsequent desire to train them to discern for themselves the guidance and help God provides through His Word.

When the work in Oakland took off, training leaders to deal with the mushrooming growth in those first Bay Area classes became an immediate priority for Miss Johnson. As classes quickly spread from California to Indiana, Arkansas, Arizona, Washington, and elsewhere, the distance to new classes prompted Miss Johnson to consider having Area Advisors to oversee new classes. Some consideration was given to training new Teaching Leaders in their own region, saving the time, money, and effort to bring them to Oakland for orientation. But Miss Johnson decided that regional offices would change the character of Bible Study Fellowship.

⟜ **FROM THE DIRECTOR**
*Wetherell Johnson:*

Every Teaching Leader should keep close personal contact
with the General Director by phone and by letter. The future
Area Advisors' work will be to advise headquarters of any real
problem in policy or procedure that arises on the field, and be a
counselor and supervisor of classes in each region.

I believe this decision proved to be one secret to the strong
relationship all Teaching Leaders have with headquarters. As
general director, I came to know and love each one and was able
to pray for them individually. We are truly a fellowship! When
triennial seminars for Teaching Leaders were instituted, the
heartwarming fellowship and testimonies gave evidence to the
links that were strongly forged during the week when "would-
be" Teaching Leaders were in headquarters for training.[1]

## The BSF Way

The decision to maintain a centralized training program,
administered at headquarters by the Director, coincided nicely
with Wetherell Johnson's hands-on approach. Although the BSF
training policy placed seemingly frustrating limits on growth,
those limits ultimately benefited the organization in the years
that followed.

As Miss Johnson asserted in *Created for Commitment*, cen-
trally trained Teaching Leaders helped preserve the organization's consistent quality and amazing growth. She could hardly
say enough about their contribution.

⟜ **FROM THE DIRECTOR**
*Wetherell Johnson:*

The Teaching Leaders give at least twenty hours or more each
week to study and meetings and find unspeakable fulfillment in

teaching a class of up to 450 members, leading individuals to the Lord and training Discussion Leaders who could one day become Teaching Leaders for another class in the area. Every one of them came into being as a "miracle" of God's circumstantial leading and personal call to a demanding and fulfilling ministry stamped with eternal value.[2]

Early on, Miss Johnson and the headquarters staff emphasized the importance of the distinctive "BSF way." An archived copy of typed revisions for a brochure about the organization, from 1966–67, reads as follows:

Classes have developed in other cities and states as experienced Bible teachers have become interested in the Bible Study Fellowship methods and material, and have met the requirements, which include a visit to the San Francisco Bay Area to observe the operation of the classes and receive first-hand experience in the methods of training Discussion Leaders and of the organization.

Already, after only a few years of existence, the implications were clear. Required training in specific methods and materials was the starting point of the BSF way.

In the remainder of this chapter and in the next, we intersperse the experiences of a handful of early TLs with some of Miss Johnson's own accounts of the who, what, where, when, and why of BSF leadership training. The combination provides an overview of what Wetherell Johnson intended training to be and what it meant to those who went through it.

## DL and TL Training

Most BSF Teaching Leaders began as class members and then were invited into leadership, first as Discussion Leaders. Miss Johnson talked often about the essential leadership DLs provide.

### ⟋ FROM THE DIRECTOR
*Wetherell Johnson:*

I taught new Teaching Leaders that the key to a fruitful ministry lay more in their training of leaders than even in their lecture. Discussion Leaders developed a relationship with each member of the small group. This fellowship counts particularly in the life of a new member who is perhaps totally unacquainted with the Bible.

I loved my own Discussion Leaders' class. They were taught never to say, "that's wrong" to a class member, and not to give out any answers. Instead, they were to look around and ask if another member might have a different opinion. In addition, every Discussion Leader was required to submit an outline of the passage to be taught.

We always kneel for prayer. I do not believe kneeling is just a matter of form; there is something of earnestness, of recognition of the majesty of God that our Western, comfort-loving Christians seem to lose. We became intimately close. I sensed that any Teaching Leader's effectiveness depends largely upon the spiritual quality and dedication of each Discussion Leader who led fifteen class members. Each discussion class has a prayer chain for those who wished to participate each week.[3]

In 1964, Miss Johnson invited Skip Brey to become a Discussion Leader for her Walnut Creek class. Here is her story:

### ⟋ IN OTHERS' WORDS
*Skip Brey:*

Before becoming a Discussion Leader, I had to have an "interview" with Miss Johnson. I was so nervous about meeting this woman face to face! She came up to me out on the patio and stood close. She took both of my hands in hers and looked me square in the eye. "Mrs. Brey, I understand that you would make a good Discussion Leader," she said.

She asked me how long I had been in church and a couple of other questions, still holding my hands. Then she said, "Now, I want to tell you this one thing. We do not 'go off picking daisies.'"

I had no idea what she meant by that, but I said, "I see."

Then she concluded, "I think you'll be just fine."

Looking back, I think she read right down into my soul and the Lord said, "She's okay; don't worry about it."[4]

Five years later, in 1969, Skip Brey trained to be a Teaching Leader. She and Jeanette Tompkins were the only two in their orientation session.

### ⟿ IN OTHERS' WORDS

*Skip Brey:*

Jeanette and I drove in every day to Oakland from Walnut Creek for three days of training. We had our meetings in Miss Johnson's house. One day we spent with Miss J, one day with Pearl Hamilton, who did the administrative training; then we went over to headquarters for one afternoon of training for the Children's Program. On our day with Miss Johnson, we got there fairly early in the morning and she handed us Teaching Leader manuals. Then she went through those manuals line by line, telling us what they were about, in detail.

We were dead tired by the time we were to go home. I don't remember "going off picking daisies." I finally figured out what that meant—stay on topic![5]

Jeanette's story of the events leading up to that training session is inspiring.

### ⟿ IN OTHERS' WORDS

*Jeanette Tompkins:* My y dear, dear Jeanette for many years. Was my area advisor. Is 92 yrs old. Now lives in Tahoe

I had gone to church and Sunday school all my life. But when my Catholic neighbor invited me to go with her to something called Bible Study Fellowship, I thought, *If a Catholic is inviting me to something at a Protestant church, the least I can do is go and see what's going on.*

I wasn't particularly interested in studying the Bible. Not because I didn't believe it was true—I did. I even believed that Jesus Christ was the Son of God and that He died for the sins of the world. And I was hoping I would be good enough to go to heaven when I die.

So, I went with my neighbor to BSF, and it was like eating one peanut—I couldn't stop. I cried through every lecture for a while. I knew the women in that class had something I didn't have. I wasn't sure what it was, but I wanted it.

BSF at that time had what was called an Assurance Letter, a sheet of paper with questions to ask yourself and Bible references to read to know that you have personally accepted Christ and are indeed a Christian. It is now called "Steps to Assurance." My discussion group leader had given it to me. I read it. And one day at home, in the middle of doing my lesson, I dropped to my knees at one of the chairs at my dining room table, and I thanked the Lord Jesus that He died for my sins. Like the letter said I needed to do, I invited Him to come into my heart, take control of my life, and help me live it in a way that was pleasing to Him.

I got off my knees that day with the assurance I would go to heaven when I died.

Miss Johnson was the Walnut Creek Teaching Leader, and we were studying Genesis in 1964 when I came to know the Lord. Two and a half years later, I was invited into leadership, as a Discussion Leader.

In December of 1968, my husband and I crashed in a small airplane. We had been given clearance to land but came into a freak pocket of fog and crashed into trees. My husband, sitting right beside me and piloting the plane, was killed. His whole side of the airplane was gone. My back was broken.

When I recovered enough to come back to class (I was a

discussion group leader at the time), Miss Johnson wanted me to tell all the leaders about the experience. When I finished, she said, "Maybe God wants Jeanette to be a Teaching Leader sometime."

That summer she invited me to her house. There were nine hundred people in her Walnut Creek class by that time. So she was dividing her class into three separate classes, and she asked me to take the one that she taught right there at Walnut Creek. The other two classes would move—one would meet in Danville and the other in Concord.[6]

Miss Johnson explained more about her intentions in training leaders.

### ⌁ FROM THE DIRECTOR
*Wetherell Johnson:*

At this point, it is important to explain the philosophy and procedure of the pattern given by God as the secret of God's blessing in the amazing expansion of the work in less than ten years. This lay largely in the fact of each Teaching Leader's dedication and reliance on the Holy Spirit's power.

Teaching Leaders and Substitute Teaching Leaders were invited to headquarters as candidates. In most cases, they paid their own transportation to headquarters in Oakland. At first, some were accommodated at the Foothill office, others in the home of friends. During this week, the staff and I grew to know each candidate's personality. Since the Teaching Leader is the key to a successful class, personality was all-important; and I, as well as others, considered their gift of communication, spiritual outlook, and agreement with the principles of procedures and policies. We considered these four orientation sessions each year of vital importance.

Often, candidates would arrive in Oakland scared! Therefore, our first mission was to make them feel accepted and at home. Marguerite Carter and Mrs. Pearl Hamilton would meet them and often have a scenic evening showing off the sights of San Francisco. As the work grew, we purchased three orientation houses, all located within easy access of headquarters and my home. Each of these houses was occupied by a staff member as her residence throughout the year, which she shared with each group of orientees during their week in training. These homes provided a natural home and gave opportunity for trainees and staff to enjoy a fellowship and love that carried into each class.

On Sunday night these groups, which grew from ten to twenty persons, would crowd into my living room. After a welcome and prayer, they would identify themselves in any way they chose. I think I loved this session second only to my teaching of God's Word. As each one spoke, unconsciously he or she revealed his or her personality, and many interesting stories emerged. Always a large percentage of these orientees had been converted at Bible Study Fellowship meetings.[7]

One Teaching Leader who trained at the headquarters on Foothill Boulevard before serving twenty-eight years as a TL tells about her involvement in BSF.

## ꙮ IN OTHERS' WORDS
*Ruth Larson:*

My tennis partner was going to go to BSF and she invited me to go. I had two young children and she said it offered "free babysitting." That was for me. I hadn't been in the class three months when I was asked into leadership as a Discussion Leader. Several years later, I trained to be a Teaching Leader.

BSF put us up in a small house, downtown. The four of us who were there for training stayed in a couple of bedrooms above where they did the printing. They would come pick us up and drive us to Miss Johnson's house on Snake Road.

When I had my personal time with Miss Johnson, I told her that I was under a TL who was so gung-ho BSF that her family was neglected. I had told the Lord that I wouldn't do that. So, I also informed Miss J of that vow.

Bible Study Fellowship changed my life because God's Word changes your life. Because I had to teach it, I had to apply it.[8]

Wetherell Johnson explained more about the training routine for Teaching Leaders.

### ⌒ FROM THE DIRECTOR
*Wetherell Johnson:*

During orientation week, all the visiting candidates attended classes, including my own, and studied administration and class finances with Miss Hertzler. These sessions also included the study of homiletics and an entire day of the Teaching Leader's manual, where I explained the "whys" of some procedures.

At leaders' meetings we do teach leaders some of the techniques of speaking, which is called "homiletics." Among other techniques, some people like to stress having three divisions of the subject beginning with the same letter for the purpose of memory. Many of our discussion leaders find this a tantalizing "brain teaser."

On Wednesday night, we all went out "on the razzle." Then, on the day of departures, I had personal interviews with each candidate. Each one would receive confirmation of acceptance, or if not, some gentle suggestion of another position of service in Bible Study Fellowship. We become intimately acquainted and subsequently frequently communicate by telephone and letter, visit classes and help Teaching Leaders by instruction and fellowship.[9]

## Miss Johnson's Stamp on the Leadership

Orientation weeks allowed Miss Johnson and her staff to know the Teaching Leader applicants personally; and, many would-be Teaching Leaders had their first opportunity to interact with BSF's national leadership.

Each Teaching Leader has his or her own story of orientation with Miss Johnson. Here is a most unusual one.

## IN OTHERS' WORDS
*Marion Mann:*

The only reason I went to a BSF class was that I belonged to the church where it met at the time. In those days, I was reluctant to do anything; I was a very fearful person. But I immediately saw this was indeed something I could handle.

However, I never would answer the personal questions or go to any of the fellowships, because that was just too threatening for me. But because I knew the Bible and answered all those Bible-related questions, they thought I had potential. And that's how I was asked to be a Discussion Leader.

When I finally went to Oakland for Teaching Leader training, we went to one house, where Marguerite Carter was house mother. I came down with stomach flu and fever. I said, "Marguerite, I am really ill."

She said, "You're going to go through the training anyway." And that was that.

On the day that we were to have homiletics with Miss Johnson, we were all herded over to her living room, and I was sitting on her couch, just leaning back. Miss Johnson stopped in the middle of a sentence and said, "Marion, my dear, what's wrong with you? You look terrible!"

My roommate said, "Miss Johnson, she's sick."

Miss Johnson said, "Oh, oh, get her a blanket! Get her pillows!"

Everybody scurried around throughout the house. People put pillows behind me, tossed a throw over me, and she went on. She did not miss two minutes of time. They propped me up the rest of the day, and I was not required to go to dinner that night.

The next day, we were to head home and I was crawling, pulling my suitcase out, to get ready to go. Marguerite came and said, "What do you think you are doing, Marion?"

I said, "I'm packing, Marguerite. We're going home."

And she said, "You're not going home, my dear. You are going up to stay here with Miss Johnson tonight. She feels you are too ill to travel."

So, when everybody else went home, I went up to Miss Johnson's house. That was God's provision because I had been so terrified of that woman. Miss Johnson put me in her own bed, and she slept on the sofa. She was so gracious. She came in the next morning and said, "I'm going to fix you something that we always use at home. We like fish. That'll help you."

I prayed one of the most sincere prayers in my life: "Please, Lord, don't let me throw up here in Miss Johnson's bed!"

So, she fixed and served me fish broiled in milk, with English muffins and tea. I got it down and I felt fine. Miss Johnson sat on the edge of the bed and we talked about books we both enjoyed. It was just a beautiful time of sharing. She even sang to me. God knew I needed to see that side of her, because that wasn't the image most people had of Miss Johnson. She served me and then sent me home.

I taught BSF for thirty-three years and retired at age seventy.[10]


Marion Mann was far from being alone in feeling fearful and inadequate to serve as a Teaching Leader. She and other TLs may have been surprised, though, to learn that Wetherell Johnson could personally relate to their feelings.


### ⌒ FROM THE DIRECTOR
*Wetherell Johnson:*

Often I comfort new Teaching Leaders by telling them how Satan attacks me before speaking in a class. Yet once one is in the pulpit with a well-prepared outline and alert to the varied expressions of the audience during the message, the Holy Spirit takes over, and teaching the Bible becomes quite definitely the

most exciting, delightful, and fulfilling work one ever does.
Then to hear of changed lives gives an unspeakable exhilaration. I am always careful to turn aside any suggestion of praise,
remembering, "God will not give his glory to any other." This is
also the reason we never advertise or solicit, for fear of touching
"the glory of God" (Isa. 42:8).[11]

The Teaching Leader who started the first BSF class in
Indiana tells about her training.

## ⌒◯ In Others' Words

*Mary Nell Schaap:*

The orientation class was small when I was there, but the
method of teaching was the same as it is now. Changes came
with growth, but BSF kept Miss Johnson's initial idea of how to
study the Bible, that she would not spoon-feed anyone. And
they were careful to utilize the very best theological input for
the training of TLs—and in the children's department. They went
to the top somehow. At one retreat, J. I. Packer and R. C. Sproul
were there. And then there was the retreat with the Schaeffers.

Miss Johnson's background gave her such a broad knowledge and insight, and what she went through as a young woman
in China really toughened her. She was also brought up with
demanding teaching in the course of her classical education—
and that impressed the men especially.

But the secret was her radiant love for the Lord and being
able to communicate that. She radiated love and humility at the
same time. She always gave you the feeling that she would be a
mess without the power of God. She didn't let anybody use her
as her model. The Teaching Leaders were all different kinds of
people. She didn't try to make them into clones of herself. She
said to Pearl Hamilton once, "You're looking at me and not the
Lord, Pearl. Don't be doing that." She didn't let anyone idolize
her or be her little groupie. She made you see the Lord and not
her.[12]

# Chapter 11

# REPEATING THE PATTERN, PART 2
## Establishing policies and an organizational culture

I n the early days of Bible Study Fellowship, the Teaching Leader orientation training was the primary means of ensuring the establishment of the "BSF way" for new classes. But it wasn't long before the organization grew to the point where additional resources were required to maintain the quality and uniformity of the BSF way among all the classes being launched around the country. Spreading the time-tested policies and procedures across the growing organization contributed to an organizational "culture"—a coherent and consistent way of doing things that God had already proved He would bless.

## The Teaching Leader's Manual
It began with the Teaching Leader's manual.

### ⌒ FROM THE DIRECTOR
*Wetherell Johnson:*

When we received more applications for new classes far from us, I felt the time had come for us to compile a leader's manual, which they would study and take home with them.

This would be a further development of assistance to them. When we compiled the manual, we asked leaders to give their contributions to its composition. I remember Mrs. Katherine Plate of Berkeley inviting several friends to her home at Mount Hermon Conference Center, where we discussed and decided upon some basic rules that we thought necessary for our unique method of study. Although the atmosphere of each Bible Study Fellowship class would reflect the Teaching Leader's personality, part of the "family" fellowship among the classes was derived from the fact that to attend one class—whether in the Bay Area or elsewhere—it would be basically the same (as another) since each class would follow the pattern God gave us, and the basic structure, later known as "Policies and Procedures." In time, there were manuals for Class Administrators and Children's Leaders, and separate manuals for men's classes.[1]

The November 1967 *BSF Newsletter* reported on this development.

Miss Johnson and Miss Hertzler were absorbed throughout June and July in writing a new Manual for TLs. As prospective TLs and AAs visit headquarters to receive the training necessary to start a Pilot Class, they find it difficult to assimilate so much information about methods, policies, and procedures all compacted into their four-day visit. Every TL now has a copy for ready reference; the Manual will not only be of tremendous help to those teaching new classes, but will also be an aid in maintaining standards in classes already established. Dr. Stevens has made minor adaptations to the Manual for the men leaders.[2]

Teaching Leaders quickly saw the value of having the policies and procedures written in manual form. Two of these early TLs share their perspectives.

## ~⊘ IN OTHERS' WORDS

*Jan Myers:*

When I started teaching, there was no limit on the number of people in a class. I had 750 women in class—for the first year! We had an introduction class every week and we put new people into discussion groups every week. We had huge discussion groups of as many as twenty-six people. Sometimes we'd have three discussion groups in a room—back-to-back.

The policies came into being gradually, as there was a need to address situations like that.

It was hard to have such huge groups. We had women coming that didn't have a Bible and had never been at church before. We didn't have any policies about attendance. Some classes seemed like a revolving door; people would come and they'd go.

I think it was my second year teaching that BSF had Area Advisors. They talked to Miss Johnson and said, "We can't go on like this, because it's unmanageable."

BSF then established some new policies. Attendance requirements were set—miss three times and you're out. We could have an intro class to integrate new class members just once a month. And headquarters decided to limit the number of people in a class to 450.

That meant I had to tell 300 women they couldn't come the following year. But the next fall Margaret Duffield started a class, which helped siphon off some of the people. And over the years when I was teaching, we kept just flaking off new classes all the time. So the size limit really did help stimulate growth rather than limit it.[3]

## ~⊘ IN OTHERS' WORDS

*Mary Nell Schaap:*

We had to learn the BSF way, and it took time. But before long, we could see the wisdom in Miss J's policies. Those policies were priceless, and even though they felt restrictive at times, they kept us in focus.

Several ladies in my class had me out to lunch one day and asked, "Why can't we stay on for questions? Why do we have to do this? Why can't we do that?"

It was such a wonderful (and simple) thing to be able to say as kindly and gently as I knew how, "We're running this like a class, and if you don't want to take it, you don't have to."

We didn't have manuals for the first few years, and that was a big thing when we put some of the policies into print. Miss Johnson would take Teaching Leaders that didn't have much Bible background, but she knew with proper training they could teach well. That's why it was so good to have the rules and the standards, because she could then use women who were not all that well informed in theology.

There is another secret to BSF. There was never any gossip. There were regular changes made—such as new Area Advisors being chosen—and there was never any talk about it. It was just amazing. Miss Johnson and Miss Hertzler just didn't allow any negative talk, and their positive attitudes filtered down through the leadership. I was totally sold on Miss J's policies because she always had good reason.

There was another side of Miss Johnson that I saw and want to comment on—that is her compassion. And when it was a choice between rules or compassion, she would break the rules. We had testimony meetings at the retreats where we could share what was going on in our classes. Miss Johnson had a clock and she would say, "We have a lot of people here. You may share for three minutes." After that, she would stop you. There was a man in Washington that had been in a bad accident. He had been through so much that he went on a good twenty minutes and she didn't stop him. I've seen her break all kinds of rules if it meant to be gracious or compassionate.[4]

Perhaps one of the hardest policies for Teaching Leaders to embrace was the attendance requirement. Class members who missed class three times were asked to drop out, making room for someone who could make a more serious commitment. But according to Teaching Leader Ruth Larson, "The attendance requirement was something that soon became an accepted part of the group, and class members realized their participation couldn't be hit and miss. In other Bible studies, people might come and go, but not in BSF. Sometimes the attendance policy was hard to enforce, but it is one of the things about BSF that makes it unique and keeps it so strong."[5]

## Changed Lives

Policies and procedures were hardly the only thing BSF leaders learned in their training. Those early TLs who went through orientation under Wetherell Johnson will tell you that the rules and regulations were not nearly as important to the BSF way as were the things they learned from Miss Johnson herself—through her example as much as through her words.

### ⌒ IN OTHERS' WORDS

*Lorrie Kemp:*

When I went to Oakland for teacher training in the early 1970s, there were probably sixteen of us. Miss Johnson did most of our training, and Marguerite Carter did the elegant serving of food. Always linen tablecloths and napkins. We felt so pampered.

By that time, BSF was well organized. We got to see the printing operation and the dedicated volunteers working together to make that happen. We visited classes together and heard a couple of different Teaching Leaders, men and women. We even went to one of the first youth classes.[6]

Many Teaching Leaders are quick to tell the ways BSF training and the experience of studying God's Word profoundly impacted their lives.

### ↶⌒ IMPACT STORY

*Mary Nell Schaap:*

Being a Teaching Leader has probably changed my life more than anybody's in my class. My faith really grew. Miss Johnson didn't want us to use commentaries or footnotes but to dig in and study the Scriptures to see what they would do in your life. God's Word is what really changes you, and what we wanted to pass on to people is that change.

I would study my lesson early in the morning and then put it away by the time my children got home. I tried never to be consumed with my studies when my kids needed me. I wanted to have the house normal. Yet, my children were blessed anyway.

Years later my daughter Julie told me, "Mama, I used to get up early in the morning, and you'd be on your knees with your Bible." That probably made more impression on her than ever saying anything.

As inadequate as I often felt, my teaching BSF was a huge blessing for my family. You cannot get up and talk about not being angry if you've just been angry with your children. That's a poor witness.

I can say that BSF really changed my life because I didn't want the women to just go out and say, "That was a really good lecture," but I wanted their lives to change. I know that only the Lord can make the blind see, but I grew conscious of that.

Miss Johnson would say to the Teaching Leader, "Your job is to study the lecture and let the Discussion Leaders handle the problems." That meant on Wednesday morning it was my job to do that lecture well and let the other leadership look after the rest of the class.

Miss Johnson gave me a lot of practical help about spending time in study and not trying to get my lecture up quickly. I needed to mull it over all week. People think that you just spit it out and it doesn't require a lot of work, but it does.

Miss Johnson was always concerned about problems you would encounter which might prevent you from "milking that passage." That was a favorite expression she would use—"You are there to milk that passage and not to get little corresponding Scripture verses." She expected you to stay focused on that particular passage.[7]

Another veteran TL tells how her BSF training and teaching experience affected her life.

### ⌒ IN OTHERS' WORDS

*Jan Myers:*

Before I started teaching, I asked Vergene Lewis, my Area Advisor, "What if I'm not a good teacher?"

She replied, "Well, you'll find out soon enough. Nobody will come!"

Fortunately, the material was good. And I learned on those 750 women who came to my class that first year. I learned that I love teaching and I love to learn, and I think that probably translates.

Before I became a Teaching Leader, I struggled with depression and fear. One day I was reading Psalm 31: "In the shelter of your presence you hide them from the intrigues of men." That was like a door opening to me. I thought, *I don't need to be afraid, because I'm putting my trust in God, and He will hide me!* That verse became such a wonderful comfort.

When I was asked to be a Teaching Leader, it was as though the Lord said to me, "Well, do you believe what I just told you? You don't need to worry. I'll hide you."

So I said, "Okay," because I thought, *If I don't believe and act on this, my comfort and confidence will go away.* So, amazingly enough, I have never been afraid or fearful when I talk.[8]

Lorrie Kemp agrees that her BSF training under Miss Johnson helped to make her a different person, a stronger Christian, and a better leader.

## ↶⸉ IMPACT STORY
*Lorrie Kemp:*

Through BSF, I learned all kinds of leadership skills! I made out a list of simple things that I learned. But there are many more.

1. Pray about everything, but be specific.
2. Have at least one job in your church.
3. Be a loyal supporter of your church.
4. Do not tell other class members what church you belong to.
5. Ask questions that really allow you to get to know your class.
6. When in group meetings, leave no cold spots. Don't leave empty spaces in your classes. People were encouraged to sit right next to other people and not to leave an empty seat.
7. Confidentiality is vital. It is never acceptable to break that.
8. Always complete the lessons for your own sake.
9. Listen, listen, listen. And when you do, hear.
10. Don't be afraid of leadership. Train for it and rely on God.
11. Always have hope for every situation.
12. Make God's Word an everyday part of your life—always!
13. Affirm when you see an occasion to encourage others.
14. Do not keep the Good News to yourself.[9]

## The Wetherell Johnson Teaching Style

Those early Teaching Leaders frequently heard Wetherell Johnson teach. In addition to their training during orientation week, TLs would regularly receive audio tapes from Miss Johnson for their further edification.

### ⟳ IN OTHERS' WORDS

*Lois McCall:*

I was preparing my first lecture for the *Colossians* pilot in Houston. It was scary, but Miss Johnson had provided tapes of her own lectures, which I listened to repeatedly. She had told me, "Now, my dear, you don't have to use my tape, but it's available. Use it as you need it."

So I did. Her images were so vivid! She described Colossae and you would feel like you were there, and then Miss Johnson would say, "You might feel that you are in a 'Colossae' right now, with little children. You feel like you were meant for greater things. But God has so much for you right where you are." I wanted to be just like her.

When I'd worked up my lecture, I asked my husband if he would allow me to practice on him. Longsuffering soul that he was, he agreed. When I got through, his first comment was "Do you have to teach with that British accent?"[11]

By listening to audio tapes, many Teaching Leaders learned Miss Johnson's artful teaching style.

### ⟳ IN OTHERS' WORDS

*Jan Myers:*

Miss Johnson was a master storyteller. Those tapes that Miss Johnson did for the Teaching Leaders were sometimes raw, but those stories she told on the tapes were her heart. She would often talk about her life in China. But, when she did, it wasn't about her—there was always the application of how God had worked. She was honest about who she was. She told the story about how she just didn't like the person she was with in China. They didn't get along, but God used that. Miss Johnson talked about herself, but in such a way that it wasn't egotistical.

I learned to teach from Miss Johnson. I learned the rhythm of teaching: she would give you the facts, then she would fill in, and then she would apply.

Sometimes she would go off on these little rabbit trails, which were the fun part because that's when you came to know who Miss Johnson was. She knew what that passage was about and how to apply it. When you listened to the tapes, you could feel the bones in the passage. I just feel so privileged to have been able to sit under her. Every time I heard her on tape, after she was gone, I'd think, *She, being dead, still speaks.*[11]

And through the legacy of training and the BSF way, Wetherell Johnson still teaches. Even today.

# Chapter 12

# AN ARM OF THE CHURCH

Bible Study Fellowship's partnership with the Christian community

When those first five women in San Bernardino asked Wetherell Johnson to teach them the Bible, she was reluctant to accept, primarily because they were churched women. After all, these ladies lived in a town with church buildings on every other corner; they had seemingly unlimited resources and a plethora of places they could go to learn the Bible. Their "needs" seemed so much less compelling than those of the students she worked with for years on the mission field back in China.

But once Wetherell sensed the Lord indeed calling her to teach those women, their friends, and countless others like them, she quickly recognized their deep need for Bible knowledge. The fact that they were churched women was never a negative, but a real plus from the start. When that first Bible Study group grew too big to meet in homes and moved into a local church, a new pattern of creating partnerships began. Churches not only provided the places where BSF classes met but they also benefited when BSF students plugged in to serve that congregation.

## The Goal: Partnership

By the time Bible Study Fellowship was incorporated in 1960, the mutually beneficial partnership between the ministry and churches was a well-understood and oft-stated goal.

## ⌒⊙ In Others' Words

*Dr. Ernest Hastings:*

The original concept of BSF was that we would teach people the Bible, and then they would go back to their churches and work and put everything they had learned into operation. I saw that happen because in each church I pastored—both in California and Washington—we started BSF classes. And the people who became BSF leaders, also became the leaders of the church. BSF not only taught them the Bible, but those who took leadership in BSF also learned skills of leadership. And people with leadership skills automatically stand out in every congregation.[1]

In *Created for Commitment*, Miss Johnson recalled her first meeting with Ernest Hastings as pastor of Melrose Baptist Church in Oakland, a church she referred to as a "flourishing congregation." She was grateful that he took the risk of inviting her, without knowing much about her, to teach a class in his church. But he made it clear that "its continuance would depend upon the elders of the church and the congregation."[2]

That understanding of goals shared by Wetherell Johnson and Ernest Hastings was reflected in the original BSF bylaws, the working philosophy of the new organization. And as BSF grew, Miss Johnson's policy toward churches was spelled out at length in leadership training and in her book.

## ⌒ From the Director

*Wetherell Johnson:*

Bible Study Fellowship aims to become a definite arm of the church. Churches welcome us. After the beginning of our work in a home, we always hold classes by invitation from the pastor of a church. Unchurched members often join the church where they attend a class; class members say that they appreciate the pastor's message each Sunday increasingly because of a personal understanding of the Bible. Always we try to train church members not simply to warm the church pew, but that each member should ask what he or she can do in his or her own church.

From the earliest days, Bible Study Fellowship has been interdenominational. Classes are comprised of members from almost all Christian denominations. Discussion Leaders are instructed never to encourage members to switch churches. So, we do not consider ourselves a "para-church" organization as much as an arm of the church.[3]

## Serving in the Church

One of the first rules of BSF was that everyone in BSF leadership had to hold a position of responsibility at church. That single principle magnified the impact of BSF on individual lives by asking those people to take what they had learned in BSF and share it with their churches.

One Teaching Leader in England explained the following:

### ⌐◯ In Others' Words
*Jan Heal:*

Application of what a person has learned is an important part of BSF to get people working, becoming involved in the leadership aspects of their churches. So that the church doesn't feel like BSF is sucking people out, it is important that the training we're receiving in BSF is being used in the church. And class members get excited about carrying this knowledge and experience out of the class and applying it to their lives and in their churches and seeing results.[4]

The leadership training gained in BSF enabled many people to take positions for which they otherwise would not have felt qualified. Barb Watson, a Children's Supervisor in England and later a Children's Area Coordinator, told of one such person.

### ∿ IN OTHERS' WORDS
*Barb Watson:*

A leader, a Children's Supervisor, had to leave suddenly for personal reasons. The class was left without. Another girl who was really quite shy, but an excellent Children's Leader, was asked if she would take over. When she did, she just grew and opened up like a flower. It was wonderful. Then she took a position in her church, which she would never had done without BSF.[5]

Another Teaching Leader in England, found that her BSF leadership training equipped her to lead in many other situations.

### ∿ IN OTHERS' WORDS
*Anita Newton:*

Early on, I found that the DL training was transferable to all similar situations.

I was asked to lead a group of about twenty people at a training day, not BSF, and all other group leaders were members of the clergy. Though my group was a mixed one of men and women, none of whom I knew, they were a typical discussion group, with some who had to be drawn out and some who had to be handled firmly. I treated it as a BSF discussion group, and the group members afterwards remarked on their satisfaction at the leading.[6]

BSF's goal was to build up and equip members for leadership—not just for their BSF class but for the church as well. As one BSF veteran put it, "All the time and effort that goes into training a Teaching Leader or a Discussion Leader identifies and brings out the innate leadership qualities God has given those persons. So, they are able then to go back into their own churches and do a bang-up job of leading. They become shining lights in their congregation and their community."

## ⤞ Impact Story

*Rollin and Marion Mann:*

*Marion:* Over the years we've seen BSF leaders change and grow from the beginning of the year to the end. Then they take that training from BSF out with them to use in a variety of settings. It helps them become leaders of the PTA and other organizations. Many of them have gotten great jobs because they've been trained to be so organized, to present themselves well, and to lead others.

*Rollin:* Ministers who have had church members active in Bible Study Fellowship love to see more of their people in BSF classes because they know that they will be well trained for leadership and that they will soon have to take a position in the church.[7]

Dr. Chuck Musfeldt, now Director of International Operations of BSF, witnesses firsthand the influence of BSF on host churches around the world.

## ⤞ In Others' Words

*Dr. Chuck Musfeldt:*

When the class I taught grew, we ended up moving from First Baptist Church, Elmhurst, to Christ Church of Oakbrook. The leaders at the new, bigger church were extremely gracious in hosting the men's class, and it still meets there today. The pastor of the church had lived in California and had known men in his previous church involved in BSF. He had seen them grow and had seen what the Scripture could do in their lives. When it came up for the vote on whether or not to have BSF use their facilities, the pastor said, "If BSF will come to our church, I'll make the coffee for them!"

BSF is really a training center. We are training the men and women of BSF to go back and pray for their pastor, and pray with their pastor, and then help their pastor by serving. If that isn't happening, then we're not meeting one of our primary goals as an organization.[8]

## Bringing People In

Another way BSF functioned as an arm of the church was by constantly and effectively reaching out in order to bring people in. A sizable percentage of people who found themselves attracted to Bible Study Fellowship were unchurched when they first came. Studying the Word of God worked as a powerful gravitational pull, slowly but surely drawing them to the truth through fellowship, teaching, and individual study. Eventually they understood their need to be connected as a member of Christ's body.

### ᴄ◯◯ IMPACT STORY

*Jerry Prenzlow:*

My sister-in-law Alice got into a BSF class, became a leader, and really changed. She was transformed into this whimsical and joyful Christian—and it tickled me. I couldn't relate to what she was talking about, but I liked listening to her. She would tell me about how God had answered her prayers and how He told her this and that. I thought, *How quaint and harmless, but cute.*

Then she started telling me, "You need to get into BSF. You like to read and learn new things. You'd love it."

I said, "No."

Then she even gave me some notes to read, though I never read them.

September 1970, she called to tell me, "There's an introductory class in your town."

I told her, "Alice, I'm really not interested."

But the next month she called and repeated the same thing.

By that time I was insulted and said, again, "No. I'm *really* not interested."

November, she called a third time. I was horrified that she

would do that. I wasn't angry by that point, but more embarrassed with myself. She was so cute—going on and on—as if she had never asked me before. Then in December, she called and did the same thing. In January, I finally decided I would go for three months. Then I could quit and tell her that I tried it, but it was not for me. And that would be the end of the whole business.

So, I went in January in Boulder, Colorado. I had a cold and a cough that first day. But the opening prayer, I'll never forget. The Teaching Leader said, "Lord, if there is anyone in this place who does not know You, please speak to them." With that, tears started coming, and I began coughing. People all around handed me cough drops and Kleenexes. I don't know what they thought, but I didn't yet realize it was the Lord speaking to my heart.

I was assigned to a discussion group. We were in Genesis, and these women acted as if they believed the stories of Jacob and Abraham. One day a bunch of us carpooled to a group luncheon, and I said, "Do you all believe these stories?"

I thought they would say, "No, not really." But they all said, "Yes."

I liked these women. We had a great time in class and I was doing my best. But I had never had such hard questions. I couldn't answer some of them. They were faith questions, so I had no answer.

Then in May, at our last luncheon, one woman asked the Teaching Leader, "I am a new Christian of two years. We have two little boys and my husband is not a Christian yet. I know we should be in church, but my husband wants to go camping on the weekends. What should I do?"

The Teaching Leader said, "For now, you have BSF. Temporarily make that your church, and go camping with your husband."

Well, my jaw must have dropped open. I had thought it was all about getting on board and going to church. I never heard another word at the luncheon. I kept reviewing what she had said and thinking, *Why would she say that?*

I started my long drive home, and on the way I prayed, "Lord, I guess I have this all wrong. I liked that answer. This is what I want: I want You."

That was it. The Lord came in. Tears came to my eyes and I could hardly catch my breath. I almost had to pull over because I could hardly see to drive. I didn't realize at first what had happened. But by that night, I was different. I was praying differently—talking to God as my Father. I reacted differently to my husband the next day. I thought, *Finally I'm getting it.* I still didn't understand that I had become a Christian.

The next fall in BSF, we went around the circle and introduced ourselves. Without ever planning to, I said, "I'm a new Christian." Then I thought, *Why did I say that?* My leader gave me an Assurance Letter, and that is when I realized what had happened that day in my car and that I hadn't actually been a Christian before.

I became a Christian one week before my thirty-third birthday. We have three sons, and the oldest one was in fifth grade. I told my husband, "I don't care what you do, but I'm taking our boys to church."

He said, "I'll come with you and the boys."

So, time went on and I couldn't study the Bible long enough or fast enough. It changed me. It changed our family. My husband became president of our congregation. My sons had been getting nothing spiritual. So I hung on Joel 2:28, where it says that God will restore the years that the locusts have eaten. Today all our boys are Christians, and their wives and their children are too. The entire family is in church and serving the Lord. Only by God's grace—at work through BSF.[9]

## The Local Connection

Bible Study Fellowship always considered itself an arm of the church, just as every BSF class, from the outset, has an arm-in-arm relationship with a local congregation. Lois McCall went to

Oakland for Teaching Leader training in 1970 in anticipation of starting a BSF class in Houston, Texas. She tells that story.

## ⌒⊙ IN OTHERS' WORDS
*Lois McCall:*

The next step was to have a series of coffees to let people know about BSF and then await the invitation of a host church. One of the women that came to the coffees was a member of a fashionable mainline denominational church in a nice residential section of Houston. So, my friend went to her pastor and told him about BSF. He said, "Invite Mrs. McCall to call me." She explained to him that, according to BSF guidelines, I had to wait on an invitation from him. He then called me and arranged a meeting. He was frank with me. He had looked at the Bible Study Fellowship statement of faith and found it "quite rigid." He added, though, that his congregation included some women who had been in BSF before moving to Houston, and what he had seen of loving kindness and a helpful spirit in those women made him want BSF in his church. "I would like this training for my congregation," he said, "and I would like this atmosphere in my church." It was clearly God's provision, because this pastor disagreed with BSF teaching on some basic theological issues. But he saw the Lord at work and was willing to host Houston's first class.

We had some interesting discussions. He was a man of great authority and respect in his church. He and I became good friends during the time BSF stayed in that church—until the church had a major expansion program and their parking lot was no longer big enough to hold all of our ladies' cars. We had grown to more than 700 by that time.

We had invitations from other churches in our area to host our BSF class, and the one closest to our first location welcomed us warmly. Everything seemed to be going well. Then we were told headquarters had established a new policy: classes had to be limited to 450 people. And if we had many more students than that, we needed to make plans to start more classes.

I was going to have to tell more than 250 women there wouldn't be a place for them the coming year. The thought of that just about killed me. I didn't want to lose any of those precious women, especially since a number of the ladies we would be turning away were members of the new host church. I knew there was going to be weeping and wailing and gnashing of teeth when the attendance list was posted. So, I went to that pastor ahead of time and showed him our criteria for attendance and participation. It broke my heart to do that, to tell him that some of his own congregation would have to leave the class. I explained that the unchurched ladies who had been coming longer, who were there all the time and faithful with their lessons, would have priority over some of his church members.

I was afraid he might be angry with me or with BSF, so I was relieved when he sat back and chuckled. "Lady," he said, "I wish I could put that kind of restriction on my church. There is nothing like making something hard to get, to make people want it more."[10]

Not that BSF's relationship with every host church's pastor is always smooth. At times, nettlesome issues, both interpersonal and theological, have created serious tensions. But one of the most helpful principles for handling such conflicts was established at the beginning of Bible Study Fellowship.

∽ **IMPACT STORY**

*Vergene Lewis:*

The pastor of the church where we were meeting in that first San Bernardino class was having a difficult time in his own life. One day we arrived at class and the doors were locked. There was no place for us to meet that morning. We immediately called another pastor in town and he said, "Sure, come to my church." We went there but left someone at the first church to inform people about the location change.

Miss Johnson, before class began that morning, took the

leaders aside and said, "No one in this room says anything against this pastor! This man is God's anointed."

I will never forget that lesson: That pastor was God's anointed. The Lord would deal with him. We just needed to pray for him. And we all did pray for him that morning.

That was a change in my understanding of how Christians should work and treat each other. I would have thought you shouldn't let someone get away with something like he had done, that something should be done to "get even" so that justice would be served. But you know, God's work wasn't thwarted. A number of us were members of that man's congregation. Some of the others chose not to go back to that church. However, my husband and I kept going since my husband was a deacon. I was upset and had to deal with my own anger toward this pastor. But in the process of praying for him, as I sat under his teaching, I learned that I could pray for him, because he was in a hard place. I understood that he, too, was a human being who needed God's grace and strength.

That incident taught me a completely new way of dealing with people in conflict situations. I have to thank Miss Johnson for that. Her strength in God's Word and her walk with the Lord allowed me to learn a valuable lesson.[11]

Other potential tension points BSF teachers deal with are a little more predictable but no less challenging. Skip Brey recalls the first BSF class she taught.

### ⟳ IN OTHERS' WORDS
*Skip Brey:*

In February 1973, I took over as Teaching Leader of the Ignatio Valley class. We had 425 members meeting in a small Baptist church where the minister had some sort of intercom setup that enabled him to listen in on my entire lecture. When I started midyear, the class was already halfway through *The Life and Letters of Paul*. So, with only three days of Teaching Leader training, I stepped in to begin teaching the book of Romans.

Everything went fine until we got to chapter six and I said something about "baptism means identification." The minister, who was listening in, evidently hit the ceiling. He immediately picked up the phone and called Miss Johnson. Then Miss Johnson called me and said she had set up an appointment for me to meet with the minister. She asked if I had used any commentaries, and I told her I had read Dr. J. Vernon Magee's commentary on Romans. Her comment was "Oh, thank goodness. Dr. Magee believes in immersion!"

So I had to go in and "defend my position" to the minister. I don't think I got out of his office in less than three hours! But that minister and I ended up being the best of friends.

Somebody from the church called me later to apologize: "Our pastor is having a tough time handling the fact that you fill the parking lot on Tuesdays and he does not on Sundays."[12]

A major goal of this arm of the church has always been to uphold local pastors and their ministries. According to various Teaching Leaders, Wetherell Johnson and the Board's goal to foster and maintain a true partnership with host pastors, and the broader Church, was more than lip service. Teaching Leaders were to respectfully work with and for the local church. From this goal came sometimes difficult, but always tactful, well-thought-out advice on creating and keeping great relationships with local churches.

### ᴄ⃝ IN OTHERS' WORDS

*Mary Nell Schaap:*

Miss Johnson used to caution us, "Don't ever use the word 'liberal' from the pulpit when you teach, because it puts a label on people." And she would say to the women who might be attending "liberal" mainline churches, "Don't go to your pastor and ask, 'Why aren't you teaching the Bible more?' Those men have given their lives and are working hard. You need to be nothing but positive if you are going to stay or teach in that church."

I thought that advice was so wise.

Miss Johnson had a heart for pastors and wanted people to respect them and support them. She wanted BSF to feed the church and never compete with it. We always tried to respect the church property. Sometimes we actually hired policemen to direct traffic and help protect property.[13]

Another TL recalls a time when her class became perhaps a bit too ecumenical in their parking habits.

### ⌐⌐ IN OTHERS' WORDS
*Myrl Glockner:*

One morning I was giving the opening devotional and this tall policeman came down the side aisle in full uniform. I stopped right in the middle of what I was saying, because he was obviously coming to commandeer the microphone. Women all over the audience started twittering and laughing—until he began lecturing those ladies about the way they were parking, not just in the parking lot (which was overflowing), but anywhere and everywhere they could find the slightest opening on side streets all around the church.

The police, and the neighbors, must have been wondering what in the world was going on with all those women showing up at church in the middle of the week.[14]

The leadership of BSF never wanted impressive numbers or the growing sense of the Lord's blessing of their ministry to translate into pride or entitlement. From BSF's earliest days, the organizational policy was to make contributions to the host church to defray the cost of using their facilities, though many churches chose to make their premises available with no remuneration, since they saw the BSF class as a part of their community outreach. Being an arm of the church meant functioning as a true partner, always striving to give greater than what was received. That kind of attitude has been key to the positive relationship between BSF and its host churches throughout the years.

## Interdenominational

Another special thing God has been doing with this arm of the church is teaching all sorts and denominations of believers to embrace each other, to pull down some of the barriers that too often separate them.

### ∼⧛ IMPACT STORY

*Lorrie Kemp:*

> One of the greatest things about BSF is that it has always been so interdenominational. Through BSF, I met many people from many walks of life whom I couldn't possibly have met in my own church experience. I became far less judgmental, more understanding, and truly excited to learn there could be other denominations that knew the Lord too.
>
> I realized how important it is to take an active role in supporting your own church, as well. BSF was always strong about that. And because everything about BSF was positive, that put you and kept you in a positive spirit, rather than being critical, which is so easy for many church members to be.[15]

When they began Bible Study Fellowship, Wetherell Johnson and the other leaders of the organization resolved to collaborate with churches, to be an arm of the church. Fifty years later, that arm is, in the minds of countless pastors and church leaders around the globe, a vital and crucial part of the worldwide body of Christ.

*Chapter 13*

# RETREATS AND SEMINARS
### Nourishing the spiritual lives of leaders

From the earliest days of Bible Study Fellowship, Wetherell Johnson made it one of her priorities to offer ways Teaching and Discussion Leaders could receive additional spiritual nourishment. Some she provided herself in the initial training process. She also distributed her own teaching tapes as inspiration and a model for Teaching Leaders.

Those leaders fortunate enough to live near the Bay Area headquarters benefited from an even more personal touch.

### ∼ IN OTHERS' WORDS
*Skip Brey:*

Every once in a while, usually on a Saturday, Miss J would have a bunch of class leaders to her house for lunch. She would tell us, "Be here at nine o'clock," because she planned an entire morning of spiritual things before we ate.

Leaders had prayer with Miss Johnson, then time alone with a Bible study guide, then a time of sharing and a meal. When we ate, there was a different Bible verse under each plate, every one of them prayed over and chosen by Miss J for that person.

There was nourishing of our faith. She got to know us, and we got to know each other in the process.[1]

Bible Study Fellowship quickly outgrew Miss Johnson's home, no longer having room for the leaders of just the Bay Area classes. So, she had to find some other means of providing the spiritual nourishment and fellowship she had made a part of her Saturday luncheons and mini-retreats.

As early as fall 1962, the *BSF Newsletter* reported the following:

Fifty-two leaders (including two from Seattle and six from Southern California) had an unforgettable experience of blessing at our two-day conference at Mt. Hermon as the Lord by His Holy Spirit manifested his presence with us, in times of prayer and quietness before him, in the stirring messages in our close fellowship and oneness, and in the awareness He gave us of His purpose for our own lives and for this work He has entrusted to us.[2]

## Regional Retreats

The continuing expansion of BSF's ministry to other parts of the country presented new challenges and led to new means for spiritual nourishment.

### ⟋ FROM THE DIRECTOR
*Wetherell Johnson:*

Our first regional retreat for leaders began in a small way in 1964. Dr. and Mrs. Wenger invited me to hold a retreat in Little Rock, Arkansas, at a beautiful resort called "Petit Jean Park." It was wonderful for me and for them to get to know each other in fellowship.

Mrs. Smucker brought two carloads of leaders from eight hundred miles away in Indiana. We met together in sharing and teaching, and I realized the great value of this relationship with classes who were far away from headquarters. We recognized the importance of establishing a close relationship with all the leaders of classes through "Regional Retreats." There were usually seven retreats between March and May. Leaders were able to develop a close relationship with other classes in their region. We from headquarters came to appreciate the leaders as our own friends. The regional schedule was arranged so that leaders from every class would be able to attend at least once in three years. From February to May, Mrs. Pearl Hamilton and other staff members would travel with me to, for example, Estes Park, Colorado; Asilomar (near Carmel), California; Seattle; Portland; Pipe Stem, Virginia; Fort Wayne, Indiana. From 300 to 600 Teaching Leaders, Discussion Leaders, and Children's Leaders attended each regional retreat.[3]

Each morning and evening at those retreats, Miss Johnson spoke on some biblical theme or subject outside of the five-year study series. Other BSF staff members conducted training workshops specifically for Discussion Leaders and Children's Leaders. Every afternoon for three hours, silence was observed on the retreat grounds as each person pondered a handful of heart-searching questions in this private time with the Lord. Afterward, all the attendees came together in small groups, called "the fellowship of fives," to share and pray together.

Each night after the evening message, the meeting was opened for a time of testimonies and sharing. As she said in her book, *Created for Commitment,* "Many of these testimonies were so moving it was hard for me to keep back the tears. To most leaders, their regional retreat is one of the highlights of Bible Study Fellowship."[4]

These regional retreats were created to enrich all the Leaders in BSF: Administrators, Discussion Leaders, Children's Leaders, and Teaching Leaders. But as their popularity grew to the point that hundreds of class leaders came to each retreat, Wetherell Johnson longed for a more intimate setting through which to provide a deeper level of spiritual nourishment and teaching only for the Teaching Leaders.

## Seminars for TLs

In 1969, BSF held its first Biennial Seminar—for Teaching Leaders only. Response to that first TL seminar was so positive that BSF held its second Biennial Seminar in January 1971, again at Mount Hermon, with 104 Teaching Leaders from across the country attending. The spring 1971 *BSF Newsletter* reported on that event.

> God fulfilled our expectations of blessing during that unique time in which He met us all. Days were filled with workshops on leadership training and homiletics, with sharing experiences and ideas, with stories of God's work in individual classes and with the warm fellowship of a wonderful "family" spirit. Most memorable were the stirring, deep messages given by Miss Johnson and the conference speaker, Rev. Joseph Carroll, Director of the Evangelical Institute of Greenville, South Carolina. They brought to us the challenge of new spiritual insights into the life that God wants us all to have in Christ. Dr. David Hubbard, President of Fuller Seminary, came one day to give a special talk on how to prepare messages. He also gave a most helpful resume of some of the crises and confusions of our present day world.[5]

For the Biennial Teaching Leader Seminars, as with everything concerning BSF, Wetherell Johnson demanded excellence. To help spiritually nourish Teaching Leaders, she invited some of the best speakers the evangelical world had to offer.

The featured speaker for the third Biennial Seminar in January 1973 was the world-renowned evangelist Dr. Paul Rees. That year, 148 Teaching Leaders from America, England, and Australia attended.

These Biennial events became Triennial before the next seminar was held at Mount Hermon in 1976. The speaker that year, Rev. Michael Baughen, rector of All Souls Anglican Church in London, delivered profound biblical truths to TLs. He was so well received that he and his wife were invited back in 1979, when 266 Teaching Leaders attended.

But the caliber of speakers was just part of the reason for the seminars' popularity. Miss Johnson incorporated many of the ingredients she'd used for successful retreats over the years, and she added some new features.

The seminars usually lasted four days, with both Miss J and the guest speaker giving morning and evening messages. Various BSF staff members conducted workshops on homiletics, children's work, and other class-related subjects.

Following the pattern so successful at the retreats, the seminars also included a time of silence for self-evaluation, after which leaders joined a "fellowship of five" for sharing. And of course, after the evening sessions, testimony times allowed people to share with the entire group. Additional seminar features included a skit night, which quickly became a tradition, and a special question-and-answer time during which Miss Johnson responded to queries submitted by the Teaching Leaders. The seminars became a cherished highlight of TLs' BSF experience.

The seminars obviously required a major commitment of time and energy on the part of the organization. Yet Wetherell Johnson, Alverda Hertzler, and the headquarters staff never seemed to begrudge the investment. Neither did they allow their special understanding of the ongoing spiritual challenges faced by TLs to let them forget the needs of the broader class leadership.

## The Ongoing Value of the Retreats

Between the biennial and triennial seminars, regular regional retreats continued in bigger and better ways, as evidenced by the following report from Pearl Hamilton in the summer 1974 *BSF Newsletter*:

> This spring, more than 2,600 dedicated leaders packed their suitcases and traveled to seven regional Retreats, from Puget Sound in the Pacific Northwest to the Ozark Mountains of the Mid-south. Miss Johnson and various staff members attend each retreat and take part in the program. Area Advisors and Teaching Leaders spend a whole day with them. In this way, we get to know our leadership as much as possible.[6]

One goal of BSF leadership meetings was to enrich the participants spiritually. The seminars also benefited attendees personally. The fellowship fostered an invaluable sense of unity, not only among leaders of different BSF classes from regions around the country but also between local class leadership and the national headquarters staff.

Vergene Lewis remembers an incident at one of the early leader retreats in the Midwest.

## ᔇ IMPACT STORY
*Vergene Lewis:*

Miss J contacted me to say, "There is going to be a retreat in Indiana, and I would like you to go with me." These people had been doing BSF for four or five years and no doubt had formed an idea of what Miss J must look like—a little old lady missionary with white hair in a bun and sturdy shoes.

The first night of the retreat, she came in. Everyone else was seated. She wore a long, gorgeous green dress. She'd had her hair done, put on lipstick. She just wowed them.

She told stories. She told jokes. This Midwestern audience was just blown away. This was not the woman who had written these serious lessons. No! Who had all these rules and regulations. No! After the meeting, I walked up to her and said, "Well, you really blew them away tonight!" Miss Johnson just grinned. She had understood all along what she was up against. So that night, she made certain people realized she was a real person and had a real message. It was precious.[7]

Another attendee at that Indiana retreat recalls her experiences.

## ᔅ IN OTHERS' WORDS
*Mary Nell Schaap:*

I remember terrific speakers. The retreats were so good for us all. I think Miss Johnson thought of us as Paul thought of the folks he mentored and left in Jerusalem.

Some of us did a silly little play one time, acting out the history of Bible Study Fellowship. Thereafter, Miss Johnson would always ask me to write a skit for the next retreat. She enjoyed having fun and laughing on skit nights. She wouldn't really plan but would call me a couple of days before and ask me for a skit. Then I would have to get busy and come up with one.[8]

Marion Mann, a Teaching Leader for thirty-three years, also remembers those retreats.

### ⌒⊘ IN OTHERS' WORDS

*Marion Mann:*

People would pass in questions, and she'd read them off and then answer them. Sometimes what they were asking about was a violation of one of the rules, but other times it was just something for which we had no policy. Miss Hertzler was always sitting in the front row, and she would sometimes say, "Now, Audrey, we'll talk about this later."

At the retreats, because of the strict dress code, it seemed someone always asked, "Why can't we wear pants in BSF?" And Miss Johnson, at every retreat, would say, "For one day of the week, you can dress up like a lady." And the men would cheer.[9]

## Miss J as Speaker

Although Miss Johnson brought in speakers to enrich the spiritual lives of BSF leaders, she also did much of the teaching herself. For most BSFers, her messages were more than memorable spiritual challenges; they gave class leaders real insight into the heart and person of Wetherell Johnson.

## ⟋⟋⟋ IMPACT STORY

*Jan Myers:*

One time when a bunch of California TLs gathered at Arrowhead Springs, Miss J taught on the feasts in the Old Testament. You would think, *How boring can this get?* Instead, it was wonderful. She had this reservoir of information and experiences that the Lord gave her. We hung on every word and wished that she could go on.[10]

Sometimes it wasn't so much what Wetherell Johnson said that made a lasting impression, but what she did—how she responded to specific people in certain situations. For example, during a time of sharing, a microphone was passed to anyone who wanted to share—for three minutes. Ordinarily, Miss Johnson monitored the time and kept things moving along, but it didn't always work that way.

## ⟋⟋⟋ IMPACT STORY

*Jeanette Tompkins:*

Miss J was always a stickler for time. At this particular retreat, one man, a Discussion Group Leader, got to sharing some personal experience and started crying. He cried and he sobbed so hard that he couldn't keep talking. We thought Miss Johnson would do something. But she had the grace to wait and wait and, I mean, *wait,* until he was composed and finished.

When she went to the microphone, she said, "It is so refreshing to see a man cry because of his love for the Lord." Those things really touched our hearts, because we so often saw her as the disciplinarian.[11]

Another time, Miss Johnson's own reaction to one of the special speakers made a telling impression on many BSFers who witnessed it. The occasion was the 1976 seminar when the rector of All Souls Church in London spoke at Mount Hermon.

### ⌇⦂ IMPACT STORY

*Anne Graham Lotz and Dottie McKissick:*

*Anne:* Rev. Michael Baughen was the teacher. He totally changed my prayer life. He had written a song, "Blessed Is the Man." Miss Johnson and Michael Baughen were up on stage, arms raised in the air, dancing out of pure love and exhilaration for Jesus. I looked at Miss J and thought, *That's what I want. To be abandoned in my love for Jesus.* I had seen it in my Mother, and Miss Johnson had that as well. I would have listened to anything she said!

*Dottie:* Rev. Baughen had published a book on the Psalms, written to hymn form. This one particular hymn, "Blessed Is the Man," is in our BSF leaders hymnal still. As we sang it, Michael did sort of a dance on the platform. Miss Johnson was obviously loving this new song. So, Reverend Baughen took her hand and they did a little twirl up there. Miss J was usually very proper, but she had that fun side to her too. We didn't get to see it too often.[12]

Even when she wasn't on stage, Wetherell Johnson had an audience. And sometimes she made the most of it. Many early BSFers still talk about one very memorable time she showed an unexpected side of herself.

### ⌇⦂ IN OTHERS' WORDS

*Anna Kingsbury:*

Miss Johnson would say, "If you were to come into the presence of the queen, wouldn't you dress your very best? Well, then, if you are coming into the presence of the King of Kings, what else?" So, we have a defined standard.

But at Teaching Leader seminars, there was one informal evening when we always did a skit about the history of BSF. Some of the principals took their own parts. When we were all assembling for our meal at the Christian conference center, she made her appearance. There she was, coming down the walk from her cabin to the dining hall, in a red double-knit pant suit. The people standing around just said, "Wow!"[13]

Truth be known, Wetherell Johnson simply loved any chance she had to offer enrichment for, or to fellowship with, BSF people, no matter where in the world they were from. And over the years, she designed a variety of programs that allowed her to do just that.

One of the most noteworthy occasions grew out of her friendship with Francis and Edith Schaeffer, when, after first visiting L'Abri, Miss Johnson and Miss Hertzler invited the Schaeffers to speak to a leader's retreat in the Bay Area. The fall 1971 *BSF Newsletter* reported the following:

> Dr. Schaeffer had accepted an invitation to speak to students in San Diego, and Miss Johnson felt it would be wonderful if he could also speak to as many Teaching Leaders as were able to come from extension classes and to our Bay Area leadership. The result was far beyond our expectations. Over seventy Teaching Leaders attended.[14]

One of those seventy lucky attendees shared these memories:

### ◠◡ IN OTHERS' WORDS

*Jan Myers:*

If we wanted to attend this retreat, we all had to read all of Dr. Schaeffer's books before the meeting. The Teaching Leaders in the Bay Area actually had to take tests on them! I understand that only two people made a perfect score. One was Pearl Hamilton and the other was June Whipple.

An amusing incident occurred at this meeting. Mrs. Schaeffer was talking about how L'Abri was established. She had spoken for about an hour to an enthralled audience. Her time was up and, as Miss Johnson was wont to do, she tugged on Edith's dress to remind her to stop. Mrs. Schaeffer just kept on speaking, and this was repeated several times. Finally, Mrs. Schaeffer turned and said rather firmly, "Wetherell, I am not done." When Mrs. Schaeffer finally ended her message, she said, "This was the introduction to what I wanted to say."[15]

## Area Workshops

Miss Johnson always looked for ways to meet the needs of the growing number of BSF leaders and to respond to their ideas. In 1972, the Deputy Director of BSF described one new method: the Area Workshop.

### ⌐⊙ IN OTHERS' WORDS

*Pearl Hamilton:*

Every year brings new developments. This fall it was an experiment to have all classes participate in Area Workshops at the outset of the year as many leaders have requested. So, it was that by the end of October every group of leaders had attended Workshops, many traveling from 100 to 200 miles. The Lord gave us such good results that we believe that what was experimental this year is worth incorporating for future years.

Thirty six Workshops were held, including one in Australia and one in England. An Area Advisor or Staff member was present at each one except in the most distant places. The Workshops serve a vital purpose in keeping our leadership current on procedures. They also maintain a close link with Headquarters through the Area Advisor or staff member. They afford opportunity for review of fundamental principles and practices of the Bible Study Fellowship. Attendance was nearly perfect in all areas. The enthusiastic response of leaders more than justified the labor that went into preparing for and conducting the Workshops.[16]

By the summer of 1974, the *BSF Newsletter* reported that, due to the amazing growth in classes, only new leaders would be invited to the retreats.

> There was a time in the early days of BSF when the *entire* leadership could gather for a retreat at someone's cabin, where all thirty of us would share the Lord's blessings. That is history. Now only new Leaders will go to Retreats because there are not facilities large enough to hold even the leadership of a given area.[17]

## Regional Meetings

By the end of the 1970s, BSF tried an entirely new format— mass assemblies in huge arena-type venues—to which class members as well as leaders were invited. In the May 1979 *BSF Newsletter*, Miss Johnson reported on the first two of these meetings.

### ⌒ FROM THE DIRECTOR
*Wetherell Johnson:*

This year we are experimenting with a new venture called Regional Meetings. This means that class members, along with some five-year BSF alumni, are provided with free tickets to attend a Saturday morning meeting from nine to twelve.

On March 31, the area was Anaheim. At this meeting there were between 7,000 and 8,000 in a huge conference center. I actually spoke for two and one-quarter hours. This amount of time was partly due to the excitement we had of three of the original five ladies who asked me to teach Colossians. They came onto the platform and looked over the vast sea of people, and we all realized what God can do from such a small thing as a request.[18]

In her autobiography, Wetherell Johnson summarized her reasons for emphasizing the ongoing spiritual training for her leaders.

## ⟜ FROM THE DIRECTOR
*Wetherell Johnson:*

One cannot give out more than what one has received, and superficiality in Christian work results in superficial fruit.

It is not enough to lead individuals to receive Christ through the Holy Spirit at new birth. Paul states, "As ye have therefore received Christ Jesus the Lord, walk ye in him" (Col. 2:6 KJV).

I believe God has a message for this age when "Christians" are increasingly caught up in the "love of emptiness" and pleasure seeking. Christians of today need help. They need study, they need discipline, and they need fellowship and love from others like themselves to become true disciples of our Lord Jesus Christ.[19]

That was the ultimate goal of all the BSF retreats, seminars, workshops, meetings, and conferences. Why? Because making true disciples of Jesus Christ was the ultimate goal of Bible Study Fellowship classes. And Wetherell Johnson firmly believed, for her leaders as well as for herself, that "one cannot give out more than one has received."

# Chapter 14

# NEW LEADERS,
# NEW CLASSES, NEW CITIES

Further U.S. expansion through the 1970s

B ible Study Fellowship printed twenty-five thousand copies of the October 1970 *BSF Newsletter* for its class members across the country. That issue commented on the current growth of the ministry.

> Last September we began with 90 classes, and this year we begin with 110. Ten new Pilot Classes are already in prospect with candidates for Teaching Leader and Administrative Assistants coming for training during the first two weeks of November. Six men will be in these new orientation groups from Indiana, California and Texas; sixteen women will come from Idaho, Texas, Indiana, Maryland, Washington, Michigan, and California, expanding the outreach of Bible Study Fellowship into three new states. We are grateful that so many are being drawn to the study of God's Word during these days of political unrest and world turmoil. Our deep desire is that this study may bring "joy and rejoicing" of their hearts (Jer. 15:16 KJV).[1]

The incredible growth of BSF in the first decade after its incorporation wasn't so much an *expansion* as it was an *explosion*. The initial blast in California scattered students and leaders across the United States.

Impressive growth continued through the 1970s. The Holy Spirit chose to bless Bible Study Fellowship and propagate its ministry in varied and creative ways, as evidenced by the sampling of testimonies in this chapter.

## Growth Stories from across the Country

Anne Graham Lotz has a most unusual story about how she came to be a Teaching Leader and how BSF expanded to Raleigh, North Carolina.

### ⌒⊙ In Others' Words

*Anne Graham Lotz:*

It became apparent to me that there was a hunger for God in our city. And clearly, I had a personal need in my own life. I wanted to be a good mother, like my own mother. I knew she was disciplined in prayer and Bible reading. And I didn't have the discipline to do it.

I spoke at this church, and a woman came up afterward to talk. But she didn't say anything about what I had said; she simply told me about Bible Study Fellowship. That night back at home, as I fixed supper, I thought, *What she described may be what our community is looking for*.

I called a mutual friend, and she arranged for the woman to come to my house. We talked some more about BSF. She showed me the material, broken down by days. She told me all about the class. Right away, I thought, *This could be an answer to my need*. I'd been looking for something that would get me into God's Word every day. And I felt this could be an answer to a greater need in the community.

The lady wrote to BSF and was told that there was a three-year waiting list.

Later that summer, I was traveling with my husband's family

up to Cape Cod. My mother-in-law was reading the Bible aloud to herself, in the back seat of the car. I happened to hear the words of Revelation 3:8, where Jesus said, "I have placed before you an open door that no one can shut."

I asked her to pass me the Bible so I could read it myself. Then I said aloud, to my husband and his mother, "I wonder if God is speaking to me about this BSF class."

It struck me that when He opens the doors, no one can shut them. Not even Miss Johnson or whoever answered the inquiry at Bible Study Fellowship.

I continued to pray. In the material I had about BSF, there was a list of classes—two to three hundred of them—and the people who taught them. In Minneapolis there was a class taught by a Mrs. R. R. Glockner. So, I picked up the telephone and called Myrl, whom I had known years before. I hadn't talked to her in fourteen years or so. She did indeed teach Bible Study Fellowship. She advised me to write another letter to Miss Johnson and said, "I'll make sure she receives it."

I wrote a letter, and in response, I got an application for a class. I called together six or seven friends and we sat down together and filled it out. I then signed it and sent it in.

I never knew that the applicant for Teaching Leader was supposed to fill out that form and send it in. Or that I was now locked into teaching the class. I just sent it off to Oakland, and my friends and I committed together to pray for a teacher. I approached everyone in that circle and some others. No one would agree to teach the class. Then something in me thought, *If I have to do this myself, in order to be in the class, I will.*

BSF headquarters informed me that it would be years before I could be trained. But then a training date suddenly opened up. I asked a friend if she would be my back-up, the Substitute Teaching Leader. She said she would, because she had never been to California.

Neither of us knew about having a calling. I had this burden in my heart and my friend wanted to take a trip.

We did not know anything about BSF. We had never been

in a class, had never heard about BSF except through this one woman who had told me about it. I traveled in pants.

The woman who picked us up at the airport in California told us that we couldn't do this and we couldn't do that. And we were telling her what we planned to have BSF change. When she put us out the door at the orientation house, she looked at us and declared, "You will never make it."

I first met Miss J that night when she came to the orientation house to take us to dinner. Everyone else was in awe, and they talked about her like she was the pope. I hung back and thought, *I wonder who this lady is.* She walked in the door and was darling, with her little curls that bounced when she talked. She seemed very lively. She spoke to me, but I wasn't in awe. I didn't know anything about her.

We went through the training. When Miss Hertzler was talking, going through the administration part of the class, I got splitting headaches. But Helen, the person I took with me, just ate it up. She was excited; she grasped all of that stuff.

When Miss Johnson talked about homiletics, she called on me. I had never done it before. And she didn't tell us how to do it; she was used to critiquing leaders who already knew the basics. I gave her a subject sentence that didn't have a noun or a verb; I don't think it was ten words. She ripped it up, in front of the orientation class. My face must have turned red. I felt humiliated. But, I thought, *I want to learn how to do this.*

Miss Johnson took me in for that final interview of orientation week. When we finished, she came out the door and hollered to me as I walked up the hill from her home to the orientation house, "Dearie, be tough!"

I imagine she thought that, when Billy Graham's daughter set up a class, it would swell and then drop off. So, her parting advice was "Be tough!"

We came back to North Carolina excited about plans to begin a BSF class, and God gave me a verse, Malachi 3:10: "'Bring the whole tithe into the storehouse, that there may be food in my house. Test me in this,' says the LORD Almighty, 'and see if I will not throw open the floodgates of heaven and pour out so much blessing that you will not have room enough for it.'" I took that to mean I should give God exactly what was His, and I thought that meant to follow the BSF guidelines and instructions and the manual to the letter. And then He would pour out the blessing.

So, I set up the class. We had twice as many sign up as we were allowed to have in class. Every year that I taught, we had twice as many to sign up as we could hold.

When headquarters decided to get every class on the same lesson series, I had just taught Genesis, and the next year they wanted me to teach Genesis again. We turned out everybody who'd had Genesis before and started a completely new class, still with a waiting list.

We did that at least twice—made all class members get out and started new classes and allowed them to go into another class to seed that class. Eventually there were about ten classes in town and all at capacity.[2]

One couple's story of becoming involved in Bible Study Fellowship in California and then taking BSF to San Antonio, Texas, is more typical of the way new classes began in the 1970s.

### ◠ IN OTHERS' WORDS

*Mary Heppes:*

My neighbor in Walnut Creek, California, invited me to BSF in 1963. I started that year in Miss Johnson's class. The first day I walked in, seven hundred women were there. Back then, there were no limits to the classes; they'd accept as many people as they had room for. I felt like I had come home.

We were studying the Minor Prophets. I'd been a Christian since I was ten and thought I was well-versed in the Bible. I quickly realized I wasn't at all. The next year I was a DL.

The day before the final luncheon that first year was the

day Larry, my husband, was saved. He got in BSF the next year too. After two or three months, they asked him to be a leader. We were in those BSF classes two years and then we moved to San Antonio. Before we left, Miss Johnson said, "Maybe you could get a class started in San Antonio. We don't have one there."

I said, "You'll have to pray for me." However, I was thinking, *No, I can't start a BSF class, but I can't live without it!*

When we moved to San Antonio, I was expecting our fourth child. So, I waited until he was two or three months old and then had some coffees and invited some ladies to my home. I'd been in a Bible study with our pastor's wife, Monica McCann, and she became our first Teaching Leader. Then Monica had to resign because her husband was going to do something else.

We were without a BSF class for about two years. All the ladies who had been in leadership were still meeting and we were praying. Then, one night, I got a phone call from a woman who told me she'd been in a Bible study with this lady who'd been on the mission field. She asked, "Have we found a leader yet? Because I think she'd be really good." She gave me Rosemary Jensen's number.

So, I called Rosemary. She said she had heard about BSF from the girl who had called me. She'd even gotten some of the notes and read them. I went to visit her Bible study, listened to her teach, and thought, *Yes, she'll do good.* Before long, she went to California for training.[3]

Rosemary Jensen became the Teaching Leader for that San Antonio class. And Mary Heppes served as Class Administrator for eleven years.

BSF spread eastward to Massachusetts through the efforts of a California Teaching Leader. Although she didn't actually teach BSF in Massachusetts, God used her and some difficult life circumstances to plant a seed. Here is her story.

## ⁓ IN OTHERS' WORDS

*Lorrie Kemp:*

In 1968, Joyce White, a friend from church, knocked on my door. She told me about something called Bible Study Fellowship. Joyce had been asked to pray about possibly teaching a class in our area of La Habra, California. She asked me, and some others, to be a part of her new team.

Joyce was a fine leader, mentoring all of us as we grew together. We met at the La Habra Baptist Church for about five years. When we passed the five hundred–member number, we found a new church, the First Evangelical Church of Fullerton, California. There, we grew to over seven hundred women, with ninety leaders. That was too much for Joyce to handle alone.

I was asked if I would pray about going to Teaching Leader training in Oakland to become an assistant Teaching Leader. That would enable us to split the leadership for leaders' meeting.

I went to Oakland and had the opportunity of training under Wetherell Johnson. That experience is a treasure in my heart—to have personally "soaked up" Miss Johnson's passion for Jesus and her vision for worldwide Bible study classes.

Later that year, Miss Johnson, faced with the huge growth of Bible Study Fellowship classes, made the difficult but necessary decision to place a cap on class membership. Classes were not to exceed 450 women. It became clear that we would have to form still another class. God opened up a church in Whittier. And I was asked to take that class.

In May of 1973, many things happened. First my husband's company was sold and the new owner offered him a position in Massachusetts—the other side of the world to my family and me. Two years earlier, my mother and father had moved to California to be near their only grandchildren (and us). On May 1, 1973, my father became quite ill and three days later went to be with Jesus.

My head was spinning. *Leave my newly widowed mother alone? Take her grandchildren three thousand miles away?*

*How, God, could all of this be happening, when You have made
me so excited about launching a brand-new class in Whittier?* It
made no sense at all.

But, in a short time, we sold our home and moved to
Westborough, Massachusetts. In my heart was the strongest
conviction that if God had allowed me to be trained to lead a
BSF class, perhaps the reason all of this took place was in order
to launch a class there in New England.

We found a church, and the seedling of a BSF class was
there. We became friends with a wonderful Christian couple,
the Caccapoutis. With the help of Elaine Caccapouti, we began
a Bible study in my home and then one in her home.

After twenty-two months of living in the Northeast, we
moved back to California. No sooner had we left Massachusetts
than Elaine received a call from BSF to come to Oakland
for Teaching Leader training. She was a TL for ten years in
Massachusetts, then an Area Advisor for another four.

I thought I'd missed out on my opportunity again. But
shortly after we came back to California, Betty Ann Roberts,
who had taken the Whittier Class as Teaching Leader, was invited to become an Area Advisor. I was asked to take the class I
had to leave behind when we moved East. In the meantime, I'd
helped get a Massachusetts class started without ever teaching
there. Isn't God awesome? At last, I understood God's plan for
me to move.[4]

Lois McCall began a BSF class in Houston, Texas, and served
as its Teaching Leader for ten years before becoming a member
of the BSF Board of Directors. By 1980, Houston had the longest
waiting list of any area in the country. Lois tells of how that class
began.

## IN OTHERS' WORDS
*Lois McCall:*

One day in early 1970, I received a phone call from an

acquaintance asking me to go to a coffee with her. I had met this young woman a couple of years before when I served on my church's visitation team. She had a joy that I had never seen before—an enthusiasm, an excitement, and a delight about life. I wondered what made her tick.

At that time, I was a hardworking church person, but there had not been a whole lot of joy in my life or in my ministry as teacher of a large adult Sunday school class. Then in late 1969, God had granted me a life-changing encounter with Him that showed me the real joy of loving and serving Him. I had been praying earnestly for an in-depth, disciplined study of His Word so that I might know Him better still.

When I got into her car for our coffee appointment, she asked, "Have you ever heard of Bible Study Fellowship?" I had not. So she explained, "It's a nondenominational, in-depth Bible study that originated in California. When we lived out there, I was in one of the classes, and it was the greatest Bible study you could ever hope to find."

There were about thirty-five women at the coffee, and many of them I knew from other Christian circles. But among them were five young women I had never seen before. They had come from different BSF classes all over the country, had moved into the Houston area, and had been praying together for a BSF class.

I listened to them. I saw the delight in their faces, and I knew that this was real and not any put-on thing. They showed me some of their BSF notes. That impressed me, because I had been teaching for years and immediately saw that this material was rock-solid in content and superb in quality. The statement of faith was unequivocal and uncompromising. This was the assurance and the certainty I had been looking for. I wanted to learn more about it.

At the end of that coffee, I said to the girls that were clustered at the door, "Be sure and let me know when you get this class started, because I definitely want to be in it." And they asked me to pray for a Teaching Leader. I went home and earnestly prayed for a week, telling the Lord all the details of what we needed—someone who

- was known and respected in Houston;
- knew the Lord personally and was experiencing Him in her life;
- had a gift for public speaking, specifically teaching;
- did not have young children, because of the time requirements.

I was pleading with the Lord to send someone like this, and one day as I was praying, a thought came: *Is it you?* I thought, *Oh no! That's not possible. I don't know enough; I'm not good enough to be a BSF teacher.* But I had heard it said that God is more interested in your availability than your ability, and what we lack, He will supply. I called one of the girls from the coffee and asked, "Has anybody come forward as a potential Teaching Leader?"

She said, "Not yet."

I told her, "I cannot believe that I would be the one. But as I was praying, the thought crossed my mind that I ought to make myself available. But I don't know whether this is what God wants or not!"

She was excited as she told me the next step—write Miss Johnson, tell her just what I had told Sally, and wait for an application. "When she gets your application," she added, "you may not know for sure, but she will!"

I went to Oakland for Teaching Leader training in November of 1970. There were seven or eight of us in that class of potential Teaching Leaders and Class Administrators. A CA was generally selected for her executive and administrative gifts, and she had to step in for the Teaching Leader if the TL was sick or out of town. My friend Bunny, who had invited me to that fateful coffee, went with me to the training class to train for Class Administrator.

We heard Miss Johnson's personal story. Then we met many of the headquarters staff, like Marguerite Carter and Pearl Hamilton. Pearl was a towering intellect and a delightful woman, a gifted pianist and a terrible driver. Pearl's driving was careful, but it was so fast that I felt survival would be a miracle indicating God's stamp of approval of my going into BSF as a Teaching Leader.

The training in Oakland was a real adventure in many ways. But I came back with an assurance that teaching a BSF class was exactly what the Lord wanted me to do. We scheduled a six-week pilot class that next spring. The week before our starting date, I took the leaders over to the church to show them their room assignments and let them become familiar with the church set-up. We walked into the gym, which was then also the church's sanctuary, and there were two women sitting in the seats waiting for us.

They wanted to know, "Are you with the Bible study? We're here and ready to start." Right now, in 2007, Houston has an abundance of good Bible studies and a number of excellent teachers, but at that time, there was little available. These women were hungry for the Word, they had heard about BSF, and they showed up a week early in their eagerness.

We explained that the class would start the following week. But we chatted, got to know them, and then all prayed together for an abundance of women to come.

At our first class session the next week, there were 188 women, and the numbers grew almost exponentially. By the end of our pilot, we had a full class. No one wanted to stop and wait until September, so we got Miss Johnson's permission to teach another six-week pilot series in Ephesians and then a five-week course in 1 John. The class just kept growing.

We started our fall class with over three hundred women, and by the end of that year we were literally spilling out of that church. Some of our class members would drive one hundred miles each way to come to class each week. They came to that first Houston BSF class from at least ten to fifteen different cities within a hundred-mile radius. The Word was going out, and it was not returning void.

Our attendance level was at 85 to 90 percent most of

the time, and we had long waiting lists. Then at the Teaching Leaders' seminar in 1973, we were told that classes had to be limited to 450. We were instructed to start more classes, but the one leader I felt was capable of taking on a new class was not ready. "I would love to do it," she said, "but I can't. We're getting ready to move into a new house and I have too many irons in the fire." A year later, she recognized a clear call from the Lord and became a Teaching Leader, saying she realized that she had been resisting God's will.

When I had to warn the women about the cutback, I said to them, "We have no means of judging who needs to be in class, except by your attendance and your faithfulness in doing your lessons and participating in class. So those of you who are here all the time, and who regularly have your lesson prepared, will be chosen to stay."

I told my class members that if they had a chronic illness or chronic problems in their families that kept them from attending the class faithfully, they should prayerfully consider giving up their places for the sake of those who could give BSF a high priority now. Some graciously did.

Even so, at the end of the class year, the CA and I had to look at all the records and make choices about who stayed and who went. I wept over that list all summer. But as hard as it was for me to see it at the time, that process was one means the Lord used to strengthen our class. A place in BSF became a coveted treasure, a privilege to be carefully guarded and nurtured.[5]

Shirley Mills began attending a BSF class in California in 1969 and possibly holds the record for starting more classes in more cities than anyone else in BSF history. She helped begin new classes in Beaumont and Houston, Texas; Wichita, Kansas; Chicago; and Washington, D.C. During her service as the head of the Class Administration Division at BSF International headquarters, Shirley told her story to new Teaching Leaders at each orientation.

## ↶ IN OTHERS' WORDS
*Shirley Mills:*

In March of 1969, my neighbor had continually been asking me to BSF. I was not a believer and I had no desire to study the Bible. But finally, I thought, *I'll go one time just to get her off my back.* I went and was overwhelmed with what I heard. The Bible was being taught and was relevant for today. For me, up to that point in my life, it was just a book.

That was on a Friday. On Saturday, I went out and purchased a Bible because I did not own one. The following Tuesday I became a believer in Jesus Christ. So, between my first and second BSF class days, I became a Christian.

I attended that pilot class and a second one. That summer I was invited into leadership as a Discussion Leader.

My husband was serving in Vietnam at that time. When he came home, he requested a transfer, unbeknownst to me. I was upset with him when I found out we were moving to Virginia, because I had lived in Virginia twice and I didn't know any Christians in Virginia.

About this time, I went to a retreat at Forest Home. At that retreat, Miss Johnson's first message was on Philippians 1. When she got to the sixth verse, 'Being confident of this, that he who began a good work in you will carry it on to completion,' that ended up being my life verse. From that point on, no matter where I was, I was confident that God was not through with me. Even though he took me out of BSF for those three years in Virginia, my heart was still with Him and with BSF. After three years, we moved back to southern California and I finally was able to join another BSF class.

I was a Discussion Leader in the San Diego Day Women's Class, then in the Vista Bay Women's Class, where I was asked to be a Teaching Leader in about 1976. Actually, I was asked to go for training to be a Substitute Teaching Leader.

I went to Oakland to be trained. And on Sunday night, I was sitting in Miss Johnson's living room with sixteen people being trained, and she wanted us to share how we came to BSF. When I shared that I hadn't owned a Bible when I started with BSF, she came out of her rocking chair and exclaimed, "What? This is so wonderful." She always felt that, in America, there was a church on every corner and everybody had a Bible. She seemed thrilled to learn that here was someone being trained who didn't even own a Bible when she first came, and now she's coming to be a Teaching Leader.

When I went for the interview, at the end of Teaching Leader training, I was nervous. But as soon as I got in her presence, I was put at ease. She was such a godly woman! I left there feeling like God had said, "Yes, you are going to be a Teaching Leader."

That was in October of 1976, and I took over the class in January of 1977 and taught that class in Vista, California, for two and a half years. Then my husband and I decided the Lord was leading him out of the Marine Corps. And God opened up a job for Leo in Beaumont, Texas.

Within four days after arriving in Beaumont, I was meeting with a woman who had been praying for four years for a BSF class. She had attended a class in another part of Texas. Things didn't move very fast in those days. Sometimes it took years to get a BSF class started. The fact that God had brought in an already trained Teaching Leader was just a wonderful answer to prayer in her mind. Indeed, plans moved quickly. She went to headquarters to be trained as my Substitute TL. Then Leo was transferred.

I was able to stay in Beaumont long enough to do everything but teach the first class. The woman who had trained as my substitute ended up teaching.

We moved to Houston, where things were growing so fast I helped start the first Evening Women's Class. Then we moved to Wichita, Kansas, where I subbed for a Day Class and then started an Evening Class.

After that, we moved to Chicago, where I met Jean Nystrand. She was my Area Advisor while I was the substitute TL for a year and a half in Winnetka, Illinois. Then Jean came to me and said, "The Teaching Leader is moving. Would you be willing to take it?"

I told her, "I will do that. But you realize that I've already been here a year and a half, and with the history we have with this oil company, I can't be sure how much longer we're going to stay."

I taught that class for three months before we moved to northern Virginia.

There I soon met a lady who had been collecting names for the first Evening Class in the Washington, D.C. area. She already had a list of about forty names. So I talked to headquarters, and Rosemary said to me, "Let's work on that Evening Women's Class, but I want it seven miles from the nearest Community Bible Study, because we don't want to take away from them or be in competition with them."

I got in my car and drove around, literally looking for steeples closer to D.C., and God opened the door. I taught that Evening Class for a year and a half.

Then we moved to Dallas, where I met another Teaching Leader, Gwynne Johnson, who had recently moved into the area. The two of us became really burdened for the wives of the Dallas Seminary students. We contacted headquarters to ask, "Could we start a BSF class on the Dallas Seminary campus?" I was the Teaching Leader of the seminary class, and Gwynne was the sub. I taught that class for about six months before we moved back to Beaumont again.

At that point, I was asked to be an Area Advisor in BSF, and for nine years (we actually lived in one place for nine years!) I served as Area Advisor for eastern Texas.[6]

## Never in Her Wildest Dreams

On December 1, 1979, at the close of the decade and near the end of Wetherell Johnson's time as General Director of BSF, she spoke at a mass meeting of BSFers in the Oakland Coliseum.

## ⌐◦ FROM THE DIRECTOR
*Wetherell Johnson:*

I never in my wildest dreams thought that teaching 5 ladies would end in 51,000, including 10,000 men, in 28 years. What do I say? The power of God's Word, the Holy Spirit, the dedication of the Teaching Leaders. To God be the glory! What great things He has done! There are 50,000 people studying in 280 different classes. I hope you'll see that the smallest thing you do for God, God multiplies. In Jesus' name.[7]

# Chapter 15

# HEADING OVERSEAS

Bible Study Fellowship moves into Australia, England, and Canada

With Bible Study Fellowship classes multiplying across the country, it was probably inevitable that Wetherell Johnson's unique approach to studying the Bible would spread to other countries. And when it did, it happened the same way BSF had grown from the beginning—through class members relocating, because of "circumstances" and "open doors," by word of mouth, in response to a declared need, and through the Lord's grace and clear leading of those He had prepared to further the ministry of BSF.

## Australia

The first class outside of the United States began in Australia, through a connection with Marguerite Carter.

By 1968, Marguerite served on staff as Administrative Secretary, in charge of the BSF headquarters office. Living in one of the orientation houses, she invited some friends, Mr. and Mrs. J. Stuart Mills of Australia, to visit her. During their stay, they accompanied Marguerite to the Walnut Creek BSF class and heard Wetherell Johnson teach on Romans 7.

Mrs. Mills, the chair of the Christian Women's Convention in Australia, was so impressed that she arranged for Miss Johnson to be a conference speaker at the Australian Christian Women's Conference in March 1969. Miss J was gone from BSF headquarters for six weeks that spring, speaking at conferences in Sydney, Newcastle, Canberra, and Melbourne as well as in Auckland, New Zealand.

In early January 1970, Australians Jean Raddon and Grace Collins, who served as Wetherell's drivers and guides in Australia, traveled to Oakland to learn how to start a BSF class in Australia. The *BSF Newsletter* for summer 1970 described the beginning of Bible Study Fellowship "down under" this way:

> Already the Australian ladies are tremendously enthusiastic about the coming classes—so much so that it is hard for Miss Raddon and Mrs. Collins to meet their eagerness to begin. In order that the Australian work may have the best foundation, the plan is to commence with only one or two pilot classes in Sydney, which will ultimately become the model classes upon which others are built up in other areas.[1]

The spring 1971 *BSF Newsletter* reported on the progress of that class.

> Australia began a pilot class in Sydney in November. We had shipped 300 lessons for their pilot series, but after their opening, they sent an "S.O.S." for 100 more lessons. Great enthusiasm is reported from "down under." By this time, they are well into their first full series on Matthew's Gospel.[2]

The first class had reached an attendance of 170, and a second BSF class began in November 1971 in the Sydney suburb of Bolgowlah. By the fall of 1972, the *BSF Newsletter* reported the following:

> Overheard in an evening class, as one enthusiastic Teaching Leader impressed the needs among our expanding classes for prayer, he said, "And now the sun never sets on Bible Study Fellowship." Each year classes are more widespread, reaching beyond the coasts of the United States and at close of our day to

daylight hours in other hemispheres—Australia and England. The contagion of response to Bible Study Fellowship in Australia has spread from Sydney to Melbourne with the opening of a Pilot Class in September, introducing 143 women to class study.[3]

In 1974, the Administrative Secretary to Wetherell Johnson reported still more growth in Australia.

### ⁀☺ IN OTHERS' WORDS
*Marguerite Carter:*

We have added nineteen new day and evening classes since last we wrote you. Included is a first men's class in Australia. Typical of the fervor of so many in all these classes is the scene of a new class Wee Waa, in the plains of western Australia, where one woman drives 160 miles round trip each week over dirt roads with two little children to reach the class she so dearly loves.[4]

## England

Ann Cook, the first British Teaching Leader, reminisced about the origins of the first class in Liverpool, England, during an interview in April 2003.

### ⁀☺ IN OTHERS' WORDS
*Ann Cook:*

From September 1969 until July 1970, my family lived in Seattle, USA. My husband is a surgeon and we were asked to go there so that Richard could teach interns at the Children's Orthopedic Hospital in Laurelhurst. We had three children at the time, ages eight, six, and two.

We went to a church in Seattle and got to know people quickly. After three or four weeks, a woman said to me, "Oh, I know what you'd like, Bible Study Fellowship. I'll come and collect you next week."

I replied, "I've got Rachel and she's two."

"Don't worry about that; there's a Children's Program," the woman assured me.

I thought to myself, *I'll go once, because she's invited me. And that will be it.*

When we arrived at the BSF class, I saw this enormous church with the car park chockablock with women and children all streaming in. I was exceedingly impressed with the Teaching Leader, Lorraine Tillman. In retrospect, I expect she was probably the most influential person in my getting involved in a big way.

Lorraine was inspirational and enthusiastic. And Rachel was well cared for. So, I went to class regularly.

In February, I was asked to be a Children's Leader.

I said, "We're going home to England in July. I don't have much time left."

I was assured that didn't matter.

I thought, *Why not? Rachel is being well looked after. I could go and look after other children.* Of course, that meant I would need to go to leaders' meetings. So, I prayed about it. Little did I know that would be the beginning of real involvement.

I attended the leaders' conference in the Northwest that year and met Miss Johnson briefly. Later, Lorraine phoned me and said, "Miss J has been praying for years that a group could start in England. We've wondered whether you could be instrumental in this."

They suggested that I zip down to headquarters, from Seattle to Oakland, to meet with Miss Johnson to talk about it. I quickly realized that they were serious about a group starting in England, but I wasn't sure I was the ideal person to start it. I had a real spiritual struggle over whether to get involved or not. We had three children under eight and were about to have four children under nine, because we adopted a little Indian girl when we got back to England. However, I said I would think about it.

We'd made many lovely friends in the United States, and I

was especially sad to leave my Bible Study Fellowship group. But we got back to the U.K., to Liverpool.

Now, I did not really want to stay in Liverpool, because we were from the south of England. One afternoon I announced to my husband that the only thing that would convince me that we were meant to stay in Liverpool was if somebody named Mrs. Poynder would call us up and tell us her house was for sale. The attraction there was that my own parents had actually lived in that house some years earlier.

About five o'clock, I was getting the children their supper, when the phone rang. On the other end, a woman said, "Mary Poynder here. I don't know if you'd be interested, but we are moving and our house is going up for sale."

I nearly dropped the phone. I had made my comment to Richard no more than twenty minutes earlier. There wasn't much more discussion about whether we should stay in Liverpool. That was 1970 when we moved into that bigger house that had belonged to the Poynders and was now ours by divine appointment.

I soon communicated with headquarters to say that I would get involved with Bible Study Fellowship. I had some coffees, trying to raise interest in a prayer group. I was the only one in England who had been to a class. It was just me selling the idea to everyone. One or two Christian doctors had moved into Liverpool the same time we had. They and their wives were open to new ideas. So, they formed the nucleus of the original Bible Study Fellowship class here in Liverpool. Still, it was really a wild idea.

We had a small group that met together for prayer. And I'd tell them about BSF and try to inspire people with this vision of what a class could be like. We finally did get a list of women who were willing to try it.

But there remained many barriers to introducing BSF in the U.K.:

- It was American. The majority of people were suspicious of anything American.

- The whole idea that you should study the Bible in a disciplined way was a new concept.
- Interdenominational organizations were rare in England.
- Some churches felt threatened.
- The idea that there were rules about how you did things and when you spoke seemed crazy.
- A lot of Christians in Liverpool were involved in the charismatic movement. BSF was not charismatic.
- We have impossible church buildings—ancient and cold, with no parking, and few smaller meeting rooms. The church we started in was totally hopeless, yet better than most.
- Few women had a car; they would have to come on public transportation.

Frankly, most people thought it was a mad idea.[5]

Yet, for years Miss Johnson felt a special burden for starting BSF classes in England, her homeland. After Miss Johnson's radical cancer surgery in 1970, Alverda Hertzler reported the following in the October 1970 *BSF Newsletter:*

> Many of you prayed especially for Miss Johnson on her illness in July. You can imagine how grateful to God we were that her doctor discovered the tumor before we left for Europe, and how we rejoiced when we learned the malignancy had not spread.
>
> Miss Johnson had to cancel her original trip to Europe, the main purpose of which was to see people who wanted Bible Study Fellowship classes in England. The needs were so urgent that Miss Johnson felt she should take this trip, and finally her doctor agreed.[6]

Ann Cook continues her story.

## ⌒⌒ IN OTHERS' WORDS

*Ann Cook:*

On June 9, 1971, we had our first pilot class on *Colossians*. Miss J visited Liverpool on June 10–13 en route to Switzerland. Lorraine Tillman, my Seattle TL, later visited on her way to Europe and did the lecture on June 30, 1971.

We had leaders' meeting on Mondays in my home. We arranged for the children to be cared for. We sang hymns in the sitting room around the piano. Then we'd go up three flights of stairs to the attic. We called it "the upper room."

BSF class day was on Wednesday in the United Reform Church. I was both Teaching Leader and Administrator for some months before we found someone to take on the role of Administrator. Crates of material were delivered to my house, unpacked by Richard, and stored here.

We gathered a nucleus of people who were keen on BSF, and they were bringing other people. God was blessing us. After the pilot class in *Colossians*, we began to grow. It was thrilling.

On September 15, 1971, BSF officially started.[7]

That new BSF class in Liverpool had a membership of sixty-five women when it began in the fall of 1971. That was a very respectable beginning, as the fall 1971 *BSF Newsletter* reported.

Miss Johnson and Mrs. Tillman were both greatly impressed by the enthusiasm and response these English women showed for this type of Bible study. A letter from Mrs. Cook says, "It is thrilling that enthusiasm continues and there is such a real unity in our group. Many of the women walk miles in pouring rain and some have to get two buses and set off at 8:00 AM to reach the class in time."[8]

While the growth was exciting, the work was not easy, as Ann Cook admitted.

### ∼◯ IN OTHERS' WORDS

*Ann Cook:*

Humanly, it was daunting. I was thirty-four years old, with four small children. My husband worked long hours at the hospital. Most of my BSF work and study had to be done between 9:30 PM and 2 AM Thankfully, I can exist on very little sleep, but after my lecture, I would be physically exhausted.

I attended one TL conference in the United States, the one with Michael Baughen. Then we had one conference in the U.K. during my time.

BSF was and is brilliant—and, to my thinking, the best way to study the Bible that I've ever encountered. In-depth Bible study, prayer, and preparation resulted in my being "innovative" spiritually and having great confidence in God's Word. It affected so many lives.[9]

A member of Cook's class tells her side of the story.

### ◠◯ IMPACT STORY

*Gwyneth MacKenzie:*

When I was invited to go, BSF sounded great to me. But my pastor said, "Be careful. Something coming from America, you never know what it might be."

I was thrilled that first day, seeing all the people gathering, the young mothers with their children, the ladies with their Bibles, all walking in. I thought, *This is the place for me.*

BSF came into my life as a gift from the Lord. My children were in their late teens and I wanted to do some study. I had thought of Bible college but knew that would be impossible. BSF became my "lay Bible school," offering rich fellowship with others like me who wanted to know the Lord and live our faith out in our lives.[10]

Like Gwyneth MacKenzie, another member of that first BSF

class in Liverpool wanted to learn more about living out her faith in daily life. She remembers her experience in that founding prayer group:

### ~⊙ IN OTHERS' WORDS
*Ann Colmer:*

Ann Cook invited me for lunch and started to tell me all about what was to me a rather strange American Bible study. She asked if I would join the first prayer group. I was happy to be part of that group, and we started to pray for a BSF class in Liverpool. The pilot was just about to start when we got our first set of questions and notes. I shall never forget sitting down in my lounge at home, starting to look at them. I went up to my husband and said, "What have I let myself in for? This is like being back at school. We've got homework. And things that look just like examination papers." But that reluctance soon disappeared as I got involved in the pilot class and began to see the impact of God's Word on individual lives.

What made the most impression on me was my acquaintance with the different denominations. Up to that time, my own experience had been just within the Anglican church. Suddenly I was with people from all other kinds of other denominations. Especially in Liverpool, a lot of people were from Brethren churches.

I'd been in Leaders for a few months, when another leader said to me, "Ann, I didn't think there were any Christians in the Anglican church, until I met you." That was a great joy.

As a Discussion Leader, I had a young Brethren girl in my group, and she sat very, very quietly. I discussed that with her one day and she said, "We don't speak in my church. I have never spoken about the things of God in a group." With a little encouragement, she began to open up. What a joy for her to be able to express her faith in a way that she had not been able to before!

Ann did a great job, being the TL, training us all.

Bible Study Fellowship was where I learned about the Bible.

I'd become a Christian in my twenties, but I'd never been in a Bible-teaching church. When I got married, my husband started to help me read and study the Bible. But my knowledge was still shallow. So, it was in BSF that I started to appreciate God's Word.[11]

From the time the pilot class began in June 1971, until half-way through the first full class year, Ann Cook served as both Teaching Leader and Class Administrator for the Liverpool Day Women's Class. In an interview in 2003, class member Gwyneth MacKenzie described that part of her life.

### ~ IN OTHERS' WORDS

*Gwyneth MacKenzie:*

To begin with, Ann brought the toys for the children, flower arrangements, labels for the group venues, a welcome board for the entrance, even toilet rolls—everything that was necessary.

Over the Christmas break, I received a letter from Ann asking me if I would go and train to be the Class Administrator. I'd never flown. I thought, *I couldn't possibly do that!*

I talked it over with my husband, John, who said he thought I ought to go. "If it was in this country, would you go?" he asked.

I said, "Oh yes!"

He said, "Then it makes no difference, this being in America. You should go."

The previous year my husband had been diagnosed with cancer and told he had only six months to live. This was less than twelve months after that. He was doing all right, but I thought, *I can't possibly go and leave him*. Yet, I felt sure that was what the Lord wanted me to do.

With his encouragement, and with great fear and trembling, I went. The trip to Oakland was a great experience for me. At that time, Miss Johnson felt that overseas TLs needed to be there three weeks and go through two orientations.

I saw the printing presses and visited different classes. I

remember Miss Johnson teaching us homiletics on Jonah. I never forgot that and quoted it so often. It was especially helpful.

I came back in February to be Class Administrator and took the lecture whenever Ann needed a substitute.

My husband lived another ten years and, in the end, did not die of cancer.[12]

When Ann Cook resigned as TL of the Liverpool Day Women's Class to return to nursing, Ann Colmer took over for the next four years. Here she talks about that leadership experience.

### ⟶ IN OTHERS' WORDS

*Ann Colmer:*

I was happily enjoying myself as a discussion group leader. I loved having a group each year, doing the coffees and the phoning. I was comfortable. Then Miss Johnson came over to lead a retreat. During that retreat, I was in a fellowship of four when suddenly the door opened and the woman who was our Area Advisor at that time beckoned me. Miss Johnson wanted to see me.

Well, my stomach went over. I went back in a little room with Miss Johnson. She told me that Ann Cook wanted to go back to nursing and would not remain the Teaching Leader. Ann had suggested that I might be the one that would take over.

I was flabbergasted. I started coming out with all sorts of reasons why I couldn't do it: "Miss Johnson, I do this in my church and I do that."

Miss Johnson said to me, "Ann, go away and pray over each of those things that you are doing now—in the light of eternity."

I said yes. And then I went off to Oakland for training to be a Teaching Leader. That was a valuable time, visiting American classes, seeing different classes and leadership in action.

I taught in Liverpool for only four years. Then I became an Area Advisor.[13]

*I had the privilege of praying on my knees with this lady when she visited our Oakland class.*

## Canada

While classes grew in Australia and England, one other English-speaking country had a new BSF class. In the fall of 1972, the *BSF Newsletter* reported that thirty women traveled by carpool across the Canadian border each week to attend the BSF class in Blaine, Washington. That core group of women formed the first class in Canada. The spring 1973 *BSF Newsletter* included this information:

> The many women who have been crossing the border from Canada to attend the class in Blaine, Washington, now rejoice in helping to start in Canada under the Leadership of Mrs. A. Gillet, a former member of Melrose Baptist whose husband has just moved from Everett, Washington, to Vancouver, B.C.[14]

## More Growth in England

In 1973, two more cities in England were interested in beginning BSF classes. The eventual Teaching Leader in Hereford remembers how the BSF class there began.

### ∾ IN OTHERS' WORDS

*Anita Newton:*

In 1973, Jessie Bentley-Taylor met Wetherell Johnson on holiday in Switzerland and heard about BSF. Following that she met with two women from each church in our area, Hereford, England. I was interested but put off following it up. Then I heard that Jessie had set up a meeting in someone's house, and I realized that I was about to miss one of the great things in life, so I quickly responded.

About seventy women attended that introductory meeting, but there was little response. However, Jessie set up a prayer group with about eight women who had shown interest. I was one of those.

Eventually a potential TL and STL were identified, and Miss Johnson visited us to meet with them. At around that time some of us traveled to Liverpool to visit the only BSF class in the U.K. There we met with the Teaching Leader, Ann Cook, at her home, along with other interested women from the city of Southport.

The prayer group continued. Then, in September, Dorothy Gell, who had been the second woman from my church to hear of BSF from Jessie became interested once again. She was given some BSF lesson notes on Corinthians to read on holiday, and when she came back, she was ready to be involved.

When Miss Johnson came over to the U.K. again, Dorothy and I drove up to the Liverpool class to visit her. I was placed in a discussion group led by a young mother. The leadership of this group enthralled me. Everyone had prepared their answers, and they were graciously drawn into discussion. Afterwards, I went to a group fellowship lunch led by the same young mother. Her name was Ann Colmer.

In January 1975, Dorothy Gell, a Teaching Leader, and Jean Latham went to Oakland for three weeks of orientation. I started as a Discussion Leader. Jessie Bentley-Taylor was our class Secretary. The pilot course on *Colossians* was under way in Dorothy's own church. Our class stayed there for about five years. It was the oldest BSF host church in the world—nine hundred years old!

We started the second year of BSF with Dorothy still leading. When Jean had to stand down, owing to illness, I became Class Administrator and Substitute Teaching Leader. I had never spoken in public before, except one or two talks to small women's groups. My first lecture was on Matthew 2, before I ever had any training.

When I went to Oakland for orientation, we had an earthquake. The next day I discovered that, during the earthquake, Miss J had wondered if the Lord was coming again, while Miss H had gotten out the suitcase she had already packed with essentials from under her bed.

I found Miss Johnson kind, gentle, penetrating, and frightening. In those early years of BSF in the U.K., our Area Advisor was Elizabeth-Ann Horsford, an Englishwoman on the staff of

BSF who came over from the United States about once a year to visit the classes.

By 1977, we numbered four classes in England: Liverpool Day, Southport Day, Liverpool Men, and Hereford. I took over as TL at Hereford in January 1979, during the study of John's Gospel. That same month there was a TL seminar at Mount Hermon in the redwoods in California, and I was invited to attend. I remember Michael Baughen preached on prayer. That was to prepare me for taking over.[15]

### ᐤᐤ IMPACT STORY
*Ann Colmer:*

One looks back and thinks of the different people who came to BSF. I think of one lady who could barely read or write. We found out after a while that her daughter at home was reading the Bible passage and the questions to her. Then she would give her answer and the daughter would help her write down something, to enable her to give an answer in her group each week. I saw those answer sheets, with such large, irregular writing. But when she shared, the depth of that woman's concepts and understanding from God's Word—it was a challenge to all of us. The Word of God cut right through that lack of education.[16]

Barb Watson was a Children's Leader in England and then Children's Area Coordinator for Europe.

### ᐤᐤ IMPACT STORY
*Barb Watson:*

It was only when I came into BSF that I began to seek the Lord's will as to what I should do. I had to reassess all the things I was involved in at church, to ask the Lord which of those things were the things He had for me to do.

When we studied Ephesians as a pilot class, the verse that

said that God had work for us to do really hit me right between the eyes. I don't know how many times I'd read those verses in my life before. But I thought, I'd better ask Him if what I'm doing is what He has planned for me to do.

I learned a big lesson. I could say no to things. I didn't have to say yes because people thought I could take them on or I was there and the job needed doing. That freed me up to do what God called me to![17]

Ann Cook, the woman who first took BSF to England, recounted the following in 2003:

### ⌒◈ IMPACT STORY
*Ann Cook:*

About five years ago, I was coming up to Liverpool on a train from London when the engine broke and we had to change trains. Everyone became friendly, because we'd all had to move. I was talking to a woman seated next to me, and she said, "I must tell you about something really brilliant. I go to a marvelous class, called Bible Study Fellowship."

This was about twenty-five years after our first BSF class began in Liverpool. So, I told her, "I actually do know about it."

But it was lovely to have someone telling me about BSF here in England. The wheel had turned round. What a thrilling moment![18]

## Looking Back, Looking Forward

Wetherell Johnson and Alverda Hertzler watched in delight as the Lord blessed their mushrooming ministry throughout the 1970s. BSF had not just gone international, but by 1979, classes throughout the United States had grown and spread to more than forty states, including Hawaii, where one Day and one Evening Class already met. The two ladies could only pray that blessing and growth would continue. But they realized their own years in leadership of the organization were ending.

In fact, just around the corner was the end of one era and the beginning of another.

# Part 3

# THE SECOND GENERATION BEGINS
## (1980–1984)

*Chapter 16*

# A CHANGE OF LEADERSHIP

Bible Study Fellowship gets its second director: Rosemary Jensen

I n *Created for Commitment*, when recalling the late 1970s, Miss Johnson admitted, "For some time I had been looking forward to finding a replacement who would be trained in the work. Yet, nothing had worked out. However, God knew that when the emergency came He already (unknown to me) had His own choice."[1]

As it turned out, the Lord had not only new leadership in mind for the organization but also a new location for its headquarters.

## Beginnings in San Antonio

That part of the story—and more compelling evidence of God's provision for the ongoing leadership of Bible Study Fellowship and its ministry—began some years earlier. A member of the first San Antonio class and part of the lunch bunch, recounts the beginning of BSF in that Texas city.

### ⌒ In Others' Words
*Betsy Wray:*

In 1969, Larry and Mary Heppes brought BSF to San Antonio from California, where Larry had been in Miss Johnson's class.

The first Teaching Leader in San Antonio was Monica McCann, wife of the Heppes's pastor.

When I attended that BSF class, it became an instrument God used to change my life. Getting into the Word of God is a transforming grace. I thought I had everything I could possibly want—friends, family, everything. But I was lacking a spiritual life. Oh, I was a Christian and a churchgoer, but I needed a transformation. I got that through BSF in every area of my life. And the same was true for my husband.

When Monica and her husband moved away, there was no longer a BSF class in San Antonio, for more than a year.[2]

Meanwhile, in 1972, some of Rosemary Jensen's neighbors and a few people from her church attended a weekly Bible study she taught in her San Antonio home. Rosemary and her husband, Dr. Robert Jensen, a former military physician, had only recently returned to the States after living nine years overseas. During their seven years as missionaries in Africa, Bob had founded the Kilimanjaro Mountain Medical Center. Then they spent two years in Okinawa before moving to San Antonio, where Bob reestablished a medical practice and taught at the University of Texas Medical School.

One week Rosemary commented to those attending her home Bible study that she was studying Genesis in her personal quiet time. Afterward, a member of the group, Brenda, came forward to say she had something she thought Rosemary might find interesting. At the next week's Bible study, Brenda handed Rosemary a bulging notebook filled with BSF lessons. Rosemary noted the thickness and weight of the notebook. When she opened it, she saw it was filled with typewritten pages, all single spaced, with many of the pages stapled in sets. There were questions, too, which Brenda had answered in tiny writing, filling up all the margins.

This simple beginning became a turning point in Rosemary's life, one she would never forget.

## ᴄꙅ Iᴍᴘᴀᴄᴛ Sᴛᴏʀʏ

*Rosemary Jensen:*

The whole thing looked rather imposing. Not the kind of material any casual reader would choose to wade into. I thought, *I have commentaries that are nice, bound books. Why would I look at these lessons?* And I set the notebook aside. However, each time Brenda showed up at Bible study over the next few weeks, she would ask, "Did you read the notebook yet?" Finally, I decided that I would peruse one lesson. Then I'd be able to truthfully tell Brenda that I had looked at the material, thank her, and give her back the notebook.

So, I began to read, starting with the lesson for Genesis 1. By the time I had finished that first lesson, I thought, *This is really good stuff. This Wetherell Johnson person, whoever he is, really seems to understand me.*

By the next week, I had read every one of the lessons—though I didn't do any of the questions—so that I could give the book back to my friend.

When I asked Brenda where I could get my own copy of the material, Brenda told me, "You can't."

I assured her, "I'll be glad to pay for it."

Brenda explained that it wasn't for sale.

In that case, I insisted, I would just write to Wetherell Johnson and request a copy from him.

"You can't do that." Brenda told me. She explained that Wetherell Johnson was a woman. Then she said, "And there's only one way you can get these lessons. You have to go to a class."

"Then I'll go to the class," I told her.

"You can't," she responded. "There isn't one here in San Antonio."[3]

Rosemary learned there had been a class, taught by Monica McCann, in San Antonio for two years, from 1969 to 1971. When the Teaching Leader and her husband moved away, Brenda and a small group of women began praying for a new Teaching Leader. And they'd been praying ever since. Her experience in Rosemary Jensen's home Bible study convinced Brenda that Rosemary might just be the answer to those prayers.

## Rosemary Jensen Joins BSF Leadership

The more she learned about Bible Study Fellowship, the more Rosemary sensed God's leading. When she contacted BSF head-quarters in Oakland about restarting a class in San Antonio, she learned about the required Teaching Leader training. That didn't discourage her a bit. In fact, she readily agreed to fly to Oakland for the next orientation session.

So it was, having never attended a class, and merely weeks after she first heard of Bible Study Fellowship (and that Wetherell Johnson was a woman!), Rosemary sat in a California living room with a dozen other would-be Teaching Leaders from across the country, being instructed in the policies and practices of BSF by Miss Johnson herself.

As with every other Teaching Leader since the beginning of BSF, Rosemary had to get the Director's personal stamp of approval at the end of the orientation session before she could serve as the TL of a new class. Miss Johnson gave her endorse-ment, and years later, after training hundreds of TLs from across the country and even around the world, she said of Rosemary: "I well remember her coming for orientation classes and how I was impressed by her life in God. Like myself in 1952, little did Mrs. Jensen realize what her leading from God to take a class would one day result in."[4]

### ⌒◯ IN OTHERS' WORDS

*Betsy Wray:*

Rosemary came home to Texas after that orientation and started a pilot class in San Antonio that April 1973, with resounding success. One hundred and fifty women attended. By the time the regular class year started that fall, three hundred women had signed up.

Those of us who'd been praying for so long about a new class were thrilled by the tremendous response. I served as a leader in that class for nine years. After just a couple of years, Rosemary became an Area Advisor, and one thing led to another. But while Rosemary was our Teaching Leader, some of her good friends would all have lunch together after class each week. I was in that group, the "lunch bunch." We became prayer warriors for Rosemary, for our class, and for Bible Study Fellowship.[5]

Despite some initial nervousness and misgivings, Rosemary soon discovered that she loved teaching the Bible in BSF. "I felt that BSF was the most wonderful thing," she said, "definitely the best way in the world to study the Bible. I just loved it, and I sensed that this was what I was destined to do."

Her new San Antonio class continued to grow. At the end of two years, it capped out at 450 members, and Rosemary was thinking of starting a second class. Then she received an unexpected phone call from Wetherell Johnson.

Although the two women had seldom talked since Rosemary's orientation, they felt an instant bond. Perhaps it was because they had both been missionaries. Perhaps because they both loved God's Word and BSF.

The phone call from Oakland came one summer afternoon in 1975. Miss Johnson wanted Rosemary to pray about being an Area Advisor.

"What is an Area Advisor?" Rosemary asked. As a Teaching Leader in Texas, she had not had an AA to help her.

"Oh, my dear," Miss Johnson responded, "there's nothing to it. It's just like being a Teaching Leader—on just a little bit broader scale."

She explained that it was the AA's job to oversee other Teaching Leaders in Texas and Oklahoma. As AA, Rosemary would visit and represent headquarters to all the classes in her area, evaluate the leadership, and mostly encourage TLs by offering help and advice with problems or questions.

Rosemary wanted to know, "What am I going to do with my own class?"

Miss Johnson's solution? "Oh, my dear, no trouble—you can do both."

It was after noon the day Miss Johnson called to ask Rosemary to pray about becoming an Area Advisor. At 6 AM the next morning, the Jensens' phone rang again. In Texas, it was six o'clock, but in California, where Miss Johnson lived, it was four o'clock in the morning. Miss Johnson wanted to know if Rosemary had prayed about the position. She didn't really give Rosemary time to answer before she added, "I need you in California next week for an Area Advisors' meeting."

So, for the next three years Rosemary taught a class and was Area Advisor for Texas and Oklahoma—both Men's and Women's Classes. During that time, she and Miss Johnson developed an even more cordial relationship.

## Miss Johnson's Health Begins to Fail

Late in 1977, Wetherell Johnson thought she was suffering from shingles. When she went to her doctor, he made the surprise discovery that, seven symptom-free years after her first bout with cancer, it had returned. Further tests revealed one collapsed vertebra and bone cancer in four other vertebrae of the upper spine.

Jane Roach remembers being trained as a Teaching Leader in Oakland when Miss Johnson had the recurrence of cancer.

#### ⟜ IN OTHERS' WORDS
*Jane Roach:*

Bob Jensen, Rosemary's husband, gave me a prescription to carry out there. I was sworn to secrecy. Nobody was to know that she was not well. So, I slipped the prescription to her.

And I remember that first night we were there. We were all meeting in the living room of Miss J's home, getting acquainted. Then we knelt to pray. We were on our knees for twenty minutes or more. She never fidgeted. She never leaned over. She was right next to me, so I could feel her presence. In all that time, she did not move despite her excruciating pain. That is the kind of strength that she had. I learned to love that in her.[6]

When Robert Jensen learned of the cancer diagnosis, he and Rosemary invited Miss Johnson to stay in their home in San Antonio while getting additional testing from an excellent specialist whom Dr. Jensen recommended. While she stayed in an upstairs bedroom of the Jensens' home during January 1978, the relationship between the two women deepened. And Wetherell Johnson began to wonder further about Rosemary Jensen's potential in BSF.

⸻ **FROM THE DIRECTOR**
*Wetherell Johnson:*

> I became conscious that God had blessed Rosemary with spiritual depth, a gift of speaking, and a gift of administration. Besides being a former missionary to Africa, she had been a Bible Study Fellowship Teaching Leader for six years and an Area Advisor for four. As I listened to her telephone counseling with some of her class members, I began to wonder if this was not the replacement God would choose.[7]

Of course, there was one major roadblock, as Miss Johnson saw it and as others would see it: Rosemary lived in Texas, but the BSF headquarters was in California. Perhaps that could be resolved somehow.

Meanwhile, on doctors' recommendation, and in hopes of slowing the cancer, Miss Johnson immediately began a series of cobalt treatments at the University of California Medical School Hospital in San Francisco. She worried at first that the five-days-a-week regimen would require a change in her plans to hold four weekend BSF retreats that spring. However, as she later reported, "God wonderfully undertook and nothing was left undone because of cancer."[8]

In spite of undergoing grueling treatments, being limited to a liquid diet, and experiencing severe physical weakness, she managed to speak as scheduled at all four retreats—in California, Indiana, Ohio, and Virginia. She later wrote of her gratitude for God's help and the support of faithful BSFers, all of whom knew that she was there only "because of adequate strengthening from God in answer to many prayers." [9]

### ⌒⊘ IN OTHERS' WORDS

*Karen Dable:*

Miss J's back was bad, and she was very weak. They had a rocking chair for her on the stage because she needed it to sit, before she would get up to talk. She'd be in that rocker and we knew she was in pain. It would come time for her to get up and speak and she'd get out of the rocker, she'd come up, and she would look a little pale at the start. But by the time she was into her message for three to five minutes, it was like a resurrection was happening before your eyes. There was power; there was pink in her cheeks. God would just fill her. That was really an awesome thing. [10]

Miss Johnson also admitted, "While I was taking meetings and concluding the cobalt treatment, I kept thinking and praying about my replacement—and Mrs. Rosemary Jensen." [11] Soon she was doing more than thinking about her. She was talking to Rosemary.

### ⌒⊘ IN OTHERS' WORDS

*Rosemary Jensen:*

From 1978 on, I talked to Miss Johnson by telephone for at least two hours every day. That lasted for years, so I knew everything that was in her mind fifty times. I'd pick up the phone and she would say, "Hello, dear, how are you?"

I'd say, "Fine."

Then she would say, "How is your family?"

And I'd tell her, "Fine."

I always said "fine" because I knew if I started to say anything else, she would immediately interrupt and begin talking about BSF. Because that's what she really wanted to talk about.

She and I never really had a conversation about anything except BSF. We talked about some doctrinal things and about the Bible, but we never talked about politics or anything else. It was all BSF, and I absolutely loved it.

I always stopped doing what I was doing when she called, sat down to talk, and gave her my full attention—because I recognized the importance of BSF. I loved every facet of it and thought it was just the most marvelous thing. I loved all the details of everything that she wanted to tell me. So, I soon knew quite a lot about the organization.

Wetherell and I became very good friends. I loved BSF and I loved her.[12]

One day Miss Johnson called to say, "Rosemary, we've just had a Board meeting, and guess who's been put on the Board?" Rosemary mentioned someone's name, and Miss Johnson said, "No dear, you!"

Miss Johnson had wanted another woman, someone not from California, on the Board. She knew that Rosemary, with experience as a TL and an Area Advisor, understood BSF's work in the field. Miss Johnson was also thinking about the future of the organization.

While staying in the Jensen home later that year, Miss Johnson told Mrs. Jensen, "Rosemary, you need to come onto the BSF Staff."

Rosemary laughed. She didn't live in California, and she didn't consider herself the same caliber person as Pearl Hamilton or Ann Horsford, who both worked in the Oakland office at the time.

Discounting any such protests, Miss Johnson added, "You know, Rosemary, you could do this job," meaning her own role.

Looking at her friend and mentor, Rosemary thought, *This cancer has hit her brain! There is no way in this world that I could do that.* Rosemary said, "No, dear."

But Miss Johnson said, "Yes, you could, dear. It is just like being an Area Advisor, just a little bit bigger scale."

## A Decision

Meanwhile, Wetherell's health continued to decline. In December 1978, she turned seventy-one years old and was not well. The Board, facing a number of serious issues, made it their priority to address the question, how do we find a replacement for Wetherell Johnson?

Everyone involved believed the Lord wanted the work she had started twenty years earlier to go on. But whom did God want to lead BSF?

Another serious challenge facing the BSF Board was the need for larger headquarters facilities. The five properties in Oakland lacked enough space; they were scattered; and the cost of adding to them looked prohibitive.

During this time, an anonymous donor offered the Board ninety-five acres of land, free of charge—just outside San Antonio, Texas—if BSF wanted to move the headquarters there. Miss Johnson saw this timely and generous overture as one more indication that Rosemary Jensen just might be the next Director of Bible Study Fellowship.

For most of 1978 and 1979, the BSF Board wrestled with these two critical issues: the wisdom of moving the headquarters, and who could or should take over the reins from Miss Johnson.

Early in 1979, at a BSF Board meeting held in Miss Johnson's Oakland home, a major part of the agenda was discussing potential candidates for a new Director. As a new Board member, Rosemary took part in that discussion. Several names were raised, but no agreement reached.

After the meeting, Dr. Ernest Hastings, who had served on the Board since the organization was founded, pulled Rosemary aside to ask if she might be willing to consider the position. He made it clear that he was not asking her to say yes or no, but merely wondering if she would pray about it.

When Rosemary reminded him that she lived in Texas, not California, Dr. Hastings inquired whether she would be willing to ask her husband to move to California.

Rosemary told him, "I will not do that. I go where my

husband is and would never ask him to move so that I could do something."

Ernest asked if she would at least tell Bob what had been said between the two of them.

"I will tell him," she agreed. "And he will laugh just as I am laughing."

Rosemary believed that God makes His will known to those who earnestly seek Him. When she got home from California and told her husband about her exchange with Ernest Hastings, Bob's response totally surprised her: "Rosemary, you know that God is not a God of confusion. If He is calling you to be the Director of BSF, then He must have something for me to do in California. You can tell them that."

"Bob, honey, I can't do this!" Rosemary protested.

He said, "Yes, you can!"

As she finally considered the possibility, Rosemary remembered something Board chair Dr. Grant Whipple once said about Miss Johnson. When he first become acquainted with Wetherell years before, she was the shyest person he had ever met. But she changed. *Perhaps,* Rosemary thought, *I can change too.*

For some time she told no one else about the decision facing her. Not relatives. Not praying friends. Only her husband and the Board knew.

Betsy Wray, one of Rosemary's closest friends, owned a beautiful place on a nearby lake. Bob and Rosemary had often gone there with Betsy and George Wray. And the Wrays had offered to the Jensens use of the place whenever they wanted to get away.

That summer of 1979, Rosemary asked Betsy if they could spend a week together at the lake. Rosemary needed some quiet time just to think and pray. She desperately wanted to hear from the Lord, to know what God would have her do.

So, Betsy and Rosemary spent a week there. Each morning, Rosemary got up early and walked to the round house on the water for her quiet time with the Lord. She cried out to God in her mind and heart, saying, "You need to show me what to do, Lord. What is it that You have for me?"

One morning, toward the end of the week, Rosemary heard God's voice, not aloud, but clearly in her mind, saying, "Rosemary,

I am going to move BSF, and I want you to do it."

Then she walked up the stairs to have breakfast with Betsy. From that point on, she knew the Board would ask her to be the Director. And she was terrified.

The following morning, she went down to the lake again and prayed, "Are You sure, Lord? You know that I can't do this, don't You? You know that I cannot teach like Wetherell Johnson. I cannot. I am not that kind of person. I don't know what I would say, and I don't know how to do this!"

That year, in her quiet time, Rosemary had been reading through the Bible. On this particular day, her Scripture reading came from Isaiah and included 51:16: "I have put my words in your mouth and covered you with the shadow of my hand."

When she read that promise, Rosemary prayed, "Lord, I know I cannot do it myself. If You will say the words, I can do it. If You will keep me covered, with Your hand on top of me, okay."

Years later, Rosemary described that memorable day this way: "I walked around with a deep peace. I did not tell Betsy or anybody. But I knew that God had given me His confirmation; I knew that it was His call for my life. And I have never questioned it in all these years."[13]

In September 1979, the BSF Board met at the Oakland airport. The time had come to discuss Wetherell Johnson's replacement. During the deliberations, Rosemary was asked to step out of the conference room so the rest of the Board could talk freely. She sat all by herself in the airport, waiting for the others to decide. Her fear was gone. She felt only anticipation and peace that God was orchestrating everything and that He would work everything out according to His plan.

When the Board called Rosemary back into the meeting, they had indeed voted to name her the new Director of BSF. But she'd expected that. To her surprise, they also had unanimously voted to move the organization's headquarters to Texas. Some of her colleagues on the Board wanted to be certain of her commitment to go wherever God wanted BSF to be. Once they had her answer and knew she was willing to move to California, they decided a move to San Antonio made a lot of sense.

The Jensens would not have to move after all—but the entire

BSF headquarters would. And that posed a completely new challenge.

When Miss Johnson introduced the new Executive Director to thousands of BSFers at the Oakland Auditorium in December 1979, she had the following to say about her successor:

### ⌒ FROM THE DIRECTOR
*Wetherell Johnson:*

You know, I never felt old. I never felt old at forty—at forty, I was beginning a new work. But when I was seventy and had cancer, I did begin to feel old. And at the same time I got to know, in a way, that cancer was a good thing. I should tell you the story. We had an Area Advisor meeting and Mrs. Jensen was there. I was supposed to have had shingles, and her husband was kind enough to send me a little bottle of something to help my shingles. So when I discovered it was cancer, I immediately thought the courteous thing was just to write to him and tell him about it. He said, "Come and see me."

Well, when I went to see them, I not only got to know Dr. Jensen and his hospital, the way he handled things and the godly man he is, but I also saw Mrs. Rosemary Jensen. I saw the intense love that the people of her area had for her. Not only that, she was a woman of prayer; she has some university graduate work as well as her own degree, Army experience, and a general view of life, having been in Africa for seven years with her husband. I saw leadership. And I saw what I value most of all: a dependence upon the Lord. I saw a family relationship with all three girls earnest Christians and all grown.

Now of course this was a Board matter; they had to think about it. They had to count the cost; they had to think about all

Wetherell Johnson's farewell in Oakland

the complications. But it was a unanimous decision. It is my very great pleasure to introduce Mrs. Rosemary Jensen. Some of you don't know her, but you will love her as I do when you get to know her.[14]

## ⟶ FROM THE DIRECTOR
*Rosemary Jensen:*

It took twenty years for BSF to be established, but that was only the beginning. As gracious as God was to give us everything we needed to get started, He was not finished. His plan was to make Bible Study Fellowship a tool for the next twenty years and, we trust, into the twenty-first century. Furthermore, His plan also included reaching the whole world with His unique method of Bible study. But, for this to happen, some things were needed.

God in His grace had already prepared Miss Johnson's replacement, and I was absolutely dumbfounded to find out it was me! I want to tell you something here, though. I loved Wetherell Johnson, and amazingly, she loved me too. I appreciated her. I knew her well, and she opened herself to me through lots and lots and lots of conversation. There were literally years that she and I talked for at least two or three hours every single day on the telephone, if we were not together. I don't know how this worked except for the fact that God put us together. God gave her a love for me and me a love for her. He gave us similar minds regarding what needed to be done in the work.

BSF was what we would discuss hour after hour after hour. I never tired of it, and I guess maybe that's why she thought maybe it would work for me to be the next Director.

In December of 1979, Wetherell Johnson retired, and in January of 1980, I officially became the Director of BSF. She was seventy-two, and I was fifty.[15]

*Chapter 17*

# THE TEXAS TRANSITION
## Reorganizing Bible Study Fellowship in San Antonio

I n her new position of leadership, Rosemary Jensen quickly learned some important lessons.

### ⤳ FROM THE DIRECTOR
*Rosemary Jensen:*

Being the Director of BSF is no more like being an Area Advisor than being an Area Advisor was like being a Teaching Leader. They are different "animals." But God wanted me to be the next Director of BSF.

When I became the Director in 1980, I had no idea how He would use me. I couldn't figure out why God put me there. I just knew one thing—I could depend on Him. And I had to.[1]

The most pressing issues the new Director needed to address were neither new nor surprising to Rosemary and the BSF Board. The biggest challenges the organization faced were part of a growth crisis that had been building for years and that finally converged to a point of urgency during 1978 and 1979.

To understand the Board's vote to move at the same time they elected a new Director requires a little historical background.

## Relieving the Training Bottleneck

Bible Study Fellowship's facilities in Oakland had been less than adequate for some time. It took a creative, committed, long-suffering staff to accommodate the amazing growth of the organization in the space allotted them.

While comfortable and homey, none of the three BSF-owned staff residences, which also served as guest and orientation houses, were close together. Each was at least a fifteen-minute drive from the administration building. In addition, Miss Johnson and Miss Hertzler divided the upstairs and downstairs of their house, which also was used during teacher training.

The training building was next door to the administration building, but the press building was located up the highway. During TL orientation, trainees had to drive, or be driven, from one location to another. No more than sixteen Teaching Leaders could be accommodated in one session, and that was crowding the facilities because staff members also lived in those houses. The kitchen facilities made feeding even that small number a logistical feat.

The training bottleneck in Oakland resulted in a serious shortage of Teaching Leaders. In Houston alone, there were one thousand people on waiting lists to get into BSF classes. Some people had been on the waiting list of Lois McCall's class in Houston for three years. Lois would hold an introduction class, and 350 women showed up, every one of them hungry to study the Bible the BSF way. But that class would have room for only fifty new members.

And Texas wasn't the only place BSF was growing. Classes across the country had waiting lists; second and third classes were desperately needed in some cities. People in places with no BSF presence wanted to start classes in their area. But new classes could not begin without Teaching Leaders.

A shortage of training facilities was only part of the problem.

Since BSF's beginning, Wetherell Johnson had trained the Teaching Leaders personally. No one anywhere in the world could teach a BSF class without first coming to Oakland and sitting at the director's feet for instruction.

Even as the demand for new classes and Teaching Leaders skyrocketed, Miss Johnson's health and strength plummeted. Repeated rounds of cobalt treatments took a heavy toll. Unable to sleep, she would get up around four o'clock in the morning. But she could hardly work with people at that hour, and she regularly took naps in the afternoon. When she had trouble working more than half a day at a time, she did what she could from home. But it grew increasingly difficult for her to keep up with the daily needs of BSF. She was simply unable to conduct additional training sessions, even if the facilities would have allowed.

All of this factored into her thinking, and the Board grew concerned that the time had come for choosing Miss Johnson's successor. Through it all, God was working out His plan to take Bible Study Fellowship to places no one yet imagined. BSF's leadership, the Board, and class members around the world, all praying for God's will to be done, were about to see His design unfold.

As a result, the confidence of BSF's leadership never faltered, even in these most trying of circumstances. Alverda Hertzler said, "As Bible Study Fellowship faces a new era of growth, some exciting developments lie just ahead. Our Board of Directors is engaged in the study of our growth and ways of meeting the challenge it produces."[2]

## Ninety-Five Acres and a Dream

The small group of women who, for years, had prayed for Rosemary Jensen each week—the lunch bunch—included Betsy Wray, Betty O'Connell, Eleanor Craven, Mary Heppes, Sissy Orsinger, and Ginny Trawick. Through these women, in the summer of 1978, Rosemary learned BSF had been offered ninety-five acres of land. She immediately told Miss Johnson and Miss Hertzler about the offer. They thought it was an interesting proposal. They, too, were concerned about the cramped headquarters and the long waiting lists of people not finding room in

BSF classes. They knew changes needed to be made, and they wanted things done right.

With Wetherall and Alverda's blessing, the prayer support of her friends, and her firm conviction that this could be God's will, Rosemary summoned the courage to present the information on the San Antonio land donation to the BSF Board, meeting in September 1979. Everyone had agreed the organization could not go on without larger, or more, facilities. At that meeting, the Board discussed the possibility of expanding or adding to their property in Oakland. Perhaps they could build a high-rise on it, to make the most of the land. They seemed willing to consider every possible solution.

### ⌒ FROM THE DIRECTOR
*Wetherell Johnson:*

> The Board needed to give much prayerful considerations before contemplating such a tremendous move that would affect all of our staff. On the other hand, the Bible Study Fellowship was growing to such an extent that almost immediately we would need once more to look for land on which to build in Oakland, and there apparently was nothing suitable available.[3]

The BSF Board sent Rosemary back to Texas to calculate the cost of duplicating in San Antonio the 24,000 square feet of facilities they had in Oakland.

BSF's business office was given the job of counting the cost of a possible move, from the California side. They evaluated the operational expenses in California and compared them to costs in Texas. They also compared a Teaching Leader's cost to travel from New York to San Francisco versus from New York to San Antonio. They compared the cost of shipping, from Texas versus from California, weekly study notes to all the classes. And they gathered realistic appraisals on all their properties in Oakland, both residential and commercial.

Simultaneously, Rosemary gathered information from the San Antonio side. In surprisingly short order, she tracked down encouraging answers to feasibility and cost questions. Several preliminary hurdles were cleared in such remarkable ways that Rosemary felt certain she was seeing God's hand at work.

The morning of that BSF Board meeting in the Oakland airport on September 10, 1979, Grant Whipple, chair of the Board, opened *The Daily Light* devotional for that day. "That we may all be one!" he read aloud. "If that isn't from the Lord, I don't know what is!" he added. And he put the booklet in his pocket. That brief prayer, "That we may all be one," was answered later that day with the Board's unanimous vote to select Rosemary Jensen as the new Director and to move the headquarters to Texas.

It would be two years before the new headquarters' dedication, on September 12, 1981. Those two years were busy—developing the San Antonio land and constructing new buildings there, selling the California property, and moving an organization halfway across the country. Meanwhile, the everyday work of BSF had to go on—the administration, the training, the classes, the printing and shipping of lessons every week to classes meeting all around world.

## Making the Transition

The move to San Antonio had far-reaching consequences. And not just for the organization. It affected all the staff members and their families. Many members of the BSF headquarters staff had worked together for a long time. They felt called by God to the ministry. Now they had to decide if God was calling them to continue their ministry in Texas.

People not moving had the concerns of finding a new job and separating from coworkers whom they loved and an organization to which many of them had devoted a significant portion of their lives. Those planning to move to Texas had houses to sell in California and new houses to buy in San Antonio. When they were at home, their houses were for sale; when they came to the office, those buildings were for sale as well. It was an unsettled and unsettling time for everyone.

Times of transition are a challenge in most organizations, because people often have difficulty embracing change. For years, some BSFers had speculated or assumed who might best succeed Wetherell Johnson as Director. Many expected Pearl Hamilton, Miss J's longtime Deputy Director, to take over. So, when the Board chose Rosemary instead, they were surprised and some had difficulty adjusting to the idea. One of these was Dottie McKissick, TL in southern California for thirty-five years. Another was Jan Myers, TL in California and AA in Hawaii for thirty years.

## ⟶⊙ IN OTHERS' WORDS

*Dottie McKissick:*

At first, I have to say, I just didn't know Rosemary well enough to feel sure about this. Then I talked to Pearl and told her, "I'm really not cool with this, but you are handling this so well and I marvel at you."

Pearl said to me, "You know, this is what the Lord has for me. I'm not the leader; I'm second fiddle." She recognized the vision that Rosemary had, which she did not have. And I appreciated that.

That conversation with Pearl helped me to let go of any resistance and begin to see Rosemary for what she really was— a woman of vision who could expand the work of Bible Study Fellowship.[4]

## ⟶⊙ IN OTHERS' WORDS

*Jan Myers:*

Those of us who knew Miss Johnson loved her. It was not that we felt howsy-wowsy about her but that we admired her so much. When she retired and Rosemary came on, I struggled with that. I really struggled. It was so difficult to think of someone else in Miss Johnson's place. So I said, "Lord, this is Your organization and what I feel is not important, so I want You to give me peace about this and help me to love and accept Rosemary." And He did just that. I came to love Rosemary, though not in the same way.[5]

When Rosemary Jensen walked into the office as the Director of BSF on January 2, 1980, she lived in San Antonio but would commute to Oakland one week out of every month. As difficult as the transition time promised to be for her, she knew the Board's decision to move would be even more difficult for some members of her staff. She believed, however, that the Lord had given her a plan to help her staff pull together through the challenging days ahead. She knew that without unity they would never be able to accomplish the move or the ministry to which God had called BSF.

So on her first morning in Oakland, after the staff had morning prayers, Rosemary told them, "We all must have the same purpose, which is BSF and not ourselves. It is not about us; it is about God and His work we are trying to do. Here is what you need to promise, and I will promise it too." Then she handed to every person in the office a paper entitled "Seven Secrets of a Successful Staff." It read as follows:

> 1. I will do my work as unto the Lord. I stand before God and not men (Colossians 3:23).
>
> 2. I will love my fellow staff members and show this love by laying down my life in generous service and encouraging words (John 15:13). The world will know we are Christians by our love (John 17:23). Further, I will assume that my fellow staff members love me and wish me no harm. (Romans 13:10).
>
> 3. I will not gossip about another staff member, nor will I listen to gossip (Ephesians 4:29). I am told not to judge others (Matthew 7:1).
>
> 4. I will not give a negative evaluation of circumstances. This shows a lack of trust in God (Exodus 16:8; Romans 8:28). When something needs improvement or correction, I will report the need to the person responsible and then do my part to fill that need.
>
> 5. I will take the steps outlined in Matthew 18:15–17 if someone on the staff offends me. Furthermore, I will

forgive others remembering how much I have been forgiven (Matthew 5:24; 6:14–15; Luke 17:3–4).

6. I will not allow resentment over anyone else's position, title, or duties to remain in my heart. It is the Lord who has given each one his work and many can be defiled by a root of bitterness (Hebrews 12:15).

7. I will thank God every day for the work He has given me to do in Bible Study Fellowship (1 Thessalonians 5:18).

Everyone who worked at the Oakland headquarters signed that pledge. And every new person hired to work in San Antonio would sign it as well.

The transition was not easy. Rosemary and her assistant, Mary Gail Campbell, worked three weeks out of every month in San Antonio, in an office they created out of the game room in the Jensens' home. For the better part of the next year, most of the headquarters staff remained in California, keeping in touch with Rosemary by phone.

The lunch bunch in 1980

Even long distance, Rosemary plunged right in to address the most pressing problems. Her first orientation for Teaching Leaders held in Texas was in January 1980, her first month as Executive Director. To host the orientees, she used the houses of three friends—Betsy Wray, Betty O'Connell, and Helen Bernhardt. Betty and Eleanor Craven prepared and served the food in Rosemary's house during the orientations. The lunch bunch was still coming through for Rosemary—big time. In a concerted effort to ease the shortage of Teaching Leaders, and to shorten those long waiting lists, Rosemary held a record six Teaching Leader orientations during 1980.

But perhaps the best measure of the enormity of this challenging transition can be found in the sobering yet positive reports written in the Christmas 1980 issue of the *BSF Newsletter*. Here is what veteran staffers wrote in the midst of all this change.

## IN OTHERS' WORDS

*Pearl Hamilton:*

God built a nation by teaching people to follow Him in the wilderness. We Californians have pitched our tents in Texas. One of the difficulties involved sale of houses in a market that was inflated and depressed at the same time. Ours sold in two months to the one and only buyer to offer. It was answered prayer. Also, Terree Williamson's house sold in three weeks to the first bidder. We are grateful for your prayers.

In mid-July, several carloads of headquarters staff members and moving vans began the nearly 2,000 mile southeast trek accompanied by teenagers, friends, dogs, and a cat. The General Director had ferried one bird, in cage, on her lap via plane, for a staff member. Sightseeing along the way at Grand Canyon and Carlsbad Caverns compensated somewhat for the heat of summer 1980, which is now in the record books. What a welcome we received in Texas! Southern hospitality is not overrated, nor is the love of those in Bible Study Fellowship. Combined, they are unbeatable.

Much of our heart remains in California. God has been good to us in leading our three grown daughters and two sons-in-law to "migrate" to Texas also. My husband, Jack, was willing to take an early retirement and begin a new career "from scratch" because he felt that this was God's guidance for us.

Since opening the headquarters in San Antonio, we have held four orientations sessions—as many as were held in Oakland in any year. Already the move is benefiting the work as the long waiting lists are being whittled down. New classes are in embryo stage—in many states and overseas. We cannot thank you enough for your faithful prayers and expressions of encouragement.[6]

### ⌒ IN OTHERS' WORDS

*Mary Siemens and Anna Kingsbury:*

Moving means many things! For the Production Division, it means discovering God's provision for "business as usual." First, as building and houses have sold, we have assisted in transferring and packing furniture and supplies, and rearranging 5707 Redwood Road to make space available for furnishings that had to be stored until the new facilities are completed.

Then, we accelerated our production schedule so we can move by May 1981 without disrupting the flow of materials to classes. Perhaps a few statistics will help you visualize this:

- In 1979, we printed 516 jobs using over 72 tons of paper. We completed shipping lessons for 1979–80 on February 6, 1980.
- In 1980, by October 23, we printed 847 jobs using over 101 tons of paper and completed shipping all lessons for 1980–81.
- Before May 1981, we will print and ship all class forms, children's materials and lessons 1–16 for 1981–82. Then we will disassemble presses and equipment; pack and ship everything to San Antonio to be installed in our new building.

We are grateful for all of your prayers for us. We've had joy and great fun in pulling this load together.[7]

## Staff Changes

The Board had to be impressed and pleased by the energy, initiative, and commitment their new Director brought to her job. At the same time, the Board chair, Dr. Grant Whipple, tried to caution as well as encourage Rosemary when he told her, "It will take five years to build the headquarters and get things running on an even keel, but I am sure you can do it."

Five years seemed an exaggeration to Rosemary. She had already established a time line for the move, began training more TLs than ever before, and started lining up new employees to fill the jobs of those staying in California. She even reorganized the headquarters staff into five divisions, with each Division Head reporting to her. Miss Johnson's longtime Deputy Director, Pearl Hamilton, graciously agreed to continue working with classes and Teaching Leaders. Kitty Magee led the children's work. Anna Kingsbury would supervise the press in San Antonio. Bob Owens stayed on as business manager. And Rosemary added a division to oversee class administration, hiring Kay Thornton for that position.

The assimilation of new staff was as important to the transition as was the cooperation of longtime headquarters staff. For new members were also willing to become part of the Master's plan for the organization. And often, God's leading was every bit as remarkable in their stories as was His help for those moving cross-country.

### ⟊ IMPACT STORY

*Steve Gately:*

> I started with Bible Study Fellowship as a class member in a San Antonio Men's Class in 1975. My wife, Gloria, attended a local Women's Class. But when Sears transferred me from Texas to Tulsa, Oklahoma, in 1976, there weren't any BSF classes in Tulsa at the time. After a couple years, Sears moved me again— to Oklahoma City, where my wife was able to attend a Women's Class.
>
> There were no Men's Classes there, but I started meeting for weekly prayer and Bible study with a small group of guys—a couple of whom, like me, had previous experience with BSF. We thought it would be great to get a Men's Class started in Oklahoma City. The more we prayed about it, the more I felt God leading me to consider being the Teaching Leader.

Before I learned Rosemary Jensen had been named the new Director, I'd known her as Gloria's TL in her San Antonio class. One day early in 1980, I telephoned Rosemary to say I was coming to Houston on a business trip and wanted to swing by San Antonio to talk about the possibility of helping launch a new Men's Class in Oklahoma City.

When we met for that initial interview, we talked about my positive experience with BSF when I lived in San Antonio. I told her about the men I'd been meeting with. And I explained how I thought God was leading me to consider becoming a TL.

She listened to everything I had to say and then she asked me, "If you could do anything you wanted right now, what would it be?"

I explained that Sears treated me well. Even so, I didn't really think I wanted to work for them all of my life.

At that point, Rosemary asked me my college major. When I replied, "Accounting," she asked if I could keep books. I said I could.

"We need a bookkeeper," she told me. "We're in the process of relocating to San Antonio, and our California bookkeeper isn't going to make the move." She wanted to know if I would like the job.

Suddenly I had a real dilemma. My appointment had been made to talk about becoming a TL in Oklahoma City. Rosemary knew that, yet here she was offering me a staff job in San Antonio. I told her I'd have to talk to my wife and we would pray about it.

Gloria wasn't against the idea, but she had concerns that I would not be paid as much at BSF as I was earning with Sears. We prayed, and the two of us sat down to take a hard look at our budget. Finally, I wrote a figure on a piece of paper and showed it to Gloria. "If she offers me a salary of that much," I said, "I think I should take it."

At the beginning of that next meeting, Rosemary raised the salary subject and told me how much BSF could afford to pay me. I'd written the exact figure on that piece of paper for Gloria.

So, of course, I agreed to take the job. But that wasn't the last sign that the Lord was in this. I had told Rosemary I couldn't move to San Antonio or start with BSF until June—after the kids' school year ended and my son graduated from high school. My wife may have even wondered if I'd lost my mind, taking a job making less than half of my salary with Sears.

On top of that, we were both concerned about selling our house. Interest rates had sharply increased—14, 15, 16 percent. Some houses in our neighborhood had been on the market for two years without selling.

Ours went in less than a week—another sign. We even got exactly what we were asking for it.

We now knew how much I was going to make. Plus we knew how much money we were getting out of our house in Oklahoma. We also knew a little something about the housing market in San Antonio, from when we lived there before. So, it was time for Gloria to go house hunting (I couldn't take any time off at the time).

We looked at the numbers and I told my wife how much I thought we could afford to offer and how much we could put down on a house. I even figured out the highest monthly mortgage payments I thought we could afford.

Four days after she got to San Antonio, a discouraged Gloria called me to say, "I can't find a single house in our price range that you or I would want to live in." The market had gone crazy.

Finally, she went to one ugly, pink-brick house. Gloria told our real estate agent she didn't even want to go in. But they had an appointment, so they took a quick tour. Gloria fell in love with the brick floors inside. And the place had a lot of other charm we could emphasize by painting the exterior and making a number of relatively minor changes ourselves. Our offer was accepted, and the mortgage payments were only four dollars more a month than the figure I'd set. But when our lender recalculated our payments the next January, they came down four dollars—to the exact figure I'd said we could afford—confirming, once again, that we were where we were supposed to be.

God engineered the whole thing. And He has more than supplied all we have needed ever since.[8]

Steve served as BSF Bookkeeper for two years before taking over as Business Manager. He eventually became the organization's Chief Financial Officer, until he retired in July 1998. He now serves on BSF International's Board of Directors and continues to consult part-time with the organization's business department.

The changes in administrative leadership proceeded so smoothly and quickly that Rosemary thought they were far ahead of Grant Whipple's five-year prediction. Only years later did she look back and say, "As a matter of fact, the interesting thing is that it took exactly five years."

Indeed the next few years held changes and hurdles, many involving the construction of the Texas headquarters. But God provided new facilities beyond all dreams and expectations.

# Chapter 18

# SIGNS OF GOD'S BLESSING
### Building headquarters in San Antonio

Throughout those months of administrative and moving preparation, Bible Study Fellowship people in San Antonio were praying. The lunch bunch was praying. A larger group of BSF graduates in Texas was also praying. And members and leaders in BSF classes across the country were asking for God's guidance and blessing.

As a result, God clearly worked at the new headquarters site in marvelous ways. But to tell this part of the story, we must again go back in time to the initial offering of the land in 1978.

## Land and Water

When she returned to Texas with the assignment to explore the feasibility of building on the offered property, Rosemary Jensen sat down with her husband and with the couple who wanted to donate it. The four of them prayed for God's will for BSF and for wisdom in how best to investigate the suitability and cost of building on that ninety-five acres.

### ⌒ FROM THE DIRECTOR
*Rosemary Jensen:*

First, we had to find an architect. Someone suggested Paul Hesson, saying that he was the best architect in town. I felt strongly that any architect we consulted needed to not only be able to give us accurate estimates and keep our initial inquiries confidential, but he should also be a member of Bible Study Fellowship. No one else would understand the needs of BSF or our dependence on God for provision and guidance.

Unfortunately, Paul Hesson was not a member of a BSF class. But his wife and two daughters were. So our group of four—Bob and I and the donors—prayed, "Lord, if Paul Hesson is the architect for this project, would You please somehow get him involved in BSF?"

Three weeks later, guess who walked into a men's BSF class? Paul Hesson. We did not know who had invited him, but our prayer group and I knew, *This must be the Lord's working!*[1]

Rosemary contacted him immediately to explain BSF's needs and to request a cost estimate, a drawing, and a square-footage cost. She showed him the land—which had no road, no electricity, no water, nothing. The property could be reached only by four-wheel-drive vehicle.

Paul Hesson looked over the land and told Rosemary, "You will need an engineer. You've got to put in roads and everything else." For that he recommended Fred Goetting.

The Jensens were familiar with Fred. The Goettings' son had dated one of their daughters for a short while. Fred's wife, Joanne, had been a leader in Rosemary's BSF class. And Fred attended the San Antonio Men's Class.

The first question needing answered was, is there water on this land? No water meant that no headquarters could be built there. Fred Goetting arranged for a geologist to check out the property. The expert offered a grim report: "You will never find clear, good water there."

Charlie Kuhn, a local well driller, was also a member of the

Men's Class in San Antonio. When he heard that BSF needed to know if there was water on that site, he offered to help: "I'll put a well in for you. You just have to fix it up so that I can get my drilling rig in there."

Since there was no road into the property, BSF needed a miracle.

Ann Biggs was in a BSF prayer group that was asked to pray about getting a road into the property. Ann's husband, Glen, just happened to be the chair of City Public Service, the supplier of electricity for the San Antonio metropolitan area. So, she offered to have her husband call Rosemary to discuss the prospect of getting a road and electricity to the site.

Glen told Rosemary that his company was currently running an additional set of power lines all the way from their nuclear plant on the Texas coast to San Antonio—and those new lines would run right alongside the existing line on the BSF property's right-of-way. Even more, before those lines could be installed, his men needed to put in a track—not a paved road, just a track—so they could get their equipment in to erect towers and string new lines.

Then the power company executive made Rosemary this offer: "I'll tell you what we can do. We can put that road in there now. My crews are working down toward the coast, but if you are willing to pay for the movement of the equipment, they can put your part in right away, then go back and finish where they are now."

When Rosemary asked how much that would cost, he said $5,000. After she offered this as a prayer request at the next meeting of her lunch bunch, the husband of one of her lunch bunch friends offered to pay the bill for moving that equipment.

Rosemary considered this provision for the road to be a wonderful example of God's "previousness"—how He knows and provides for our needs even before we are aware of them.

The power company cut the road, and Charlie Kuhn brought in his well-drilling equipment. He drove to the first level place he found and set up his equipment.

All the BSFers in that part of Texas were praying for water. Some found Bible verses about water and wells, streams in the desert, or living water to claim for the new site.

When Charlie Kuhn drilled down, water came up. Not sulfur water, as the geologist had predicted, but pure, drinkable water. And that first well produced enough water—five gallons a minute—to meet the requirement to build on the land. Rosemary, Miss Johnson, and other members of the Board saw this as yet another strong recommendation to accept the property and move BSF headquarters to San Antonio.

When the building committee of the Board examined the land, they actually had a picnic on the grounds. Though they arrived by four-wheel-drive vehicles over a primitive road, the visitors got a bird's-eye perspective of the land and the rugged Texas hill country surrounding it on a helicopter engaged to deliver Miss Johnson and Miss Hertzler.

Rosemary Jensen and Wetherell Johnson taking off to look over the land for the future headquarters.

### ∽ IN OTHERS' WORDS

*Betsy Wray:*

I will never forget seeing that helicopter land with those two dear women in it. They couldn't have looked more tickled if they had arrived on a magic carpet. I think that Miss J and Miss H were just blown away by the whole idea of a headquarters' building, the property, and the entire area.

Another time, George and I took both ladies out to our country place. There were masses of bluebonnets. I took this picture of A&W (that's what we called them—A&W, Alverda and Wetherell) standing together in this huge field of bluebonnets.

When they got back to the car, Miss Johnson exclaimed, "Oh, my dear, it's just like Switzerland."

We had to laugh. Texas was just so hot, and there were no Alps in sight. We thought it was such a joke. Then we realized Miss Johnson was referring to the beautiful flowers. However, from then on, whenever we went back there, our family would say, "Oh, it's just like Switzerland." And we'd laugh. But Miss Johnson and Miss Hertzler loved it. We took them on a boat ride and they loved that. They were grateful for everything. But most of all, they were grateful for what was happening with the land and the new headquarters. I have never seen such appreciative people. They really lived their lives to give God the glory.[2]

## The Lord Provides

God continued working in the lives of people involved with the new San Antonio headquarters, including the man who built the facility, Harvey Hancock. The tale was recounted at the BSF staff Day of Prayer in May 2000.

> Rosemary felt strongly that whomever they hired needed to have some BSF connection. So, the Board agreed not to put the job out for a bid. Instead, they asked Paul Hesson to suggest three contractors he felt good about. All three of the men he recommended were either in BSF classes or their wives were. One possibility was Harvey Hancock, who was not in BSF, but his wife Kathy was a Discussion Leader. Harvey and Kathy also attended the Jensens' church.
>
> After the worship service one Sunday, Kathy pulled Rosemary aside and asked if she would be willing to pray with her about something: "I know that Harvey is being considered as the builder for the BSF complex. Will you please pray that if he gets that contract God will use it to get him into the Word of God? Or else that Harvey will *not* get the contract?"
>
> Harvey was eventually chosen as the contractor.

Because of their interaction on the project, Paul
Hesson asked Harvey to go to BSF with him. Harvey
joined that class and stayed in it through the entire
five-year series.

On December 10, 1979, the BSF Board held its first Board
meeting in San Antonio, at Rosemary and Bob Jensen's house,
which they referred to as the "San Antonio office." During that
meeting, the Board met with the architect, Paul Hesson, the
engineer, Fred Goetting, and builder Harvey Hancock.

The Board asked Harvey how long it would take to build the
headquarters complex, start to finish.

He replied, "Thirteen months."

They all smiled and nodded and then asked again, "Harvey,
how long do you really think it will take? You contractors never
finish when you say you are going to finish."

Harvey answered, "I really believe we can do it in thirteen
months." Then he laid the plans out for the Board as well as his
estimated cost.

The Board smiled and asked, "But, Harvey, how much do you
really think this will cost?"

Harvey's answer astounded them: "This is the price we have
negotiated, and I believe this is what it will take. But I'll tell
you what I will do: if I can save any money, I will give it back to
you."

At that point, BSF had only enough money to begin building.
They required the money they hoped to get from the sale of their
Oakland properties to pay for remaining expenses of the new
buildings. Yet, the Board decided to step out in faith, confident
now that moving to San Antonio was the Lord's will and that He
would continue to provide.

When ground was broken and the building began on April
14, 1980, Rosemary was still working from California one
week out of the month. She decided that it was time to move
the Business and Training divisions to San Antonio. The Press
Division and the shipping operation couldn't move yet, of course.
BSF could not stop printing the materials that had to go out to
the classes.

Rosemary began looking for temporary office space for the parts of BSF that could move. One day she stopped at the Blanco Feedstore, a building near the site of the new headquarters. The owner had built a two-story addition on top of an old icehouse, and it appeared to be vacant. Rosemary took down the phone number and called the owner.

She informed him she was looking to rent seven offices for one year. She asked how much the rent would be.

"How much are you willing to pay?" he wanted to know.

Rosemary had not expected that question, and she had no idea what a reasonable price would be. But God gave her a figure. "Twenty cents a square foot, and that's it. But you have to pave that driveway."

When the owner hesitated, Rosemary asked, "Do you have anybody else?"

The owner was still not sure. "Do you have the authority to make the decision?" he wanted to know.

"Yes, I do," Rosemary told him. "And you would be fortunate to have us—we take good care of things. We don't smoke and nobody will be coming in with alcohol, so you are not in any danger. We'll take care of everything, and we pay our bills. You will be paid on time."

"Where do you get your money?" the owner wanted to know.

"Oh, the Lord provides for us," Rosemary assured him.

So, with the Lord's provision, Bible Study Fellowship's headquarters began the actual move. But that divine provision was evidenced not just in the details of the transition, in the lives of the many BSF staff members migrating to Texas, and in the hiring of the architect, the engineer, and the contractor for the entire project. God, it seems, was also definitely working in the lives of others who would play key roles in establishing the new San Antonio headquarters.

## Called to Be Part of It

In April 1980, Rosemary received a letter addressed "To Whom It May Concern." The letter was written by Richard Walenta, a builder, who told how much BSF had meant to him and to his family. He went on to say that he was interested in helping work on the new headquarters.

Rosemary sent a letter in reply, saying she appreciated his letter but that BSF had already hired a builder.

But that wasn't the end of the story.

## ᘾ Impact Story

*Richard Walenta:*

I had been in the Seattle Evening Men's Class probably five or six years. Because of my involvement with BSF, I felt that God was calling me to do something, and I thought it was missions— foreign missions. So, I checked into the different opportunities through my church, but nothing worked out.

Sometime in 1979 we heard in our BSF class that head-quarters was asking for prayer about moving from Oakland to San Antonio. The first time I heard that, I thought, *I need to check this out.* I sent the letter.

When I received Mrs. Jensen's reply, for a day or so I thought it was another closed door. But God had stirred my heart and I just couldn't let go of it. I thought to myself, *I guess they really don't understand what I am offering to do.*

At that point in my life, I had determined that God had blessed me so much that I wanted to do something for him for a year, like a tithe for ten years of blessing.

I wrote another letter to Mrs. Jensen. And she wrote to me again and said, "We have a contractor and he has all his people. However, if you send me a résumé, we will keep it on file. If we ever need somebody with your expertise, then we could call you."

A friend helped me do the résumé, and I put down everything I had done. I grew up as the son of a mechanic and worked in his service station with him. I fished commercially in Alaska for five years. My next career was to build houses.

I sent off my résumé. I was excited because I just knew that Mrs. Jensen would invite me to come to San Antonio. But her next letter said, "I guess you might want to look on a map. San

Antonio is not anywhere close to any water, and we really don't need any commercial fishermen." She also said again that they did not need any more people to work for the contractor.

Now this had become a challenge to overcome, a mountain to climb. With every letter, I kept getting more determined and more certain that this is what God wanted me to do. I thought, *I am through writing to this lady. I am going to call her.* Several minutes into the conversation, she said, "We are looking for a printer. Have you ever considered printing?"

"No," I replied, "I haven't considered printing. I am a builder, and I am interested in building." As we talked, I was standing outside on a beautiful day in late spring. I was looking at the Olympic Mountains and everything was beautiful! The air was fresh outside, and she was telling me about this printing job. I could hardly believe what I said next. "I've never thought of being a printer, but I probably could do that; I've done a lot of things."

By the time the phone conversation was over, she had me believing that I not only wanted to be a printer but that I was *born* to be a printer, and that with the Lord's help, I was going to be the most fantastic printer in the world! By the time I got from the phone up to the house where I was working, I thought, *I don't want to be a printer! What in the world have I agreed to?*

A couple days later I called Rosemary back to break the news that I didn't want to be a printer—I just wanted to build. And, in the course of that conversation, I said, "I believe that God has called me to come down there and help out with that building."[3]

That comment finally made Rosemary realize that Richard was in earnest and had really prayed about this. She called Harvey Hancock and asked, "Is there anything that this man can do for us?"

Harvey said, "We're going to need a night watchman—somebody who can stay on site to watch over all the equipment and materials. I can get an unfurnished trailer out there for somebody to live in. It won't cost you anything."

About that time, BSF had a regional meeting in Seattle, with 4,500 attending. Richard made an appointment to meet with Rosemary Jensen afterward. When Miss Johnson thanked everyone for putting the meeting together, she added, "I understand that Richard Walenta is the person who built the platform, put in all these beautiful rhododendrons, and arranged all this. Richard, will you please stand so we can say thank you?" Rosemary, sitting on the platform, looked up to see Richard Walenta for the first time.

That evening Richard and his wife gave Rosemary a tour of Seattle before sitting down together for a cup of coffee. Rosemary described the situation in San Antonio, the job of night watchman, and the small trailer that would be available for them to live in. She told them, "There is no electricity. We'll have to put in a generator, and you'll get water with a hose from the well. It will be hard living there for a year. I don't know whether you'd want to do that."

Richard's eyes filled with tears as he explained, "You don't understand! We've already rented our house out, and we're asking God to give us a place to live. And this sounds wonderful." It was settled. The Walentas took the job.

The Walentas intended to stay a year or so, long enough to see the construction finished, and then return to the West Coast. After just one week of observing his work, Harvey Hancock asked Richard to be in charge of all the carpenters. Then, when Rosemary found out that the plant manager in Oakland was not moving to Texas, she asked Richard if he would pray about staying in San Antonio as the plant manager.

"When Rosemary asked if I would pray about staying on after the construction was finished, I told her, 'No, I won't pray about it. God has already confirmed to me on the way down here that I would not be going back to Seattle.' I believe this is what I am supposed to do."

And that's what he did—for the next twenty years of his life.

## Getting It Right

One prayer the lunch bunch prayed throughout construction was, "Please, Lord, let us avoid any mistakes in this building process." That prayer received a specific answer one day—in one of many ways the leadership helped to make sure the building project started and finished in a God-directed way.

### ⌒ FROM THE DIRECTOR
*Rosemary Jensen:*

I went out to headquarters most days, during my lunch break, to watch the building process. One rainy, cold day, I started to not go but immediately thought, *I had better go on out there.* The builders were working in the room that is now the library of the Manna House. In that large room, over a fireplace, a cross is inset in the stone. The plan was to light it and, oh, it would be a beautiful thing—a subtle, worshipful touch to the room in which teachers would be trained.

Construction progress on the press building in 1981

When I walked into the room that day, the stonemasons were working on the cross. They had decided to fill the cross with small, bright-red stones. I took one look and thought, *That is garish!* I tried to persuade the stonemasons to stop. They didn't pay attention to me. So, I sped back to our temporary offices and called the contractor. "Harvey, you can't let them do that! Once they finish, it will be in concrete."

So, Harvey spoke to the stonemasons, who removed the red stones—leaving the cross as it had been planned.

In planning the project, Rosemary worked closely with Paul Hesson on his architectural drawings. Having seen the way the operations worked in Oakland, Rosemary had clear ideas of how the new building should be arranged in order to facilitate production and to enhance teacher orientation and training.

To create a warm, family-like atmosphere, Rosemary wanted several separate cottages to house the teachers. Those cottages were to be adjacent to each other and connected with walkways. The printing press needed to be close to the administration building so the flow of work between the two would be efficient and smooth.

## The Grace of God in Action

Slowly but surely over those next few months, all the plans and dreams began to take shape. And the progress inspired everyone involved. This was certainly true for Rosemary.

### ⌒ FROM THE DIRECTOR
*Rosemary Jensen:*

Each time I go out to our land to see the progress of the building of the new Bible Study Fellowship headquarters, I am reminded of the organization itself and this tremendous calling. As I step over boards and try to dodge trucks bringing in materials, the sequential orderliness of construction impresses me.

First, the foundation was poured and as we watched literally hundreds of truckloads of cement being firmly anchored to prepared bedrock it made me think of the "Foundation" of Bible Study Fellowship, Jesus Christ.

Next came the framework and as each board was cut into just the right length and nailed into its prescribed place I could not help but think of the framework of Bible Study Fellowship— Miss Johnson and Miss Hertzler in the beginning—now the Board of Directors, the Headquarters Staff, the Area Advisors, the Teaching Leaders, and all the leaders in each class—each one perfectly fitted and joined together to make the shape of the organization.

Now, even as I write this letter, the stones are being placed one by one in the walls and I think of you, each one of you who comes to class as living stones all being built up together into a spiritual building to be a holy priesthood (1 Peter 2:5). I am struck with the fact that it's the stones that give beauty and substance to the building. Each stone is unique with a different shape and hue and the combination of them gives interest and loveliness to the whole. I am grateful to each of you for the place you have taken and continue to take in the building of Bible Study Fellowship.[4]

Years later, Rosemary Jensen recounted a less poetic summary of how it all happened, between the groundbreaking in April 1980 and the completion of the buildings the following year.

### ⌐⌐⌐ FROM THE DIRECTOR
*Rosemary Jensen:*

Talk about the grace of God! Now, you've all heard this story. I hope you don't mind hearing it again, because I love to tell the things that God did for us.

When we decided to build new facilities in San Antonio, we agreed that we needed twice the floor space that we had in Oakland with all the combined buildings that we had there. We had negotiated with our builder and come up with a set amount for the building. Of course, we had to sell our Oakland properties in order to pay for the San Antonio buildings. The Board had stepped out in faith and had hired an architect and a builder and trusted God to sell our property in California.

Now, because God had been so gracious already in so many small ways, I expected Him to bring in one buyer who would say, "We need all of those buildings in Oakland." The facilities were all separated everywhere and money was tight at that time, but I expected that because I knew nothing is impossible with God. I've seen him do too many things that I thought were impossible. But God is so much wiser and He is much more creative than we can even imagine.

He didn't sell all of those buildings to one person or even sell them all at the same time. Do you know what He did? He sold a building just before we needed to make a payment to the architect. It was incredible! We had enough to start. We had enough money to hire the architect, but we didn't have enough money to pay for the building. So, God would sell this one just at this time. We were praying, but He was not only faithful; He was gracious to do it when we didn't even know what to pray for.

The amazing part of this though is the result. When all the buildings were sold and paid for, we ended up with $300,000 more for the buildings in Oakland than it cost us to build the buildings in San Antonio. We had twice the floor space and we had much better buildings, all in one location, and they worked. You all know that because you have all been there to see for yourself. Is that the grace of God, or is that the grace of God?

Let me tell you something else. We negotiated the amount for the San Antonio buildings, and when we were working on that negotiation, the builder said that he would try to save us as much as he could rather than just taking the whole amount. Have you ever heard of that? At the completion of the building, the builder returned to us $30,000.

The grace of God. Not only was the grace in the financial area; God brought us those who should build it—BSFers, the architect, the builder, the engineer—and He brought a number of people to Christ even in the building process.[5]

One of those people was a man named Tony. He didn't know he was there to find the Lord—he just wanted some work!

### ᴄᴏ IMPACT STORY

*Tony Zepeda:*

In 1980, I was a carpenter and high-rise construction worker, taking jobs all around the San Antonio area. One day, between jobs, I went by my union hall and I heard someone say there was work to be found out at Blanco Road and Highway 1604. I knew where that was: out north of the city in the middle of no-where. *What would anyone be building out there?* I wondered. When I asked the question aloud, someone replied, "A church. They're building a huge church."

If that was true, the work might last a while. I decided to drive up there and check it out. When I got there, I thought, *This is a strange place for a church.* There was not a house anywhere around. Just low, rolling hills covered with live oaks and cedar trees, scrub brush and cactus—stretching as far as you could see. At the end of the road I stopped and got out in the middle of what felt like a real wilderness.

I spotted a small crew of men setting some forms, so I walked over and asked who was in charge. A gentleman by the name of Richard Walenta introduced himself. I told him I was looking for work. He asked me a few questions about my construction experience. Then he offered me a job starting right away.

I soon found out the building we were working on wasn't going to be a church at all. It was an office building, the headquarters of an organization I'd never heard of—Bible Study Fellowship. According to Richard, there would be other buildings to come. Maybe I could work there for a long time! I hoped so.

There was just something special about this new job from the start. I didn't mind the drive at all—the setting was so beau-tiful and peaceful.

But I didn't know what to think when, just a few weeks after I began working for him, Richard asked me to go to a Monday night class with him. My first reaction was, *Class? That sounds like school. I'm a journeyman carpenter; what do I need a class for?* I told him I had other plans.

Richard didn't give up. He invited me again the next week. And the next. And the week after that. "Tony, why don't you come with me? Just once."

Finally I thought, *Okay, I'll get this guy off my back. I'll go with him to his class once. And that will be it!*

When I realized it was a men's Bible Study Fellowship class, I wasn't sure how I felt about that. I had read the Bible and gone to church earlier in my life. Yet, I'd never heard anyone talk about the Bible or the Lord like they did that night. God's Word just came alive for me. I couldn't wait to go back the next week.

One day on the job—after I'd attended that BSF class for maybe four or five weeks—I was working alongside Richard. We fastened two beams together to create a rugged wooden cross. Once we'd assembled it on the ground, we hoisted the cross up, into what was going to be the prayer tower at the top of the headquarters building.

As we finally stood it in place there at the center of that prayer tower, I looked up at that cross. Tears filled my eyes and I became so moved that I fell to my knees. "Richard," I said, "I want to accept Jesus Christ as my personal Savior." So, that's just what I did. Richard prayed with me, right there in the middle of that construction site. That was the turning point in my life. I'd been heading in the wrong direction for a long time. Thankfully, God does allow U-turns. That's what happened in my life—I made a complete U-turn.

After that, I had even more reason to be grateful for the privilege of working on the BSF project. It also meant a lot to me when Miss Johnson and Miss Hertzler would come out to wander around the property and inspect our progress. As they walked past, I would overhear them talking about what this would be and where in the building that would go. They seemed so excited, so pleased by everything that was happening.

I remember watching them and praying, "Lord, if there is ever anything for me to do at BSF, even if it's just mopping floors or washing dishes, please open the door for me to work here." I was willing to do any job just to be working with people like them and to help an organization that had played such an important role in my life.

We eventually finished the offices and the big production building. But my time at BSF wasn't over. At each stage of the headquarters construction and expansion, every time there was a new structure to put up, I'd get a call from Richard Walenta asking if I wanted to be part of the job. I always came. Over the years, I helped build the cottages, the House of Heroes, more cottages, and then the big auditorium. Then, in 1992, Richard called and asked if I would work for him full-time in BSF's Building and Maintenance department.

I remembered the promise I'd made to God years before, that I'd be willing to do anything if He would allow me to work for BSF. I also remembered as a kid, praying in my backyard, "God, if You're listening, I want to go up to heaven with You. Even if I have to be a janitor in heaven, I just want to be with You."

I prayed both those prayers, and now that's exactly what I'm doing. What a wonderful answer to prayer! And what a great example of God's grace to allow me to work every day in the maintenance department of Bible Study Fellowship![6]

The headquarters staff began moving into the new facilities in May 1981, just one week beyond the thirteen-month deadline the contractor Harvey Hancock had promised. The landscaping wasn't yet in and additional finish work needed completing. And then there were a few special touches God graciously provided before the new headquarters was dedicated later that year.

# Chapter 19

# PUTTING ON THE FINISHING TOUCHES

Furnishing and dedicating the new headquarters

I n May 1981, the BSF staff at last moved into the new head-quarters in San Antonio, Texas. On the day the big moving vans arrived from California with the printing presses, the temperature registered a sizzling 102 degrees. Quite a warm welcome to Texas! Half the staff had already relocated; but the production staff and all the printing equipment had remained in California, continuing to produce the needed class materials until the buildings were completed and ready for occupancy. So, after almost a year and a half of transition, the staff members were finally together—with the equipment on site as well.

### FROM THE DIRECTOR
*Rosemary Jensen:*

Sometime that summer, about the time of the dedication, I remember Board member Ray Stedman standing with me outside of the headquarters. Looking around at the new buildings, he said, "Rosemary, this absolutely blows my mind!"

I think that was the moment when the rest of the Board

realized this move was God's will. The last thing we wanted to do was ruin this wonderful organization by uprooting it and moving it where it didn't need to be. But seeing the buildings in place, seeing all of this in stone, wonderfully done, was just great.

Originally, we had decided to get cost estimates on what it would take to duplicate what we had in Oakland. But we did not want it just duplicated. We wanted to build something bigger; we almost doubled the floor space from 24,000 to 42,000 square feet.

We had all the buildings in one place, where we could go easily from one building to the next, making a smooth transition for our training. We had our first three cottages—Matthew, Genesis, and Minor Prophets—which gave us room to house twenty-seven people for training sessions. We also had the Manna House, which we used for training and meals. We had the administration building and a huge new press and production building. The final building of this first phase was the caretaker's house.

And all the buildings were much better quality buildings than we had in Oakland! Our new headquarters is literally built on a rock! And better yet, in San Antonio there are no earthquakes.[1]

Before and after the big move-in day, the Lord showed that He was not finished blessing BSF by giving unexpected gifts of generosity and care to headquarters.

## Surprise Blessings

Early in the building process, architect Paul Hesson met wth Rosemary Jensen at his office to discuss furnishings for the headquarter buildings—wall coverings, carpets, and such. Paul had some ideas and samples for Rosemary to see.

At the time, workmen had just poured the concrete slab for the office buildings. So, Rosemary had been discussing with various staff members the work flow between the various buildings.

Because she found it challenging to shift her attention from work flow to interior design, Rosemary invited two of her lunch bunch friends, Betsy Wray and Eleanor Craven, to join her in meeting with Mr. Hesson.

When the three women arrived at Paul Hesson's office, he had carpet and wallpaper samples laid out for them to see. He had envisioned all three cottages being decorated exactly alike—with dark brown carpeting and brown plaid wallpaper for the bathrooms. The three women, looking at the samples, agreed they would make the cottages look like an economy motel. That was definitely *not* their vision for the cottages. They wanted a homelike atmosphere.

They asked Paul if they could work on the design for the cottages. The architect gladly turned that part of the job over to the women. Rosemary, in turn, delegated it to Eleanor, who worked to give each cottage its own flair—each painted a different color, with different colors of carpet, distinct wallpaper, and even different styles of furniture.

This story was told at the May 2000 staff Day of Prayer.

> Rosemary confronted a similar problem with her office, where Mr. Hesson selected brown carpeting and brown herringbone wall covering. Rosemary explained that she didn't want her Executive Director's office to look like it belonged to a man. She wanted it to be blue. And the small study adjacent to her office, which had been built as a place to pray, study, read her Bible, and get away from the telephone—she wanted that painted yellow.
>
> Betsy Wray was with Rosemary when she met with Paul Hesson about the Director's office. When Rosemary talked about a blue office, the architect seemed taken aback. So, Betsy mentioned that she had seen "the most beautiful blue carpet in the San Antonio Country Club on the stairway addition that comes down to the new addition." Betsy knew Paul Hesson had built that addition.
>
> So, Betsy and Rosemary left the architect's office

and went to the country club for lunch—and to see that blue carpeting. Both women thought the carpeting was beautiful but probably too expensive for the BSF Director's office.

After lunch, as they left the country club, they strolled across a series of beautiful Persian rugs, one right after the other, just inside the club's entryway. Rosemary stopped, turned to her friend, and said, "Ah! You know what would be nice, Betsy? I think I need a Persian rug in my office. Don't you think so?"

Betsy responded, "Oh, right, that is exactly what you need."

Both women laughed at the outlandish idea.

From the country club, they headed to Rosemary's house. As they walked in the door, the telephone rang. Betsy walked into the living room and stretched out on the sofa while Rosemary answered the phone.

The caller was a man whose wife had been in Rosemary's BSF class and had died of cancer the year before. Rosemary had spent a lot of time with her during her last year of life. He had decided to downsize his home and queried Rosemary, *Could Rosemary use the Persian rug, from his home, at the new BSF headquarters?*

Rosemary knew that Betsy could hear her end of the conversation, so she asked, "Did I hear you correctly? You want to give that Persian rug in your living room to BSF headquarters?"

Betsy rolled off the sofa and hit the floor. Only thirty minutes earlier, Rosemary had made her laughing comment in the San Antonio Country Club about the Persian rugs there.

"You won't believe this," Rosemary responded to the man on the phone. "Just this morning, Betsy and I were talking with the architect about what we want to put in my office. Would it be okay if I put that Persian rug in my office?"

At that, the man started to cry! He said, "Rosemary,

nothing would have pleased my wife more than seeing that rug in your office. She loved you and she loved BSF. I think it will be wonderful. Would you please come over and take a look at it and see if it will fit?"

Betsy and Rosemary drove to their house immediately to look. Of course, it was exactly the right size for the Director's office.

Then the donor wanted to know, "What are they planning to put under the rug?"

The women explained that the architect was planning dark brown carpet for that office.

"No," he insisted. "You should have this rug on parquet flooring." So, he donated the parquet flooring to go under the Persian rug.[2]

Meantime, Deputy Director Pearl Hamilton was praying about musical instruments for the new headquarters. Everyone thought the headquarters would need a piano, but no one was thinking beyond that—no one except Pearl. As a talented and dedicated musician, it mattered to her that BSF have quality instruments.

One day Rosemary received a phone call from a class member who said, "The Lord has put it in on my heart to give BSF a piano—a grand piano!"

Rosemary knew that Pearl, in the next office, could hear her side of the conversation, so she repeated: "You want to give BSF a grand piano?"

The woman then asked Rosemary and Pearl to meet her at the San Antonio Music Company that afternoon to pick out the piano.

At the store, the generous young woman told them to look at the Steinway grand pianos. She understood that Steinways were the best, and she wanted to give BSF the very best.

While Pearl excitedly flitted from one piano to the next, trying to make a choice, Rosemary checked out the price tags. The would-be donor suddenly retreated to an office to make a phone call.

Rosemary wondered if she was okay. Perhaps she, too, had seen the price of the pianos and was having regrets about her offer. Maybe she was calling her husband in a panic, wondering what to do because she hadn't realized how much her gift would cost.

But when the woman returned, she explained that she'd been talking to her sister, also a member of BSF. She told her sister about giving BSF a piano and then asked her sister, "Don't you want to match the gift—and give BSF an organ?" Indeed she did.

Rosemary and Pearl were invited to also pick out an organ for the headquarters. An Allen organ, she insisted, since they were known for their quality.

The three women had met at 3:00 PM, and by 5:30 PM, they walked out of the store, having selected a Steinway grand piano for the administration room lobby and an Allen organ, which now sits in the dining room of the auditorium.

## Dedication Day

Reestablishing the organization in another state was an important transition that could not go without special recognition. Those who attended the dedication ceremony remember it as a time of reflection, of praise, and of joy.

### FROM THE DIRECTOR
*Rosemary Jensen:*

On September 12, 1981, we held the dedication service for our new headquarters. We invited Francis Schaeffer to be the speaker because Wetherell loved him, and I was so thrilled for Wetherell to see that. So to have him there for the dedication service in the huge new press building was a thrill for her. And a thrill for me to see her enjoyment and amazement at the finished facilities.

We hung a giant banner across the press room, "To God Be the Glory," for the dedication ceremony and decided never to take it down. It has been there since 1981, constantly reminding us of God's gracious provision for our buildings, grounds, move, and every other detail of our San Antonio headquarters.[3]

The dedication ceremony was an organization-wide celebration. The list of people who addressed the crowd was a "Who's Who" of BSF history. The following is a sampling of what was said that day.

### ~© IN OTHERS' WORDS

*Dr. Ernest Hastings, Kay Gudnason, Paul Hesson, and Dr. Grant Whipple:*

*Dr. Ernest Hastings:* Our purpose today is not to try to glorify Bible Study Fellowship but to bring glory to our Lord Jesus Christ, who we believe used Miss Johnson to found Bible Study Fellowship. During the years that most of you have been teaching or working with Bible Study Fellowship, there have been literally thousands upon thousands of people who have come to know our Savior as their own Redeemer and their own Lord. Today, as we come to dedicate these buildings, we believe God will take our dedication and He will consecrate it for the continuing of His ministry and His work throughout the world.

Alverda Hertzler, Wetherell Johnson, Dr. Grant Whipple, Dr. Ernest Hastings, and Rosemary Jensen at the dedication

*Kay Gudnason:* I think it is significant that I found above me, when I came this morning, the words "To God Be the Glory," and we will be experiencing Him and His glory in many ways today, I'm sure. We are here to dedicate a very significant complex of buildings, which are built for the ongoing of His work and to His glory. We gather today to honor Miss Wetherell Johnson and Miss Alverda Hertzler, who had a dream and faith to pursue it. Now we see the reality, although not the complete fulfillment, because surely the impact of this organization is going on into eternity.

*Paul Hesson*: As you know, Dr. Whipple, we as the architects and builders for this facility have felt God's hand in it from the very beginning. Now it's finished, and I'll hand you the keys, knowing that it will be used to God's glory.

*Dr. Grant Whipple:* All this started when this beautiful property was offered to Bible Study Fellowship as a gift. A dramatic change has taken place since the first time we met here on these grounds for a picnic. We were given a ride by helicopter to get the perspective of the land and the area round about. I would like to mention our new Director Rosemary Jensen, together with her whole staff, who undertook this horrendous job of looking after all the details involved in the building of a complex of this kind, and did this simultaneously with taking on the Directorship being transferred from Miss Johnson to Mrs. Jensen, and also made the move simultaneously from Oakland to San Antonio. You can hardly imagine all that was entailed with all of these things going on at the same time.

There are so many indications and evidences that God was in this that I just have to say this. It costs money to produce a complex of this kind. The Lord in His graciousness has enabled Bible Study Fellowship to accumulate a little reserve that allowed us to get started in the construction work. But we knew that we needed the proceeds from the sales of the properties in Oakland to pay our bills and see our project through, but I'd like to report this morning that the proceeds from those buildings, together with gifts that have come in from you friends and others, are enabling us to complete this headquarters in its entirety with all expenses paid. This has been an illustration of this truth from the Word—that we're truly workers together with Him. And except the Lord build a house, they labor in vain who build it.[4]

Miss Wetherell Johnson gave the dedicatory prayer.

> O, Lord God, there is no God like you, in heaven or in earth who keeps His covenant and shows mercy unto your servants that walk before Thee with all their hearts. And Lord, oh, how wonderful it is, that we have been chosen, before the foundation of the world, by Thee! That we have been adopted into Thy unique family, as each of us Thy child. O God, as we think together of all that Thou hast done; as I think of the five women that knew and were hungry for the Word of God; and that my heart was for pagans and didn't want to teach, in '52; and thou, O Lord, I had no idea what You would do all through the years. And then as we think of this building and we think, Lord, of all the prayer and the miracles Thou hast done in all this building. O God, Thou art the God who answers prayer and has fulfilled all You promised us, and even more than we expected. And we praise Thee. O, Lord, we come unto Thee and we pray Thee that, in a very unique way, we—everyone who is working here, who comes here—may so feel the presence of the Lord here that we would dedicate ourselves to You.
>
> O, Lord, we pray You that everyone who comes here may see You and Your Glory. And Lord, as we think in the old days, of how when the temple was dedicated, the glory of the Lord filled it.
>
> And Lord, who are we? But Thou art grace. And we pray You as we dedicate this whole building that Your Word might go out to all people to the biblically illiterate people of today. We pray that may be fulfilled. And Lord, we rejoice with You today. We rejoice in all You've done. Lord, may we rejoice!
>
> And then, Lord, we pray that Your glory may fill this place and this day. In Jesus' name.[5]

Following Miss Johnson's prayer, all assembled sang the hymn "Great Is Thy Faithfulness." Then Ernest Hastings approached the microphone again to say the following:

The names Bible Study Fellowship, Miss Johnson, and Miss Hertzler are almost synonymous. Knowing them as well as I do, I'm sure that the last thing these two ladies want is to attract attention to themselves, but we're going to do that anyway.

There have been many suggestions as to what we should call this new headquarters complex. To date, no official name has been adopted. But there are two buildings that we are going to officially name today and dedicate as we dedicate the rest of the headquarters complex to the Lord.

If you walk over to the Administration Building, in the reception room you'll find a plaque. On that plaque, you'll find these words: "Johnson Center, to the glory of God, in honor of Wetherell Johnson, founder of Bible Study Fellowship, 1959–1979." And as you leave this building, you'll find at the entrance another plaque, which reads, "Hertzler Press, to the glory of God, in honor of Alverda E. Hertzler, Administrator of Bible Study Fellowship, 1959–1979."

And so, we're very happy at this time to present these two ladies with these two plaques naming these two buildings in their honor.[6]

Francis Schaeffer was the main speaker of the day. He challenged those present with this message.

The Bible is God's written communication and language that tells us of the universe, of man, as he was intrinsically made in God's image and yet now fallen. It tells us of God's solution to man's true moral guilt in the substitutionary death of Christ.

What a gracious gift of God! Without His Word, many basic questions would be without possible answers.

Without what God gives us in His Word, we have no answer for the brokenness of the world. You have nothing to say to your neighbors when they cry, "Life is absurd, life is absurd."

Without God's Word, they're not wrong; they're absolutely right. But with God's Word, it is not so. With God's Word.

- Suddenly human life is not absurd. Human life has unique value and dignity.

- There is a basis for values, morals, and law that is not purely arbitrary.

- Human relationships are more than the biological.

What is this Book and why study it? This Book doesn't only tell us how to go to Heaven. The Book gives us the answers to why life now, in the midst of all the tears, is indeed worth living. Why should we study the Bible? For no less a reason than it gives us the answers to the total of reality and the answers to every one of the really big, human, important questions of life.

How fortunate you and all those who have had the opportunity for this study are. Through the unusual gifts the Lord has given to Miss Johnson, supported by Miss Hertzler, and then shared by many of you, thousands have had the opportunity of knowing what the Bible truly says. With careful study, so that it is not something lightly pursued or only a vague religious experience. But you know the content of the Bible from one end to the other. Surely, this has been, and is, and—God willing—will continue to be a gift of God to nothing less than the whole church of Jesus Christ.

We can understand what a glorious thing the Bible Study Fellowship has been given from the hand of God. The thousands who have had and are having this study, have the opportunity of knowing what this truly wonderful book of God's communication to people really teaches. Isn't that wonderful? How wonderful to be able to study in detail what it really teaches. And that's what you have in the Bible Study Fellowship.

Once we realize indeed what this Book is, we must truly live under its teachings. Now, that's so for personal salvation. But that is also equally true for all of life.

Let us be glad for such Bible study as those fortunate enough to have had the Bible Study Fellowship courses have had. It is eminently worthwhile because the Creator God does exist and in His love has communicated to us in this Book. And then, once we have that precious knowledge which God has given us, let us live under it as to God's commands as to what is for our personal good and for the good of society. God's laws aren't just negative. Indeed, to go against them is sin. But He who made us gave us the law. He knows what would fulfill us, individually and in society, and to go against His commands is sin. To live under the Word is to have that which the Creator, who knows us best, tells us it is for my personal good and for the good of society. The Bible, as the great God's written Word, is a tremendous gift, first to be known and then to be lived under in the whole spectrum of life. To this end, I pray the Lord will use this property that you dedicate today, in the Bible Study Fellowship, in the days to come.[7]

# Chapter 20

# SETTLING IN
## The early years in San Antonio

Dedicating the impressive new headquarters was an important milepost on the organizational journey. But it was not the end of the transition. Immediately after the dedication, Rosemary Jensen and her new administrative team (along with the Board) confronted significant decisions and developments that would determine the direction as well as affect the ministry of BSF for years to come.

Rosemary Jensen with the Board in 1981

These challenges required novel thinking, fresh resources, and additional personnel. But most of all, they required a God-given, 360-degree perspective that could look back to recall the lessons of BSF's past journey; look around to recognize the reality of its present position; yet look ahead to anticipate the organization's future needs and mission.

Most people interviewed for this book had already recognized Rosemary Jensen's vision for Bible Study Fellowship. One Teaching Leader who served under three directors said, "Rosemary was a visionary in the purest sense of the word."

Rosemary could indeed look back to recall the lessons of BSF's history, recent and not so recent.

### ⟿ FROM THE DIRECTOR
*Rosemary Jensen:*

There was no question that God was in charge of this move—from the building of the new campus to the selling of the old buildings. God was gracious to allow us to depend on Him, to seek Him fervently in prayer, and to watch His way of providing for us—a way that far exceeded our simple imaginations and feeble requests. To God be the glory!

We ended up not in debt at all; we actually ended up with money in reserve. By the time we finished the construction, we had $350,000 in reserve.

It reminds me again that God has had His hand on BSF from the beginning. Wetherell Johnson was a normal person; she was no more a saint than any other Christian was. All of us are human beings; I am a human being. But God has had His hand on this thing and made it this way, not because of anything that anybody could do.

That is not anything for us to be proud of—all the glory goes to God! He did it all! But He has had BSF in His mind from eternity past. He knew exactly what was needed at this time in history. He brought Wetherell Johnson along; at exactly the time He wanted, He brought me along, knowing that He could get a lot more glory from me, because weak things are glorifying to God.[1]

As Rosemary Jensen took stock of the organization during the first years of her administration, she saw many people excited about Bible Study Fellowship. But repeatedly she reminded others of the proper perspective by asking, who could have done all this except the Lord?

## Filling the Teaching Leader Gap

Despite the exciting and positive things happening, Rosemary and her Board realized that the growth issues needed to be solved quickly in order to then look ahead to BSF's future needs and ministry—and to even more growth.

So, Teaching Leader training became an immediate priority for the new administration. Even during the height of construction for the new headquarters, Rosemary and her administrative team conducted more orientation classes than BSF had ever had before. And with three guest cottages completed in the first wave of construction, headquarters could now comfortably house more orientees than they ever could in Oakland. So, with more and larger orientation classes, the TL shortage began to ease.

Yet, Rosemary Jensen wasn't content with one strategy for tackling the problem. The TL shortage seriously deterred BSF from expanding into new areas; it also threatened the survival of existing classes.

Before Rosemary became the Teaching Leader of her San Antonio class, the class had been disbanded for two years due to a lack of trained leadership. Because of that experience, Rosemary was particularly sensitive to the plight of other classes that had to dissolve when a TL moved, retired, or was otherwise unable to continue in that leadership role. Here's how she described the problem of one such class.

⟜ **FROM THE DIRECTOR**
*Rosemary Jensen:*

In July 1980, I learned of a Teaching Leader in Fort Wayne, Indiana, who was resigning. So, we were going to have to close that class. I had started out my administration in January of 1980 with 286 classes, and to me every one was precious. I really didn't want to close that class. So I prayed, "O, Lord, what can we do about this?" And I thought, *What if we had somebody from headquarters who served as a sort of ambassador, someone who could go and hold open these classes where a Teaching Leader was leaving, until we could train new leadership? That would be a wonderful thing to have.*[2]

As the buildings were going up at the headquarters in Texas, Rosemary envisioned this potential solution to a recurring problem and tapped Susy Harbick to execute the experimental idea. Susy tells how she came to be involved in this plan.

### ᘰ Impact Story
*Susy Harbick:*

I had been in BSF seven or eight years. My first class was a combined Men's and Women's Evening Class with Jack Hamilton as my Teaching Leader. Then I was part of the first Young Adult Class. I had been a Discussion Leader, Secretary, Class Administrator, and eventually became a Substitute Teaching Leader.

BSF was my passion, second only to nursing. I was a registered nurse in medical ICU and CCU. Probably about two years into my BSF experience, I became a roommate with Anna Kingsbury. We had bought a home together and were well established. All of a sudden, I started hearing about a move to San Antonio, Texas, being planned for BSF. That turned my perfect world, of which "I" was in control, upside down. I had no idea what was going to happen. But I knew the Lord did!

I started praying, and He clearly showed me that I was not going to move to San Antonio with my BSF staff friends—June and Pearl and Anna—as a nurse. Since nursing was my profession, I decided that I needed to consider what God had for me. Over the course of that year, I resigned from my head nurse position and trained my replacement.

Before I made any decision about what I would do career-wise, I came to San Antonio to unpack June's and Pearl's moving vans. I committed two weeks to help them, packing them up in California and then unpacking them in Texas.

On a Sunday evening in San Antonio, June and I were staining bookcases in the living room of her new place with the air conditioning on full blast because it was one hundred degrees outside. Suddenly the phone rang. I did not hear an audible voice, but in my heart I knew God was saying to me as the phone was ringing, "Are you going to pursue what you want, or are you ready to do what I want you to do?"

As I pondered that thought, June answered the phone and turned to me. "It's Rosemary. She wants to talk to you!"

I took the phone and Rosemary asked, "Could you come over?"

As Rosemary and I sat on the swing in her backyard that evening, she talked about the BSF class in Fort Wayne, Indiana, that was about to be closed for lack of a Teaching Leader. She mentioned her idea for a traveling Ambassador, a trained Teaching Leader, who could go and fill in until a replacement could be trained for classes whose TLs had to move or became ill. She asked me, "What do you think about the idea?"

I exclaimed, "I think it's a wonderful solution!"

You can guess what she said next. "Would you like to be the first Ambassador?"

I went to Fort Wayne, Indiana, for the first six months of the 1980–81 class year and then to Colorado Springs, again as an Ambassador, to teach another class for the remainder of the year. I had the privilege of teaching in two different series back to back and then went around the world teaching for seven years as an Ambassador.[3]

## FROM THE DIRECTOR
*Rosemary Jensen:*

I have always asked God, in anything I've ever done in my life, "Lord, if You are calling me to do things that are way too hard for me, would You please give me people to come alongside and help?" He has been faithful to do that, and Susy is just one of many that He has brought to help me.

So, God was beginning to pull people into place; it was just wonderful! This was a good thing for BSF.[4]

## Teaching Leader Institutes

Rosemary Jensen was concerned not just about the *number* of Teaching Leaders trained. She was also concerned about the *quality* of their training, their relationship with headquarters, and the ongoing support these dedicated volunteers needed to carry out their teaching ministry effectively. She had another new idea that would address all those issues.

### ⟵⟶ FROM THE DIRECTOR

*Rosemary Jensen:*

I remembered what it was like for a Teaching Leader to go for an orientation to the headquarters in Oakland for that one week and then never to get back there! Occasionally, there was a seminar where the Teaching Leaders would come together to hear some speaker Miss Johnson would invite.

But even as we were in the middle of construction in December of 1980, I had thought: *Wouldn't it be wonderful to let the Teaching Leaders come back and have a week at the headquarters where they have been trained, so that they can be reacquainted with headquarters staff?* Of course, everyone had been trained in Oakland up to that point, so they could come to San Antonio to see what our new headquarters is like. And while they are here, we could have a special speaker who could provide specific teaching on the book or books they would be teaching in their classes in the coming year.

I was often reminded that our Teaching Leaders are all lay-people, because this is a lay Bible study. So, they felt the need for further enrichment and knowledge.

We could call these Institutes for Teaching Leaders.

I also recognized that, not only did they need some teaching and to be reacquainted with what was going on at the headquarters, but also many Teaching Leaders were very tired by summertime.

Being a Teaching Leader is tough. They are Teaching Leaders, they are married, they may have a job, and they may have a family with children at home. Plus, they are teaching a BSF class, which takes twenty hours a week. No wonder many of them are exhausted! An institute could give them a week's break—a week-long "vacation."

I went to the Board and asked if we could do this at BSF's expense. We had ended up with some money in the bank, and we wanted to use that money on ministry as much as possible. What better use could there be?

Pearl Hamilton, Alverda Hertzler, Rosemary Jensen, and Wetherell Johnson at the 1981 Teaching Leader Institute

When I made the proposal to the Board, they decided we could try the idea on a limited scale to see what the interest would be. In June of 1981, we had thirty people attend the first pilot institute at our newly finished headquarters in what we now call the staff lounge.[5]

The Teaching Leaders loved it! For five hours each day, a Bible scholar and various staff members covered the material TLs would teach in the coming year. Each afternoon, TLs had free time to wander the headquarters property for a time of personal reflection and meditation. Rosemary had personally walked through the property to flag the trees where she wanted a walking trail and to mark areas for meditation benches, giving Teaching Leaders a place to be alone with the Lord.

## ⌒⤍ FROM THE DIRECTOR
*Rosemary Jensen:*

I had these benches in my mind, and all along this trail, where people could sit out by themselves—these Teaching Leaders, who are just busy all the time.

One day I got a call from the husband one of my class leaders. This man was one of the kindest, most loving, wonderful men you can imagine. But he had developed cancer and was close to death. So I was surprised to hear his voice on the phone saying, "Rosemary, I want to come out and see you. I want to bring you something."

I said, "Are you sure you want to come out here?" I did not want him to use his precious energy for a ride in the car.

"Yes," he insisted, "I'll get my wife to drive me out."

He came in his pajamas, sitting in the passenger seat. His wife had a little wooden box, which she had sewn a little flower on the top. He handed me the box and said, "I want to give you this. It's something I want you to have." He did not even get out of the car. He just handed me the box and they left.

I walked into the house and opened the box. There was a check in it for $5,000. My heart almost sank and I thought, *What is he doing?*

I called him and said, "I'm coming down to see you."

So I went to their home and told him, "I don't think you want to do this right now. I mean, this needs to be for your family."

"Yes, I do want to do this," this generous man insisted. "And I want you to cash that check right now before all my cash is frozen in the bank in the estate."

"Well, what do you want me to do with it?" I asked.

He told me, "I want you to do with it whatever you would like. What's on your heart, Rosemary, that you would really like to do?"

I said, "Let me tell you. I've been thinking about benches— meditation benches—for the Teaching Leaders to sit on in the woods on the trail. I want Teaching Leaders to come here and have benches to sit on and be alone with God. How would that be?"

He said, "I think it is an absolutely wonderful idea." Then he added, "My wife can take care of that for you. You go ahead and cash the check and then she will see to getting the benches made."

That man died the next week, and his wife did get the benches made for us in Mexico and brought them up to us. We still have those benches around our headquarters today.

I love this story because it shows people's hearts that have been touched by God and His Word so much that they want to give back to Him and His work. And I never will forget that family's gift, because it was such a gracious provision of God for this desire of mine.[6]

That 1981 pilot institute with thirty Teaching Leaders from the Southwest Region was such a success that Rosemary and her staff expanded the institute prototype for the following year. By the time the headquarters was dedicated that September, plans were already in the works to build a "speaker's quarters" and additional cottages to house Teaching Leaders for the larger institutes to come. But that was hardly the end of the new plans Rosemary Jensen had for BSF and her headquarters staff.

### ⌒ FROM THE DIRECTOR
*Rosemary Jensen:*

By Thanksgiving of 1981, we had just finished building Paul, the new speaker's quarters. And we were preparing for a Teaching Leaders seminar in January 1982. So much was happening that I felt like I was holding on by my fingertips alone! That's when I found out that I needed to have a complete hysterectomy, because of some precancerous cells.

"Thanksgiving," I said, "is the only time I can take off for a few days. At least I can work it out at that time."

So, I had surgery. After the surgery, lying in the bed, I was talking to the Lord about another concern I had for BSF: "God, what are we going to do for these people that we are making graduate from BSF?"

At that time, when someone completed the five-year cycle of classes, they had to graduate, to leave BSF, to make room for new people who wanted to do the study.

I'd first confronted this issue when I had graduated from being a Teaching Leader three years earlier. There had been over a hundred women who graduated with me. So I met with all of them after a class at the end of that year and told them, "Now, you need to get out and use what you've learned in the community or in your churches."

They looked at me with blank stares and said, "What do we do?"

I said, "You might start by teaching a Bible study. After all, you have had five years of Bible Study Fellowship. That should have prepared you for service throughout the world—whatever you find to do."

But they asked, "What material should we use?"

I told them, "You know that black book that says on the front of it, 'Holy Bible'? That's the material you use."

But they said, "We really don't know how to do that." These people were not class leaders, but they were class members. This was in 1978.

I said, "I'll tell you what. I'll teach you to do homiletics and that will help you." So I did. I met with them once a month, and we went through a couple of books. But they were still floundering.

Now I was in bed by myself all day, asking, "Okay Lord, what are we going to do with people we are making graduate?"

One day the answer was just as clear as a bell!

"Ah! This is what you do! Show them what they need to know. They need to know three things: (1) They need to know what the Bible says—the content of it. (2) They need to know what it means in principle. (3) They need to know how to apply it in their lives."

That's really all they needed—three things.

I decided that what BSF needed to do for our graduates wasn't to teach them how to do homiletics but show them how to use these three simple questions to lead a Bible study. *What does it say? What does it mean? How do you apply it?*

I got excited about that. When I returned to the office, I said to the staff, "Let's pick a book of the Bible and ask those three questions of ourselves; we will do it in our staff prayers." We did just that with the second Gospel and developed the Mark Study Series, which we are still using to this day.

Later on, the Graduate Program was expanded to a five-part program, which is now called Graduate Seminars. But that's how and when it began—back in 1981 at the end of a busy year, a year of experiencing God's grace in extraordinary ways![7]

The year 1982 got off to an eventful start as well. Rosemary prepared for her first Teaching Leaders seminar as Director of BSF. All the Teaching Leaders from around the world—about three hundred by then—went to Austin, Texas, for the seminar. And it snowed!

### ⟵⟶ FROM THE DIRECTOR

*Rosemary Jensen:*

This may not seem unusual to some, but for South Texas, snow is a big deal! We rarely have snow in San Antonio, and when we do, it barely covers the ground. But it snowed the entire seventy-five-mile drive to Lakeway, where the seminar was held!

I drove my car with Alverda and Wetherell sitting in the backseat. And they were praying, because we were on roads that were covered with snow and it was really scary! Great big trucks were just sliding all over the road and blocking the traffic. I'd never driven in snow, because I've always lived in the Tropics or Florida or South Texas. So, I was praying silently.

Meanwhile, I could hear Wetherell and Alverda praying

fervently in the backseat. It soon became hilarious, because I kept saying, "God's going to get us there. Don't worry."

They would reply, "We know, dear. We're praying for you!"

We finally did get there, and by the next morning, all of the Teaching Leaders had arrived safely. Allan Redpath was our special guest speaker. We had Wetherell give one talk at the seminar as well.[8]

Indeed these were great days for Bible Study Fellowship as an organization. Exciting and significant changes were taking place as well as a new surge of growth.

When the baton passed from Wetherell Johnson to Rosemary Jensen, at the beginning of 1980, there were 286 BSF classes. Because of the new emphasis on Teaching Leader training, by 1983 there were 350 classes.

Meanwhile, headquarters, for the first time, began training Area Advisors. As Rosemary laughingly said, "Area Advisors were already supposed to know everything, as each of them has been a Teaching Leader—right? Wetherell had always told us, 'Just go out and do it.'"

And according to Rosemary, "We also started training Area Class Administrators (ACAs) and Children's Area Coordinators (CACs) to work with AAs as a team. We initiated the whole ACA program in 1980 and hired Kay Thornton to oversee that area of the work."[9]

Headquarters hosted four Teaching Leader Institutes in the summer of 1983—one for each region, since each region at that time was on a different study in the five-year cycle.

## Letting the Leader Lead

When Steve Gately, BSF's new Business Manager, represented the organization in the local business community, people were always asking, "Who is the CEO?" So, he recommended changing Rosemary Jensen's title from General Director to Executive Director, a change that took place in 1983.

During this transition period, the Board was getting used to the new Executive Director and she to them. Rosemary felt that the Board supported and encouraged her, in part, because "they recognized that moving was hard work and I had a lot to do." She felt they were developing a nice working relationship.

### ⟿ FROM THE DIRECTOR
*Rosemary Jensen:*

In 1983, I asked the Board if we could consider expanding overseas. We had only a few classes in England and Australia. I hoped we could begin classes in either English-speaking countries, which I knew included a number of African nations, or places where there were large English-speaking enclaves.

The Board was quite happy to do that, as they realized I had this international kind of mindset from the beginning. Indeed, the fact I had lived on four different continents was part of God's preparation of me to be the Director of BSF. No experience is ever wasted with God, who orchestrates our lives.[10]

According to Ernest Hastings, because of Miss Johnson's illness during the last years of her tenure, the Board became a little too involved in administration. But along with Rosemary's appointment, the Board made a crucial decision.

### ⟿ IN OTHERS' WORDS
*Dr. Ernest Hastings:*

We decided that the Board is responsible for policy. The Executive Director may recommend policy, but the Board makes the policy. In turn, the Executive Director is responsible for the administration of that policy.

So at that point there was a fresh commitment made, which we carried through for the next twenty years, that the Board would stick exclusively to policy making and we would expect the Director to administrate the policy and support her 100 percent in how she went about doing that. I think that was one of the keys to so many years of smooth leadership and real advancement in God's blessing.[11]

## Putting Together the New Team

Another key to the early successes of Rosemary Jensen's administration—the seamless leadership transition, the smooth relocation of headquarters to Texas, the application of fresh solutions to old problems, and even the management of impressive growth—was the blended team she put into place in San Antonio. Loyal holdovers from Oakland provided both continuity and a strong personnel foundation on which the new administration could build. But an influx of new faces and new life helped propel BSF into greater ministry in the years that followed.

Behind every new face was an interesting story of the Lord's grace, providence, and preparation. Here is just one example.

### ⤳ IMPACT STORY

*Jane Roach:*

My BSF story actually started in 1974 when my husband, Jim, and I joined a different church. The first thing I did was join the choir, where I met this woman who invited me to "come to this really good Bible study that a lot of us go to." I didn't like women's groups. I thought I knew a lot about the Bible already, so I just wasn't particularly interested in going to a Bible study.

This woman persevered, but I kept ignoring her. Every Wednesday night at choir practice, and every Sunday morning, she would say, "Now, the first week in February, we are going to have an introduction class. If you don't come then, it will be another whole month before you can come."

I went to the introduction class at the beginning my eighth month of pregnancy with my son James. I had never in my life sat through a sermon where my thoughts were not racing off to all kind of things. But sitting in that BSF class that day, my mind did not wander once throughout the whole lecture. Nor did I do all the things pregnant women do to be comfortable. I was absolutely caught by every word being said!

I still remember the principles given in that lecture, because they answered some specific questions on my heart at the time. But the thing that astounded me most that day was when I walked in and realized the person teaching that class was the person who had "nagged and dragged" me there—Rosemary Jensen!

She lectured that first week on the second half of 2 Corinthians. We started the following week on Romans, so my first study questions covered the overview of Romans.

My first week in the discussion group, the leader announced they were going to have a luncheon the next week. I thought, *Oh my! What have I gotten myself into?* The one thing I hated worse than women's groups was luncheons! So I just didn't go. I simply said I couldn't make it. After my third week, I dropped out of the class because it was almost time to have the baby. But my Discussion Leader kept calling me week after week after week to find out how I was doing, how the baby was doing. And at the end of the year, in May, she wanted to know, "Can I register you for next year?" That was how it was done then.

I said, "Sure, sign me up," because I thought if I said no, she'd call me all summer! By this time, I had my son James, and that is an understatement! Though he is a precious young man now, he was one horrible baby—from the first day! So, when September came around, I was ready to go to Bible Study Fellowship once a week, just to get a break from him. And that is the truth.

The first week of class that fall, our assignment was to skim the book of Matthew. That was the first time I had ever read the Bible where I felt God speaking directly to me. I read in Matthew 11, where Jesus says, "Come to Me, all who are weary and heavy-laden, and I will give you rest" (NASB). I had left my career as a mathematics teacher, and suddenly I was home caring for two little children all day with lots of time to think about where I was going in my life. Reading those words in Matthew 11 comforted me.

But all too soon, I got to Matthew 23, which is the chapter about all the woes to the scribes and Pharisees that Jesus called "hypocrites." Again I thought, *God is speaking directly to me! Whoever wrote this book is seeing into my head and my heart.*

At some point in the fall of 1974, I realized my own depravity in a way that I hadn't before. I also recognized the magnitude of God's love for me in a way I hadn't before. I understood that I was part of the world for which Christ had died. I had known that He died for the world; I just had never seen myself as being part of it.

Suddenly everything started falling into place in my understanding. The years of church and Sunday school attendance suddenly began to bear fruit in my thinking and my life. At the end of that year, Rosemary asked me to be a Discussion Leader.

Finally, at church one Sunday, Rosemary asked me, "Well, are you going to do it?"

I told her, "Yes."

My husband, Jim, was in the Men's Class at that time, and Bob Jensen was his Teaching Leader. So, Rosemary and I were both home alone on Monday nights. My children went to bed early, so she called me frequently just to talk. I thought perhaps she did this with all the Discussion Leaders, but then I decided she probably just picked the most needy one—me. My first couple of years in BSF, everything that I had believed in my life was challenged as I read the Scripture for myself.

After three years as a Discussion Leader, she asked me to become a Teaching Leader. I taught a BSF class for seven years and it was wonderful! I loved everything about it.

I got to be part of the first institute, where Rosemary challenged us to give some thought to what our life purpose was. Why God had created me? And what did I want to do with my life? I left that institute feeling that God wanted me to do something different, but I didn't know what it was.

At that time, Rosemary was meeting with me once a month for lunch, just to make sure I was staying on track. I told her, "I don't know what it is that God wants me to do, but I have the sense that He wants me to do something more than what I am doing now."

The next year our family went on vacation and came home on Saturday night. At church that Sunday morning, Rosemary said, "We need to have lunch this week."

I somehow knew God was going to tell me something in that lunch. But I was shocked when she asked me if I would come on staff as Division Head in charge of new classes. I had never started a BSF class; I had never even been in a pilot class.

However, a month later, I began as the New Class Division Head. I served as part of the training staff that prepared Teaching Leaders at orientation. I was also in charge of supervising pilot classes.

My new position was a half-time position. But after about two weeks on the job, Rosemary asked what I thought about the program. I told her that I believed it was very valuable.

Rosemary asked, "Do you think that you could handle the Graduate Program, too?"

I was thrilled at the prospect. So, in a matter of two weeks, my half-time position became all morning and half of the afternoon! When Pearl Hamilton retired in 1987, I took over some of the things she was doing as well.

Sometimes it seems that every year in BSF I have been given a little more to do. And one of the things I was asked to do, early, was to be a proofreader.

I love thinking about the previousness of God in my life! My father was a printer and linotypist long before the days of computerized typesetting and spell-checkers. He would bring home things from work and have me proofread them with him. So, when I was asked to be a proofreader, I knew what to do because I already had done it.

I also had an aunt who was a stickler for grammar. Growing up, if I ever said anything incorrectly, she would stop me and make me say it correctly. So, I had a good command of the English language and logical thought processes, which were not only necessary but also invaluable in the creation and editing of leadership materials.

I loved my years as a Teaching Leader in BSF and had thought I would be one until I died. I loved teaching the Bible. I enjoyed training my class leaders at leaders' meeting. So being able to train orientees how to do leaders' meetings has been wonderful.

Two of the things I knew I would miss when I gave up being a Teaching Leader were the leaders' retreats and the Teaching Leaders' Institutes. But God graciously called me to be a part of the team that goes to all of the retreats throughout the world! He also has allowed me to administer the institutes, which includes attending all of them each summer to be with the participating Teaching Leaders.

At every retreat, I tell the leaders that I first went to BSF because I thought that if I didn't go, Rosemary Jensen would never leave me alone. After twenty-six years, she still hasn't left me alone. Only God knows whether that will ever happen—I hope not![12]

The remarkable transition between BSF's first and second generations of leadership was a true highlight in the organization's history. Many people—from the Board to the Directors to the old and new staff—played significant roles. God was obviously blessing BSF and beginning to do new things. Many of those things began with the new leadership He provided.

### ⌒◯ In Others' Words

*Jane Roach:*

Rosemary has an incredible sense of vision, which stems from an intimate relationship with God. We used to laugh and say, "Oh, please, God, don't let Rosemary have any time alone with You, because that's going to mean more work for us."

Every time she would go and be alone with the Lord, she'd come back with this new idea of what to do. That is one of her strengths. She has an idea that she believes comes from God, and in her mind, it's a done deal. Her faith is incredible.

Of course, there are always a few little revisions of the done deal as you're working out the details. But Rosemary is not daunted by what it's going to take to make it happen. If this is what God wants, let's do it—whatever it takes.

She models what our vision statement calls for: *a passion to commit without reservation to lead in the cause of Christ in the world.*

Working at BSF headquarters presented challenges. But we got to see God's faithfulness. If we'd been thinking about how hard it was, we would never have done it. I'm grateful that Rosemary didn't think like that. From the beginning of her time as Director, she would say, "This is what God wants us to do, and now we're doing to do it."[13]

*Chapter 21*

# GOD CLOSES A CHAPTER
Audrey Wetherell Johnson goes to be with her Savior

In February 1980, with Rosemary Jensen as BSF's new Executive Director and BSF moving its international headquarters, Miss Johnson and Miss Hertzler felt God calling them to relocate to San Antonio. They sold their home in Oakland and purchased one near the Jensen's residence. In her autobiography, Wetherell wrote, "We both felt this was God's will and would indirectly help to preserve the sense of continuity of the work of Bible Study Fellowship."[1]

Although her life was nearing its end, Wetherell Johnson had not yet finished being of service to BSF and the people closest to her.

## Wetherell Johnson's Final Acts of Service
BSF's founder had been a teacher, speaker, and writer all her adult life, and so she continued until the end.

When new Teaching Leaders came to the San Antonio headquarters for orientation, Miss Johnson invited them to visit her home. There, as long as she was able, she challenged them and assisted with their training.

Jerry Prenzlow was a Teaching Leader in Colorado, while Jane Roach was head of the training division. They paint the picture in their own words.

## ⤫ IMPACT STORY

*Jerry Prenzlow:*

When I was in San Antonio for my TL orientation, Miss Johnson had us to her home for tea one afternoon.

Miss Johnson stood at the door with both of her arms out, as though welcoming a child, just as Jesus would. We all sat in chairs in her living room, in rows, and she sat as though she was giving a lecture to us. She told us a Bible story—I'll never forget it. It was the story of Jesus stilling the storm in the boat, and then, she said, "The storm stopped."

She went on to tell us, "When you have a storm in your life and things look pretty bleak, dearies, all you need to do is to ask Jesus into your boat. And the storm will stop." She had us spellbound!

While she was telling the story, all of a sudden, she would jerk and sit up straight. We knew that was the pain from the cancer. We were there in the morning, because by afternoon she couldn't do much.[2]

## ⤬ IN OTHERS' WORDS

*Jane Roach:*

I loved Miss Johnson's passion for God. When she said the word "God," people just sat up and listened. She taught me to love God.

On each of my birthdays, I adopted the practice of giving a gift to someone who had blessed me that year. When Miss Johnson moved here to San Antonio, and I was a Teaching Leader, that year I decided to give her the gift of fruit.

When I delivered my gift to thank her for the blessing she had been to me, I also told her that I had begun that annual practice based on something she had once said in a lecture.

She responded, "Oh, my dear, it's your birthday. I've got to give you something."

I said, "No, no, no. I'm giving you something."

But she insisted I take her commentary on Hebrews by F. F. Bruce.

So I have in my personal library a commentary on Hebrews that came out of Wetherell Johnson's library, simply because I took her a basket of fruit on my birthday.[3]

In addition to helping with Teaching Leader training, Miss Johnson continued to accept speaking engagements. She served as a member of the International Council on Biblical Inerrancy. And she worked on her autobiography, which was announced in the May 1983 *BSF Newsletter*.

> The eagerly awaited publishing of Miss Johnson's book *Created for Commitment* took place last fall. The publisher, Tyndale House, honored Miss Johnson with a reception at headquarters, where she signed many books for the guests. Sales necessitated a second printing. Miss Johnson recently gave Bible messages in Dallas, and San Antonio and was the speaker at a three-day conference in northern California. Miss Hertzler attended the conference with her.[4]

In 1984, as her cancer progressed, Miss Johnson and Miss Hertzler made the difficult decision to move back to California. Again, the *BSF Newsletter* reported the incident.

> In March 1984, Miss Johnson moved to Carmel, California, where she began radiation treatments following colon surgery. In April, Miss Hertzler also moved after overseeing details of packing and closing the sale of their house in Texas. They had long anticipated that one day they would retire to Carmel.[5]

In the same issue of the newsletter, Alverda Hertzler wrote her impressions of being back in California.

*Alverda Hertzler:*

Since I lived in California over fifty years and spent many vacations in Carmel, it seems like home. The climate and the shade of the forest trees are both helpful. Our new home isn't as large; distances to church, stores and the sea are only five to ten minutes away.

We have rejoiced to be here, in San Antonio, these four years, seeing the exciting growth of BSF under the leadership and wisdom of Rosemary Jensen and her excellent staff. We shall miss them all very much.

Being near friends in the Bay area again will be lovely. God has so blessed us with friends in our BSF family.[6]

## Wetherell Johnson's Death and Remembrance

In December 1984, Bob and Rosemary Jensen were traveling with their friends Bob and Kitty Magee in Africa, exploring the possibility of starting BSF classes there. Rosemary's secretary, Mary Gail Campbell, called from San Antonio to tell her, "Wetherell is in the hospital, and she is dying. You need to come home."

Neither the Jensens nor the Magees felt they had finished what God sent them to do in Africa. They needed another four to five days to conclude their trip. So, they asked God to keep Miss Johnson alive until they finished their work in Africa and got back to the States.

God granted that request. The Jensens arrived in Texas on December 18, and on December 21, Rosemary flew to the West Coast to see her friend, mentor, and predecessor. Ernest Hastings, the longtime chair of the BSF Board, met Rosemary there, and together they visited Miss Johnson.

Rosemary told her all about the trip to Africa. Then she asked, "Wetherell, are you looking forward to seeing Jesus?"

Miss Johnson looked up and exclaimed, "Oh! Isn't everybody?"

Dr. Hastings and Rosemary had a time of prayer with Wetherell, said their goodbyes, and left the hospital that evening after ten o'clock. Wetherell Johnson died the next day.

In her book *My Heart's Cry*, Anne Graham Lotz gave this report of Miss J's death.

### ⁓ IN OTHERS' WORDS
*Anne Graham Lotz:*

Miss Audrey Wetherell Johnson lived and died by that promise of heaven. She was the very godly woman who taught me how to teach the Scriptures. She founded Bible Study Fellowship, directing that powerfully challenging ministry for thirty some years, and she wrote the commentary notes that have been life-changing for so many. While she was intellectually keen to the point of brilliance, she did not teach from her head, but from her heart. And she lived out a life of such vibrant faith in God's Word that it was contagious.

On many occasions I heard Miss Johnson say that she was confident when she closed her eyes to this life she would be opening them to the face of Jesus. As she struggled with a recurrence of cancer, many of us prayed that her eyes would be opened to His face even before the moment of death, to give comfort to herself and those of us who loved her.

On the morning of the day she went to our Father's house, she sat straight up in bed, joy radiating from her eyes and a thrilling smile on her lips as she exclaimed, "I see Jesus! He has come for me!" Then she fell back on her pillow and was gone![7]

Wetherell Johnson went home to be with the Lord on December 22, 1984. Her funeral was held just after Christmas.

### ⁓ IN OTHERS' WORDS
*Larry Heppes:*

I was a pallbearer at her funeral. Wendell Hawley was the Senior

Editor at Tyndale, and he and I had gotten very close because I was his back-and-forth to the ladies on the manuscript. He was going to go out to the funeral also, so he called me and said, "Why don't you meet me at the airport in San Francisco." My plane got in early—you know I had to be on time for Miss Johnson—but Wendell's plane was late.

We drove out to Carmel. Wendell needed to stop and check into the hotel, since he wasn't dressed for the funeral. It was getting later and later. Finally, we got down to the main street in Carmel and there was a traffic jam. Here I am a pall-bearer and the funeral is going to start in about fifteen minutes! I jumped out of the car in my suit and ran to get to the church. I was scared that she was going to sit up in her coffin and say something about my being late!

But it was a beautiful service.[8]

BSF held a memorial service for Wetherell Johnson on December 27, 1984, at the headquarters in San Antonio. Her funeral was held on December 28 at Carmel Presbyterian Church, in Carmel-by-the-Sea, California. Following that service, a procession drove to the El Carmelo Cemetery in Pacific Grove, overlooking the ocean. A service, called "Witness to the Resurrection," was conducted at the grave site. On January 12, 1985, another memorial service was held at Walnut Creek Presbyterian Church, host congregation for one of Miss Johnson's earliest and largest BSF classes.

## Alverda Hertzler's Death

Alverda Hertzler continued to live in Carmel, California, until her death on February 14, 1991. This letter, entitled "In Memoriam: Alverda Elizabeth Hertzler," was distributed to BSF class members.

Alverda Hertzler had the vision for BSF and helped set its course. How grateful all of us are that God called Alverda Hertzler into the work of Bible Study Fellowship! From 1959 until her retirement in 1980, she completely handled the business administration. She had a strong conviction that the Lord's work should always be excellent, never second best or shoddy workmanship. This conviction was reflected in every facet of Bible Study Fellowship, from physical equipment and furnishings to production of materials and preparation for activities of personnel. She had a rare capacity to love and accept the love of others.

A favorite verse of hers was Jeremiah 29:11: "'I know the thoughts that I think toward you,' says the Lord, 'thoughts of peace and not of evil, to give you a future and a hope'" (NKJV). That future and hope are her present reality.

Miss Hertzler lived several years after Miss Johnson was laid to rest. But with the passing of these two, an era in BSF history ended.

Following Miss Johnson's death and funeral, as 1985 was about to begin, the BSF Board and Rosemary Jensen experienced a real sense that God was ready to open a new chapter, to do a new thing in BSF. Indeed, they soon learned He had already planted the seeds for *several* new things.

# Part 4

# A New Era of Growth and Change
# (1985–1999)

# Chapter 22

# ON THE SAME PAGE

Coordinating age groups, classes, and study series

In the first quarter century of its existence, Bible Study Fellowship grew so rapidly that, inevitably, some inconsistencies developed across the organization. While some of these inconsistencies posed no problem, others were beginning to threaten the continued effectiveness of the organization. It was time to consider where BSF needed to bring greater coordination and uniformity to its teaching program.

These attempts at coordination were just one way the organization entered into a new era of growth and change, in a large degree forming the Bible Study Fellowship that we know today.

## Creating the "Green Sheets" for Families

By 1984, BSF was on the verge of making a wonderful addition to, and a major change in, the Children's Program. The preschool curriculum had long been a significant part of the Women's Day Classes, but neither the Men's nor the Women's Evening Class offered anything for children. The people in those classes were begging for help in teaching the Bible not only to their preschool children but also to their school-age children.

Rosemary Jensen understood their concerns well. She remembered family devotions with her own children when they were teenagers; she too had wished for materials more suitable and interesting to that age. Bible-story books for preschoolers and materials for adults were easy to find. But for children in between, from age six through the teen years, little was available.

So, BSF committed to take from the adult lessons three good questions and a main principle for families to discuss in their devotions. The questions would be tied to the current lesson for parents, so they would be prepared to provide background information to their family and to share what they had learned in class.

Rosemary called Jan Myers, an Area Advisor in California, to write what came to be know as Home Discussion pages, or "green sheets," because that was the color of paper on which they were printed. Jan tells the story.

### ⌒ᴑ IN OTHERS' WORDS

*Jan Myers:*

> When Rosemary asked if I would be willing to write principles for the lessons, I had a question for her: "How do you know I can do that?"
>
> She said, "I just know."
>
> So, I wrote one sheet, a sample, and sent it to her.
>
> She read it and said, "Yes, come."
>
> I would travel to San Antonio and live in the housing unit named Paul, where there was a little kitchen, and I would write. At first, I was only responsible for the principles, and someone else was writing the accompanying questions. But I soon told Rosemary, "I have to write the questions, too. It feels too choppy, too disjointed, to have two people writing one page." So, I would go and stay for a week and come home. Then I would go for another week and come home. Eventually, I created five years of Home Discussion pages.[1]

By the end of 1984, Home Discussion pages were finally available in all BSF classes. The *BSF Newsletter* at that time stated the following:

For family members who wish they could study the Bible along with their loved one who attends class, and for class members who wish they could share effectively what they are learning each week in class, there are now available Home Discussion pages, a brand new item to meet the need and accompany each lesson.

Home Discussion pages contain mini-scripture selections and two basic questions for each day. Class members may pick up a Home Discussion page when they pick up their lesson. This page is intended for sharing the weekly BSF lesson from God's Word with household members, particularly school-age ones who are either too old to be in our children's program or too young to be in an adult class. Early response has been favorable and enthusiastic. There are even reports of spouses, in some cases previously uninvolved, who have become curious to the point of participating.[2]

The green sheets became an instant success with class members. The May 1986 *BSF Newsletter* included excerpts from letters received from BSF members, responding to the new Home Discussion page (HDP).

- The HDP is a systematic guide that has enhanced our fellowship with each other and communion with our Lord. I did not know what the reaction would be from my family, but when they were asked about using it, they all agreed.

- HDP taught us to apply the Scripture. For example, we were in a car accident. At the time, we were studying how Noah was kept safe in his ark. Our family was better able to see how God kept us safe from harm and helped us to not blame the other driver. It was a profound lesson.

- Our entire family, plus a visiting grandmother, received great reward and benefit from the daily study. We did it each morning at the breakfast table. It was a grand way to begin the day. Our grandmother is of a different denomination, and this is the first time we have been able to study the Bible in unity. It was fantastic.[3]

## Coordinating the Children's Program with Adult Lessons

In 1984, the Children's Program for preschoolers had a one-year series of lessons for two-year-olds and a three-year series for three- to five-year-olds. They were good lessons but not coordinated with the women's studies.

### ⟜ FROM THE DIRECTOR
*Rosemary Jensen:*

Kathy, my second daughter, was living in Galveston, Texas, where her husband was in medical school. Tiffany, my first grandchild, was two years old and went to BSF with Kathy. One day Kathy asked me, "Mother, why doesn't BSF have the children studying the same thing as the adults? I have forty-five minutes in the car with Tiffany after BSF class. I could reinforce everything that she is learning, but when I ask Tiffany what she learned at BSF, being a two-year-old, all she says is that she learned about God."

Kathy's question started me thinking: *Why don't we put them all together?* We had the adults in the classes, and we had started the Home Discussion page for use with the rest of the family. The only ones not in the same study were the preschoolers. We want BSF to draw people together as families! One way that happens is when they study the Bible together.[4]

Rosemary discussed the issue with Kitty Magee, head of the Children's Program. The two of them decided to enlist the Children's Area Coordinators to help write one study each year.

Kitty started the project in early 1984. And by Christmas 1984, she reported on the changes being made.

## ∼ɛ IN OTHERS' WORDS

*Kitty Magee:*

We are fairly bursting with excitement as the new vision for the program takes shape. New manuals are being written and new Bible lessons and Home Training Lessons are being edited and made ready for printing.

It is not an easy task to bring the five adult lesson series to the understanding of preschoolers, but as the Holy Spirit gives understanding, we see it being accomplished.[5]

When Kitty and Bob Magee were called to Africa in 1985 to spearhead the BSF beginnings there, Janice Pinckney, a Children's Area Coordinator, followed Kitty as head of the Children's Program. Janice wrapped up what Kitty and Rosemary had begun—new home training lessons, with a Bible story and hymn manual, to match all five BSF series. Janice tells that story.

## ∼ɛ IN OTHERS' WORDS

*Janice Pinckney:*

In the spring of 1985, Rosemary asked me to take on the position of Children's Division Head, and I came on staff June 3 of that year. We were in the process of revamping all the children's materials.

We changed that entire curriculum into what it is now. We kept the same basis philosophy: Teach the Bible. Introduce the children to a Bible verse. Don't emphasize memorizing the Bible, just show it to them. Let them hear it. What we do in the classroom goes home, and the moms do the follow-up and repetition. Two hours is a brief time, alternating active and inactive time, having a structured hymn time that corresponds to what is being taught. And singing pieces of music that contain biblical truth.

We created a curriculum to correspond with our adult lessons. The year that the adults study *Israel and the Minor Prophets,* the preschoolers are being taught *Israel and the Minor Prophets*. Not in the same depth, of course, but the same passages.

We teach an abbreviated version for the two-year-olds, an expanded story for the fives, and for the school-age children, we go into the whole passage.

Our hymn time is rather unique; we teach two-year-olds how to sing "Holy, Holy, Holy" and "Great Is Thy Faithfulness" and "Trust and Obey." The leaders talk to the children about the content of the hymn, how it relates to what they are learning, and how it applies to their lives.

In the Preschool Program, we open with free play, then a focused activity, followed by the Bible story, the Scripture verse, a snack, outside free play or some large-muscle activity. When they return, we have hymn time.

Another unique thing is that we require a quiet time. We tell the children that they may not sleep. "This is your time to think about God and to speak to Him in your hearts." So we are introducing, even at age two, what it means to have a quiet time.

We conclude with rhythm time or some other large-muscle activity, and they go home.[6]

By Christmas 1985, the newsletter reported, "More than 15,000 children are being taught weekly in BSF classes." And the numbers continued to climb from there. According to the September 1991 Board report, there were by that time 31,631 children enrolled in 435 classes.

## Getting All Classes on the Same Page
While changes and additions were being made in the Children's Program, an even bigger transformation was brewing for the BSF adult classes. When Rosemary began as Executive Director, BSF had a series of five Bible studies:

- *Israel and the Minor Prophets*
- *The Life and Letters of Paul*

- *Genesis*
- *Matthew*
- *John*

But there was no system to which of those five a class might be studying.

### ⌒◯ In Others' Words

*Anna Kingsbury:*

> While Miss Johnson was Director, someone might go through Teaching Leader training, and others in that area would be doing *Israel and the Minor Prophets,* usually considered BSF's hardest course, and this poor fledgling Teaching Leader would say, "Miss Johnson, I don't understand this." And Miss Johnson would say, "Oh, you could do *John"*—knowing that would be easier.
>
> So, some Area Advisors would be supervising classes covering three different series during the same year. In the production department, it certainly was a major challenge to keep things straight, when we had multiple studies going on concurrently.[7]

Having different lessons going at the same time created problems for more people than just those who printed and delivered the materials. When class members moved from one region of the country to another, they sometimes could not join another BSF class to continue the same series of lessons.

This problem became apparent at headquarters because BSF had many classes reaching out to military families in San Antonio, where military people came through on active duty for a few weeks or months at a time. But if they were from another BSF region, they couldn't drop in on the local classes for those weeks because the San Antonio classes might be in a different series. So, they would simply have to miss those lessons.

As early as 1980, shortly after Rosemary became Executive Director, she and Anna Kingsbury discussed getting all the classes across the country on the same yearly study series. But, at that point, they decided it would be too big a change to make on top of the move to San Antonio. Instead, BSF spent the next three years grouping classes throughout the United States into four regions and then getting all the classes within each region on the same study. That involved some classes having to skip a lesson series.

By 1984, Rosemary and Anna realized that for BSF to continue to grow in the dramatic way the organization was already expanding, all classes around the world needed to be on the same lesson each week.

Rosemary proposed that her headquarters staff spend one month praying over the decision. And she declared that when the month was up, in order to proceed, the decision to do so would have to be unanimous. And that unity would be BSF's cue that the change was God's will for the organization.

At the end of that month, the vote was unanimous. And in time, nearly everyone realized the helpfulness of the decision.

### ⟨∞ IMPACT STORY

*Jane Roach:*

Changing all the classes to the same study was incredibly hard to do. There are always people who resist change.

It had taken a prodigious amount of work to publish four different lessons simultaneously! We did not have the equipment or the personnel that was needed to keep doing that. And there were only two hundred classes; now we have almost one thousand. We could never have grown to this size if we had not taken that difficult step.

That change took real resolve and strength on Rosemary's part, and her being willing to be criticized. But we could never have gotten where we are today if we hadn't done that.[8]

## IMPACT STORY

*Anna Kingsbury:*

Moving everyone to the same study reshaped and changed the profile of BSF in more ways than many of us anticipated. Some classes had to redo a series of lessons. Others had to skip a series. But our quality and efficiency improved so much! We quickly discovered that bringing everyone on the same page made us stronger.[9]

# Chapter 23

# MAKING MORE ROOM

### Expansion and additions at headquarters

J ust as the number of Bible Study Fellowship classes grew, so did the need for space and facilities at the new headquarters in San Antonio. Even though the ministry had just moved in, the leaders and Board members were ready to adapt headquarters to better serve the ministry. This took several forms.

## Gaining the High Ground

In January 1981, even before BSF moved into its new headquarters in San Antonio, the BSF Board began discussing buying more land. Adjacent to the original ninety-five acres given to BSF, another ninety-five acres had become available.

### ⌐⌐ From the Director

*Rosemary Jensen:*

Our new headquarters buildings were built on the edge of the property line of the first ninety-five acres we had been given because that was the highest portion of our property. I began to look at that. We wanted to maintain a retreat-type atmosphere. What if somebody bought the ninety-five acres next to ours and built high-density housing or high-rise apartments right there next to our headquarters? Those adjoining ninety-five acres were actually higher than our first ninety-five acres. Several of us began to pray that God might give us that land.[1]

By the May 1981 Board meeting, God had answered that prayer. BSF had been named beneficiary in the will of a class member. The Board voted to use that money to purchase the adjacent land.

Within months of moving into its new facilities, BSF had already outgrown the first three cottages—named Matthew, Genesis, and Minor Prophets—which together housed twenty-seven people for training sessions.

At their September 1981 meeting, the Board authorized building two more orientation houses.

In the *BSF Newsletter* of May 1983, Rosemary described integrating another feature into the BSF headquarters.

### ⟶ FROM THE DIRECTOR
*Rosemary Jensen:*

One of the newest additions to our headquarters building complex is a beautiful stone entryway. Our architect and our builder gave it to us and the landscaping and lighting were gifts from classes in Washington and Oklahoma. To reach the headquarters, it is necessary to drive off the main highway a mile down aptly named Wilderness Way through trees, bushes, stones, and wild grass, then half a mile down a hill of the same until rounding a curve at the bottom you are suddenly startled by the unexpected beauty of the entryway facing you. But even more startling is the contrast between the wildness outside the gate and the gentle landscaping inside. Some visitors have said it is like entering a completely new world.[2]

Two more orientation houses, Philippians and Ephesians, were completed by November 1984, providing space for an additional twenty-four people.

## A Place for Volunteers to Stay

As classes continued to expand, Rosemary Jensen and the BSF Board began discussing what new buildings would be needed to respond to that growth. Everyone realized that the increased workload had resulted in a dramatic increase in the number of volunteers coming to headquarters. The BSF volunteer program continued to be an amazing story.

When Anna Kingsbury first worked for BSF, beginning back in Oakland, she had supervised the work of those volunteers. She recalls that unique aspect of Bible Study Fellowship.

### ~⌒ In Others' Words

*Anna Kingsbury:*

The work of BSF has always depended on volunteers. In the beginning, back in the Bay Area, everyone was a volunteer. Then three or four people drew salaries; all the rest were volunteers. It's unique to BSF, the fact that we allowed volunteers to operate equipment. Volunteers did almost everything—not just the teaching of the classes all over the country, but also the production of all our materials, the printing, the shipping, and more.

We had one volunteer named Monique, and at that time, we used an eight-sheet collator. When she came in, if we were having problems, she would kick it. And the collator would begin working again.

In 1979 the Board did a feasibility study, and at one point Sandy Sanderson asked me, "What will you do if BSF doubles?"

And I said, "We'd double the number of volunteers." That was an incomprehensible idea for a banker, to run any kind of business or organization with volunteers.[3]

Miss Johnson publicly paid tribute to BSF volunteers at the Oakland Coliseum, December 1, 1979.

## ⟵⟶ FROM THE DIRECTOR
*Wetherell Johnson:*

Now I'm going to ask a very precious group of people to stand. You know that every one of your lesson sheets is stamped. They're collated; they're packaged; they're shipped. And we have over one hundred groups who come and just volunteer, just plain nitty-gritty stamping things all day, or dragging out the lessons you send back and putting them in the right place.

What we'd do without our one hundred volunteers, I don't know. But it's a witness of how people love to serve the Lord. They don't just listen and take; their love for the Lord is such that they give and they give.[4]

## ⟵⟶ IMPACT STORY
*Dr. Ernest Hastings:*

There is no way that BSF could have developed without volunteers. From the beginning, the idea was that it was like a church. After all, Sunday school teachers are volunteers. So Miss Johnson thought, *We can do this with volunteers.*

Rosemary is the one who thought in terms of volunteers coming to headquarters for a week at a time. Some of us on the Board thought it was almost sinful to invite people down and then expect them to pay all their own expenses while they were working for free. But Rosemary got away with it. BSF always had all the volunteers they needed.[5]

## ⟵⟶ FROM THE DIRECTOR
*Rosemary Jensen:*

Once we moved to San Antonio, the volunteer program began to expand to the point where we wondered about a place for volunteers to stay when they came to work. People from out of town wanted to stay at the headquarters, but we didn't have any room for them.

I went to the Board and asked, "Do you think we could build a place for out-of-town volunteers, where they can come and stay for some length of time?" I proposed charging the people a small amount to rent the places if they wanted to volunteer at BSF. I had worked out the math, figuring if we built a fourplex, we could pay it off in ten years.

Ray Stedman asked, "Rosemary, do you mean to tell us that you think people are going to come at their own expense and pay to stay in a place at the headquarters just so that they can volunteer their time?"

I said, "Yes! That's what they will do, because they are so grateful to God for what He has done for them in BSF!"

I think there was a feeling among a number of the Board members that perhaps I was being a little bit unrealistic about this. So the Board said, "Why don't you rent an apartment as close to the headquarters as you can you find and lease it out to people?"

The Board members were and always have been careful to be wise stewards of the money that has been given to BSF. We found the closest place and rented one apartment. As soon as the word got around that it was available, it was filled all the time. We almost immediately needed to rent a second apartment. Then one lady came in and said, "I need an apartment for nine months." She was a widow and planned to volunteer for nine months.

When we were getting ready to rent a third apartment, I brought my original proposal back to the Board and asked: "May we just go ahead and build this thing?" The Board quickly agreed that it would a worthwhile use of our resources, and we built the House of Heroes. It has been used regularly since its dedication in 1986, first by volunteers and also, some years later, by overseas staff who were home on furlough or waiting to go out on their first assignment to a foreign country.[6]

## ᜒᜒ IMPACT STORY

*Carolyn Edwards:*

When I was a Teaching Leader, I would often take a group of Discussion Leaders to Texas in the summer to be volunteers. Working as volunteers at headquarters really gave these gals a greater vision and helped them see that BSF is truly bigger than their class.

They helped pack up the lessons for going overseas or served the meals for some other group that had come for a seminar. We not only got a lesson about table etiquette, but we got a feel for the organization as a whole.[7]

## ᜒᜒ IMPACT STORY

*Jeanette Tompkins:*

I started BSF in 1964, in Walnut Creek, California. The study was Genesis, and I did not yet know the Lord Jesus as my Savior. Through the "Assurance Letter," now called the "Steps to Assurance," I was assured of eternal life. But little did I know the joy unspeakable God had ahead for me.

Five years after becoming a Christian, I was asked to be a Teaching Leader and continued teaching for fifteen years. I then served as an Area Advisor for seven years. But in May 1991, I came to headquarters for my last official visit as an Area Advisor, retiring because of my age. Between dinner and our first session, Rosemary said, "Why don't you move to Texas?"

After I became a widow, I had managed a court of duplexes for twenty years, paying only $150 a month for my own rent. But just the week before that visit to San Antonio, my landlords had taken me to lunch to inform me they were in negotiations to sell the property. So I knew, once that sale went through, I would have to move within about six months.

Now, unexpectedly, Rosemary is making me this proposition.

I admitted to her that I had just learned that I would have to move but that I had a lot of speaking engagements back home.

"You can always fly to those," she told me.

But I still wasn't sure.

A few minutes later, however, as Rosemary started the first session with the Area Advisors, she said, "We're saying goodbye to Jeanette. She's retiring as an AA, but she will be moving to Texas." All weekend long, Rosemary kept making remarks about my coming to Texas.

I went home confused. I knew I was too old to be on staff now.

So I prayed, "Lord, if this is not of You, let Rosemary forget about it or change her mind, or have the Board say no."

That was the first weekend in May. On June 15, I received a note from her. Before I even opened it, I held it in my hand and said, "Oh, Lord, she has not forgotten. She has not changed her mind. The Board probably doesn't have to make a decision, but if You're asking me to move to Texas to be a volunteer, You'll have to speak to me about moving."

I walked over to my desk and took out Oswald Chambers's book *My Utmost for His Highest,* June 15, and the first words on the page were: "Get a Move On." The reading explained that one of the greatest hindrances to spiritual character is that we think of common, daily, ordinary things as drudgery, so we look for big things. But Jesus took a towel and washed the disciples' feet. I had my answer, not only to move, but that it was a servant's position.

I walked the floor in my little duplex, just saying, "Oh, oh, oh." That's all I could get out. I finally stopped right in the middle of the room and said aloud, "I've got to get busy and study my Sunday school lesson for my kindergartners tomorrow." What was the lesson? Abraham being called out to leave his family and go to a new land—in his old age, too!

My family had a hard time accepting the idea—at my age to be moving so far away. But I knew I was supposed to go, that it was God's will for me.

I had claimed a Bible verse long before and put a book-
marker right where the verse was—Isaiah 43:18–19: "Do not
remember the former things, nor consider the things of old.
Behold, I will do a new thing, now it shall spring forth; shall you
not know it? I will even make a road in the wilderness and rivers
in the desert" (NKJV). I had saved that verse for my retirement,
thinking, *He's going to do something new.*

After I got to San Antonio, I realized that the road going
back to headquarters is Wilderness Way—"a road in the wilderness." There's a river in downtown San Antonio. God had even
told me geographically where I was going to go.

Rosemary informed me that she could not offer me a paid
position.

I said, "That's fine."

So I arrived in San Antonio, not knowing where I was going
to live or what I was going to do. I told Rosemary, "I've asked
God to allow me to reveal His glory somehow to the end of my
days. But I don't know how He will want to do that. I do like to
do outside speaking."

She asked me to be a headquarters hostess and to help
the Volunteer Coordinator. At that point, the House of Heroes

Obadiah

was for volunteer housing,
although they were already
planning a new, even larger
building—Obadiah—for the
volunteers.

I lived in Joshua, one of
the two-bedroom, two-bath
units in the House of Heroes.
I got to work with staff and
volunteers who love God
and love His Word.

One of my favorite
assignments was to be the
regular tour guide for visitors who came to see our headquarters. I showed them the grounds and buildings and told them

of God's gracious provision and faithfulness down through the history of this wonderful organization.

Once two Russian pastors visited San Antonio, and a woman from their host church brought them out for a tour of BSF headquarters. They could not understand English, so she called the university and asked if they had a Russian-speaking student. The translator the school provided was a Russian Jew. He had to interpret everything I said, and every time I'd say the word "Jesus," he'd look at me and grin. Then he'd go on translating the story. So, that Russian Jewish student heard the whole tour. I thought, *God is so good! He wanted that man to hear the gospel. What he's done with it, only God knows. But he heard it that day.*[8]

The bountiful fruits of BSF volunteers' labors can never be fully weighed or known. But a sampling of newsletter reports over the years provides a measure of insight into the great debt owed by BSF to its amazing volunteers.

1970: "Over 25 tons of lessons and other materials were printed and handled in storage and shipping this past year. About 5 million pages. More than 5,000 Manuals were printed and bound for BSF leaders. Our office 'team' of four full-time workers carry through all the various facets of the work of the Headquarters with the assistance of a corps of volunteers, a total of over 200 throughout the year."

1978: "More than 400 people volunteered at some time during the summer."

1990: "Last year over 800 volunteers gave over 22,000 hours of work alongside the staff to do the work of BSF."

1996: "1140 persons volunteered for nearly 27,000 hours in 1995."

2001: "In the year 2000, there were 1,505 individual

volunteers at Headquarters who worked a total of 28,725 hours: 241 days in the press preparing and shipping materials, 66 days in food service, and 62 days in housekeeping. Other volunteers have come from as far away as Australia, Canada, Hong Kong, Tokyo, England, India, Singapore, and Malaysia.

"Last year these people helped prepare and ship over 176 tons of parcels to our classes around the world."[9]

## Building the Memorial Auditorium

At the January 1985 BSF Board meeting, the Board discussed issues related to the tremendous growth of BSF classes and the large numbers of Teaching Leaders being trained at headquarters. They voted to remodel the Manna House kitchen, providing space for more people to be served during orientation. They also authorized payment for an architect's preliminary plan of an auditorium to be built at headquarters.

By May that same year, Rosemary Jensen proposed holding off on the remodeling of the Manna House kitchen and using that money instead for an auditorium that would seat and serve meals to three hundred people. She explained to the Board that the building could be designed with dividers to accommodate one hundred, two hundred, or three hundred people. Manna House could remain as it was to feed or seat smaller groups.

### ⌒ FROM THE DIRECTOR
*Rosemary Jensen:*

During this time, I was thinking a great deal about the training of our Teaching Leaders. As the orientation groups increased in size, Manna House (where we served them meals) became pretty cramped. It was also difficult for the staff to have our lunch in the press lounge, but that was the only space available. There was one small room for the training, but we wanted and needed more with greater numbers of Teaching Leaders coming.

Every time we had an orientation session, I realized, *We need a better place to do training.*

Having a good Teaching Leader who can teach the Bible well is what BSF is all about! I had the Teaching Leaders in my heart—to help them bring glory to God and to train them well in the truth.

I remember standing on the spot the auditorium is now. It was the highest spot of our land at that time. I stood there by myself and asked God, "Would You give to us a place up on the top of this hill? Please give us an auditorium that we can have on this very spot."[10]

In their May 1986 meeting, the BSF Board voted to proceed with construction of the auditorium. On August 11, 1986, site preparation began. The BSF staff planned for it to be finished and dedicated during the regularly scheduled Area Advisor meeting on May 15, 1987. But unusually heavy rains brought one delay after another, until, by early May, meeting the target date for completion seemed impossible.

### ⌒ FROM THE DIRECTOR
*Rosemary Jensen:*

God provided the key that turned the tide of each person's morale. I suggested that staff members who wanted to, and who could break loose from their daily tasks, should volunteer to help in any way. As usual, the staff came running with the willingness to do anything and everything to meet our self-imposed deadline. The witness this was to every workman present was unbelievable. They seemed revived with a new spirit to meet the challenge, spurred on by observing the staff working at every possible task with a cheerful, joy-filled spirit.

In that final two weeks, the building was transformed from a mass of disarray to a building of order, a place that as you entered brought a calmness to one's soul, suitable to the going forth of the Word.

At 6:00 PM, Friday, May 15, 1987 the Memorial Auditorium was ready to receive its first guests of 110 Area Advisors, staff, Board members, and builders for the dedication. This building, completed by God's enabling, will be one from which Jesus Christ, the Word that became flesh, will be proclaimed until He returns.[11]

BSF's Training Division Head, also remembers that time in BSF's history.

### ⌒◯ In Others' Words

*Jane Roach:*

The dedication of the auditorium was in conjunction with the Area Advisors meeting. Three hundred people had already received printed invitations for dinner and this dedication. Two weeks ahead, the auditorium site was a mess. There was no carpet on the floor, no tile on the floor. The ceiling tiles weren't in place; there were buckets and piles of bolts and nuts all over. Richard Walenta, who was supervising the construction, came to Rosemary and said, "There's no way we're going to be finished."

She said, "Yes, we are. We're all going to help."

So, for the next two weeks, staff members came in our jeans and tennis shoes. We burned brush; we cut down trees; we filled up buckets of trash and moved them out of there. We swept floors, washed windows, and cleaned mirrors. It was so strengthening to be able to work together. We would take moments where we'd all stop and we'd pray, and then we'd go on again.[12]

But Rosemary and her staff kept quiet about one major setback. Two days before the dedication, the kitchen in the new auditorium exploded.

Someone from the gas company had come for a final inspection and test. He had gone to the propane tank, behind the parking lot, to hook up the line. When he came back into the kitchen, he lit the stove. And the gas line blew. The wall exploded. Gas spewed out of the open pipe. A BSF volunteer ran to an emergency lever and pulled it, which instantly shut off the gas and dumped powdered chemical down on the stoves, dowsing the flames. Amazingly, no one was injured.

Later that day, supervisors from the gas company got the gas line back in working order. But the new kitchen was covered in chemicals that were difficult to scrub off the floors and counters. Rosemary told her staff, "Let's clean it up and not tell anyone. So God will get the glory."

One Young Adult Class came to work, and some AAs came early to help. Many staff members stayed and scrubbed through most of that night. At 5:30 Friday evening, they finally finished. And dinner began at 6:00.

## Other Milestones of Growth at Headquarters

Over the years, other improvements have been made at the San Antonio property to better serve the ministry. The following are some of the more notable milestones:

1989: A third well was drilled at the high point of the property, between the auditorium and the newest cottages.

1989: Colossians, the seventh cottage, was finished in the spring.

1990: Another 10,000 square feet was added to the press building.

1992: The organization purchased yet another 95 acres of adjacent land, for a total of 285 acres.

1992: Builders completed Obadiah, a housing unit that accommodates sixteen volunteers.

1995: BSF purchased additional adjoining property, for a total of 325 acres.

Bible Study Fellowship is not about its buildings or property.

It's about people—and what God wants to do in their lives through the study of His Word. But God's continuing provision for the ministry at its headquarters reveals His desire to see the ministry fulfill its assigned work in His plan.

This it continued to do—at home and around the world.

# Chapter 24

# A UNIVERSAL BODY

Bible Study Fellowship moves into more of the world

Bible Study Fellowship began establishing classes outside the United States as early as 1970 (see chapter 15). Classes in Australia, England, and Canada became the first steps that moved BSF toward becoming BSF International. The ministry became truly global in the 1980s as BSF made a major move into the world.

## Expanding into Africa

The first piece of international expansion fell into place in the spring of 1984 when Dr. and Mrs. Jensen hosted visitors—a Dr. and Mrs. Walker. The two couples had been missionaries in Tanzania at the Kilimanjaro Christian Medical Center (KCMC), a hospital Dr. Jensen started while they lived in Africa. During the Walkers stay in the Jensen home, Rosemary took them to visit a BSF class. The Walkers were enthralled and asked Rosemary, "Is there any possibility we could have one of these classes at KCMC?"

More pieces of the international puzzle came together, as, around the same time, BSF received letters and phone calls from people in South Africa, Kenya, and a military base in Germany. These people had attended BSF classes in the States but now lived overseas. They said they missed BSF and wanted to start classes in their new countries.

The financial piece of the puzzle fell into place when Rosemary received a phone call from a woman who had heard Rosemary give her testimony about being a missionary. This caller told Rosemary, "I would like to see BSF send missionaries to teach BSF classes in places where they do not have them. I know I cannot go, but, I would like to send a large donation so somebody else can go." A check for $100,000 soon arrived at headquarters for the express purpose of taking BSF to other countries.

All of these events coming together seemed to be God's leading. So Rosemary asked the Board to authorize her to go with her husband, Bob, along with Kitty and Bob Magee,

Children in Tanzania

on a fact-finding trip. The Magees had also served as missionaries to Africa—in Zimbabwe. Kitty was now head of the Children's Program.

The Jensens and Magees left Texas on December 3, 1984, and headed first for West Berlin. BSF had received a request for a BSF class from some American military people stationed there.

### ⌒ FROM THE DIRECTOR
*Rosemary Jensen:*

> In Berlin, we did not find leadership we felt we could count on. So, we went to South Africa, but again, they weren't ready. We arrived in Tanzania to find the people there were eager for a class. We even met with a woman who had been a Children's Leader for one of the first BSF classes in Australia. She told us she would be delighted to come to KCMC for a BSF class.
>
> From Tanzania, we went to neighboring Kenya. I will never

forget the meeting with our contacts there. When I described the BSF way of Bible study and what it could do for them, these three young women started to cry. "Please do something for us," they pleaded. "Our husbands are pilots, and they are gone all the time. We have nothing here, nothing to feed us spiritually. Will you please do something?"[1]

When the BSF Board met in January 1985, shortly after Miss Johnson's death, Rosemary reported on the overseas trip. She stated that the time was not right in Berlin and South Africa, but in Tanzania and in Kenya, the opportunity was ripe. She reminded Board members that BSF now had donated funds dedicated to the project.

A number of Board members expressed concern that BSF stay true to its original calling. They saw BSF primarily as a Bible study, not a mission-sending agency. But they were willing to assign Kitty and Bob Magee to Kenya as Area Advisors for Africa and to pay them a salary. The Magees could administer a "branch office" of the organization in Nairobi and lead BSF classes there.

In the May 1985 edition of the *BSF Newsletter*, the Magees wrote of their perspective on the new opportunity.

### ∽ IN OTHERS' WORDS

*Kitty and Bob Magee:*

What an exciting prospect! The doors to the continent of Africa are opening to Bible Study Fellowship, and we expectantly look toward what God will do by the power of His word in that continent. Our plan is to live in Nairobi, Kenya, and from there respond to the requests that have reached us from Africa asking for classes. We would like to be in Kenya by August 15 if that is God's timing. Will you pray with us for the establishment of Bible Study Fellowship classes in Africa?[2]

In that same newsletter, the "Remarks from Rosemary" column provided additional background.

## ⟶ FROM THE DIRECTOR

*Rosemary Jensen:*

Many of you know that my family and I spent eight years in Tanzania, Africa as missionaries. During this time, it was often lonely and I longed to have something that would nourish me spiritually as I attempted to minister to Africans. Few sermons were preached in English, books were scarce.

When we left Africa, my heart's desire was to do something to help those who minister so faithfully to others, but have so little for themselves. At that time, I knew nothing of BSF. I have not stopped praying for Tanzania. And God answers prayer. Today there are those in several countries in Africa who are asking if we can start BSF classes where there is a large English-speaking population. Prayerfully this part can be accomplished within the next six months.[3]

Back in San Antonio, Rosemary talked with her sister and brother-in-law, Cecil and Reynolds Young. They had been missionaries in Pakistan for twelve years but were back in the States, unable to get visas to get back into Pakistan. Rosemary asked if they might be interested in going to KCMC, where Reynolds could work at the hospital as a doctor and they could each teach BSF classes. The Youngs went to the leadership of their home church and asked that the congregation support and send them to KCMC.

So a few months later, the Youngs, with another couple, Sharon and Larry Messer, headed to Africa. Cecil and Reynolds would be Teaching Leaders, and Sharon and Larry were Substitute Teaching Leaders. They worked at the hospital and began BSF classes in Moshi, Tanzania.

Pearl Hamilton, Deputy Director of BSF, wrote about the start of this work.

## ⌒ൟ IN OTHERS' WORDS

*Pearl Hamilton:*

Bible Study Fellowship is established in Africa just one year after sharing with you the hope of the Lord opening the door. Much has happened since then by God's grace. In August 1985, Bob and Kitty Magee left the USA and headquarters staff to live in Nairobi, Kenya. A pilot class there is now completed with over seventy women from Europe, America and Kenya attending.

In Tanzania, Kenya's neighbor to the south, the Kilimanjaro Christian Medical Center in Moshi recently added to their staff Dr. Larry Messer, an orthopedic surgeon from Texarkana, Texas. One year ago, nothing was farther from the minds of Larry and Sharon Messer or their three children, Amy, Shelley, and Buddy, than moving to Africa. How, then did it happen?

As Children's Supervisor in Texarkana, Sharon Messer attended the leadership retreat in Oklahoma in March 1985 as one of hundreds of leaders last year who heard about the possibility of God's opening a door for BSF in Africa. Returning home, she told her husband. The Lord began to speak to their hearts. They could not forget the vision for Africa! They began to pray about going and asked their children to seek the Lord's guidance individually, which God gave. Larry reported this to Rosemary Jensen and began attending the closest Men's Class in Little Rock, Arkansas, 150 miles away!

In October, Larry and Sharon Messer came to headquarters for orientation, qualifying them to begin Bible Study Fellowship classes. In January, Harold Hansen, director of the Lutheran World Ministries, and John Moshi, administrator of Kilimanjaro Christian Medical Center, met with the Messers and Rosemary Jensen at BSF headquarters, a thrilling moment for the staff.

In March 1986, the staff held a reception for the Messers bidding them Godspeed. The next day, the five Messers flew to Tanzania. All praise to God![4]

According to the following excerpts from BSF Board reports, steady growth continued in Africa.

September 10–11, 1987:

- "Three pilot classes in Africa were graduated to established-class status."

- "The Nairobi Women's class opened in September with 39 ladies and closed the year with 78 enrolled, representing 15 denominations and 18 nationalities."

- "The Nairobi evening men's pilot class was held in July and will begin a regular class year in September. The membership is about one-half African and one-half European."

- "Mrs. Magee has started a prayer group for a possible Nairobi evening women's class."

- "The pilots for the Moshi, Tanzania women's and men's classes have been completed."

August 26–27, 1988: "Ambassador Sue Williamson went to Jos, Nigeria and Cairo, Egypt to assist with the pilots for those cities. There are now seven BSF classes in Africa. A retreat and an international meeting will be held in Nairobi in October."

January 9–10, 1989: "Mr. Gately, BSF's business manager, has investigated the possibility of purchasing fax machines for the headquarters in San Antonio and in Nairobi."

September 2, 1989: "At the conclusion of the class year in 1989, the Africa Division had ten established classes."

## Expanding into the South Pacific

In a recent interview, Cheryl Hutchinson and Pat Edwards recounted BSF growth in Australia and then into the South Pacific.

## ⌒ In Others' Words

*Cheryl Hutchinson and Pat Edwards:*

*Pat:* In 1972, there were already three BSF classes in Sydney and one class in Melbourne. Cheryl and I joined the class in Melbourne, and then started the second class in Melbourne. Before that first class in Melbourne began in 1972, we went to a coffee. There must have been forty or fifty people there. By the time they had explained what goes on, we were just dying to be a part of this.

I'd only been a Christian a short time, so I wanted to learn as much as I could, and I wanted a Bible study that made me work. I did not want to stay on the surface. That is what attracted me to BSF.

*Cheryl:* Shirley Tembe, the Teaching Leader of the first class in Melbourne, rang me and asked me to be a Discussion Leader for the pilot. She asked me to pray about it and discuss the decision with my husband.

After she'd asked me three times, I said to my husband, "Shirley's rung again, and she wants to know if I could do this, just for five weeks."

My husband looked at me and said, "Well, I suppose you can do anything for five weeks."

*Pat:* Five weeks was enough time to be totally hooked in.

*Cheryl:* I was a Discussion Leader for the pilot, and then I did a year in that class. But when Shirley asked me if I would be a Teaching Leader for the second class, I cried on the way home. I live near mountains called the Dandenong—I looked at them and thought, *I will lift up my eyes to the hills. From whence is my help come?* That was all I knew. So, I went home, grabbed a concordance, and found where it was in the Bible.

When I looked it up and read it, that passage was my call.

The promise went on to say, "The Lord will guard your going out and your coming in, from this time forth" (NASB).

I was in my garden pulling up weeds and saying to the Lord, "I can't even do homiletics!" when one of my discussion group members rang me. She asked, "Is there something I can pray for you?"

I told her, "Yes, I'd like the Lord to give me some clear guidance about a matter."

And she replied, "Well, He doesn't put neon lights in the sky, Cheryl."

I knew I had really heard the call already. And God gave me promise after promise. "When you are weak, I am your strength." All those. My call was very much of Him.

Then, like every new Teaching Leader, I needed to find the person to work with. I prayed about it, and every time, Pat's name came into my mind. I said, "No, Lord, she can't do it." Because Pat had a handicapped daughter, deaf and blind from rubella. I kept thinking, *I couldn't even ask her.*

Finally, I said, "Lord, if You really mean this, bring Pat here, to my house." We really didn't have much contact at that point. I had moved and she had moved since we'd even seen each other. The next day, a little Volkswagen drove in my drive, and I thought, *I wonder whose car that is.* It was Pat.

*Pat:* The night before, Sunday evening, in our church, we'd had a visit from the youth group of the church where Cheryl went. We got talking with our visitors, and I mentioned Cheryl's name. They knew her, so I asked, "Where is she living now?" A member of the group told me, and I thought, *I'll call and see her sometime.*

The next morning I had to take my handicapped daughter to school, a one-hour drive each way. I didn't have time to go home before I needed to be back at the school to pick her up, so I thought, *I'll look for Cheryl—she doesn't live far from here.* So, I went to her new house that morning.

So the two of us started the second class in Melbourne. Our

pilot was in 1974. The big class started in February 1975.

*Cheryl:* After four years, I was asked to be our Area Advisor. At that point, there were four classes in Sydney and three in Melbourne. And in 1978, a class had started in Adelaide. Pat became the first Area Class Administrator—ACA. Rosemary learned what Pat was doing and thought it was a good idea.

In 1982, the first New Zealand class started. In 1984, we began a class in Brisbane, the capital city of Queensland.

In 1985, Rosemary came to Australia for a retreat. She had a meeting with us and asked us to be staff members, not just AA and ACA.

*Pat:* Cheryl became the Division Head and I became the Business Manager. We ran the office. We bought a house in Melbourne, and it was big enough to store the materials. A class started in Perth in 1986, after an American, Kay Nolan, moved there from San Antonio, where she'd been in a BSF class. She started the prayer group in Perth and helped get the class started. Then she moved to Singapore and said to me, "Can we do it again here?"

So, we started visiting Singapore after Kay had a prayer group there. And in 1987, the first Singapore class began.

Another class began in the Philippines in 1988. In 1991, Canberra, in Australia's capital, began. In 1996, a class started in Samoa.

We just grew. The amazing thing is, we never sought any growth. It just came. People are hungry. And when they get satisfied, they want to bring other people. Our biggest problem was finding churches large enough to house us.[5]

One member of the prayer group and the first BSF class in Singapore went on to become a Teaching Leader and then an Area Advisor with BSF. She tells her story here.

### ⌢⊙ IN OTHERS' WORDS

*Shirley Tan:*

Quite early in our married life, my husband worked for Dow Chemical in Midland, Michigan, for three years. A friend from our church invited me to a prayer group, to pray about the start of Bible Study Fellowship. We had our pilot class in Midland, and several of us were trained to be Discussion Leaders.

I was in only that pilot class in Michigan before my husband's company sent us to Hong Kong again. When I left Midland, the girls in the class said, "We're going to pray for a class in Hong Kong." I told them to pray for a class in Singapore. So, they started praying for a class in both places. We went back to Hong Kong, but there was no BSF class in Hong Kong. After a time, we moved to Singapore, where my husband is originally from.

In Singapore in 1984, I began talking to people about BSF because I really was keen to have a class there.

I talked to friends, and they would brush me off and say, "Yes, yes, yes. We know all about Bible studies in a church, and we have enough."

But I said, "This is a different kind of Bible study."

One day I talked to a friend of mine, who had met another friend from Australia, Kay Nolan, who was also talking about BSF. My friend said, "I'll have to get you together."

When I met Kay, she told me about a group that had just been organized to pray about starting a BSF in Singapore. So, I met with that group, and we prayed for two years before the class was established.[6]

Kay Nolan was the Teaching Leader for that first pilot class in Singapore. And Susy Harbick, BSF's first Ambassador, helped to get the class started.

### ⌢⊙ IN OTHERS' WORDS

*Susy Harbick:*

After Rosemary asked if I wanted to be BSF's first Ambassador,

I would travel and be the TL for classes that had lost their Teaching Leader, until a new one could be trained. Or I would help them start new classes. I had the privilege of doing that for seven years.

I went north in the winter, south in the summer, from the East Coast to the West Coast. I helped to start the first classes in Singapore and in the Philippines at the Subic Bay Naval Air Station. I went to Europe and to the U.K. Several years later, I went to Singapore again and helped develop the Asia office.[7]

BSF classes continued to grow and spread in the South Pacific, as reflected in Board minutes.

September 11–12, 1986: "The South Pacific division now has 26 established classes and six pilots."

September 2, 1989: "The South Pacific division has 34 BSF classes and 2 pilots."

January 4–6, 1990: "Attendance of 550 at the Australian retreat."

## Spreading from England to Europe

After Susy Harbick taught the pilot class in Singapore, she spent Christmas 1986 at home. But by January 4, 1987, she was in Basel, Switzerland, to teach the pilot class there. While BSF was being founded in Africa and expanding in the South Pacific, it was also spreading from England to the continent of Europe.

In May 1986, Rosemary Jensen invited Kitty Magee, Division Head for Africa, and Ann Colmer, TL from Liverpool, to attend the leaders retreat in Australia. While they were there, Rosemary asked Ann to be the Division Head for Europe and Cheryl Hutchinson to be the Division Head for the South Pacific.

### ⌒ꝋ In Others' Words
*Ann Colmer:*

At the same retreat where Rosemary Jensen asked Cheryl

Hutchinson and me to become Division Heads, we were given computers. In that day, they were really rare. We had this thing called Easy Link with which we could communicate back to headquarters in Texas. One of our computer-literate trustees came to instruct Gwyneth MacKenzie and me how to use this machine. I can still see us, sitting at a table, with him patiently trying to teach us. He must have spent the whole morning with us. Suddenly, he banged the table. "Stop! Now let's get one thing straight. This is a man-made object. We are created beings. Now, let's start again."

In 1985, we opened a division office in Britain, not far from my home. It had been an apartment above a shop, lovely, but with damaged carpet. When Rosemary came for a visit, I showed her around and said, "We plan to cover the damage with a rug."

And she said, "No, you are going to have new carpet. We need to have the best for the Lord."

So, we went to this huge carpet warehouse, and the two of us were kneeling on a piece of carpet. Suddenly this voice said, "You're not going to be kneeling, saying prayers at your work, are you?" We fell apart laughing. That *was* what we would be doing.

Not long afterwards, someone gave us a gift of money to furnish the office. I went to a carpet dealer, and he had a job loss that was a good piece of carpet, and it was just the amount of money we had been given. It covered not just the one room, but also the whole office suite, even enough to do the stairs that led up to the office and the landing. God provided for that office in an amazing way.

That became a little hub. It opened in 1985, and in 1986, we had our first class in a non-English-speaking European country—Belgium. The Brussels class started, and it just seemed to grow from then on. We soon had other classes in Switzerland, France, Holland, and Germany. In the Paris class, the ambassador's wife started the prayer group. They had been praying for a long time. Suddenly, Carolyn Ratcliff was there with her husband, and they had the Teaching Leader they needed to begin a class. We saw God's provision in each of these places.

For some women in the Swiss classes, English was perhaps their fourth or fifth language. They struggled over their study questions—not just reading in English, but doing their answers in English and sharing in English in the group. It was an interesting experience.

I'd seen members from different denominations at the beginning in England. Now we were seeing all these nationalities. The Basel class had fifty members and nineteen different nationalities represented at one time.

I asked one French lady, "How do you manage? Do you understand everything that is said?"

She smiled and told me, "I just pick up the crumbs under the table."

Another French lady would go home every week and write up her own Bible study based on what she'd learned in BSF that week. But she'd do it in French. She'd have her neighbors round and do her own Bible study with them each week. There was such an excitement among those classes. They wanted to take it out into the community where people couldn't speak English.

Kay Jones, the Teaching Leader in the Basel class, and in the Zurich class too, was giving the lecture in perfectly good English. She was describing a particularly difficult concept to the class and suddenly started translating it into German for the benefit of some in the class. She really wanted them to understand.

Out of the Basel class came Barcelona. A Teaching Leader moved from France to Switzerland and got involved in BSF. Then they moved to Spain and she started a prayer group in Spain and taught the class there for some time.[8]

Holly Holmquist, eventual Area Advisor for Europe, told how classes often got started on that continent.

## ᴄ᷒᷒ꞷ IMPACT STORY
*Holly Holmquist:*

Vickie McIntire, who was with Greater Europe Mission at the time, started the first class in Brussels. She had been in a class in Memphis, Tennessee, and moved with GEM to Belgium and helped get the class started in about 1986.

Often, Americans who were involved in BSF in the States start new classes abroad. God uses Americans who are too dumb to know that it won't work, so they do it anyway. Europeans say, "Oh, that will never work in France or Germany." But Americans, even though they may know the culture well, jump right in. The woman who started the French BSF class was an American married to a Frenchman. God uses us Americans to start things and then will often hand it off to a national person to grow.[9]

One class in Germany was able to continue when God sent a replacement Teaching Leader from Korea. Anita Newton, then the Area Advisor for Europe, tells the story.

## ⌒◉ IN OTHERS' WORDS
*Anita Newton:*

We had two classes in Germany, a Day Women's and Evening Men's at the U.S. base at Kaiserslautem. These two were started by Nancy and Dick Tyler, who had originally gone to Romania with Flo Zander to investigate the possibility of a BSF class, but on leaving Romania temporarily at Christmas had ended up in Kaiserslautem. So they ran a pilot each and then taught the classes for a year. No Teaching Leader could be found to continue the Men's Class, but the Children's Supervisor became the women's Teaching Leader for two years before she moved away. Then we were stuck. These military classes are so mobile.

I was sure that the class was not dead, but in May we were left with a Discussion Leader, a Secretary, and a Children's

Leader. We had the manuals returned to the U.K. office and waited, having told the class to hold on. In June we heard of a Teaching Leader moving from Pusan, Korea, to Frankfurt who was keen to continue teaching. Rosemary approved. In July I had a long telephone call with her, the upshot of which was this: if she, the in-transit Teaching Leader, was at our European workshop in Zurich in late August, she could teach the class. She was and she did.[10]

BSF continued to grow in England and to spread throughout Europe, according to Board minutes.

- In 1986, the European division had seven classes.
- In 1987, BSF added three in England and one in Switzerland.
- In 1988, a class started in France.
- In 1989, four more classes were added in Europe.
- In 1990, another five classes started in Europe.

As BSF branched out into other countries, the decision was made to keep BSF lessons in English. One reason for that decision was the concern that if lessons were translated into a variety of languages, the ministry could not be certain that the translations remained faithful to the message of the original. Here's a little history behind that decision.

### ⌒⊘ In Others' Words

*Dr. Ernest Hastings:*

Miss Johnson had a heart for China, and wanted to start classes in China. When BSF was maybe five years old, we decided that we would allow her lessons to be sent to China and there translated and taught in China. It took about a year to realize that this was a bad idea. We had lost all control over what makes a Bible Study Fellowship class work as a BSF class. And in so many areas, there are such a variety of dialects. It would be difficult to choose. There has to be a common language so that we could know that everything was being presented the BSF way. English became an attraction and a unifying factor in our overseas classes.[11]

Because BSF classes were conducted in English throughout the world, many nationals attended just for the opportunity to improve their English language skills—discovering God's truth in the process. Keeping the lessons in English also fit into the mission of BSF in surprising ways.

### ⟶ FROM THE DIRECTOR
*Rosemary Jensen:*

Several years ago, God put into my heart a renewed concern for English-speaking enclaves within non-English-speaking countries and for countries where national leadership and professionals speak English. English is the language of the educated in many countries throughout the world. BSF could provide one kind of in-depth Bible teaching, which these countries need. Furthermore, by confining the teaching to English, we would be able to reach the leadership of these countries, who, in turn, could then reach their own people in their own language.[12]

The Area Advisor for Latin America had a close-up perspective on this issue.

### ⟶ IMPACT STORY
*Linda Hunt:*

Many people go to BSF classes because they want to learn English. Latin America wants to be like Americans, so, any way they can learn English, they take full advantage of it. When the School Program was introduced in these countries, especially in São Paulo, there would be children in the School Program who couldn't speak any English. And these children now have learned English because they weren't allowed to speak Portuguese at BSF.[13]

By the end of the 1980s, Bible Study Fellowship was truly an international organization. Indeed, Wetherell Johnson would have been thrilled to hear Barb Watson's summary observation: "I remember sitting in leaders meeting, all the different countries and all the different classes, just looking out at all the different women, so different in age and colors of the skin and outlooks. Yet all being one—all doing the same thing, following the same study. We all wanted to love the Lord more. We were truly a universal body in Christ."[14]

*Chapter 25*

# PERSON TO PERSON
### How Bible Study Fellowship grew

W hen Rosemary Jensen became its Executive Director in
January 1980, Bible Study Fellowship claimed 280 classes,
with 51,000 people attending in four countries. By the time she
retired two decades later, there were 212,526 members enrolled
in 971 BSF classes in 30 countries.

God had utilized Rosemary's skills of organization and
leadership to expand BSF dramatically in the 1980s and 1990s.
Just before her last class year, Rosemary reminisced about those
years, going all the way back to the beginning of her term as
Director.

### ⌒ FROM THE DIRECTOR
*Rosemary Jensen:*

When I began as Director, the chairman of the Board at
that time, Dr. Grant Whipple, charged me with the task of better
organizing our ministry so that BSF could expand. Everybody
wanted more classes, but such growth takes much organization,
especially if you're going to maintain the high standards BSF
had set in the early days. We needed facilities, personnel, and
systems before we could being to grow.

God, in His grace, provided the money and the construction expertise to build housing. By the end of the 1980s, we were able to house seventy-one orientees. We also needed a place to feed them and to train them. So, in 1987, we completed the auditorium.

There was a need for more materials and the ability to print them. God, in His grace, gave us an addition on the press building, which increased from twenty-seven thousand square feet to thirty-seven thousand square feet of space. This should accommodate the printing needs for at least five hundred thousand lessons.

Numbers were never our primary concern—except for the fact that we did want more numbers to hear the truth. So we prayed for our classes, that they would grow in size, because we certainly wanted everyone to get the advantage of the teaching. But, of course, to grow required more personnel. God, in His grace, brought us a wonderful headquarters staff. Right now, in 1999, we number thirty-six, and grace upon grace upon grace, we all love each other.

One of the first things we had to do back in the eighties was to develop an organizational chart and write job descriptions for each of our staff members. We found that job descriptions helped people know what they are supposed to be doing.

In 1980 there were twenty-four Area Advisors; now there are seventy-seven. In 1980 there was no such thing as an Area Class Administrator, and there were only three Children's Area Coordinators. We added a new person in the early eighties to the headquarters staff to work with the ACAs and one to work with the CACs, and now all of our area teams are complete.

Excellence is our goal, because this is the Lord's work. BSF is not just an organization; it's a tool in the hands of the Lord. A few other developments in BSF were needed to make it more effective. God, in His grace, helped us start some of them right away.[1]

Two things soon became clear to many of those who observed and worked with Rosemary. First, God gifted Rosemary Jensen with the managerial and organizational skills required by BSF during this time. And second, He provided her the strength of character and determination to apply those abilities to challenge others and effect change.

## Filling Out the Organizational Chart

Early in the 1980s, an additional layer of supervision and guidance was added to BSF in the form of area teams, comprised of Area Advisors (AAs), Area Class Administrators (ACAs), and Children's Area Coordinators (CACs). These area teams supervised and encouraged local BSF leaders in dealing with the explosive growth in the numbers of classes and the increasing size of those classes.

One BSF veteran, an ACA, explained.

### ⁓ IN OTHERS' WORDS

*Gwyneth MacKenzie:*

The new three-person area teams were invaluable to BSF. The classes felt like we were somebody on their side, someone they could relate to. We visited them regularly. They got to know us. So anything that cropped up that they did not understand, or something that needed clarifying, we would do that. It saved a lot of confusion. We, the three members of the area team, traveled together and had quite a lot of time waiting in airports to talk and to help each other with the different aspects of the class.[2]

BSF began inviting Area Advisors, Area Class Administrators, and Children's Area Coordinators to headquarters to learn how to minister to the BSF leaders under their supervision. Candy Staggs, now Director of Domestic Operations for BSF, describes that training.

## ∼◯ IN OTHERS' WORDS

*Candy Staggs:*

What is now in place is that we train the three parts of the area team who travel together. We bring them back to headquarters for a few days to give them some fine-tuning, a few tips on how to switch roles from being a Teaching Leader to now helping someone else do their very best in teaching.

They are invited back on a Sunday, and through Wednesday we train separately for each of those positions. We give the big picture, our philosophy. And we work on relationships, because that is a lot of what area people do—have relationships with people. Then we give them tools to let them know what problems to look for, how to be an encourager, how to give the Teaching Leaders support in this work that God has called them to do. And how to make that Teaching Leader and that class the most attractive and to bring the most people in to study the Bible.[3]

The current Area Advisor for Europe had a unique experience while training as an AA.

## ∼◯ IMPACT STORY

*Holly Holmquist:*

I had heard about BSF when we lived in California but never got involved until I moved to Europe. My husband and I originally went to Belgium as missionaries with Greater Europe Mission. I heard about a Bible study that was being offered and learned that they were studying the Minor Prophets, so I was interested. I went to the classes, and in listening to the Teaching Leader, I thought, *Boy, have I come home! This is the place I want to be.*

I became a Discussion Leader and eventually a TL, and I taught for six years before our mission agency relocated us and I had to resign from my BSF leadership. Then I was asked to substitute for the Area Advisor. Now, I'm in my third year as an AA.

As a new AA, I was supposed to come to the States for AA training, and the dates conflicted with when I was supposed to go to the Ukraine and teach at our mission school. Rosemary said that if I didn't come to the meetings I couldn't be trained in the BSF way. That was such a grief for me! But she got back to me and said that if I could get to the States on these certain days, which were different than the regular training, and then she would personally train me. So I flew into headquarters in San Antonio and spent one whole day with Rosemary and the training manual. To think that she was willing to train me one-on-one! It was terrifying but very special to me. She even had me to her home and cooked the evening meal—ostrich stew. That was way beyond the call of duty.[4]

## One Heart at a Time

The Lord had prepared the organization in many ways for the tremendous growth He planned for BSF through the 1980s and 1990s. But the growth itself followed some of the word-of-mouth patterns typical in the early days of BSF, as evidenced by this story about the first Men's Class in Tulsa, Oklahoma.

### IN OTHERS' WORDS
*Gordon Ziegler:*

My wife, Linda, had a Fuller Brush route, and one of her customers was Deanna Rogg. Deanna's husband, Ron Rogg, is on the BSF Board now. Deanna was in BSF and kept witnessing to my wife, until one day, my wife finally accepted the Lord. That was on a Thursday or Friday, and on Monday my wife was in a BSF class with her friend.

In no time, I could tell this class was changing her life and making a difference. But she also talked about all these guidelines and rules: how she had to answer questions every week and wasn't supposed to speak up unless she had something written down. I thought that was too weird to be normal.

We moved from Wichita to Tulsa, Oklahoma, in 1978. My wife started going to a women's BSF class there. And there was a group of men praying about starting a Men's Class in Tulsa. One evening Linda told me that they were going to have coffees, because they had someone to be the men's Teaching Leader. I told her I did not care.

Not an hour later, I got on the phone. I can't tell you to this day why I did this; I'm not even a guy that likes to talk on the phone. But I started calling men in my church, and I got seventeen guys to go with me to a BSF coffee. At that time, cards would be left out at the coffee, and people were told that if they knew someone who might make a good leader, to put that person's name down. These seventeen guys who came with me all put my name down.

I was asked into leadership, and by the time the full class started, I had gone from being a Discussion Leader to being the Class Administrator in the first Men's Class in Tulsa.

Later that year, in March 1985, at a BSF retreat, Rosemary mentioned that Bob and Kitty Magee were getting ready to go to Africa and that BSF needed someone to take Bob's place. Rosemary cornered me one night at a dinner and we talked. That was on March 28, and on July 8, I started work at BSF headquarters, working in shipping and receiving.[5]

While wives were getting their husbands into BSF classes, others were doing their part to bring their family members to a BSF.

### ⟡ IMPACT STORY
*Linda Hunt:*

I had a cousin that lived in San Antonio and worked at headquarters. She would say, "Come see me sometime. I'm at Bible Study Fellowship." That is how I first heard the name.

At that same time, God put such a hunger in my heart for His Word. I'd never gone to a Bible study in my life. I'd never even read the Bible much, except when I went to Sunday school as a kid and got bars for attendance.

One day another cousin, Leslie, who also lived in San Antonio, brought her children to see me. I went out to greet her in the driveway that day and asked, "Leslie, you go to a Bible study, don't you?"

She replied, "Yes, I do, and I love it. But I have driven three hours without air conditioning. Could I come into the house and get some water before we talk about this?"

I must have been quite intent to run out to her car and ask her that question without even saying hello first. When we finally got to talking, she said that she went to Bible Study Fellowship. We decided to go together so I could visit the class, which was studying the history of Israel and the Minor Prophets that year.

If I say that I was biblically illiterate, then I certainly was with Micah. The Teaching Leader prayed and used words like "the blood of Jesus Christ." I knew absolutely nothing about what she was talking about, but I knew I was home. So I registered and went to the introductory class, and I was called by the Discussion Leader two months later and put into a class.

I never missed, because it changed my life completely. I had a long drive each week—three hours each way. Then God moved me to the Rio Grande Valley, five hours from San Antonio. But I wouldn't have cared if it had been a ten-hour drive; I kept right on going. Little by little, I dropped out of other things. I would even change vacation times so that I didn't miss a week. I was that starved for God's Word.

I did not know it, but people had been praying for eighteen years for a BSF class in the Rio Grande Valley. I filled out a form with my address, for my class in San Antonio. My leader said to me, "I need you to call Flo Zander, because I think God is calling you to be a Teaching Leader."

She kept on until I finally called Flo, whom I'd never met. Flo came to the class in San Antonio to interview me, although I didn't know it at the time. She and I became good friends.

She was the Area Advisor, so when a new class finally started in the Rio Grande Valley, in McAllen, Texas, I became the first Teaching Leader there—from 1982 to 1988.

After that, I was asked to become an Area Advisor. I taught my seventh year while also serving as the Area Advisor for Latin America.[6]

Of course, not everyone was invited to BSF by relatives. Some came through the influence, the invitation, and sometimes even the insistence of neighbors, friends, or coworkers. Whatever the route by which they started, new class members often became recruiters of those in their own circle of family, friends, and acquaintances. Indeed, much of BSF's growth through the years can be attributed to such personal yet powerful connections.

Here's the testimony of a woman who went to class at the urging of a fellow Navy wife. Then she carried BSF with her when she and her husband moved to his next assignment.

### ⌒⊘ IN OTHERS' WORDS

*Donna Read:*

I lived in the Bay Area of California from the mid to late seventies, only a mile and a half from Miss Johnson's headquarters. I was asked to go to BSF there in Oakland, but I never went.

Then when the Navy transferred my husband to Hawaii, the wife of the engineer on his ship was a Discussion Leader in BSF. She invited me, and I went to BSF for the first time the next month. The Teaching Leader of that Hawaii class was Nan Sancher, and as she gave her lecture, the Holy Spirit spoke to my heart, saying, "Donna, you've been so far from where I want you to be." I literally walked out of class that day already reading Miss Johnson's notes for *The Life and Letters of Paul*.

The next year I was asked into leadership. We were transferred in December of that year to an area where they had been praying for a BSF class for nine years. I joined a Community Bible Study where the children's supervisor, the class administrator, and I had all been in BSF before.

The Navy soon reassigned my husband to San Diego, where I served as a BSF Teaching Leader, until we moved to Atlanta, Georgia, when my husband left the Navy in the mid eighties.

I was flabbergasted that at the time, in the whole state of Georgia, there was only one BSF class—the one I attended in Atlanta. I began to pray for another class in Georgia. And the next year, when my husband's company transferred him to a nuclear plant in south Georgia, I began praying specifically for a class there.

I remained a Discussion Leader in Atlanta, and on Wednesdays I would leave after class and drive 197 miles south to my home in Vidalia, Georgia. Then I'd drive back to Atlanta again the next week in time for the weekly leaders' meeting.

Our Area Advisor called on a Monday and asked if I'd be willing to help with a new Macon class. A trained Teaching Leader was now living there. I went to headquarters in San Antonio the following Thursday for STL training. The people in Macon had prayed specifically that by the first of December an STL would be trained. I was that person, although we had never met.

When the Teaching Leader found out that I lived one hundred miles south of Macon, she thought it would never work. But it did. We held the pilot class in early 1988 and began the regular class in that fall with the study of Matthew. Three months later, the Teaching Leader's husband was transferred to Raleigh, North Carolina. I became the TL of that Macon class for seven years.

Then my husband was transferred to Birmingham, Alabama, where he was able to get back in BSF. And in Birmingham they needed a Teaching Leader for a Women's Evening Class. I took the Evening Women's Class, and we launched the School Program in Birmingham.[7]

While most people come to BSF through the influence of friends or relatives, a complete stranger invited a woman who eventually became Area Advisor for the United Kingdom.

## ⌒◯ IN OTHERS' WORDS

*Jan Heal:*

I got a phone call one Monday morning from a lady that I didn't know—Gwyneth MacKenzie, who was running a prayer group for BSF in Chester, England, the town where I live. This group was looking to get a base from several different churches. Gwyneth called early that morning. The prayer meeting was scheduled that same morning. We had a problem with our central heating system, and I needed to call the gas board to come and have a look. But before I did, I prayed, "Lord, if You want me at that prayer meeting, I'm handing this to You on your timing."

I rang up the gas people after 9:00 AM. Much to my surprise, the gas man showed up at 9:45, fixed whatever was wrong, and was off by 10:15. So I got onto my bike and made it to the BSF prayer meeting in time. I had a real sense God wanted me there that morning.

One of the women in this prayer group invited me to go with her to a BSF class that was about fifteen miles away, so that I would have some idea what it was we were praying for. On that next Wednesday, I went to an introduction class and started BSF.

A lady named Janet felt God was calling her to be the Teaching Leader of this new class in Chester. But they still needed a Substitute Teacher. Once I started to attend this nearby class, I began to wonder if God was calling me to this. That conviction continued to grow.

About five or six weeks later, I was at a tea with Janet. We sat and chatted, talking about BSF. She waited for me to say something about being an STL, and I waited for her to bring it up. In the end, she said, "Have you ever considered a leadership position in BSF?"

We took it from there and contacted the Area Advisor, had an interview with her, and then filled out an application form. That was in October 1988. In January, Janet and I went over to the States for training to start the pilot class.

We did one pilot in Philippians and then started the class the following September in Genesis. I subbed for three years. During those three years, I was asked to be the person who trains the other STLs in her area. Initially, I did that just for the European classes, not for the U.K. ones, as someone else was doing that. But six months later, the other girl resigned, so I covered both the U.K. and Europe, which I thoroughly enjoyed because I got the bigger picture of BSF in Europe. Sometimes I would travel with the Area Coordinator teams to train STLs, and I enjoyed that.

I loved being an STL because I got to lecture every now and again but didn't have the full teaching responsibilities. Before my first lecture as an STL, however, I wondered, *How am I going to do this?* I went to the bathroom just before the lecture. There was a door going out of the church between there and the sanctuary. If I could have escaped out that door, I would have. But after that first lecture, I thought to myself, *I can do this!* Well, I couldn't, but God could.

About Christmas of our third year, my Teaching Leader came to tell me that her husband had been transferred down to London, so she was going to have to move. I didn't think I could take over and become the teacher. It took about six weeks for the Lord to convince me that I could do it.

I took over the class in September 1992 and taught it for the next eight years.[8]

Barbara Chrouser had attended the first BSF class outside the state of California. Years later, she played a part in starting new classes in Texas.

### ⌒ In Others' Words
*Barbara Chrouser:*

We moved to Texas so my husband could teach there. The first person who came to visit me in our new place was from the faculty wives. She stayed just a few minutes and we had coffee.

Then, as she was leaving, she asked, "Have you ever heard of Bible Study Fellowship?"

I told her that I had been in classes in two different places. A group of interested people asked me teach a Bible study. That developed into a BSF prayer group, then I helped start the BSF class in Tyler, Texas. Several of us drove back and forth to that Tyler class for several years before starting our own class in Longview. Eventually, my husband also started a Men's Class.[9]

## Growth in Evening Women's Classes

In 1981, 1983, and 1989, reports to BSF's Board concluded, "The greatest growth has been in the Evening Women's classes." After serving as a Discussion Leader for years, Carolyn Edwards helped start one of those Evening Classes for women in 1984, in Bloomington, Indiana.

### ∽ In Others' Words

*Carolyn Edwards:*

When Sarah Buzzwell and I went to Texas for training, I was the first to go in for my interview with Rosemary, who said to me, "I think we have two Teaching Leaders here."

I told her, "No, I just want that class to start, and I'll do whatever you want me to do."

So Rosemary asked Sarah to be the TL, and I was her STL.

Sarah was a brilliant teacher, but she left after three years and they asked me to take over the class. I ended up teaching for ten years.

BSF was the most wonderful part of my life. I loved every minute of it and saw lives changed, because God changes people.[10]

After years of attending BSF classes, Chris Morris also felt the call to begin an Evening Class for women.

## ᴑ◯◯ Impact Story

*Chris Morris:*

I was raised as a Christian and thought I was. When I got married, my husband was in the Air Force and we went to England for thirteen months. While we were there, I sensed something was drastically wrong with my life. Without any fanfare, no one even around, I accepted the Lord.

When we came back to the States, I felt the need for study. I went back to college for a year and thought, *This isn't doing it.* A neighbor hounded me about this Bible study. I had a two-year-old son at the time, and my neighbor told me there was a program for him, too. I went to get her off my back.

The class was in this huge church, and I arrived to see five hundred women all going into the church at the same time. I wondered what was going on and *Where is the little room downstairs where the Bible study is?*

Fifty women were in the introduction class; they told us there wouldn't be room for all of us and that some of us might not be placed. Although I hadn't wanted to go in the first place, when they told us we all couldn't go to the class, I said, "What do you mean I can't get into the class?" I was completely captivated by that point, and that's how I got into BSF.

I never had been to anything like that before. I loved the international aspect of it and meeting women from such different backgrounds. I loved the focus. There was no chitchat or even coffee; we were there to study. God stirred up a need in me for study and a need for Him, and that all came together in BSF.

After that first year, I was invited to be part of the class leadership. Then we moved to an area that didn't have BSF, in the high desert in California. The first person I met there had been in BSF, and she and I began to pray together that God would bring BSF there, and He did. A Day Class started there in 1982.

In 1986, we had a senior and a sophomore in high school, when my husband and I were offered a baby to adopt. My friends threw a baby shower for me. Then, at the last minute, the girl kept her baby. I went into a two-month mental decline, thinking, *What's in this life for me?*

The Teaching Leader talked me into attending the BSF retreat that year. But I went with a terrible attitude. The focus was on worship, and I soon realized that I didn't know anything about worship and that God was stirring me up to have a relationship with Him.

On Saturday night they had an opportunity for everyone to share. People lined up on the sides to talk at the microphone for a couple minutes. I thought, *I can't do that!* But the Lord's voice was so clear.

Rosemary told me later that when I stood up and started talking, she thought to herself, *She needs to be teaching a class.* As Rosemary was shaking my hand at the end of that weekend, I said, "This has been a wonderful retreat, but I am resigning this year. We just don't have the population base for an Evening Class, and yet I feel led to start a Bible study for working women."

Rosemary said, "Call me Monday." And then she wouldn't let go of my hand until I promised I would call.

Rosemary had insight. She could read people so well! With her encouragement, a friend and I started an Evening Class for working women in 1987.[11]

The Teaching Leader of the first Evening Class in Liverpool, England, first heard about BSF from Ann Cook back in 1970 and had been a Discussion Leader in the morning class in Allenton. Finally, in 1986, things came together for an Evening Class.

### ⤶ IN OTHERS' WORDS
*Val Atkinson:*

Ann Colmer started a prayer group for the Evening Class. When summer came, several of us kept praying, going along as if we were going to start the Evening Class. For sixteen years, Leslie, a woman I'd never met, had been praying for an Evening Women's Class in Liverpool. She didn't know anything about our prayer group. But at the beginning of August, at the point we decided to go with it, Leslie felt God saying, "You can stop praying now. I am taking care of this. It is on its way."

Ann Colmer knew Leslie and was in touch with her. At the same point we told Ann we were going ahead with the class, Leslie told her what she had heard from God. That was a big confirmation sign for Ann.

We did the training. We held the coffees. We identified about five hundred people who said they were interested. When the time came to go to San Antonio for training, there were still a couple of things I was concerned about whether or not I could go along with certain BSF policies. I determined not to tell anybody about my concerns. But they were answered explicitly, one by one, each day during the week. By the end of orientation week, I was convinced. They had removed any misgivings.

I went to orientation with Carol McAbee, and we were not sure who would be what. I went thinking that I would be the Substitute Teaching Leader. But during the week, listening to the job descriptions for STLs and TLs, Carol and I came to the same conclusion at the same time. She said, "I can't be the Teaching Leader." And I said, "I can't be the STL."

Finding a church was a last-minute thing. We had people coming from a wide area, so it had to be somewhere people from Southport to Manchester could get to. But at many churches, the elders had never heard of BSF and didn't want to get their own programs swallowed up. Not until the last week before class started did we settle on a location. We found a large, old church, part of which was derelict, with a small congregation, one of whom wanted to come to class. That was the minister's wife, who was desperate for spiritual input.

The church was located in a poor area in Liverpool. Because it was such a rough neighborhood, we had husbands patrolling the streets every night we were there.[12]

## Different Arenas

In addition to growing in numbers of classes around the world, BSF also branched out into different arenas of ministry. In 1984, BSF started the first class inside a prison (in Boise, Idaho) and the first class for the military (at the Presidio, in California). By 1985, a second prison class started at the women's prison in Raleigh, North Carolina. In addition to the military class at the Presidio in San Francisco, pilot classes were in progress at Hill Air Force Base in Utah, at Central Oahu in Hawaii, and at Fort Leonard Wood, Missouri. Another pilot class was planned at the military base at Subic Bay, Philippines. A retired colonel's wife was trained as a military Ambassador.

The *BSF Newsletter,* May 1989, told this moving story from one of the prison classes.

> Let me share with you just one story of a class member who came to class a few weeks after her incarceration. Jill was extremely frightened, having been assaulted by two other inmates numerous times. She came to our class because it was a safe place, but each week her roommates would steal her completed lesson before she came to class. One night Jill seemed especially distraught. So we prayed together and I encouraged her to seek God's comfort by spending time in the Psalms.
>
> That week Jill again completed her lesson, and again it was stolen. When Jill returned to class, however, she was joyful, for the Lord has enabled her to be an "overcomer." Jill had stayed up each night until 3 AM in order to memorize her lesson and the Scripture so she could participate in her discussion group! She realized no one could take from her what she had hidden in her heart.
>
> I visited Jill after she was transferred to another prison for protective custody. She told me she didn't hold anything against those who had assaulted her because they had forced her to memorize the Bible, which had become a regular part of her discipline.

Jill also told me it was during the week she first memorized her lesson that she committed her life to Christ. She said, "You know why I came to your class? Because it was safe. I came to find a safe place. What I found was Jesus."[13]

# Chapter 26

# GROWING A DIFFERENT WAY

Focusing on larger, stronger classes

By the late 1980s, the tremendous growth in the number of BSF classes became a regular topic of reports and discussion at BSF Board meetings. Seventy new classes began in the fall of 1988, for a total of more than seven hundred classes. In January 1989, Dr. Ernest Hastings asked the Board to consider whether growth should be limited, or encouraged. Fred Goetting suggested some long-range strategic planning. Rosemary Jensen believed that God would lead BSF step by step, but she thought the Board should examine the organization's mission statement to see how growth might best be handled.

In January 1991, Rosemary Jensen reported to the Board, "BSF is growing and will probably have 1,000 classes in the next few years. Last year over 66 classes were added and the staff is praying for 75 new classes this year." She suggested that growth was reaching the point where their focus would need to be on increasing the size, rather than the number, of classes. She was not ready for the organization to stop growing, but she was concerned with the quality control of the classes.

In May 1992, she told the Board, "BSF is coming to a crisis point in growth." The decision was made to close any class with fewer than seventy members. That meant closing ten classes.

In May 1993, the Board decided that new classes would need to have seventy-five members, and existing classes more than five years old would need one hundred. That would mean closing twenty-two or twenty-three classes. Rosemary assured the Board, "BSF will not stop growing but will grow in a different way."

## Maintaining Quality

As Rosemary Jensen pointed out, the new emphasis on larger classes was all about quality control.

For one thing, the organizational system of Area Advisors, Area Class Administrators, and Children's Area Coordinators continued to keep BSF standards high in the face of phenomenal growth. People acting in those roles around the world made sure the BSF way was upheld.

Furthermore, the BSF Graduate Program, started by Rosemary in the early 1980s, helped strengthen BSF classes and class members. Later called Graduate Seminars and then BSF Seminars, these sessions enabled class members to more effectively transfer the skills and spiritual lessons they learned in BSF to their churches and communities.

### ⌒◯ IN OTHERS' WORDS

*Jane Roach:*

The year I started on staff, we made some huge changes in the Graduate Seminars, and I got to be a part of that. At first, it was truly a program for graduates, people who had finished the five years of BSF and had graduated. We were asking people to leave once they completed the five-year cycle of studies, in order to make room for new class members. Near the end of the class year, the Teaching Leader would hold two meetings with the people who were going to graduate and teach the graduates how to do our three-question method:

- What is the passage about?
- What do I learn from it?
- How can I apply it to my life?

I was a Teaching Leader then, and I got to see how that worked and I loved it.

But many Teaching Leaders didn't want one more thing to do at the end of the year. So we chose what we called the Area Graduate Supervisors. The Area Advisor would train them, and they would train the graduates.

By the time I came on staff, this program had been stretched to four weeks, to include a spiritual gifts inventory. And work had been done to expand it to ten weeks, and we piloted that in a number of cities throughout the United States, one session per week in the fall, for people who had graduated the previous spring. The next year, we did it everywhere.

That's when we started getting feedback that this was too much to learn at one time. Some people did not have time to do it. And others wanted to add more things.

One day Rosemary sat next to a pastor at a meeting, talking about BSF and the Graduate Program. That pastor suggested, "Why don't you give them a little bit of that every year, while they're in class, so they don't have to wait till the end." After discussing that change one day at a Division Head meeting, we decided to do just that.

It was March and I was thinking, *I have a whole year to put this in place.* But Rosemary said, "No, I want to do it at the end of this class year."

I said, "Rosemary, that's just two months away."

"Yes, it is," Rosemary agreed. In her mind, if you have an idea, you go ahead and do it.

I countered with "If we're going to do that, we need to bring the Area Graduate Supervisors back to headquarters, so they understand what we're doing. They are the ones who will have to make it happen."

We looked at the headquarters calendar, and one weekend was not already filled with activities. Rosemary told us to do it then.

I went immediately to my office and sent out a letter inviting twenty-eight of our thirty Area Graduate Supervisors. We did not invite the two from overseas, from Australia and England, because there wasn't time to arrange their travel.

Twenty-seven of them were able to come on late notice. They
dropped everything.

We also decided that ten weeks of Graduate Seminars was
too many. We could combine them into five. We had "Personal
Quiet Time," which was personal Bible study and prayer. We
had what we called "Evangelism," which is now "Sharing the
Gospel." We had a "Homiletics" session and one on "Leading
Others," which was the three-question method and principles
of leadership. The "Spiritual Gifts Inventory" was last.

One day I went to Rosemary and said, "I don't think the
Spiritual Gifts Inventory is what we want." Some people were
going to their pastor and saying, "I can't do that; it's not my
gift," instead of saying, "Whatever you need me to do, I will do
it." So we came up with a personal evaluation for a servant of
God, which focuses on serving others and being a servant of
Christ. Anyone could take whichever one they wanted to, but
we suggested they take one session a year.

The idea is that, if you take one of these a year, and really
start applying what you've learned in the summer between one
BSF year and the next, you can really master that skill and it is
yours for the rest of your life.[1]

Another successful addition to BSF's calendar was the
Institutes for Teaching Leaders. The pilot institute, launched in
1982, was such a hit that by 1983, headquarters hosted four institutes, inviting Teaching Leaders to see the new headquarters
and giving them a week of spiritual retreat mixed with training.

### ⌔ IN OTHERS' WORDS
*Jane Roach:*

Our Institutes for Teaching Leaders served as their ongoing
training. We brought them to headquarters to encourage them,
give them a time of rest and a foundation for the next series they
would teach.

When Teaching Leaders come here the first time for their
orientation week, they're tense, nervous, and scared. Then they

teach for a whole year, and the next year, when they come to institute, sometimes I don't recognize them. And it is not because
they have a new hairdo. The look on their faces is so different
because they have experienced the faithfulness of God, thirty-
two weeks in a row, in putting together leaders meetings and
giving lectures. The peace and the maturity on their faces—it's
just amazing. I see it every year.[2]

## Advantages of the New Emphasis

In the early 1990s, when BSF shifted its focus from growth in
numbers of classes to growth in the number of members in each
class, many good things began to happen. For example, Chuck
Musfeldt, now Director of International Operations, learned that
*taking* people to BSF could be much more effective than just
*inviting* them.

### ⌒☺ IN OTHERS' WORDS
*Dr. Chuck Musfeldt:*

In 1989 we lived in the western Chicago suburb of Naperville,
Illinois. I had an MBA and was working with Ernst and Young's
health-care consulting group during the week, and then practic-
ing as a family physician on the weekends.

My wife, Linda, joined BSF that year and soon became a
Discussion Leader. She informed me about a men's BSF class
only forty minutes away. But I said, "There is absolutely no way
I'm going to a Bible study in another suburb on a Monday night
in Chicago traffic." She and the other BSF leaders got onto their
knees together and prayed that one day I would go to BSF. So I
guess I really didn't have a chance.

Two years later, a man in my church named Bill Littell said,
"Chuck, how about if I come by on Monday nights and pick you
up after work? We'll get some dinner and I'll bring you to BSF."

I enjoyed going to Chicago Cubs games with Bill, so I said,
"Okay."

Often it takes a man to get another man into a Bible study. I learned there is the difference between inviting someone to BSF and bringing someone to class. Going with Bill took many of the unknown factors out of it for me. We stopped to eat, so there was food involved—another plus. And I didn't have to walk into a strange place alone. I went with my buddy.

I had become a believer in Christ when I was nine, so I knew Christ as my Savior, but I wasn't involved in any study, and I knew that I probably needed that. I was attending and active in church, and I read the Bible every day, but it was more as a historical document that was true than something I could apply to my life. I really loved my class once I started going, but I wasn't a good BSF student my first year. I waited all week and then I did the entire BSF lesson in fifteen minutes before class, in my car in the parking lot at church. The problem was that I kept leaving my dome light on in my car, so they frequently called out my license plate number during announcements, saying, "Somebody needs to go turn off the light in their car."

When my Discussion Leader would call me on Sunday night and ask me if I was having problems with the lesson, I'd look at my blank lesson and say, "No, not at all."

After that year, I started working on my lesson through the week. That was a good accountability check for me—to have a quiet time each day and work on the lesson little by little. I also enjoyed talking about the lesson with my wife and even took one of my daughters with me to the School Program.

I was in the Men's Class for two years as a member, a Discussion Leader for another two years, and then taught the Men's Class in Chicago for five years.

My first Teaching Leader, Harry Hoffner, was a professor of Near Eastern history at the University of Chicago. I realized that he knew a lot more about the Bible than I did. So when I was asked to pray about being the new Teaching Leader, I told Harry, "I don't have any background in Hebrew or Greek. Your illustrations were about Near Eastern history; my illustrations will all probably be about the Cubs."

But Harry said, "God has given you different gifts, and He will use that in a different way that will bless the class."

I came to the TL orientation not completely convinced that I was supposed to be the TL; I still couldn't see myself filling the shoes of my predecessor. But during one of her lectures, Rosemary looked right at me and said, "Do you think that God is confused? That all these situations that have been put together, and all these people that have recommended you to become the TL, are all wrong? Or could it be that you're confused, and God and all these other people have it right?"

That was a real turning point for me. I was able to commit without reservation to become the TL. Then we sang "No Turning Back" and I really was committed.

What Rosemary did so well was to show you what God had in store for you, that you don't want to miss. The verse she gave me at the end of the orientation was Isaiah 42:6: "I, the LORD, have called you in righteousness; I will take hold of your hand. I will keep you and make you to be a covenant for the people and a light for the Gentiles."

When I was a TL and they'd bring me the announcements that someone had left the light on in his car, I had to smile. I knew how that had happened. I'd read the license plate number and say, "Would the future Teaching Leader of this class please go out and turn off his dome light?"[3]

Even in England, where BSF classes tended to be smaller, the organization experienced encouraging growth.

### ⟨∽⟩ IMPACT STORY
*Barb Watson:*

My most vivid memory was when I went to San Antonio for training in 1983 to become the Children's Area Coordinator for the UK. During the training session, Kitty Magee said, "You have to have vision for the work." I am not visionary. I didn't know how to get the vision. I came home a bit burdened by this. In my prayer time, I said, "Lord, I've been told that I have to have a vision for this work. I don't know where to begin. What's Your plan for BSF's children here?"

Then I just stayed where I was. I was waiting there, when into my mind came an outline, a map, with a compass and flat dots. Then the Lord spoke into my mind and said, "I want you to think of all those little black dots as groups of children who need the pure Word of God, growing up into men and women who will honor Me and turn this nation into a Christian nation again."

I literally said, aloud, "Wow, Lord! And You've chosen me to set that in motion?"

That was not my work; it was His. I was privileged to set it in motion.[4]

BSF grew in its impact not only on individuals but also on churches, communities, and families.

### ᨐ Impact Story

*Dottie McKissick:*

One thing that has impressed me is how BSF gets into and affects entire families. One particular friend was a leader in my class, and her children never were interested; they considered BSF something their mother was involved in. That family moved and my friend became involved in BSF in Michigan. When my friend moved back to California, for a time her daughter's family lived with her, including a two-year-old granddaughter. My friend took her granddaughter to our class, just for six weeks. And the change in this little girl so impressed the mother that, when the family was settled in their own house, she started going to class.

The mother eventually recruited her sister and her husband. Next, the husband's brother and his wife and preschooler went. The first daughter now has three children in the program, and her husband is going and taking the oldest one.

That, I think, is fun to see—how BSF grows and touches

whole families and how the Children's Program is significant in drawing their parents into BSF.[5]

## Still Seeking Growth

Throughout the decades of the 1980s and 1990s, the BSF staff prayed for more class members and for more classes. The Executive Director set the tone of those prayers, as shown in this column in the *BSF Newsletter*.

### ⌣⟶ FROM THE DIRECTOR
*Rosemary Jensen:*

As the Christmas season approaches I am full of joy just thinking of all of you who will be worshipping our Lord Jesus Christ more fully this year because you have been studying and learning of Him in BSF. Jesus tells us that His Father seeks worshippers such as you are (John 4:23). Therefore, we are praying for 10,000 more class members this year than we had last year (Psalm 138:3)! We are praying this knowing that more members mean more lessons, more teacher training, more equipment, more housing, more staff, more volunteers, and more food! Even as we grow in the classes, so we also must grow at the headquarters.[6]

These figures, taken from BSF Board meeting notes, document the growth of BSF in the 1980s and 1990s.

1979–80: Average attendance of 51,896

1980–81: Average attendance of 54,004

1981–82: 316 classes

1982–83: 350 classes

1983–84: 385 classes; 77,222 members plus 12,566 children

1984–85: 449 classes; 13,808 children

1985–86: 512 classes; 91,570 members; 25 new Evening Women's classes

1986–87: 548 classes; 25,181 children enrolled

1987–88: 596 classes; twelve nations; 25,608 children

1988–89: 650 classes; 100,000+ members; 2 new states, Nevada and West Virginia

1989–90: 720 classes; one new state, New York

1990–91: 768 classes; 118,210 members

1991–92: 825 classes; 120,622 members; 31,631 children; Maine now has a BSF class and so does New York City

1992–93: 857 classes; 122,094 members; May 1993: 22 or 23 classes closed, due to low enrollment

1993–94: 866 classes; 134,362 members

1994–95: 882 classes; 200,000+ members; 32,809 children

1995–96: 885 classes; 259,746 members; many graduates came back for the Moses study

1996–97: 903 classes; 176,017 members; 50,650 children

1997–98: 914 classes

1998–99: 945 classes; 194,029 members; 57,853 children; 20,000 in the school program

1999–2000: 971 classes; 218,428 members; 64,565 children

Focusing on larger, stronger churches turned out to be not a deterrent to growth, but the only possible way to let growth continue—and to maintain the traditional quality of BSF teaching.

*Chapter 27*

# MISSION TO DEVELOPING NATIONS
Forming Rafiki and The World Outreach

Beginning with Wetherell Johnson and continuing through the ministry's history, BSF leaders and class members have had a heart for the world and to spread God's love and Word through BSF classes everywhere. Chapters 15 and 24 chronicle some of BSF's initial expansion around the globe. And the organization's ongoing growth (see chapters 25 and 26) extended its ministry to even more countries and continents.

By the mid-1980s, Rosemary Jensen became convinced that Bible Study Fellowship's overseas ministry required and deserved additional attention, consideration, and support of its leadership—from headquarters and the Board.

## Being a Friend
Years later, BSF's second Executive Director reflected on that period of growth and organizational evolution in BSF's overseas work.

## ⌒ FROM THE DIRECTOR
*Rosemary Jensen:*

In 1986, when we were just beginning our BSF classes in Nairobi and in Tanzania, my husband and I, my brother, and Richard Walenta made a visit to these countries.

On that trip we identified two specific needs: practical help required by developing countries in medicine, in education and in economics. The second need concerned our BSF leaders. These two families were sent out by their respective churches to teach BSF classes, but also to work in the hospital. We discovered when we were there, it was a makeshift arrangement. We recognized the need for consistency. These people were going to stay for four years and then going home for a year, as many missionaries do. They had to be able to take their furlough and deputation time when we weren't having class time. It was complicated.[1]

On the long flight home from Africa, the Jensens, Richard Walenta, and Rosemary's brother Don discussed the challenges they'd seen and agreed that the Lord was leading them to start a nonprofit foundation in response. The first purpose of that foundation would be to fund needed medical, educational, and economic projects in developing countries. Its second purpose would be to serve as the sending agency for BSF leaders into Third World countries.

Early in 1987, the Rafiki Foundation (*rafiki* is the Swahili word for "friend") incorporated and registered in Texas as a 501(c)(3) organization. But as was the case with BSF, the story of Rafiki's birth and early growth is best told through the personal stories of its people. Here is one of those stories, told by a BSF Teaching Leader who spent ten years in Africa.

## ⌒ IMPACT STORY
*Chris Morris:*

As a Teaching Leader, I came back to headquarters in 1990

for an institute. Rosemary had just gotten back from a trip to West Africa, and she kept tantalizing us that she was going to tell us about her trip. Monday she said it. Tuesday she said it. And Wednesday. By Thursday, I was thinking, *So what's the big deal about West Africa?* Then she told about the people she had met there and how they had said, "If you can send us teachers, we can start fifty classes in Lagos, Nigeria, alone." Lagos had a population of 20 million and an evangelism explosion but no teaching going on. At that time I had just fifty women in my class. All I could think was, *There are plenty BSF classes here. Why not go where there aren't any?*

After Rosemary dismissed us, I went up to her and asked her what to do. She told me to start pushing on doors, and every door God opened, to go through it. The first door was my husband, John, who met me at the airport. I hadn't planned to say anything about this until we got home, but in the airport parking lot, I said, "What would you say if I told you that I thought that God might be calling us to Africa?"

John answered, "I've been ready for years! You've been the holdout."

Our initial assignment was to Nigeria, but before we left, the Muslim-Christian conflict blew up. They redirected us to Accra, Ghana. We landed in November 1991, and in our initial team of seven, four were medically trained: a doctor, a medical technologist, a nurse practitioner, and my husband, an RN. We were taken to the main teaching hospital and introduced to all sorts of people, one of whom was a cardiac thoracic surgeon. This Ghanaian doctor was ready to open a cardio-thoracic unit in this Third World hospital, a state-of-the-art, air-conditioned unit with new monitors and equipment. He was getting ready to do open heart surgeries in January 1992, with only one problem: he had no one to train the nurses in how to care for the patients after surgery.

This doctor asked John, "What do you do?"

And John answered, "I've been an ICU nurse for years."

The doctor was Christian and told John, "You're an answer

to prayer!" But he also said, "You're not going to recognize these monitors, because they all came from Germany."

The hospital where John had worked for the six years before we left for Africa had nothing but German monitors! So John walked over and started fiddling with all the knobs, totally at home in this ICU unit in Accra, Ghana.

We got there in November, and I was to start a new BSF class. I had all my leaders trained, and the class was to meet on the grounds of this teaching hospital. But I realized these nurses and doctors had strange schedules. Then the week before our pilot class started, there was a national nurses' strike and none of them went to work for six weeks. The pilot class was five weeks. The week after we finished the pilot, they all went back to work. We had one hundred women enrolled in that pilot BSF class, and all of them had perfect attendance.

We raised our financial support before we went, so John volunteered his time at the hospital. And starting in September of 1992, he taught the men's BSF class there in Accra.

We lived in Ghana for ten years and the last two years we were there, the Rafiki projects had started. I was the project director for acquiring land for the children's center, as well as carrying on our BSF work, besides living in a Third World country and all the challenges that brings.

In October 2000, God made it clear that we were to go home. We flew out on June 10, 2001, five days after the children's center was dedicated. By then there were around 250 women in my BSF class, and we had a School Program of about 140 children.[2]

In Rafiki's earliest days, Rosemary did the administrative work in her "spare time," in addition to leading BSF through its amazing growth around the world.

## Clarifying the Relationship

The September 1989 BSF Board meeting was held in Liverpool, England, at the offices of the European Division. Later that fall, Dr. and Mrs. Ernest Hastings, again chair of the Board, attended the Australian BSF retreat and traveled from there to visit classes in Singapore and Taiwan. By the following spring, Fred Goetting, also a Board member, had traveled to visit the BSF work in Africa.

After all this exposure to international classes, the May 1990 Board meeting was a major turning point in the Board's view of the overseas work. Fred Goetting gave a video report of his trip to Africa. Rosemary told about her recent trip to Nigeria and showed a video of classes in Jos. The Board considered a request for a BSF class in Romania, viewing a third video on the needs there. At the same meeting, requests were received for classes in Japan, Brazil, and Uruguay. Rosemary also reported on the progress of establishing an office in Singapore, to handle the needs of classes in Asia.

Then, during the Board's discussion of business and budget issues, the overlap between Rafiki and BSF became apparent. Rafiki missionaries were being sent to do Rafiki work and to teach BSF classes. They raised funds to pay their own expenses. Many had sold their homes to help pay for their work, which meant that when they returned to the States on furlough, they had no permanent residence in which to stay. Many were staying in the House of Heroes at the BSF headquarters in San Antonio.

At one point in the meeting, Board Member Dr. Jim Boice asked if the Rafiki Foundation should continue, or if it made more sense for BSF to take over the overseas operations. After extensive discussion, the Board approved the transfer of missionaries from Rafiki to BSF. They also commissioned Rosemary and Board member Steve Gately to bring a plan to the next Board meeting, held in September, outlining the changes in the overseas operations.

The minutes of that September 1990 Board meeting read as follows:

> Mrs. Jensen reported that at the last Board meeting, the transfer of missionaries from Rafiki to Bible Study Fellowship was approved in principle. The mission ministry is to be a separate division under the

administration of BSF International. Missionaries
will continue to raise their own funds to go out and
no funds will be solicited through BSF classes. The
Rafiki Foundation will continue to exist but will not
be publicized through BSF. Rafiki will provide supplies for special projects, such as medical supplies.
Funds will be raised separately.

The Board felt that the mission program should be called
TWO (Third World Outreach) and that "BSF" should not be part
of the name.

Years later, in a talk given near the end of her term as
Executive Director, Rosemary gave this additional explanation of
the relationship between the TWO divisions of BSF and Rafiki.

### ⟜ FROM THE DIRECTOR
*Rosemary Jensen:*

By the grace of God, one of our Board members suggested that
BSF become the sending agency for our BSF teachers. I knew
it had to be the Lord who put that thought in the mind of our
Board member.

We named the division TWO, meaning Third World
Outreach, but later changed it to The World Outreach. The
Rafiki Foundation remained intact in order to continue to fund
the projects in which the TWO missionaries would work.[3]

## TWO in Action

In 1993, Susy Harbick returned to BSF headquarters from
Singapore to administer the TWO Division. She tells that story.

### ⟞ IN OTHERS' WORDS
*Susy Harbick:*

I was called into Rosemary's office. She asked me if I'd be
willing to come back to headquarters and take over the TWO

Division. I had the privilege of working with TWO for seven years. We administered the funding for the overseas BSF teachers. In developing countries there's a hunger for God's Word but little opportunity to study it.

Every place I went, and not just in developing countries but also as an Ambassador, people would say, "BSF is Western."

And we would say, "No, this is Scripture. You need to learn to think differently."

Sometimes it took five years for people to understand what we were trying to help them to learn in the Scripture and how the study pattern worked. And I watched that evolution, that outreach, happen. It wouldn't have happened without TWO.[4]

BSF, through the TWO Division, administered funds for the Rafiki Foundation. And Rafiki opened doors for BSF's people to enter developing countries.

### ⸻ FROM THE DIRECTOR
*Rosemary Jensen:*

Political situations were getting tighter and tighter, and persecution was getting greater and greater against Christians, especially in developing countries. So it was increasingly harder to get Christian missionaries into these countries. Rafiki could get BSF people into developing nations because Rafiki is listed, not as a Christian organization, but as a charitable organization, doing something for the country. They would be teaching BSF classes on their own time—just as people in the United States do—and their job would be with Rafiki. Their passports truthfully stated that each was a businessperson or a project director or whatever for one of our Rafiki projects.[5]

Two such missionary-teachers, Barbara and Dan Chrouser, had been long-time BSFers. Here is their story.

### ～◯ In Others' Words

*Barbara Chrouser:*

When my husband and I were graduate students at Indiana University in the late sixties, the church I attended hosted a BSF class, and I became a Discussion Leader in Mary Nell Schaap's Bloomington class. When we moved to Texas, I became involved in the BSF class in Tyler and then started a BSF Women's Class in Longview. My husband started a class for men in the same city several years later.

We were asked by Rosemary Jensen to consider going to Uganda with the Rafiki Foundation in 1992 and pilot BSF classes there. We started a Women's Class one year, a Men's Class the next, and then taught them for about eight years.

In Africa the challenge is, How do you get visas? How are you going to live there?—that sort of thing. So my husband and I went into Uganda as teachers at Makerere University. He taught physical education teachers, and I taught math. We had work permits under the government, and our connections with the university gave us credibility.

The first year, we just learned a lot, got to know people, and prayed. We came in the fall and didn't start the introduction coffees until March. Long years of war had destroyed whatever infrastructure Uganda ever had, so not a single person we knew had a telephone. We had many difficult, sometimes humorous, adventures, delivering BSF invitations out to villages and driving on bad roads during the rainy season.

Some people back in the States couldn't imagine how we could start a class where people didn't have cars or phones. But we saw God make connections.

We also faced the challenges of not having reliable electricity. Many times we would get up at 2 AM and work on our lectures because we didn't have electricity any other time. It was common in Uganda to have electricity twelve hours on and then twelve hours off. Other times, we might go four or five days without electricity. Our host churches would sometimes lose power right in the middle of everything. I can still see the children in our School Program sitting around doing their lessons with little candles in the middle of the table.

In Africa, pastors come to BSF classes because other theological opportunities are very limited. One of my husband's most faithful class members was a pastor who had a radio program in the Luloh language. He would take the training in BSF and then give a radio talk about what he had learned. He was able to reach thousands of people we could never reach.

When we left Uganda, our church there held a dinner for us. The pastor of the church, which had three services for more than a thousand people, told us how suspicious he had been when we arrived eight years earlier. He had felt sorry for these two people coming to Uganda to have a Bible study that met every week. He just knew that Ugandans were not going to come to a Bible study. And they certainly were not going to be on time. Then he admitted, "I am so grateful that I was wrong. The leadership of our church today has been trained by BSF." What a special gift from the Lord, for us to see the effect of BSF—that objective work of Scripture and God's Spirit in so many people's lives.

Once things were growing in East Africa, we moved to Cape Town, South Africa, and started classes there. But the BSF story there actually began years earlier with a young South African woman who had a friend who was a Teaching Leader in Sydney, Australia. She had visited there and attended an introductory class in Australia. After she returned home, she prayed for years that somehow we would have a BSF class there in South Africa. So when we arrived there with two other Rafiki Teaching Leaders, we discovered this very strong prayer group already in existence—waiting and anxious for classes to begin.

By 2003, we were Area Advisors there, for eight classes, two Day Women's, three Evening Women's, and three Men's Classes. Two are in Cape Town, three in Zimbabwe, and three in Madagascar.[6]

The BSF Board held its January 1993 meeting in Kampala, Uganda, and visited class sites there and in Kenya and Tanzania. While in Uganda, they met with the president's wife, Janet Museveni, who gave the Board her testimony as a Christian and then asked to hear theirs. When they visited a Kampala orphan-age sponsored by Mrs. Museveni, they learned that Uganda, a country of only 17 million people, had 1.5 million orphans.

Bible students in Uganda

One of the most memorable and moving moments of that trip occurred on the thirteenth floor of the hotel where they stayed. From that height, the Board members looked through a window over that city wracked by AIDS and poverty, with all those orphaned children. They prayed for Kampala, asking God to give the city to BSF—for His Word to go out there so that people's lives would be changed for Christ.

For the 1991–92 class year, BSF had begun a class for Liberian refugees at a refugee camp in Ghana, hoping that when the political situation settled in Liberia, doors to BSF classes would open. A TWO couple, then in Ghana, planned to begin the class in Liberia when that opportunity came.

The *BSF Newsletter* of May 1993 printed this letter from a male member of the Accra/Liberian refugee class.

> I write to say "Praise God for BSF" and many thanks to the administrative Board, both international and local, for their kind consideration given to us Liberian refugees. I must admit that I was envious of the ladies when they first started but now enjoy the rich spiritual dish that I've tasted of for these few months spent with BSF. My sincere prayer is that BSF will

flow on each continent, and be established in each country including Liberia.

May God continue to bless you as he uses you as a tool to build his kingdom on earth. May he also meet the many needs of this ministry, BSF. And who knows, perhaps God has called us to this position as refugees for such a great fellowship (Esther 4:14).[7]

While the African ministry was taking root and spreading throughout the continent, the first BSF-TWO teachers in India also began their work.

### ∽ In Others' Words
*Genelle and David Pipes:*

*Genelle:* In 1977, I joined a BSF class in Navajo, California. Within two years, I became a Discussion Leader, and a couple of years after that, I became Teaching Leader of that class and taught it for the next eight years.

*David:* I came home from work one night and my wife said, "There's a BSF class at the Presidio in San Francisco." So I went, and in the next five years, I missed only twice. By the end of year one, I was a DL, and then I became an STL.

In late 1992, a man from India who was the general director of the India version of InterVarsity, came to the United States to have eye surgery. He stayed with one of our AAs, and they told him about BSF. He called Rosemary Jensen and asked how to get BSF classes started in India. She told him that we would try to have someone in India by September 1993.

Before that time, Genelle and I had told the BSF leadership we were willing to go overseas. When I went to headquarters for my Teacher Leader orientation before starting a pilot class in Marin County, Rosemary and I chatted for a few minutes. She said, "I thought you wanted to be a missionary."

I told her, "We've said we were willing to go anywhere, but you've never come up with any overseas assignment for us."

She said, "You'll be in the field within a year."

Eleven months later, in 1993, we went to India with TWO and started BSF classes there. We were there for five years.

*Genelle:* India doesn't take missionaries, so we went originally as tourists. Eventually we got positions as educators. David taught at a small theological school for eight years; he was their entire English department. I also taught theology classes using BSF material.

Soon after we arrived in India, an Indian man who introduced us to five Indian couples befriended us, and all of them had introductory coffees. Out of those coffees we got enough names to start a class. This same Indian friend had numerous connections with colleges, in particular Christian colleges, throughout India. So we soon had a great base of people to draw from. We launched both Men's and Women's Classes at the same time.

Another couple, Michael and Beth Kegler-Gray, came from the States to help us about a month after we got to India.

*David:* Our fifteen-year-old daughter, Ashley, had been apprehensive about going to India, thinking it was a truly backward country. One morning, as I was going to leaders' meeting, I remember asking her, "Is there anything I can pray for you today?"

She said, "Yes, pray that I will be willing to go to India."

The Lord changed her heart after an Indian man in our church came over to our house for dinner. Ashley nailed him with all these questions. But he evidently answered them to her satisfaction. And by the time our friend left, he assured me, "She's going to be okay."

*Genelle:* By the time we got to the LA airport, leaving for India, and turned to say goodbye to our nineteen- and twenty-two-year-old sons, we were all crying. But Ashley grabbed my arm and nodded toward a huge group of Indians boarding the plane. "Look at them!" she told me. "Their saris are so beautiful." The Lord used her to help me look away from my sorrow and toward the future.

We taught BSF in India for five years in the city of Madras, now Chennai. Then we were asked to become Area Advisors for India and Southeast Asia. And we've been that ever since.[8]

## Developments in the Overseas Work

In the April 1998 *BSF Newsletter*, Rosemary Jensen gave an additional report on overseas activities.

### FROM THE DIRECTOR
*Rosemary Jensen:*

The Rafiki Foundation was incorporated in 1987. Its objective was to support projects and to be a sending agency for BSF Teaching Leaders. Rafiki now focuses on the development, implementation, and maintenance of projects that would facilitate the placement work of these BSF sponsored professionals.

The Rafiki Exchange is the most recent project to evolve in the ministry. It is a store that provides a retail outlet for the purchase of crafts made by those working in the Rafiki craft centers located in various developing countries. One hundred percent of the profits generated at the Rafiki Exchange are reinvested in the ministry of the Rafiki Foundation, Inc.

Rafiki Brazil will develop a vocational training center at La Efrata Orphanage. Initial plans are to begin with English instruction and to include the purchase of computers in the long-range plan. Future expansion includes development of a craft industry with the first handcraft to be birdhouses.

Rafiki India has established a jewelry-making center for disadvantaged women who work from their homes. They currently produce 2,200 beads each week, which is the basis for approximately 100 necklace and earring sets.

Rafiki Zimbabwe is in the process of establishing an ostrich farm and a cooking school. Rafiki Nigeria produces craft projects, including placemats and napkins and note cards in the Nigerian batik. In Mexico, Rafiki personnel have established a Bed and Breakfast and produce luggage racks, ceramic plates, doorstops, and placemats. Rafiki Kenya sponsors a dental project with Dr. Greg Crawford doing work in several orphanages.[9]

In 1990, Bible Study Fellowship changed its name to Bible Study Fellowship International. This wasn't a hopeful repositioning of the ministry. It reflected what God had already done. The ministry *was* international; the name change merely caught up with reality.

Two years later, when the Board adopted a new vision statement for the organization, the international nature of BSF's work was written into the very core of what BSF was trying to do: "One thousand training centers, teaching the Bible, to produce in all participants a vibrant relationship with God and, in as many as are called, a passion to commit without reservation to lead in the cause of Christ in the world."[10]

Map of BSF work as of December 2008

# Chapter 28

# WELCOMING THE NEXT GENERATION
Bible Study Fellowship launches the School Program

What do you suppose was the most important achievement during Rosemary Jensen's tenure as Bible Study Fellowship's Executive Director? The construction of a beautiful international headquarters in San Antonio? Her efficient administrative reorganization? Bible Study Fellowship's continuous record of growth? The expansion of ministry overseas?

Most people interviewed for this book answered with none of these. They believe the most significant development was BSF's School Program. In this program, school-age children could accompany their parents to Evening Classes to study the Bible with children their age in age-appropriate—but by no means dumbed down—ways.

## The Instigation

Susy Harbick remembers an experience while traveling overseas with the Executive Director that helped trigger this crucial new BSF ministry.

## ⌒⊘ In Others' Words
*Susy Harbick:*

The desire for a School Program was starting to percolate in the eighties. People in the States wanted their kids to be able to go beyond the Preschool Program, and the kids wanted to keep going.

I was with Rosemary in Africa when I overheard a discussion between her and this African woman, talking about teens who really needed an understanding of the Scripture. The lady insisted that BSF had the tools to meet the need. Just listening to the way the conversation went, one of my friends and I looked at each other and thought, *Here it comes.*

Even though Rosemary told the woman the idea would have to come later, we knew that there would soon be a BSF School Program. Sure enough, it became the next thing to do.[1]

At a major BSF event in 1999, Rosemary reviewed how that began.

## ⌒ From the Director
*Rosemary Jensen:*

Miss Hertzler started the preschool Program, which would be more than babysitting for the children of class members. Then in the eighties, there came the time when my own grandchild was in the Children's Program. She went all the way through the Preschool Program. She's in college now and has arranged her college classes so that she can go to BSF. She told me the other day, "Grandmama, I have so much fun because I can tell the class that I started BSF before any of them."

Eventually people began asking for something for their school-age children. I listened carefully, because it was clear our young people are growing up today with little understanding of the love of God. So, with great fear and trepidation, but believing, with all our hearts, that God was leading us, I went to the Board and asked them if we could start a school program. We hired someone to write the material. Of course, many details had to be worked through; however, the overwhelming response to the concept of such a program has been very positive.

We all can see the value of training Christian young people to lead the next generation; to me, it's one of the most exciting of all BSF developments. Last year we added level four. The program has been successful, especially in the Men's Classes. This past year there were 16,000 children enrolled; just think of how this might affect the future of our world.

Of course we have much greater numbers than that in the Preschool Program, but the children who come in the Preschool Program want to continue. It will take only a few more years and we will have even more in the School Program. The School Program is meeting the need today for our class members' children, and all of this is by the grace of God.[2]

## The Launch

Rosemary took the initial proposal for a Grade School Program to the BSF Board meeting in September 1995; BSF piloted the program in January 1996—just four months later. She suggested a three-level program—one for first and second graders, another for grades three and four, and the next level for fifth- and sixth-grade students. In her column for the Christmas 1995 newsletter, Rosemary announced the new program.

### ⌒ FROM THE DIRECTOR
*Rosemary Jensen:*

One of the commands the Lord gives us is to train our children in the ways they are to be fitted for heaven (Deuteronomy 6:7 and Proverbs 22:6). We in BSF believe that God is leading us to take a greater role in the training of today's children. Therefore, the exciting news I want to share with you is that beginning next class year we plan by God's grace to start a program for the grade-school children of parents in our evening classes. The program will be carried out in both Men's and Women's Evening Classes. As you know, Preschool Programs are operating at present in Women's Day Classes. The new grade-school program is a huge undertaking, and we will need plenty of help; but if God is in this, as we believe He is, it will help to meet the needs of children and parents alike.[3]

At the January 1996 BSF Board meeting, Janice Pinckney and Daphne Terrell gave a report on the new Grade School Program, which they were about to launch. The San Antonio West Evening Women's Class had been chosen for the pilot, due to begin later that month. Their report to the Board said the following:

Each class will have two leaders and all leaders will have a background check. The program will include a hymn time with some teaching on hymns, group participation, a Bible story, a short lecture with points of application, a highlighted Scripture verse, and, for the fifth- and sixth-grade levels, some homiletics. There will be a page to take home with questions and a lesson for the following week.

Some people thought it wasn't realistic to introduce homiletics to grade school children. But in an interview years later Janice Pinckney remembered the successful execution of those plans, saying: "We introduced the 3rd and 4th graders to homiletics by explaining that it was a systematic way to study the Bible by outlining passages and analyzing the content of it. We would ask them, 'What is this about, if you had to condense it down to a few words? And what does this mean to you? Now what are the main principles or truths that are in this passage? Then how does that apply to your life?'

"A lot of adults don't like to do homiletics, because it means they have to think. But we found that kids ate it up and did great! They were challenged. They got to do something that their parents were doing. And a lot of the time they did it better."[4]

By May 1996, the Administration Division had approximately

fifteen thousand children registered for the launch of the School Program that fall. Children's Supervisors of Day Classes offered their expertise, through workshops, to the Class Administrators of the Evening Classes, who had to provide classes for children and recruit Children's Leaders. Sixty-nine Children's Area Coordinators (CACs) attended a special two-day session held in March to train for their role in the School Program.

The May 1997 BSF Magazine recounted some of the practical aspects of seeing the School Program through its first full year.

### ∽ IN OTHERS' WORDS
*Susy Harbick:*

> When word came from headquarters that the next generation was to be reached through the School Program, beginning with *Israel and the Minor Prophets,* everyone in the Administration Division began counting. How many classrooms were available if discussion groups were arranged differently? How many chairs needed to be added as Children's Leaders joined the leadership meeting? More leader's materials, name tags, "Come and See" invitations, registration cards, and "Welcome to BSF" brochures needed to be ordered, and registration cards for children and forms for the School Program needed to be produced.[5]

Adding materials for an additional fifteen thousand young class members created new challenges for the Printing and Production Division, as these two staff members recount.

### ∽ IN OTHERS' WORDS
*Anna Kingsbury and Eileen Smith:*

> A new program! Stop the presses! No, *start* the presses! But first, . . . What? How many? What colors for the three levels of study questions, for Homiletics, for levels two and three, for administrative forms and leadership training manual?
>
> In the press, there must be a way to easily differentiate School Program materials from Preschool materials. Then, too,

the questions for the several levels must be easily distinguished from one another. Color-coding—that will work. Many people have prayed for this program for a long time. Surely the response will be enthusiastic and bountiful, so we'll provide for an average of thirty students and leaders for each level for every Evening Class. The questions must be previewed through actual use; the headquarters staff will use the questions for level 3 for their daily prayers.[6]

Here's how that time was remembered by the person who served as head of the Children's Division when the School Program was introduced.

### ◯ IN OTHERS' WORDS
*Janice Pinckney:*

For years, I would receive letters from people, especially working mothers and single moms, asking, "Can't BSF have something for our school-age children?" I would write back to say, "That's a splendid idea. But our program is for preschoolers and that wouldn't work in the evening late hours. We have no way of training leaders for that time." I had many reasons why a School Program would not work.

I still remember, following a Board meeting, Rosemary telling the Division Heads some of the decisions the Board had made, when she said, "We are going to start a School Program." She almost had to scoop me up off the floor.

We did a pilot in one Evening Women's Class here in San Antonio, starting in the winter of 1996. The next fall, all our Evening Classes had a School Program. Traditionally, women, not men, teach children. When we announced that the School Program would be in all the Evening Classes, a significant portion of our Men's Classes said, "We did not hear you correctly. Who is doing this in our class?"

It was a major hurdle for them to understand that the men in those classes would be teaching the children. They saw it as an unrealistic expectation. Unprofitable. Unnecessary. Just not workable.

I can count on the fingers of one hand the classes that have that attitude now. I have had Teaching Leaders come up to me and say, "I don't know if you remember me, but back in 1996 I was saying that this absolutely would not work. I have come around 180 degrees. This is the greatest thing that has ever happened to our class."[7]

## The Benefits

One of those skeptical but willing Teaching Leaders told how the School Program was initiated in his Danville, California, evening class for men.

### ⌒ IMPACT STORY

*Norm McBride:*

One of our most difficult times was when BSF decided they were going to have a school-age program. We had many leaders, probably thirty-five guys at our Saturday morning leaders' meeting. You know how people are—"Don't change nothing. Leave it alone." I listened to the objections for a while, then I said, "Look, we are going to do this and there're no ifs, ands, or buts about it. It's needed." As it turned out, I believe the School Program was one of the great blessings of BSF.

God led me to choose Herb Hong as the Children's Supervisor. Herb had four boys, was a strong Christian and well organized. He's a strong guy—kind, but definitely strong. The guys we asked agreed to be trained as Children's Leaders, but some of them went with trepidation and doubts.

We had the lessons and all the tools. One of the things that BSF did right was the training. I went through the training. Those kids were there from seven to nine in the evening, and then some of them had to ride an hour home. They were getting to bed at ten o'clock on a school night, and they had a BSF lesson every week on top of all their school homework, but God just blessed and blessed.

One of our Children's Leaders was Ken Cook, a great big ox of a guy who had been a wild man—into drugs and alcohol—before he came to know the Lord in BSF. He had been a Discussion Leader and then a Children's Leader.

One Saturday at leaders' meeting he said, "Let me tell you about these kids and how well they learn." He went through *faith* and *sanctification* and *glorification* and eight or nine other phrases that were in our lessons. Words that if you asked the average adult Christian, they couldn't tell you. But these fifth and sixth graders defined these things, no problem.

One of the benefits of the School Program was that fathers were responsible for helping their kids with their lessons. What we saw, then, was a growth in the dads while they were helping their kids.[8]

Carolyn Edwards and her husband, Charles, TLs in Indiana, soon saw cross-generational benefits of the new School Program.

### ᴄᴥ IMPACT STORY
*Carolyn Edwards:*

The new School Program was the greatest thing BSF had done. When we were instructed on how it would work, I admit that I thought, *There is no way these little first graders are going to be able to handle these books like regular lessons.* Much to my delight, they not only grasped the ideas but they also were the ones influencing their mothers or their grandmothers so much. And then to see the men working with children was absolutely the greatest blessing in the world.

We had one man who played the piano for Charles's Men's Class. When his kids were grown and gone, he stayed to play the piano. Then he started bringing his grandkids—here was this grandfather bringing these little kids. It's a fantastic program.

The kids so often are the ones who are caught up in it and encourage the parents to stay put in their class and not leave. Instead of the parents pushing the kids to come to class each week, it's often the kids saying to the parents, "Well, I don't care if you don't have your lesson done, we've got to go!"

One group from the next county over would carpool with their moms to come to our Evening Class. They would practice homiletics on the way—and did them in rap. Adults would complain about homiletics and say, "That's too hard." The kids were having a ball with it.

My own enjoyment of the process goes back to Pearl Hamilton because she always did her homiletics in alliteration. Since that's how she taught me to outline a passage, I found it easy to think through my words and so often it came out that way. And the ten-word summary sentence was a fun thing to come up with. All in all it was a good learning system for adults and for kids.[9]

### ⟿ IMPACT STORY

*Shirley Mills:*

One of our headquarters IT guys is a Children's Leader, teaching level two, which is third and fourth grades. He tells about a boy who had been in his class several years ago. When the boy's father was asked to be a Children's Leader, he told his son, "I don't know about teaching children. I would have to teach them homiletics, and I don't even know how to do homiletics."

The little boy said, "Dad, I can teach you how to do homiletics; I've been doing it for three years."[10]

When Rollin Mann was the Assistant Supervisor for the Children's Department in Glendale, California, their average attendance for schoolchildren was fifty-six. His wife, Marion, had been a TL for thirty-three years.

## ⌒⊙ IN OTHERS' WORDS

*Rollin and Marion Mann:*

*Rollin:* Children's classes add new life to the Evening Classes. The most significant thing Rosemary did was introduce the School Program.

*Marion:* We put a title on men, saying they are supposed to be the "spiritual leaders" of their families, but most men don't know how and therefore they avoid that. The School Program gave them the tools to take up that leadership. The husband can take the children to class, and then they have homework to do together—something concrete, something specific. That makes a huge difference.

If she had to choose, a woman would rather have her husband go to BSF and drop out herself than the other way around. You cannot imagine how many women find that husbands' taking their children to BSF introduces a huge difference in their family.

*Rollin:* Men's Classes have actually increased because of the School Program. The Evening Women's Classes, too.

But it puts a strain on leadership. As a Teaching Leader, before the School Program started, I had fifteen discussion groups with fifteen Discussion Leaders. But, with the addition of school-age children, we also need two leaders for every children's class, plus the other staff. We have five children's classes right now, so that's ten more leaders we have to recruit. It's tough enough to get guys out on a Tuesday night, and to get them to do their homework, and then to have them come out on Saturday morning for leaders' meeting. When you think about it, the commitment to Bible Study Fellowship is really a commitment.

As far as I'm concerned, the school leaders work harder than the regular Discussion Leaders. They have to prepare their own lessons. Each class has to have someone to lecture each week and the teacher's alternate weeks.[11]

Classes in Africa faced unique challenges with their School Programs, but they also reaped unique benefits. In the May 1997 Newsletter, BSF's Africa Division Head reported on the beginnings of the School Program there.

### ⌒ In Others' Words
*Susan Crawford:*

For most African children in the School Program, English is their second or third language. In one class the children eagerly share their answers by candlelight, because the electricity is off most nights.

Since many churches in Africa do not have Sunday school classes, the School Program fills a great void. Parents are excited to know their children are capable of understanding and articulating spiritual truths. Men are even willing to do something "culturally different" in bringing their sons and daughters to class and in becoming Children's Leaders.

Children are excited because they are encouraged to express their opinions, think about issues, and apply what they learn at home and in school. Involving children is an approach different from that used in most schools in Africa. They learn about the character of God and how to define issues such as sin, faith, prayer, judgment, and repentance.[12]

Children in the BSF School Program in Europe seemed to enjoy homiletics as much as children in the United States did—according to the report from the Europe Division Head at the time the School Program started.

### ✑ Impact Story
*Ann Colmer:*

In Europe, a large percentage of children know nothing of God or Jesus Christ other than to use the names as swearwords. In the United Kingdom, about 90 percent of young people are untouched by the church. In the light of these facts, we praise God that many thousands of preschool children have been grounded in God's Word through the Preschool Program and now for the opportunity for all six- to eleven-year-olds to attend the School Program. In this division we now have only two Evening Classes, but our small beginning has been an encouragement.

Most of the children have all their questions completed each week and are keen to share their answers. They enjoy the fun ways of memorizing Scripture and are beginning to sing some hymns from memory.

The children enjoy homiletics, which they refer to as "hieroglyphics." Leaders have remarked on the lovely way the children have answered concerning the attributes of God.[13]

## The Vision

In 1998, just two years after the School Program began, BSF added Level 4 classes for grades seven and eight. And two years after that, in 2000, the Senior Level began for the four high school grades. BSF's offerings for all age levels were complete—for boys and girls, men and women, from the preschool years until the end of life. The School Program had filled in the last glaring age gap.

At the end of its first year, Rosemary shared her ongoing vision for the School Program.

### ⌒ FROM THE DIRECTOR
*Rosemary Jensen:*

"And I will do whatever you ask in my name, so that the Son may bring glory to the Father" (John 14:13).

A few years ago when we believed Jesus meant this verse for BSF and began to ask for a school program, we knew He would hear our prayers, but we had no idea how quickly He would put an excellent program together. In short, the school program has been enormously successful. We want you to know of a few ways that the Father is glorified by answering our prayers made in Jesus' name.

Over 14,000 children studied the Bible in this new program this year. Some of these children received Christ as Savior and Lord. All of them received uncalculated knowledge of God, His plan for the world, and His relationship with human beings. They learned to study, to think, to sing great hymns, to memorize Scripture, and to organize their time. God is glorified as young hearts and minds seek after Him.

Thousands of parents all over the world praise God for what their children are learning in their classes about the Lord and His ways. These parents are also pleased as they study lessons with their children and grow together in love and harmony. God is glorified as parents express thanksgiving and praise for what He is doing in their families' lives.

Our prayers should be that the Lord will be glorified through the lives of these young people who are being trained today to be Christian leaders for tomorrow. The future of the church will be in their hands. What an awesome responsibility we have, but at the same time, what a privilege![14]

# Chapter 29

# NEW IN THE CYCLE

Introducing lesson series on Moses and Romans

During the early years of Bible Study Fellowship, Miss Johnson wrote five series of lessons:

- John
- Matthew
- Israel and the Minor Prophets
- The Life and Letters of Paul
- Genesis

Each series consisted of thirty-two weekly lessons, which took class members one school year to complete.

BSF also had three series of pilot lessons:

- *Colossians*
- *Ephesians*
- *Philippians*

These were each taught for five to six weeks, and they were taught months before launching the class as a way of recruiting class members and creating or gauging interest for the class.

The lessons were revised over the years. But most changes

were minor, usually just a matter of improving clarity. Questions were sometimes reworded to make them more relevant or understandable. And some of Wetherell Johnson's original notes were shortened or sharpened in focus. Yet, the basic BSF class materials remained essentially unchanged from the time they were written in the 1950s and 1960s until the 1990s.

In 1992, BSF updated two lesson series—*Israel and the Minor Prophets* and *Matthew*. The Board also okayed changing the Scripture references from King James Version to the more accessible New International Version. Of course that required significant revisions not only in lesson notes and discussion questions but also in peripheral materials, such as the Home Discussion pages and the children's materials.

By anyone's standards, those changes combined didn't add up to a major change, even with the editing done to lessons over the first three to four decades of BSF's history. However, unprecedented things were about to happen that would become major developments in organizational history.

## The Life of Moses

As usual in this stage of the ministry's history, the latest change began with Rosemary Jensen.

### ⌒ FROM THE DIRECTOR
*Rosemary Jensen:*

In the early nineties I said to the Lord something a little dangerous: I wanted Him to use me, in the years that I had left to live, to do His will for BSF, no matter what it cost me.

Some months later at a retreat in Spokane, I had a little "alone time" in my room. As I was praying, the Lord put the words in my mind that He was going to do a new thing in BSF. And some things I would have to put aside in my personal life in order to do this.

I didn't know what this new thing might be, but I went home and eliminated a couple of things that were taking up time in my life. I wanted to make room for this new thing. I said nothing to anyone about this, but there was just this sense of excitement in me as I waited to see what it was going to be. A few months after that, I knew what it was.

At the next Board meeting, with a sense of real inadequacy, I proposed to our Board that we add a new study into the BSF curriculum. I explained that our vision statement spoke of two goals for those involved in Bible Study Fellowship: one is a vibrant relationship with God, and the other is training and leadership.

So I said, "What better way for people to understand what it means to have a vibrant relationship with God than to study the Pentateuch, the whole sacrificial system and the law. How can anyone understand our relationship with God until they grasp these things? And what better way to train people to be leaders than to give them the example of the greatest leader who ever lived in history?"

God is wonderful to surprise us sometimes. When I presented this to the BSF Board, immediately they said, "Go for it!"[1]

At the outset, the thought of adding another series seemed a daunting task, and not just because of all the work involved. Those first five series, written by Wetherell Johnson, had meant so much to so many people over the years that adding a new series *not* written by her seemed to many, if not quite sacrilege, at least a departure from the "official" BSF material.

To counter such concerns, Dr. James Montgomery Boice and Dr. Walter C. Kaiser, both widely known and highly respected members of the BSF Board, were contracted to work on the new lessons. Dr. Boice wrote and Dr. Kaiser edited. Rosemary Jensen worked on the questions, and other staff members created the Home Discussion pages, children's materials, and teaching aids for Teaching Leaders. The headquarters staff used the new discussion questions in their morning prayer time, and changes or clarifications were made as needed. The new series of lessons took a full year to prepare.

In the May 1994 *BSF Newsletter,* Rosemary introduced the planned change to BSF class members around the world.

### ᒧ FROM THE DIRECTOR
*Rosemary Jensen:*

"See, I am doing a new thing! Now it springs up; do you not perceive it?" (Isaiah 43:19).

What's happening in BSF?

In person, on the telephone, or in correspondence we hear that question almost every day at headquarters. There are many God-directed "happenings" I could mention, but probably the question most of you have is, "What's happening with the new Moses study?"

I am involved up to my ears in teaching *The Life of Moses* in one of our BSF classes in San Antonio. *The Life of Moses* is the study we believed was needed to complete our understanding of a vital section of the Bible. The Law and the sacrificial system are essential to understanding the gospel of Jesus Christ. Certainly Moses as the greatest leader in history should be studied in detail by anyone who wants to lead in the cause of Christ in the world. Most of all, the Pentateuch gives, as nowhere else in Scripture, knowledge of the personal, yet holy, God in His glory. All the material is new and done by BSF for BSF—with God receiving the glory. It was decided that I should teach the study in one of the classes this year as a pilot and that all other classes would have it next year.

We are thrilled with the materials the Lord is enabling us to prepare and hope you will find the study instructive and helpful in your own life.[2]

Jane Roach, as BSF's Training Division Head, helped implement the new study. She and other BSF staff members attended the San Antonio class when Rosemary Jensen piloted *The Life of Moses* study.

### ᒧ IN OTHERS' WORDS
*Jane Roach:*

Our vision statement is to have "a passion to commit without reservation to lead in the cause of Christ in the world." Rosemary has that passion.

Writing that new study, *The Life of Moses,* was huge. Rosemary's passion was that people would understand the sacrificial system of the Old Testament and how it pointed to Christ. The new study provided a missing link in people's understanding of the New Testament.[3]

A year after *The Life of Moses* had been taught in every BSF class around the world, Rosemary Jensen gave this report on the study's success.

### ⌒ FROM THE DIRECTOR
*Rosemary Jensen:*

To God Be the Glory, Great Things He Has Done! Remember what Moses and Miriam sang after crossing the Red Sea? In Exodus 15:11, Moses puts into words these thoughts, "Who among the gods is like you, O LORD? Who is like you—majestic in holiness, awesome in glory, working wonders?"

As we look back over the past year in BSF, we are amazed at the wonders God has done. Surely He should receive the glory! Let me mention only a few of the things He has done for BSF so that you might be informed and rejoice with us in His amazing grace.

This past year began with great anticipation over the newly written study of *The Life of Moses.* There was great excitement over the way the new study provided for greater participation in discussion groups. Many lives were changed because of applying the truths taught. A large number of people wrote to the headquarters expressing how much more understanding of the Person of God they received from the questions and notes. For this we say, TO GOD BE THE GLORY.

We expected the new study to bring back many graduates who would want to take *The Life of Moses.* However, not only did the graduates return but also many new people came—over

200,000 members in all. We experienced a 37 percent increase in enrollment over May 1994. For this we say, TO GOD BE THE GLORY.[4]

By the fall of 1995, just months after the completion of the newest BSF series, Rosemary Jensen reported to the Board that she had received hundreds of letters from class members telling of changed lives because of the study of *The Life of Moses*. During that Board meeting, Mrs. Kitty Magee said, "During the past year, for the first time in most of their lives, BSF class members in Africa began to learn to know the character and person of God. They also discovered that the life of Moses is relevant today."

Soon BSF was considering another new year-long study. But the impetus for that addition came only in part from the success of *The Life of Moses*. There was also a sense of the deep and urgent need.

## Romans

Each spring, the headquarters staff conducts special weekend retreats for all BSF class leaders in three North American areas. Each fall, similar retreats are held for leaders of international classes. That means that once during the course of a three-year cycle, every area in North America and the rest of the world has its own retreat where local class leaders can interact with and be trained by headquarters staff. They can meet, be inspired by, and learn from BSF leaders on the front line of classes around the world.

It was out of these interactions that the idea for the next study series arose.

### ⟢ IN OTHERS' WORDS
*Jane Roach:*

During a three-year retreat series, we conducted a survey to see what our class leadership knew about doctrine and church history. We were astounded to find that they didn't know much. Those findings became a big part of the motivation for developing yet another new year-long study series—this one an in-depth study of the apostle Paul's letter to the Romans. Of course, any new separate study on Romans would also entail a significant revision of our existing series on *The Life and Letters of Paul,* which already devoted a number of weeks to Romans. When we took out those lessons, we had a big gap in that series that needed to be filled with lessons on other letters. And since the added letters weren't all Paul's writings, we changed the name of the series from *The Life and Letters of Paul* to *The Acts of the Apostles.*

Those revisions meant we had to also revise the children's lessons and Home Discussion pages and all the accompanying materials. And we had to do all that before we even began the entirely new *Romans* study, which was an even bigger undertaking. Writing *Romans* lessons for two-year-olds was a challenge. But we got to see God's faithfulness. If we'd been thinking about how hard it was going to be, we might never have done it. I'm so grateful that Rosemary doesn't think like that. She just says, "This is what God wants us to do, so now we're going to do it."[5]

As Jane explained, adding the study on Romans resulted in a cascade of other changes. New lessons had to be written for the renamed *Acts of the Apostles* series—covering Hebrews, 1 and 2 Peter, James, and Jude. The pilot series on *Ephesians* was retired. Again, Dr. Boice and Dr. Kaiser were contracted to write those new lessons.

The revised series, *The Acts of the Apostles,* was piloted during 1996–97 and taught to all BSF classes during the 1997–98 school year. Then in 1998–99, the new year-long study of Romans was piloted, again with Rosemary Jensen teaching the material in her original BSF class in San Antonio.

At the end of the *Romans* pilot year, a special Romans Institute was planned at a large conference center and resort in San Antonio. According to notes from the April 1999 Board meeting, "Mrs. Jensen said that the cost of the institute is now well-funded. Dr. Boice and Dr. Kaiser will be speakers and Mrs. Jensen will also speak at the institute. Dr. Hastings will give a talk on the grace of God to BSF in the first forty years. All Teaching Leaders are required to attend except in case of emergencies."

The Romans Institute indeed turned out to be an important milestone in the history of Bible Study Fellowship. An eventual headquarters report stated that 991 Teaching Leaders from around the world, plus 75 Area Advisors, 35 staff, and 6 Board members attended the institute. It was during her talks there that Rosemary Jensen provided even more background and motivation for the new study.

### ⌁ FROM THE DIRECTOR
*Rosemary Jensen:*

Our doctrine determines our behavior. We behave as we behave because we believe as we believe. I was concerned that, even in BSF, we might be teaching a lot of *application* of the Bible (the how-to), but not enough of the doctrine that literally changes our lives. Some of us became keenly aware that, although BSF was presenting the gospel, our members were often perceiving it in different ways.

Since BSF is interdenominational, we wanted to be careful to present to our class members what the *Bible* says that the gospel is. And where is the gospel better explained than in the book of Romans?

In Romans we learn about the grace of God. We learn about ourselves. We learn about the world in which we live. We learn about our need, our desperate need, to be saved from the wrath of God, and we learn about God's plan to save us. We learn the truth about Jesus Christ, His love for us, His atoning work on our behalf, and His open return. In Romans we see God's plan for all the world, for all history.

What better time than today to make the truth of the Bible known and to take it into this world of lies and confusion. Romans is the truth. It's truth because the Bible says so.

Romans teaches about God, especially His sovereignty, His

grace, His love, His glory. Romans teaches the high view of God.

At the Board level, we made the decision to write the material and to teach the book of Romans.

Some of you have asked if I enjoyed teaching Romans. I want to tell you it's the most enjoyable thing I've ever done in my life. God, in His grace to me through your prayers, kept me perfectly healthy the whole year—thank you for praying!

Now, I will not pretend that it wasn't hard to teach Romans, but you know, as I know, that the harder we have to study something—the more it takes from us—the more we get out of it. I want to tell you that it has changed my life.[6]

For Bible Study Fellowship, the 1990s ended as the 1980s had begun—still under the energetic leadership of Rosemary Jensen, still growing, and with the Lord's help, still doing new things. Membership had mushroomed to well over the 200,000. More than 64,000 kids were enrolled in Children's Programs. The 1999–2000 class year began with 971 classes.

And just over the horizon of a new millennium, another major change was coming.

# Chapter 30

# A FAREWELL

Rosemary Jensen retires

W hen Rosemary Jensen took over as Executive Director of Bible Study Fellowship in 1980, she had thought fifteen years would be the length of her service. But when she reached that milestone, in 1995, *The Life of Moses* had just been introduced and plans were underway to add the *Romans* study. The organization was in the midst of major changes, and clearly much remained for Rosemary to do. Neither she nor the Board wanted her to retire at age sixty-five.

Thoughts of retirement, however, were on Rosemary's mind. During the January 1996 BSF Board meeting, she proposed a tentative class schedule for the coming years as the revised *Acts of the Apostles* and then the *Romans* study were introduced into the cycle. As she laid out her plan on a five-year calendar, she reminded the Board that she would turn seventy, the mandatory retirement age for BSF, in just four years.

As the Board and Rosemary began to consider a transition of leadership, the spring of 2000 seemed to them a logical time. Rosemary would then be seventy years old and celebrating her twentieth year as Executive Director. She taught the pilot class for the *Romans* study in 1998–99 and conducted the Romans Institute in July 1999. Then she saw her last major initiative to completion with the worldwide introduction of *Romans,* during the 1999–2000 class year.

The search for Rosemary's successor began well in advance of the target date for her retirement. The Board asked their executive committee to serve as a search committee and to discuss the qualifications they would look for in the organization's third Executive Director. They also asked their second Executive Director to recommend three names to be considered for the short list of possible replacements.

## Repositioning Rafiki

Many details needed to be worked out with the cooperative relationship between Bible Study Fellowship International and the Rafiki Foundation. This clarification was complicated by the fact that, while Rosemary intended to retire from BSF, she anticipated devoting more time and attention to the Rafiki Foundation for as long as she had energy to do so.

The new Executive Director of BSF and Rosemary Jensen would have to deal with the parameters of the relationship between the two organizations, which is why the BSF Board negotiated and signed a contractual agreement with Rafiki.

According to the negotiations, TWO (The World Outreach)— the division of BSF that provided personnel for Rafiki projects— would be transferred from BSF International to the Rafiki Foundation. The missionaries and their support funds would simply be moved from one organization to the other. The BSF Board also agreed to provide ongoing financial support for some Rafiki development projects, to make a sizable contribution for funding of Rafiki's administration costs, and to cover expenses for Rosemary's international travel.

Rafiki also sought BSF Board permission to purchase five acres of headquarters property on which to build their own headquarters. But rather than sell property, the board agreed to build, at BSF expense, a second headquarters complex near one corner of the San Antonio property and lease that facility to Rafiki.

The eventual contract between the two ministries spelled out other details and allowed either party to dissolve the agreement if it no longer fit either organization's needs or goals. But the primary intent of the covenant was to reaffirm and formalize BSF and Rafiki's intentions to maintain a cooperative and supportive relationship.

## Announcing the Change

By their April 1999 meeting, the search committee received the Board's approval of a revised plan. The search committee's choice for Executive Director would be presented for final approval at the January 2000 Board meeting. Rosemary Jensen would continue her regular BSF duties, including speaking at the spring retreats held through the end of the 1999–2000 class year, when the new Executive Director would officially take office on July 1, 2000.

As had been the case before Wetherell Johnson's retirement, there was speculation throughout the organization (most of it unvoiced) during Rosemary's final years as to who might become the next Executive Director of BSF International. Once again the selection process proceeded with prayerful, thoughtful discretion.

The Board's decision caught many people by surprise. Indeed, most Board members didn't know the search committee's final decision until the January 2000 Board meetings in Chicago. (For details on that announcement, the decision process, and background of their choice, read chapter 31.)

Only then did plans for the transition become official and public. In Chicago, Rosemary presented a letter of resignation, asking the Board to accept her retirement as Executive Director of BSF International, effective June 30, 2000. She thanked them for their wise direction, warm encouragement, and loving support extended to her the past twenty years. The Board, in its turn, expressed deep gratitude for the leadership Mrs. Jensen had given to BSF International.

When Rosemary returned to San Antonio after that Board meeting, she gathered the headquarters staff to announce her retirement. At the same time, she informed them of the Board's unanimous choice of Mrs. Jean Nystrand to follow her as BSF's Executive Director. Then she emailed a letter to the Area Advisors and posted a letter to BSF Teaching Leaders announcing the change. BSF leaders then heard the news before coming to the retreats that spring, when Rosemary publicly introduced the incoming Executive Director to the entire BSF family. She asked them to support Jean in the same way they had supported her for the preceding twenty years.

Months later, in the May 2000 *BSF Magazine*, Rosemary bid a fond farewell in a letter to BSF class members around the world.

Jean Nystrand and Rosemary Jensen

## ⌒ FROM THE DIRECTOR
*Rosemary Jensen:*

This is the last letter I will write to you as Executive Director of BSF International. It comes with some sadness, but with a great deal of joy. My sadness comes from knowing that I will not be in close touch with you after June 30, 2000. God has given me a great love for BSFers and I have enjoyed personal interaction with many of you for more than twenty years; thus I am grieving over the closure of what have been the most thrilling and meaningful years of my life.

But at this time there is also much joy in my heart. First, I believe that the various tasks God called me to do in BSF have been finished this year with the completion of the Senior Level in the School Program and the *Romans* study. Twenty years ago I was keenly aware that I was not capable of improving BSF in any way and certainly not capable of leading such a wonderful organization. However, by God's grace the various tasks that He had ordained for me to do are finished, and I was able to enjoy every minute of it!

Second, God has prepared and chosen the perfect successor

as Executive Director of BSF. Her name is Jean Nystrand, and you can read about her in this magazine. I am thrilled with the privilege of supporting and encouraging Jean in this new role. I know that you will also support and encourage her in the years ahead.

We know that God's Word changes the world as He changes individual hearts. The strong stand for truth that BSF has established will be maintained through Mrs. Nystrand.

Third, God, again in His grace, has prepared a way for me to continue to support BSF by working full-time as the Executive Director of The Rafiki Foundation, Inc. As you know, Rafiki is the sending agency for BSF leaders who go to developing countries to teach BSF classes and to contribute to these countries by working primarily in Rafiki Women's Centers (RWCs) or in Rafiki Children's Centers (RCCs). Although I have been leading Rafiki alongside BSF for thirteen years, the magnitude of both organizations is now of such proportions that it is necessary to divide the workload.

My heartfelt thanks go to you class members, the class leaders, the area personnel, the headquarters staff, and the Board of Directors for the love each has extended to me during my twenty-year tenure as Executive Director of BSF International. I urge you all to continue to study and apply the Scriptures knowing that our gracious God will reward you richly.[1]

## Remarks about Rosemary

The greatest legacy of Rosemary's leadership may be seen in the lives and heard in the words of those who worked for, with, and alongside her—not just in the San Antonio headquarters, but also around the world.

There was an inside joke among many of those who knew her best and loved her most. With apologies to Bill Bright and his *Four Spiritual Laws,* many BSFers were known to chuckle and offer their own paraphrase: "God loves you, and Rosemary has a plan for your life." When asked about that statement, one longtime staff person laughed and protested: "No, no, no! We used to say, 'God loves you and has a plan for your life. But Rosemary knows what it is!'"

The serious point behind these humorous statements is best expressed in the lives and words of the following members of Rosemary Jensen's BSF family.

### ∼◯ IN OTHERS' WORDS

*Susy Harbick:*

One of the things Ernest Hastings said at Rosemary's retirement was that she had this gift for spotting people God could use, challenging people to do more than they thought they could do, and then encouraging them to do it. She got that from her experience, or her training as a teacher, or her training as an occupational therapist, or her time on the mission field, or her time everywhere. God has given her that gift and she uses it. The Holy Spirit provides discernment in her that just sees to the heart of an issue. And she is courageous enough in the Lord to say what He convinces her needs to be said. Rosemary simply says, "Here is an opportunity I'm presenting to you. Have you thought about this? I can see you doing this in this place for the Lord." She just lays out the possibilities.

Rosemary is a godly woman who has a passion for people within the body, within the church, to be out doing what the church needs to do. She nailed me on that all the time. She would ask, "Susy, why are you doing such-and-such? Is that really eternally beneficial to kingdom work?"

That kind of leadership is God-given. Rosemary prays and listens, and God puts it together. God reveals His heart to her and she rises to the occasion. Rarely have I known her to be wrong on this kind of issue.[2]

### ⌒◌ IN OTHERS' WORDS
*Dr. Chuck Musfeldt:*

Rosemary could get your mind straightened out to where you were focusing on God instead of on yourself.

She made sure that she asked good application questions, which in turn taught me that the heart of good Bible teaching is asking those questions. I saw her do it, and I learned to do the same thing. God used those application questions, along with Scripture, to change the lives of men in my class.

Guys would tell me they had ended an affair they were having with their secretary. Or they had quit going to the casino. Or they had moved back home with their wife and kids after being separated. It was wonderful to see God at work, and He certainly gets all the glory.

In 1999 my good friend, mentor, and Area Advisor Bill Edwards died of pancreatic cancer. Rosemary asked me to be Bill's replacement as the Area Advisor for the Men's Classes in Minnesota, Wisconsin, and Illinois. I realized that job was much bigger than me, but that with God's help I could do it.

I'll always be grateful for the way Rosemary challenged me toward leadership. She had a lot of vision and passion, and she instilled that in others.[3]

Ernest Hastings offered a historical view on BSF leadership.

### ⌒◌ IN OTHERS' WORDS
*Dr. Ernest Hastings:*

Rosemary had a larger concept, and BSF will always be indebted to Rosemary for her leadership. Rosemary was God's gift to BSF. When she took over in 1980, BSF was on a plateau. She took it global. And with her organization of things, the Area Advisors and all, she made possible a larger BSF that could go out into the world.[4]

## ⟨∞⟩ IMPACT STORY

*Shirley Mills:*

We were studying the book of Hebrews in *Acts of the Apostles,* when I read the verse in chapter 10 that said, "Here I am, I have come to do Your will." It's Jesus talking to the Father and it's repeated twice. For some reason, God impressed on my heart to pray that prayer. I didn't have a clue what I was praying. I just said, "Here I am, O God. I've come to do your will. I don't know what that means. It might mean not being an Area Advisor anymore. It might mean going overseas and not seeing my grandchildren." I went on and listed all the things I thought it might mean.

That was Monday, December 1, 1997.

On Thursday, December 4, I received a call from Rosemary Jensen asking when my husband, Leo, was retiring.

I told her, "He's thinking of retiring in August 1999."

She said, "Can he retire early?"

"I don't know, Rosemary," I responded. "What's up?"

She went right on. "Well, if he can't retire early, could you live apart?"

Again I replied, "I don't know, Rosemary. What's up?"

She finally said, "Well, I'd like you to come on staff at headquarters. Come take a training course and become the Class Administration Division Head."

"Rosemary," I exclaimed, "I've never worked in class administration. I've been a Discussion Leader, a Teaching Leader, and an Area Advisor."

"I know," she admitted. But she went on to tell me she thought I could do the job.

As she talked, I remembered that prayer I prayed just three days earlier. So I said to Rosemary, "Let me tell you what God did on Monday, when I was studying Hebrews 10."

Right away I felt, *Yes, I'm supposed to do this.* My heart had been prepared three days earlier. So I called my husband to tell him about the call and the prayer I'd prayed.

Immediately he told me, "Call Rosemary back and tell her yes. I'll work on retiring early."[5]

## Farewell to a Beloved Staff

The love, respect, and appreciation the BSF staff had for their Executive Director was certainly reciprocated, as evidenced by the following farewell comments Rosemary made to her staff just ten days before her official retirement.

> God has helped me. I have no question about that. I have the perfect staff. This staff works like a well-oiled machine. I don't mean that we don't run into problems. We do. Sometimes buildings aren't finished or equipment breaks. But there is a huge amount of love here for one another.
>
> There is an appreciation I have that I cannot describe. But there is a way we work together that makes things smooth and wonderful. What I have wanted to do is to be able to hand over this beautiful organization of people, which is you—it's not just the work, it's the people—to Jean. I wanted to say, "Here's a gift. Now you take it and do with this organization what God has for you."[6]

# The Third Generation and Beyond
# (2000–2010)

# Chapter 31

# ANOTHER CHANGE OF
# LEADERSHIP

Bible Study Fellowship gets its third Director: Jean Nystrand

At the same Chicago board meeting where Rosemary Jensen officially presented her retirement letter, the search committee presented Mrs. Jean Nystrand's name. She accepted the full Board's subsequent invitation to become the Executive Director of Bible Study Fellowship International.

Announcements were made to BSF leaders in various settings and meetings over the next few months. And then, in the May 2000 *BSF Magazine,* by way of a small photo and a brief biography, Jean Nystrand was introduced to BSF class members and leaders around the world. An article said the following:

> Throughout BSF's forty-year history, God has faithfully chosen its leaders. Thus, at the January 2000 meeting of the BSF Board of Directors, Mrs. Jean Nystrand was selected to be the new Executive Director of BSF, beginning July 1, 2000. Jean is a natural for this position and well qualified by her experience and her love for the Lord. She is a native of Elkhart, Indiana, and is married to Dan Nystrand, who is the retired owner/president of a general

construction firm. They have three married children
and eleven grandchildren.

Jean has a degree in English and has been active
in music and Christian education for many years. She
started BSF in 1969 in Elkhart, Indiana, where she
later served as a Teaching Leader and Area Advisor.
She is currently serving as the Division Head for
Europe, Area Advisor for the United Kingdom, and
Teaching Leader for the London Day Women's Class.
We trust that the Lord will cause Jean to take BSF
to greater heights and that she will find great joy in
serving the organization and the Lord. We are sure
that every BSFer will encourage and support her in
her task.[1]

Such a simple introduction to the new Executive Director
must have seemed particularly fitting to those in BSF who knew
Jean Nystrand through her seven years as a Teaching Leader,
her twenty years as an Area Advisor, or in her more recent role as
the Division Head for Europe. Note this reaction to her appointment from one of the BSFers who had known Jean longest.

### ∽ IN OTHERS' WORDS
*Carolyn Edwards:*

Jean Nystrand was a Discussion Leader in northern Indiana the
same time I was a Discussion Leader in Bloomingdale, and I
met her at a retreat, where she helped with the music. Jean was
just one of us.

That's one reason I firmly believe Jean is just the person to
lead this organization at this time and BSF is in great hands. Of
course, God already knew that! So I looked at Jean as the new
Executive Director and I thought, *This is great and God had
already planned it.*[2]

## A New Leader for a New Stage of Growth
The steps the Lord used to bring BSF's third Executive

Director into her new role are best understood as Jean shares her own story of Bible Study Fellowship's effect on her life through the years.

### ⌒ From the Director
*Jean Nystrand:*

I grew up in a strong Christian home and a Bible-believing church. I sat under strong teaching, went to lots of Bible conferences, and thought I knew a lot about the Bible. I always felt drawn to the Bible. I accepted Christ when I was very young because of a Sunday school class. Yet I never developed the discipline of a daily quiet time with God.

I had many facts in my head and I enjoyed studying. I was also very musical and enjoyed playing the piano and organ, and my church let me do that from time to time as a teenager.

Then I went to the University of Illinois for college and got involved right away with a campus ministry group. That broadened my worldview and sharpened my desire to know God. I met my husband at the University of Illinois, and we were married after I'd been there just two years. He graduated and we moved to the Chicago area, where he took a job and we started having children. I had three children in five years, and we plugged back into the church, doing teaching and a lot of musical work.

In 1969, we moved to Elkhart, Indiana. I felt as if we had moved to the end of the world. Our children were nine, eight, and six years old. I had never heard of BSF; there were no classes in the Chicago area at that time. However, God had been already working in my life in ways that I can only describe as a holy discontent. I knew there was something missing in my life. I told God that I really wanted to do whatever I needed to do to get growing in my Christian life. That "whatever" was cleverly disguised as this "life tragedy" of moving away from my friends, beyond the broadcast range of my Christian radio station, and well out of my comfort zone.

In August 1969, after the move, we visited a church in

Elkhart, a rather small congregation where the pastor was very much into the Word. In late October, one of the ladies from that church came to visit. She mentioned a Bible study she attended and asked if I might like to come with her.

My first reaction was, *I know all about the Bible. Why should I go?* But when she said that they were studying *Israel and the Minor Prophets,* I thought, *I don't know a whole lot about the Minor Prophets. I might learn something after all.*

The fact that it was called "Bible Study Fellowship" appealed to me, too, because I was feeling pretty lonesome there in Elkhart and really needed fellowship. So I decided I might as well go, since she invited me.

I sat through the introduction class where they explained what BSF is all about. Then I listened to the lecture. They were studying the life of Solomon. I was wowed. The Bible came alive to me. It was as if this woman teaching that class knew all about me; the applications applied directly to me and spoke to my heart. I took the lesson home and did the entire thing that very night; I was so excited to dig into this study. After that I tried to back off and space out the work over a week like I was supposed to do. That became a great exercise in discipline to make myself do just part of the study each day.

The fact that I had to study the Bible by myself and find my own answers was also very good for me. I was hooked from the start. I loved the study and I loved the way the notes presented the Bible. Before BSF, I had everything that I needed in life—except an intimate relationship with God. That finally came through my involvement with BSF. The study of the Minor Prophets was incredible and made a huge difference in my life. The first time I was invited to attend a leaders retreat, Miss Johnson was the teacher. Miss Johnson had a presence about her. When you got to know her, she was very warm and enjoyed a joke and had a good sense of humor. But when she spoke about the things of the Lord, her demeanor was very commanding. She was winsome but authoritative; you sensed she deserved so much respect.

On Saturday night of my first leaders retreat, Miss Johnson talked about John 12:24 and how, when you have the cross in your life, you cannot go around it; you have to go through it. And Christ is there with you.

At that point, she invited people to pray the prayer that she had prayed when she finally surrendered her life to God. "I am willing, Lord, at whatever cost, for Thy death to be worked out in me, in order that Thy resurrection life may be manifested." I prayed that prayer, and it was a very moving moment. God really touched me.

Jean's life began to change, and her husband eventually got involved with BSF too. She was involved as a class member for several years, then as a Children's Leader for a couple of years. She served as a Discussion Leader for one year.

During this time, a group of about eighty women drove from South Bend to her class in Elkhart. They wanted to start their own class, but they couldn't find a Teaching Leader.

### ⌒ FROM THE DIRECTOR
*Jean Nystrand:*

My TL contacted Miss Johnson about starting a new class in South Bend and recommended me to be the TL. I wrote to Miss Johnson asking for a Teaching Leader application in 1972. Then they sent me an application. When I sent it in, again, I didn't hear anything. I thought, *They don't want me after all. Lord, if that is what You want, that's okay.* The Lord used that as a lesson to teach me dependence on Him and not on myself.

I finally received a letter in January 1973, apologizing that I hadn't received a timely response. And I was invited to an orientation week in April 1973.

At that point, I did not teach a pilot class, like we do now. I just started the South Bend class. We already had the eighty ladies who had been coming from South Bend to Elkhart. Another hundred women showed up for the introduction class on the first day. I didn't have a Class Administrator or a Substitute Teaching Leader at first, but the Lord answered my prayers. Within a month, He provided a Class Administrator.

I taught in South Bend for five years and then the Elkhart class for another two years. I taught all five of our studies—starting with *The Life and Letters of Paul* and right on down the line.

Before BSF, I had taught children and worked some with adults in a Sunday school setting. So teaching BSF was very different and daunting. I loved teaching and I loved talking to my AA about BSF. I'm happiest when I'm studying the Word and learning for myself.

In the late seventies, at a conference in Green Lake, Wisconsin, Miss J took me aside and said, "I have plans for you, Jean. Would you be interested in being an Area Advisor?"

I replied, "Miss Johnson, whatever the Lord wants I'd be happy to do." She left it at that, and it wasn't until months later that I got a phone call from her asking me to come to an Area Advisors' meeting in Oakland.

When I'd first been approached to be an Area Advisor, I thought, *I cannot live without teaching.* Teaching was my first love. But I chose to be obedient, and God gave me the desire to become an Area Advisor. He gave me a satisfaction in being an AA that was exciting.

It's thrilling to see the ripple effects of the ministry when you are visiting sixteen to twenty classes in various places as an Area Advisor. You hear so many stories and realize how many individuals God's Word is transforming; families are changing and people who are trained in BSF are affecting entire churches. That was always exciting for me. BSF experienced tremendous growth in the Midwest during those years, especially in the Chicago area. I would say that the number of classes in our area probably tripled. Not because we were out there beating the bushes; people simply learned about BSF and God drew them to the classes.

I was an Area Advisor for twenty years, until 1998.

Sometimes people would ask, "How long are you going to do this?"

I would tell them, "Until God makes it clear to me that I am supposed to leave."

Dan eventually retired early as head of his construction company and began doing consulting work out of our home. In 1995 he trained to be a Teaching Leader and discovered he really enjoyed it.

In early September I received a phone call from Rosemary informing me that the Board of Directors wanted to strengthen the work in Europe. They wanted someone to be Division Head for Europe and to serve as Area Advisor for the classes in the U.K. Rosemary suggested that Dan could train to be my Area Class Administrator, so we could travel together. It meant moving to England and a four-year commitment. And Rosemary told us she needed to know our answer by Friday.

Dan and I prayed about it, and it was a good exercise in God's leading. I was sure that we could never know by Friday. But the next day, I was doing the first lesson of *The Acts of the Apostles*. I read Acts 1:8, which tells us that we will receive power to be witnesses all over the world. *This is interesting,* I thought. Other things happened that week, and I quickly realized that when God asks you to do something, you certainly can.

We made our decision together, and by Friday we informed Rosemary that we'd be willing to go. God arranged it so that we sold our house and we sold our cars. We had lived in our home for twenty-nine years, and it was truly our family home. That was very emotional.

It wasn't easy to think about leaving our children and our eleven grandchildren to live overseas for four years, but we became more excited about our plans as time went on.

We went to London in 1998, and sometime in July of that year, Rosemary called me to say, "By the way, in addition to being Division Head for Europe and Area Advisor for England, we're going to need you to teach the Day Women's Class in London."

"Rosemary," I said, "I couldn't possibly do all that." But I did as God provided.

England was a wonderful international-living experience. And I had the chance to teach again for two years, which brought me back to my roots and my love of teaching. During the twenty years I'd been an AA, I kept telling people I didn't ever want to forget what it's like to be a Teaching Leader. Teaching that class in London proved a perfect reminder. So that was a real blessing from God.

Amid the excitement and energy of serving in London, I began to sense that a change might be coming. In September 1999, I received a call from Rosemary, who said, "I have Dr. Ernest Hastings here with me." And she turned the phone over to him.

Dr. Hastings informed me that Rosemary had submitted her resignation, that the Executive Committee of the Board was conducting a search for her successor, and that I was one of the people who had been recommended. He asked, "Would you be willing to pray about becoming the new Executive Director?"

I told him I wasn't at all sure they had the right person. That I did not see myself as the visionary that Rosemary was.

Dr. Hastings replied, "We are not looking for a Rosemary; we are looking for the next Director."

So I agreed to pray about it.

When Rosemary got back on the phone, I asked her *how* to pray about it.

Rosemary said, "You need to love BSF, and you need to want to do the job."

Loving BSF was a no-brainer, but wanting to do the job was challenging. I didn't feel adequate at all, but there was a growing desire to do the job.

Dan and I prayed about it, and God gave me the verse of Psalm 32:8, "I will instruct you and teach you in the way you should go." I agreed to be interviewed by the Executive Committee. We had to be secretive about it; we could not tell anyone. We flew to the States and met with the Executive

Committee. Later that day, after much prayer, the committee recommended me for a vote of the full Board at their meeting two months later.

We went back to England and waited—still unable to say anything to anyone. In January 2000, I flew to Chicago, where I was introduced and then interviewed by the whole Board.

Once the meeting ended, the word went out. Rosemary was free to tell staff and anyone else. But I returned to London until mid-April. Then the first week of May, we moved to headquarters in San Antonio. The staff was wonderful in helping me adjust to the routine of the job. And God provided all that I needed.[3]

## The Board's Perspective

The longtime secretary of the BSF Board gives this insight into the executive committee's thoughts and procedures during its search for an Executive Director.

### ⟳ IN OTHERS' WORDS

*Suzanne Sloan:*

During Rosemary's tenure, there was an explosion of growth, with so many new things going on: the Children's Program expanded, the Evening Classes, the new studies, Rafiki, and more. So much had been happening that we felt, when she retired, what we needed most was a time of stabilization and consolidation. We were more concerned about maintaining excellence than doing many innovative things. We needed to make sure that the things that had been put in place in the recent years would be maintained.

So we weren't looking for a visionary, although you always want a leader to have enough of a vision to be able to move forward. But we felt the Board could provide a lot of that necessary vision. We were looking for a strong organizer and administrator, someone who could critique and tweak the different programs we already had. That's what we were looking for, and that's what we found in Jean.

Following someone who had led any organization for twenty years can be a daunting challenge. We knew it would require a special type of person. But we covered our decision in prayer. And so many things about Jean appealed to us. She really had the complete package of experience as well as a deep spirituality. We believed she had the kind of personality that would make the staff comfortable. She had a quiet, even nature, and at the same time she was very, very strong. The kind of pragmatic person who really thinks things through carefully. We expected her to help Bible Study Fellowship to stay focused on what our mission is. And she has done that very well. Her mantra has been a call for excellence across the board. People rise to excellence when their leaders hold that standard high. That's what we were looking for and hoping for. And she has done that from the beginning.[4]

As he had done so many times throughout the organization's history, Ernest Hastings offered his unique perspective on three generations of BSF's leadership.

### ⌒◯ IN OTHERS' WORDS

*Dr. Ernest Hastings:*

Miss Johnson was an excellent Bible teacher, and I think God led her in writing the lesson materials. He also led her in founding Bible Study Fellowship, and she brought it along for twenty years to a stabilized level.

Then God led us to Rosemary Jensen as Executive Director, and at that point Bible Study Fellowship took off under her administration and spiritual leadership.

So Miss Johnson took us one step of the way for twenty years. Then Rosemary took us the second step for another twenty years. BSF walked with Wetherell Johnson. BSF ran with Rosemary Jensen. Now we pray it will fly with Jean Nystrand.[5]

*Chapter 32*

# THIRD-GENERATION VISION

Jean Nystrand helps the ministry listen for God's will

During the months BSF transitioned from the retirement of its second Executive Director to the selection and installation of its third, the everyday work of BSF continued. Classes grew. Headquarters staff planned and led retreats. Teaching Leaders attended orientation trainings in San Antonio. The press printed and shipped lessons. The annual magazine was written, printed, and distributed to class members. And, as always, God transformed lives around the world through the study of His Word.

More change was coming to the organization. But it wasn't coming recklessly or carelessly. Jean Nystrand took a humble, thoughtful, prayerful approach to what God might have for BSF in the years ahead.

When Jean Nystrand spoke at her first Teaching Leader Institute as Executive Director, she began by introducing herself to the TLs.

### ⟝ FROM THE DIRECTOR
*Jean Nystrand:*

God is not finished with me yet. Although I don't ever *intend* to make any mistakes as director of BSF, I have a feeling that I will. I trust that, in God's mercy and forgiveness, He will keep BSF going in spite of the fact that there is not a perfect person in charge of the organization.

I think many of you would like to know how I was called to be the Director of BSF. I had never thought of myself as being in the running for Executive Director, because I was not the visionary that Rosemary is. After I received the phone call from Dr. Hastings asking if I was willing to be considered for the position, my husband came home from a church meeting and I said, "I think you'd better sit down, because I've had one of those phone calls." Bless his heart, he said right then, "If this is what God wants, we'll do it. But we need to find out if this is what God wants." As we prayed and talked to God, He kept coming into my mind with a verse from Psalm 32:8: "I will instruct you and teach you in the way you should go; I will counsel you and watch over you." I was confident that if God, indeed, was going to open the way, then He would use me to do what He wanted.

I'm a happy, challenged, and dependent person. I'm delighted with my work. We have a magnificent staff and wonderful Area Advisors.

We have the most important ministry in the world—the Word of God. I'm spending time learning what goes on here, as well as grappling with some of the issues that just keep popping up because I'm the Director.

It's been a wonderful time of transitioning. Rosemary has done all she could to make the way smooth for me. I am enjoying working with her as we are separating the functions of BSF and Rafiki. It's going to be a delightful time as we maximize our effectiveness in having two of us.[1]

As their Directors began establishing a working relationship, the Rafiki and BSF Boards hammered out the details of what BSF's interaction with Rafiki would be, now that the organizations had different Directors. The contract the BSF Board signed with Rafiki in 1999 (see chapter 30) had spelled out the intent and the basic outline of their ongoing association. Now the specifics had to be defined and implemented. To start with, BSF built Rafiki a separate headquarters complex near the entrance to the BSF property.

While all the usual BSF programs and ministry continued, plans were underway for new and improved ways for BSF to meet the challenges of growth. Throughout the months the Board prepared for Rosemary's resignation, selected Jean Nystrand as Executive Director, implemented the transition, and established a new working relationship with Rafiki, there were many other noteworthy accomplishments.

- The Senior Level of the BSF School Program had been decided on, the materials were written and printed, and that level was implemented in September 2000.

- The Harris 1500 press was renovated, just-in-time shipping was implemented, and new software was developed.

- Two new cottages, Moses and Romans, were built on the headquarters property. Now 96 Teaching Leaders could be housed for each institute.

## Changes on the Board

Amid all these changes, another consequential organizational development took place in the year 2000. Within weeks of Jean Nystrand assuming the Executive Director's office, a new chair was elected to the organization's Board of Directors.

Ron Rogg, a lawyer and a judge, has served as a member of the Bible Study Fellowship Board since 1996. His BSF history began in a memorable way.

### ⌒ In Others' Words

*Ron Rogg:*

My first exposure to BSF came when my wife took our one-week-old baby to a new class just starting in Wichita, Kansas, in 1968. After she had been attending class for a while, her life began to change. I did not know what to think of this. I hadn't grown up with a strong Christian background where the Bible was taken with authenticity. I was, frankly, one of the least likely people to have ever gotten into Bible Study Fellowship.

But I was suddenly curious about it. My law office was only four or five blocks from the church where Deanna's BSF class met. One morning, without saying anything to Deanna, I took my Bible and walked to the church. I entered from the front of the sanctuary, because the main doors of the building were there, and was surprised to see the place filled with all these ladies. I quickly walked along the aisle until I found a place toward the back to sit down just in time for the opening. No one questioned what I was doing there; in fact, they included me in the intro class that morning and placed me in a discussion group that met in a children's Sunday school room with little chairs. I was actually a member of a women's class for about six weeks. Then I thought, *I really don't belong here.*

I soon connected with some guys who were praying for the start of a Men's Class. We started the Wichita Men's Class four or five years later, and I became the TL. I trained with Miss Johnson in California and thoroughly enjoyed leading that class for more than ten years before Rosemary Jensen called and asked me to became an AA. I did that for fourteen years and during that time first got to know my fellow AA Jean Nystrand.

Early in my tenure as a TL, Miss Johnson called and asked if I'd be okay with her putting my name forward as a potential member of the Board. But then she retired and I didn't hear another word on the subject until I was asked to join the BSF Board in 1996.

In 2000, I was asked to replace Ernest Hastings as chair, so I began my term as the chairman of the BSF's Board, and Jean started as our Executive Director that same summer.[2]

Bible Study Fellowship's governing Board had enjoyed remarkable stability over the years, and some of those veteran members, including previous chair Dr. Ernest Hastings, remained on the Board to give wisdom and oversight during the transition. Newer members had joined during Rosemary's final years, bringing fresh insights to help this third generation of leadership face the challenges of a new millennium. One of those "newer" members shares his story here.

### ⟜ IN OTHERS' WORDS
*Dr. Garth Bolinder:*

I came on the Board in 1998 along with Suzanne Sloan. But I had been a fan of BSF long before that.

My first exposure to the organization came in Grand Rapids, Michigan, working as an associate pastor right out of seminary. My wife got involved in a local Bible Study Fellowship class, and that was a positive introduction for me as well. Several years later, when I pastored a Covenant Church in Modesto, California, a Women's Day Class met in our building. That gave me an up-close and personal six-year exposure to Bible Study Fellowship. During that time, I saw more and more people from our congregation come out of that class to become key leaders in our church.

When I moved to suburban Kansas City, the church I pastored hosted a Men's Class that made an even deeper impression on me. Five hundred men would gather in our sanctuary on Monday evenings. They'd come from work. They would be eating their fast-food dinners in their cars in our parking lot while looking over their notes. Then they'd stream in and take over our entire building with their children's ministry and their discussion groups. They'd pack the pews every week. When they would sing, I remember thinking, *What a powerful movement of men!* It was very impressive. On Monday nights, our sanctuary would smell like a sanctified locker room.

While I was pastoring in Kansas City, BSF invited me, along with other pastors of host churches, to come to headquarters for a special Pastor's Institute. While in San Antonio on that trip, I became reacquainted with Bill Garrison, whom I'd met a couple of times earlier. A Board member of BSF, Bill had also been chairman of the Board at Dallas Theological Seminary and chaired the Board of Young Life for years. An attorney in Fort Worth, Bill was a wonderful Christian statesman, full of wisdom. To make a long story short, I got to know Bill Garrison as he and I talked quite a bit during that institute. I'd also known Walt Kaiser, another member of the Board.

Yet it was still a surprise and a high honor when I received a letter a few years later inviting me to serve on the BSF Board alongside such people as Bill, Walt, Jim Boice, and the legendary Dr. Ernest Hastings, a man of vision and courage who had stood alongside Wetherell Johnson at the birth of Bible Study Fellowship. (Ernest is worth a book all by himself.) That's how it all happened, how I became privileged to be associated with this wonderful work.

I am such a fan of Bible Study Fellowship because I have both seen and experienced the huge impact of Bible Study Fellowship on churches I have pastored. Back when I was associate pastor of my first church in Grand Rapids, I realized the church members who were BSFers were people of real leadership and influence in the congregation. The same was true at the church I served in California.

Then in the Kansas City congregation I pastored for fifteen years, we had the Area Advisor, a BSF Teaching Leader, and at least a dozen people who were leaders in the community as well as in our church—professionals, doctors, attorneys, and others—all of whom had come to personal faith in Jesus Christ through BSF. They'd been invited to come for a Bible study; they had checked it out, loved the environment; they started participating and eventually realized that they needed a personal relationship with Christ. There was a period of time when I would say probably two-thirds of the elected elders in our congregation were all BSFers, either graduated or currently participating. So it was just profound to see the impact of BSF on the leadership and the life of our church. But just as meaningful to me was the realization that every Monday night, from September to May, our sanctuary would be filled with men who were there, saturating the building, praying together, and studying the Bible.

Then, when I'd get up on Saturday mornings to go to my office, I thought I'd get there early, like at 6:30. And there would be all these guys—the class leaders had already been there for at least an hour, doing their weekly leader's meeting training, going over their lesson for the coming week. But primarily, on Saturday mornings, they prayed. No wonder BSF had such an impact on those men and their churches.[3]

That kind of endorsement both heartened Jean Nystrand and reminded her of the awesome responsibility she had been given to lead such an organization. While she realized she had much to learn, she knew she would not be alone. Jean had a quality Board and a terrific staff. As she told them all repeatedly, most important of all was the assurance that she and BSF had a great God to depend on.

Jean articulated her dependence on God to the TLs attending the Teaching Leader Institute in San Antonio that summer of 2000.

### ⟶ FROM THE DIRECTOR
*Jean Nystrand:*

I don't consider myself the visionary that someone like Rosemary is. So I am depending on God to do *through* me *for* the organization. I am confident because He has called me. My concern is to be sensitive to Him, so that I can decipher what it is that He is saying. One of the items on my job description is to perceive the will of God for BSF and to communicate it to our constituency. I do take this seriously. My greatest fear would be that God would remove His hand of blessing from BSF under my leadership.

One of the questions the Board asked me as they interviewed me was "What do you expect to change about BSF?"

And I told them that I have been content over the years to follow Rosemary's leadership. It's been stretching in some ways, but I have been comfortable with that.

When I knew that I was going to take this job, any business-man with authority over people and running an organization that I met in contact with, I always asked, "Do you have any advice for me, as I think about being the Executive Director of BSF?" They said it in different words, but each said, "Take your time. Listen and ask a lot of questions before you actually decide on a course for the organization."

I do take that advice seriously, because it would be drastic if I decided tomorrow to change some major things. It would be hard for you, it would be hard for our staff, and it would not be honoring and glorifying to the Lord. So I don't intend to do that.

I do know one thing: we will continue to teach God's Word, the Truth. This is what we've been called to do and this is what we do best.[4]

# Passion, Excellence, and a Common Denominator

The spirit that Jean Nystrand demonstrated, and the determination she voiced, were affirming for everyone, from class members to Teaching Leaders to headquarters staff. Jean had, according to Garth Bolinder, exactly the style and approach to leadership the Board had been looking for in a new Director.

### ⁓ IN OTHERS' WORDS

*Dr. Garth Bolinder:*

In looking for the next Executive Director, we had prayerfully decided we needed somebody with strong BSF roots, who had been a proven leader and teacher. Ideally, we wanted someone who would be able to put her arms around BSF International and its growing international dimension. We were looking also for an Executive Director willing to consider and even address some of the structural and missional issues we felt required attention at headquarters as the organization headed into the new millennium. We wanted someone who would sustain the primary mission of BSF by leading the people already in place but who, at the same time, would not be afraid to make some systemic adjustments, some structural changes to develop and build up the organization on the foundation that had been provided.[5]

The tone Jean Nystrand set for her administration was evident from the start. As appreciative as she was of the historic foundation of BSF, Jean was determined to consider every aspect of the ministry, to analyze what worked well and what didn't, and to look for ways to make everything better. The things she intended to do personally, she required from her staff, and she expected from her working relationship with BSF's Board.

After a little more than two years as Executive Director, Jean Nystrand felt confident enough in her job to publicly review the learning curve she'd been through and to begin articulating her own vision for the third generation of BSF leadership.

### ⟶ FROM THE DIRECTOR
*Jean Nystrand:*

I am grateful that I'm past the "new" stage with regard to what I do here at the headquarters and what I do with people on the field. We've had a couple of years of what I think have been very solid consolidation of training and of refining.

I'm also grateful God puts people in my life whom I can trust and who guide me in ways I believe are from the Lord. The Board and I are now working to answer questions such as *Who are we as an organization? And where does God want us to go?* I've had a couple of very stimulating ideas along the way that I would share with you.

About a year ago, one of the friends of BSF spent some time with our Division Heads and me. He does business seminars on leadership and how to direct organizations. He donated his services, and during his time with us, he talked about "third-generation leadership."

I'm the third generation of BSF Directors, so I listened very carefully to that as this gentleman asked those people who had been here for a long time, "What's happened in the time that you have been here? What changes have been made?"

It was spectacular to put in one long list all that God has done in over forty years. He challenged us that there are several things that organizations stand at the crossroads with concerning what they do in the third generation.

The first generation of any organization is the *entrepreneurial stage*. Somebody has a vision and it begins to develop. That certainly is what happens in BSF, is it not? I don't know that Miss Johnson ever had a vision of 988 classes throughout the world, but she did have a vision that she was pressed into, as we know the story, by five women in southern California who wanted to study the Bible. That was the entrepreneurial stage: we try things and get things set up.

The second generation spans the *developmental process:* you repeat what works and you get rid of what doesn't. That's exactly what happened in the years Rosemary was here with us. We repeated what worked and got rid of what didn't. We set up guidelines to help us maintain the structure. We codified it and standardized our thinking.

So, the first stage is entrepreneurial. The second is the developmental stage. Then our consultant told us, "Stage three, leadership, can go one of two ways. An organization can either institutionalize the process and the rules that have already been established so that becomes the goal of the organization, or it can move forward and combine the vision that the entrepreneurs had with the process that's been developed in the second stage and move into the third stage—what I would consider organizational 'overdrive.'"

That was the first little seed planted in my thinking on this third-generation leadership thing.

The second seed planted was when one of our Board members gave me a business book titled *Good to Great*. This book compared great companies that had outstanding results with other companies in the same field and analyzed what these "good to great" companies did, that the others failed to do, to make the leap from "good" to "great."

There are three circles of interest: the commonality that these "good to great" companies had were, first, "What are we passionate about?" Second, "What can we be the best in the world at?" Third, "What do we need to thrive and be profitable?"

So the three circles that needed to intersect were passion, excellence, and a common denominator that drives the entire heart of the organization.

Then next, we're interested in how do we, in BSF, meet the challenge of where God wants us to go? How can we be moving from this second generation, that was so beneficial to the organization, and not institutionalize all our rules and regulations, but instead use those to pursue this vision and become the very best that we can be?

I believe that at this point in our history we are the very best Bible study in the world. But I think we can do better at that. I believe that as you work with the classes, you will see that, on a case-by-case basis, we can do that.

If God is who He is and man is who he is, then excellence should be our goal. We won't be apologetic about raising the bar for each leader in this organization. So my mindset is not on training, but on focus. My question to our board is, how does God want to work through BSF in this third generation?

We are God focused, we are prayer driven, and we are analytical in structure—and we make no apologies for that. I don't see any of that changing. Because that is part of what God has given us to do. If we change anything, that change will all be driven by our passion to be the best in the world at what God has called us to do.

I want you on board with me. I want you to be part of

this next generation. I believe God has called you to do that. I want us to prayerfully do this together as we seek what all God actually wants us to do in the years ahead.[6]

# Chapter 33

# GROWING SEPARATE WAYS
### Bible Study Fellowship and Rafiki formally divide

B ecause both Bible Study Fellowship and Rafiki were growing organizations, sorting through the details of their relationship would take several years. According to the Division Head for BSF's TWO, separating some functions of BSF and Rafiki was already taking place by 2000.

### ⌒ IN OTHERS' WORDS
*Susy Harbick:*

When the discussion of Rosemary's retirement began, Rafiki was getting ready to grow. BSF was going to be separate, and Rafiki was what Rosemary would be doing. The BSF Board decided to ask the Rafiki Board if they would take the TWO missionaries with Rosemary. That decision was made at that time, because, although many of the Rafiki overseas staff were also BSF Teaching Leaders, all of them were involved in Rafiki projects. So when Rosemary retired from BSF, my division came with her to Rafiki, and I stayed with the missionaries.[1]

At the Teaching Leader Institute in the summer of 2000,

BSF's new Executive Director elaborated on the ongoing relationship she anticipated for the two organizations.

### ⟳ FROM THE DIRECTOR
*Jean Nystrand:*

> We will also joyfully work with Rafiki, planting classes in developing countries. There is a challenge that Rosemary and I are grappling with right now, sorting out who does what and how the responsibilities work out. I cannot imagine how that woman did these two jobs for the past few years. She is magnificent.
>
> Of course, Rosemary has the vision for the Rafiki ministry. She and I both are concerned that we find just the right people to be Rafiki overseas staff. Because we only consider people who are qualified for BSF leadership, BSF and Rafiki will be working closely together with regard to recruiting people for the Rafiki ministry.[2]

## Two Ministries

Although BSF's Board of Directors had affirmed the ministry of Rafiki, they recognized the challenge their new Executive Director faced in establishing an efficient and integrated working relationship between the two organizations.

As one Board member put it, "It had become clear to our Board that Rafiki had grown into a hybrid—a mercy/development agency that offered a Bible study ministry—with a mission very different, or at least more complex, than the central purpose BSF had pursued throughout its history."

By 2001, the BSF Board made the difficult decision to exercise the option given to both organizations in the legal agreement signed by both Boards two years before. They voted to dissolve the formal bonds between Bible Study Fellowship and Rafiki. Here's some of their rationale:

### ⌒⊙ IN OTHERS' WORDS

*Suzanne Sloan:*

The different ministries required two different skills sets. Imagine running an orphanage, overseeing a busy relief program, and, in addition, administering and teaching a BSF class, training the class leaders, shepherding the leadership team, and fulfilling all of the other responsibilities of a Teaching Leader—all the while trying to adapt to the daily challenges of living in an unfamiliar Third World culture.

Many of the people who had been sent out by Rafiki naturally felt a heavy responsibility to make that work their highest priority. In many cases we felt as if the BSF ministry suffered. There were other Rafiki overseas staff whose primary calling and motivation was to teach the Bible; there may well have been times where their priorities interfered with their Rafiki responsibilities.

We wanted to remain supportive. We allowed BSF staff to go with Rafiki if they so chose. At our expense we built a headquarters facility for Rafiki on our property and leased it to them for eight years. We voted to follow through on our original plan to provide other substantial financial support for Rafiki for a number of years as the original contract had called for.

When Rosemary was starting and staffing Rafiki, the people she knew were often BSF people, so she relied on them. In the years since we went our separate ways, Rafiki has grown and is thriving now outside BSF.[3]

Of course, policy decisions made by any Board, no matter how carefully considered, always have ripple effects, sometimes around the world. In 2000, Ron and Barbara Reoach moved to South Africa with Rafiki. Their story illustrates the dynamic that Suzanne Sloan talked about.

## ⤳ IMPACT STORY

*Barbara Reoach:*

It troubled both Ron and me to think there were people around the world who wanted a BSF class but didn't have one. God was creating in our hearts a great desire to go with Rafiki. We didn't know much about what it meant to be a missionary. We were just a regular middle-class American family. We had three children. We had two dogs and a regular house in a regular neighborhood. Ron was at the height of his professional career, and he enjoyed what he was doing. We had a wonderful fulfilling ministry teaching in BSF. But God was doing something new and different in our hearts.

Ron took early retirement. It seemed illogical for us to do that. Ron was the quality manager for Dow Chemical's Midland, Michigan, plant. He liked his job and was not looking for a way out. When we left, he missed the work and the people there, but he never looked back or regretted it. He was caught up in the thrill of going to a new country and acclimated to the new culture more quickly than I did. It took me a long time just to learn to drive on the left side of the road!

In the year 2000, Ron, our daughter, and I left to begin our new work in Cape Town, South Africa. When we got there, we met with a group of people, men and women, who had been praying for a BSF class *for almost three years*. We began praying with them, and both the Men's and the Women's Cape Town classes started the next year.

A Rafiki women's center was our day job. Ron oversaw a soap-making business that provided financial resources for the center and income for the women. He also taught computer skills and assumed management and administrative responsibilities. With my nursing background, I offered basic health services and taught classes in health and hygiene.

As both the Rafiki Women's Center and the BSF classes grew, we often felt as if we were being pulled in two directions, each requiring a different mindset. Rafiki was a relatively new ministry where everything seemed dynamic, very fluid, including its still-evolving mission and strategy. What began as a women's center eventually became a girls' center, and there was discussion about the possibility of more changes ahead.

In contrast, BSF was a stable ministry organization with well-established expectations and patterns as to what we did and how we did it. And one of our main goals was to help instill BSF's tried-and-true methods in the class and in the national leadership we were charged with training.

So the two ministries demanded different attitudes as well as different skills. We continued doing both, but our energies and time were divided.

When we'd been there four years, Rafiki redefined its mission. The new focus was to establish children's centers in ten African countries. South Africa was not included.

As much as we loved our Rafiki ministry, from the outset we'd felt called overseas to provide BSF classes that would mean as much for South Africans as our classes had meant to us.

We could not abandon the BSF classes we'd started. Not just because we felt teaching the Bible was our primary calling, but also because we had already seen such heartening progress.

All four ethnic/racial segments of South African society attended our classes: Black; mixed-race "Coloureds"; Whites (both English heritage and Dutch, who had their own history of conflict); and a smaller number of Asians (Indians, Chinese, and others). Among those groups, we also had representatives of every economic strata; a number of women (both black and white) attended along with their maids or other house-help. With all four racial segments represented in most discussion groups, some interactions had been a little tense at first. But it was wonderful to see how the Holy Spirit worked in people's lives to create a true Christian fellowship most class members had never known or imagined possible before.

We stayed with BSF in Cape Town without ever having any doubt that was the right decision for us. We realized how much more of our energies we could now invest in our BSF classes.

We nurtured deeper personal relationships that strengthened us and helped build up our class leadership as well. We even had time to get more involved in our church's ministry and outreach into the community.

When the BSF Board officially designated us as Foreign Resident Ambassadors, they also decided to fully fund our work and that of other FRAs around the world from what is now called the BSF International Fund. Ron and I stayed in South Africa and experienced the blessing of teaching our Cape Town BSF classes for a total of seven years—clear through the BSF rotation. In June of 2007, the Women's Class I had been teaching was ready to be led by a South African, our goal from the beginning. With trained national leadership in place to carry on the BSF ministry, we came back to the United States.[4]

## Foreign Resident Ambassadors

The Reoachs' story illustrates the practical conditions that birthed the Foreign Resident Ambassador program. Here the BSF Director of International Operations adds more about the beginning of that program:

### ⌒⊙ In Others' Words
*Dr. Chuck Musfeldt:*

When Rafiki decided to focus on ten countries in Africa, people working with Rafiki in India and Malaysia and Latin America realized, if they moved with Rafiki to Africa, some of their BSF classes would collapse.

Some people went with Rafiki. Others stayed where they were to teach BSF classes. For those people, the BSF Board and Jean created the position of Foreign Resident Ambassador. FRAs stay for about five years and then hand the classes off to nationals. Ambassadors then have the option of coming home or going to another country to start BSF there.

A great story is that of Ty and Georgine Lunberry, who'd

been serving in Dar es Salaam, Tanzania, for several years. Ty and Georgine told their congregation, a small church of about fifty people, that they were leaving, handing their BSF class to nationals. Then they announced they had been assigned to Hyderabad, India, where there was a prayer group for someone to come and start a new class.

When an Indian man in their congregation heard that, he jumped out of his seat for joy and raced up to them. He told them his mother and his aunt had been among that group of people in Hyderabad praying for years that BSF would send someone there. So when Ty and Georgine got off the plane in Hyderabad, the man's relatives were waiting, with a contingent of other folks from the prayer group, to welcome Ty and Georgine to Hyderabad with a welcoming dinner and help get them situated.[5]

Parting ways with Rafiki and retooling BSF's overseas ministry through the Foreign Resident Ambassador program created financial ramifications for headquarters and its FRA staff around the world.

### ⌒ FROM THE DIRECTOR
*Jean Nystrand:*

Our Board was aware that God had blessed the organization; we found ourselves with a significant surplus of funds. As a nonprofit organization, we knew we shouldn't be sitting on money, but using it. So we prayed, "Lord, what is it that You really want us to do?"

When the decision was made to separate from Rafiki, we had all these Teaching Leaders in the field who had gone out with BSF/TWO because they were passionate about their call to teach the Bible. As they had been transferred to Rafiki, it became clear to them that God was underlining their call to teach. I felt strongly that, because we sent them out, we needed to find a way to fulfill our obligation to them.

I went to our Board and told them that I felt God would provide for us to support these people in the manner of Hudson Taylor, that legendary missionary whose example inspired Wetherell Johnson to establish our policy of never soliciting funds for the ministry. That's how we began using the resources God had provided us to support the expansion of that ministry overseas. We have continued to use what we call our BSF International Fund to support our Foreign Resident Ambassadors.

Indeed, I believe one reason we're an international organization today is that God has given us the primary mission and the necessary tools to train leaders. Naturally, one of our goals needs to be training national people to take over the classes, rather than expecting expatriates to carry on and on with the work.

Our International Fund started out in 2001 as a means of sustaining the former Rafiki people already on the field. We came up with the concept of Foreign Resident Ambassadors in 2003 as part of overseas strategy and committed our International Fund for planting classes. Our FRA program has grown. But God continues to provide enough over and above our general needs so that we can still fund the expanding international work. So we do not ask our overseas staff to raise their own support.[6]

Board members, in looking back over Jean Nystrand's administration, acknowledged her role in clarifying BSF's work nationally and internationally.

### ⌒⌐ IN OTHERS' WORDS

*Garth Bolinder and Dr. Ernest Hastings:*

*Dr. Garth Bolinder:* One of Jean's most significant accomplishments has been the way she fully engaged the Board in helping her determine and refine the direction, policy, and vision of the organization. She championed and gave renewed clarity to BSF's central and original mission. Internationally, she did that by developing BSF's Foreign Resident Ambassador program with the understanding that we are foremost a training center, not a mercy ministry.[7]

*Dr. Ernest Hastings:* One of the most crucial decisions we ever made was to stick with what God called us to do in the first place. But sticking to those goals does not mean that we were no longer going to be open to new ideas. It just means that any new ideas have to fit our organizational structure and original mission.[8]

*Chapter 34*

# ONE THOUSAND CLASSES
and milestones beyond

By the beginning of the new millennium, BSF was approaching the milestone of one thousand classes—the goal incorporated into BSF's vision statement in 1992: "One thousand training centers, teaching the Bible, to produce in all participants a vibrant relationship with God and, in as many as are called, a passion to commit without reservation to lead in the cause of Christ in the world."

At her first Teaching Leader Institute in the summer of 2000, Jean Nystrand affirmed BSF's vision of one thousand classes: "One of the reasons God has blessed us over the years is that we know what we have been called to do and we do that well."

But after forty years trying to keep up with incredible growth, the Board paused to survey the course ahead in light of that goal. BSF leaders agreed that God did not call them to limit the number of classes to just one thousand. The chairman of the board explains that perspective.

### ⟶ IN OTHERS' WORDS
*Ron Rogg:*

Jean Nysrtrand was open to a SWOT analysis—measuring our

Strengths, Weaknesses, Opportunities, and Threats. One of the first decisions coming out of that analysis was that if God wants to move to larger numbers, then we'll do that. We now say that a thousand classes is not a ceiling. In the process, the headquarters auditorium has been expanded and more campus housing has been built. As we are now looking ahead on campus size and buildings, we agree that if God is not in it, it's not going to happen.[1]

## National and International Development

In May 2003, the Board revisited the findings of the SWOT analysis. They agreed that one of the greatest opportunities was to further develop BSF's international work. Jean Nystrand came out of that meeting with the Board's direction to create two key staff positions, both reporting directly to her.

In June 2004, Candy Staggs filled one of those positions as Director of Domestic Operations. The following August, Chuck Musfeldt filled the second as Director of International Operations.

Candy talks about her BSF background.

### ∽ IN OTHERS' WORDS
*Candy Staggs:*

My involvement with BSF began in the San Francisco Bay area. I was on maternity leave from teaching, and I had a neighbor that kept calling and inviting me to this women's Bible study. I finally accepted. Then I wanted to kick myself for not having gone sooner. BSF was so much more than I had ever thought.

The Children's Program was tremendous; I didn't want my child to miss it. Before long, a life transformation took place in me. Changes were obvious, particularly to my husband. He would come home and say, "Oh, you must have had Bible study this morning." I evidently had a different look on my face, a more pleasant tone in my voice. He eventually joined the nearby Walnut Creek Evening Men's Class. He trained as a Substitute Teaching Leader and I was a Discussion Leader. Then my husband was offered a career advancement opportunity—not in California, but in Pennsylvania.

Most of our family lived in California and Arizona at the time, so they were not exactly in favor of our moving across the country. Yet we truly had peace of mind this was the right thing for us to do.

At least I had great peace until I saw the moving truck. I suddenly panicked, wondering, *What are we doing moving so far away?* But right there on the back of the mud flaps of the moving van, in big letters, were the words "Jesus carries this load." For me that was confirmation.

Leesburg, Pennsylvania, had no BSF classes. My husband wondered if God was calling him to start a Men's Class, but nobody seemed interested. He couldn't even get any men to pray with him for a BSF class.

I soon got involved in a home Bible study, and that group of women grew until I had thirty women from different churches meeting at my house. One day God just hit me between the eyes: I already had a core group to form a BSF class.

In 1985 we began a Women's Class in an average-sized church. We outgrew that facility within two weeks. Three or four years after that, a man called my husband and asked, "Why do the women get to have this? And why can't we?"

My husband said, "I have been waiting for a call."

My husband got a Men's Class started. Another woman started a Women's Evening Class. In 1992, I was asked to be an Area Advisor. Twelve years later, in February 2004, I received a phone call from Jean Nystrand, asking me to consider this new position created by the BSF Board—Director of Domestic Operations. We moved to San Antonio in May 2004 and have been here since. My husband retired early and says he is now doing the significant part of his life. He does volunteer work—not all with BSF—and is a leader in one of our Men's Classes here. He loves it.[2]

Dr. Chuck Musfeldt served for years as an Area Advisor in the Midwest (see chapter 26). He now oversees BSF's international ministry.

## ⌒◎ IN OTHERS' WORDS

*Dr. Chuck Musfeldt:*

In 2004, my wife Linda and I both felt that God might have something new and different in mind for us. Our girls were graduating from high school. I still enjoyed being an Area Advisor, but I told Jean Nystrand that whatever she needed I was willing to do. A couple of months later, she asked me to move to San Antonio as the Director of International Operations.

As of 2008, our BSF international operations encompass 154 classes. I oversee fifteen international Area Advisors, who themselves oversee the leadership of all those classes. I also oversee the Foreign Resident Ambassadors—Teaching Leaders who have moved overseas to help get BSF classes started.

I travel to connect with our international AAs and the FRAs and drop in on as many classes as possible outside North America to pray with TLs and their leadership teams. I visit prayer groups that want to start new BSF classes.

Right now there are more classes and people in BSF outside North America than at any time before in our history. Interest seems strongest in Asia, India, and Africa—where classes, on average, have enrollments in the mid two hundreds, and many are at capacity with five hundred.

In Madagascar, hundreds walk to our three BSF classes there, clutching Bibles that have been sent to them because there isn't a single Bible bookstore in the country. A couple of years ago, I saw in Kampala, Uganda, a Class Administrator named Grace riding sidesaddle on the back of a motorcycle taxi in the rain to a leaders meeting. She was holding an umbrella over the box of lessons so they wouldn't get wet, while she was drenched. To complete that picture, you have to know one more thing: Grace is seventy years old!

In India I saw women and men riding four to a motor

scooter, wearing their beautiful saris and silk shirts in the rain to go to BSF. I asked a man in Chennai, India, "Why?"

And he said, "We are thirsty for the Word of God."

We have a BSF group in Ho Chi Minh City, Vietnam, a Day Women's Class and a men's prayer group. The pastor of the host church said the remarkable thing for him was seeing people pray with their eyes closed and their hands *not* on their Bibles. The people in the congregation prayed with their eyes closed but would keep their hands on their Bibles for fear of them being stolen. In that church, over the last thirty years, there were only eight Bibles in the church and one of them was handwritten.

In Harare, Zimbabwe, where there is hardly any petrol for their cars, women and men walk for miles to BSF with children on their backs. One of the women told me, "God's Word is our lifeline."

In a Central American country, where we have BSF now, a pastor came, bringing people from his congregation to the BSF prayer group. He said, "Only by people studying God's Word does our country have any hope at all."[3]

## Changes on the Board

BSF's Board attempts to bathe in prayer every aspect of the organization. New ideas might prompt vigorous debate, but the Board conducts BSF business with the understanding that final decisions must be made in a spirit of unanimity. So, cordial relationships among members of the Board have deepened through the years—into what several members describe as true "collegiality."

Ron Rogg has this to say about a different kind of growth he and his colleagues on BSF's board have experienced.

### ⌒⊙ IN OTHERS' WORDS

*Ron Rogg:*

We just recently made a deliberate effort to include more

international people on the Board. Jean first suggested that Bruce Smith from Scotland come on as a Board member. I first met John Amuasi from Ghana at the retreat in Nigeria. Shortly after that, Jean nominated him, and now he has joined us on the Board. Anthony Tan, who is Chinese living in Singapore, also has become a Board member—as of our May 2008 Board meeting.

These new international Board members offer us valuable, fresh perspectives. They simply see things differently because they understand their cultures.[4]

## The Role of Men

Now, with less emphasis on adding new classes, the greater focus has become strengthening and improving the quality of individual classes. Part of the strategy to increase the quality of Men's Classes has been to provide enough male area teams to oversee all the Men's Classes—to include guys not just as AAs, but also as Area Class Administrators (ACAs) and Children's Area Coordinators (CACs).

In the following stories, two men speak of their BSF experience as AAs, and they paint a picture of the effect today's Men's Classes are having. Nick Sennert is an Area Advisor in North Carolina; Gary Liaboe fulfills the same role in Minnesota.

### ⟡ IMPACT STORY

*Nick Sennert:*

I came to the Lord in 1988 at thirty years of age. My wife had accepted Christ some months before that. We lived in Danbury, Connecticut, at that time, and some people moved into our neighborhood from California. Sue got to be friends with the woman. We soon learned this lady and her husband were "born-again Christians."

Halloween came, and the lady from California decorated her yard with Halloween stuff—ghosts, goblins, spiders, and pumpkins. Sue went to the California lady and asked, "How is it that you're a Christian but you have Halloween stuff in your yard?"

Her new friend told her, "Whether or not I go to heaven doesn't depend on my yard decorations. I am going to heaven because Jesus died for my sins and I've accepted his free offer of salvation. I gain entrance to heaven only through His blood."

*Ding!* A light went on. Sue was saved.

I was traveling back and forth between Danbury and Mexico for work at that point. In the late eighties, they were blowing up cafes and whatnot in Mexico, which really worried Sue. She wanted us to go to this nondenominational church before I went back to Mexico again, because now that she knew she was going to heaven and why, she didn't feel too good about my chances.

Their congregation met in a high school, so we showed up at the high school, and there were maybe three hundred people there. I was feeling pretty out of place when who should walk up to me but the vice president of the company I worked for! He and I had traveled back and forth from Mexico together. I thought, *If Dan goes to church here, it can't be too odd.* We sat down, sang a couple of songs, and then a guy got up to preach. He opened the Bible to Romans and started reading and talking about it.

I was stunned. All we did was sing a few songs and talk about the Bible. I thought, *That is pretty much what I always thought church should be like.* Dan, the company vice president, came to me sometime later, really humble, to apologize that "All the time we traveled together, I never once shared my faith with you." That had a pretty strong impact on me.

After Sue came to the Lord, our friend from California took Sue to a BSF class in Deerfield, Connecticut. Sue loved it! I got into a Bible study of the book of John, led by the pastor of the church. And God drew me to Himself. I made my own profession of faith in January 1988.

By that time, we had decided to move to Raleigh, North

Carolina, where we started attending this little church of twenty families. Sue was dying to find a BSF class, so one day, in this group of maybe fifteen to twenty women, she asked one lady, "Have you ever heard of Bible Study Fellowship?" Sue went on and on, giving the lady the sales pitch about how great BSF is.

The lady listened politely, then told her, "There's a BSF class on Thursday mornings and you can transfer into it."

Sue was ecstatic. She showed up Thursday morning to discover that the Teaching Leader of the class was the woman she had talked to at church. And, while her old BSF class in Danbury had around forty women enrolled, this new class had five hundred.

Sue wanted me to go to BSF, but I was resistant. They were having a sign-up, and I kept blowing it off. Finally I went to BSF, and by the next year, I was enthralled.

Within a couple of years, my Discussion Leader called to ask me to pray about being a Discussion Leader. At my first leaders' meeting, when it came time to pray, all these guys knelt down on the floor. I had never seen such a sight in my entire life. It just blew me away.

From that leaders' meeting on, everything changed. God used my leadership training in BSF to mold my spiritual life and my understanding of how you study the Bible and how you conduct yourself.

I was a Discussion Leader for some years before they asked me if I would pray about being Teaching Leader of that class. After five years as a TL, I was asked to become an AA.

During my time in BSF, I saw the same story repeatedly. Maybe I'm the poster boy for it. Guys who have grown up in church, who think they know how to run their families. They think they know what it means to be a member of a church. Maybe they've read the current crop of men's books and think, *I've done this for years and have it down.* But they are clueless until they get in contact with God's Word. Then we see a transformation. Guys who talk about Scripture as if it is alive and active in their lives. They've eaten the Word, and it has become so much a part of them that they can't help but let it pour out from them and overflow from their heart.[5]

### ⤳ IMPACT STORY

*Gary Liaboe:*

When I was a TL in Minnesota, I wasn't aware that our Men's Class had the largest School Program in the world—two hundred and a waiting list. I thought all BSF classes were that size. I saw these fathers and grandfathers become fluent and comfortable with children. And I would hear stories about how they had started teaching children in their church.

I had six years as a TL before Jean called me one day at work to ask if I'd be an AA. I was in tears because I did not want to stop being a Teaching Leader. I wrestled with the decision for a whole week, praying, "Lord, I love this. I love the men that I'm with. I love the growth, the dedication I see."

Then God tapped me on the shoulder and said, "Do you hear yourself? There are too many *I's* in there."

Then I could say, "Lord, if this is what You want me to do, then I will call Jean and say yes." I've been an AA and finding even greater rewards ever since.

Nothing else has had a bigger impact on my personal life, on my spiritual discipline and my willingness to take serious things seriously—than BSF. I see a growing vitality in the Men's Classes, and men are inviting more men. If it's approached well and right, we can bring men into BSF through first an appeal to know the Scriptures well and then how to apply what they've learned in their own homes.

I don't know any other organization that challenges men enough. To do it right means we have to be willing to sacrifice time and energy in leadership and in study itself. Guys want that challenge. I'm in the Northwoods area, so when I want to feel manly, I get my chainsaw and look for something to cut. We need to define where in BSF is the "chainsaw" for men. To me, it's being the spiritual leader of your home. BSF is a whole package of training men to live out their faith in a dynamic way.[6]

## Staffing for the Future

In addition to adding a new level of administration, the Directors of Domestic and International Operations, Jean dealt with the steady changeover of staff members as veteran staff retired. For example, after Janice Pinckney, long-time head of the Children's Division, retired, Jean asked Barbara Reoach (whose FRA experience in South Africa was detailed in chapter 33) to assume that role. Here Barbara shares about recent landmarks in BSF Children's Program and the influence of this ministry on the lives of young people around the world.

### ᴥ IMPACT STORY
*Barbara Reoach:*

For BSF's Children's Division, 2008 was a milestone year because that was the first year that a high school senior could graduate from BSF, having started as a two-year-old and come all the way up through the School Program. A number of such graduates are actually students in adult BSF classes now.

We have received scores of letters from or about young men and women who've gone through the School Program. For example, I have a friend whose daughter learned how to do homiletics. When she went away to university and could no longer attend BSF, she kept doing homiletics in her daily quiet time. Soon other young women on her dorm floor realized they didn't have that same quality time with God that she was having. They wanted to know what she was doing, so she began teaching her dorm mates how to do homiletics.

Other stories recently sent to the Children's Division include the following:

- "I have been in BSF since I was two-years old, and I am completing the School Program. Through BSF and the study of the Bible I have developed character, strength, and perseverance in all aspects of my life. My BSF leaders have helped me grow spiritually. These godly teachers have been an example to me of how to live my life for Christ."

- "The past sixteen years of my eighteen-year life, I have spent in Bible Study Fellowship. As life passes, I find myself in various situations, causing me to turn to the Scriptures for answers with each unique problem. Each time I turn to the Bible for guidance, I find the wisdom I need."

- "I was in first grade when I started BSF, and today I am in the Senior Level. My involvement in BSF has helped make Jesus real in my life. Because of BSF I have led a friend to Christ. I pray that I will continue to grow in my relationship with Christ throughout my life. Who knows? God may call me to be a BSF Teaching Leader someday."[7]

The impact of BSF on young people today holds great promise for the Bible Study Fellowship of tomorrow.

*Chapter 35*

# LOOKING TO THE FUTURE
New challenges, new opportunities

A s Bible Study Fellowship International approached its golden anniversary, its administration and Board decided another in-depth self-examination would help them prayerfully consider the organization's next fifty years of influence in the world. During the 2007–2008 class year, headquarters staff distributed a survey worldwide, giving leaders and class members a chance to offer opinions on what they most appreciate and what they would like to see refined about BSF.

Over 150,000 questionnaires were returned, providing a wealth of helpful, heartening, and somewhat overwhelming feedback. And at the August 2008 Board meeting, Jean Nystrand led the Board in another SWOT analysis.

### ⌒ IN OTHERS' WORDS
*Dr. Garth Bolinder:*

To be encouraged about the future of Bible Study Fellowship, all you need to do is go to a Teaching Leader Institute or a leaders' retreat in any part of the world. The last retreat I attended was in Kuala Lumpur. Fifteen hundred men and women were there, educated, gifted leaders in their own societies. To see these men and women commit themselves to the ministry of BSF with such devotion and courage and commitment is inspiring.

At the Kuala Lampur retreat, I sat next to a lady from Burma—now Myanmar, a nation effectively closed to the outside world. I wouldn't dare give you her name, but her story of what it's like to teach a BSF class in that oppressive environment was unbelievable.

Sitting on the other side of me at that same breakfast was a businessman from Singapore, who moved to Shanghai, China, and opened a new plant for his company—so that he could start a class for expatriate men there. Just meeting BSF people from around the world is a great source of optimism about our future.

A major challenge for us will be figuring out how BSF can engage "the next generation," primarily in North America. Connecting with the younger generation has not been a problem in Asia or in Africa. The challenge is North America, and it's an issue the church is facing as well.

And yet our greatest reason for optimism about BSF's future is theological. We know God loves His Word. And in Isaiah 55, He says, "As the rain and the snow come down from heaven, and do not return to it without watering the earth . . . so is my word that goes out from my mouth: It will not return to me empty, but will accomplish what I desire and achieve the purpose for which I sent it (vv. 10–11)."

If there is one reason why BSF has flourished—and this is both theological and empirical—it is because, from the beginning, Bible Study Fellowship has had one purpose: to help people learn the written Word of God.

BSF has always been a ministry that gathers people around the Word of God. And it helps those people engage the Word of God both personally and in community. BSF also provides the discipline and structure for the kind of leadership training and life change every pastor would love to see among his congregation.

One more important organizational trait is a confidence that God is at work through BSF, that He can and does accomplish powerful things through weak people, and that He answers prayer. The result of this understanding is that BSF prays more and looks for God to work more than most para-church ministries I've been aware of. If we continue to hold to that, BSF's future will be bright indeed.[1]

## What People Said about BSF, c. 2007

At the 2007 Teaching Leader Institute, Jean Nystrand addressed the future of Bible Study Fellowship with Teaching Leaders from around the world.

### ⟜ FROM THE DIRECTOR

*Jean Nystrand:*

BSF in the twenty-first century is a wide, wide topic, especially at this juncture in our journey as a para-church organization. Our Board of Directors is especially interested in what we can be in the future, in order to respond to the call of inviting people to get to know God through the study of His Word and applying that Word to their lives.

We are trying to see what it is that we have, what are our strengths, what are our weaknesses. What do we need to minimize? How can we best be relating to the generation that is coming up?

We want to be sure that we keep the system that God has used in so many different ways. We want to preserve the core while we stimulate progress, a core that is important to us and that God has seen fit, in His grace, to use.

But also we want to stimulate progress. First, what are the immutables of BSF? What will we not change? The Board and I have been working on this, developing a statement of what our core values are, trying to assess what it is that really makes BSF, BSF. Our Board has enunciated it in this statement:

> We exist to glorify God by depending on Him for directions and for the working out of this ministry. We

glorify God by encouraging excellence in all that we do. We demonstrate integrity in the ministry and we maintain constancy in the approach to study God's Word and to training leaders for Christ's kingdom.

Finally, in all we do, we seek to demonstrate caring for the individual. While we do have a structure, we understand that that structure and all of the guidelines that we have are to be administered in the spirit of truth and grace, because we care about the individual. We're a unique Bible study, characterized by high standards, a training center concept, denominational diversity, and expectations for class members that maximize their participation.

I also wanted to be sure that we continue recognizing the basic beliefs on which Bible Study Fellowship's ministry is built. I've identified these six:

1. First, the Bible is God's Word, revealing God as the source of absolute truth, and lives are changed by the power of the Holy Spirit as He applies these truths to believers. We are not going to change that.

2. Every member participates and benefits from the study. Our guidelines are directed toward making sure people participate.

3. Members are directed to discover biblical truth for themselves, with no spoon-feeding. They are going to dig and discover biblical truth for themselves.

4. The key to a fruitful ministry is in training leaders.

5. God supplies the resources for His work, whether they are in financial terms, volunteer terms, or leadership.

6. Finally, we are an interdenominational arm of the church.

At retreats in recent years, I have conducted focus groups for people ages thirty-five and under to answer four questions:

- Why or how did you come to BSF?
- Why did you stay?
- What about BSF is off-putting to friends you'd like to invite?
- How could we fix that?

I've had some fascinating discussions. And several items have come to me out of those focus groups.

I've discovered that many come because of family members' invitations. Some were in the Preschool Program. All stayed in class because of the valuable in-depth study. They said the discipline was hard to learn, but once they got into it, they were excited and it paid off for them.

One sad thing was that many were reluctant to invite their non-Christian friends. That jarred me, because one of BSF's strengths over the years—with the other generations that we have served—is that many people come to BSF as non-Christians and come to the Lord because of their study. Historically, BSF has been a terrific evangelistic tool. One previous survey showed that 12 percent of our people had received Christ as Savior while they were in BSF.

I discovered that community and relationships are important to this generation. They'd like more time with fellow class members to develop in-depth relationships. They do feel that the opening time, singing together, the opening, the lecture, and being together in the big group is a plus for them.

The introduction class is not inviting—too much information and strongly presented rules. They would prefer a guest day or night, when people come to class and experience it, go into a discussion group, see what's happening, and then, if they choose, go to an introduction class. We need to reassess what it is that we offer in the introduction class.

Then music can be a barrier for the generation that's accustomed to praise teams. And yet, once they get used to singing hymns, they love it. It is important that we have good music done well. We certainly can pray that God would guide us to the kinds of music that would be invigorating and encouraging and uplifting for our class members.

The next thing is that many see BSF as almost secretive, with many rules. I wondered how we could more effectively publicize and make available testimonials of our satisfied customers. We also need to know if there is a more effective way to get information about BSF to local pastors.

Other feedback I've received is that the Day Women's Preschool Program is attractive to young moms. Some people would like a School Program during the daytime, because so many home-schooling parents are coming to our classes now.

We really need to be assessing what it is we can offer. We don't want to just lop off a particular generation because we haven't been willing to creatively consider what it is we can do for them.

The last thing: younger people have said they would like us to rethink our stance on using electronic communication, email and text messages, for the weekly contact of the Discussion Leaders to their group members. I think we can, in this area, find how we can best use modern technology to strengthen our BSF ministry.

This is the "State of the Union" of BSF. First we are global. About sixty thousand volunteers in over thirty different countries, with about 200,000 constituents, lead us. We have about one thousand training centers in this global venture, and a growing headquarters staff serves all of this.

BSFers demonstrate changed lives and use their Bible knowledge and training to serve in churches and in other organizations. We see ourselves as offering a season of preparation for a lifetime of ministry.

Our standards are high for ourselves and for our participants in the classes. In many ways we are countercultural, because a biblical worldview is countercultural.

The system that was developed through Miss Johnson, honed with Rosemary, and built upon in this era has been used by God to produce heroes of the faith. Miss Johnson was willing to give flat-out all for God. The elements that she taught those five ladies in San Bernardino are the same elements that we consider the immutables of BSF.

We are focused on a high view of God as He reveals Himself in His Word, and we train people to embrace a God-honoring authority structure. We understand that God's Word, applied by the Holy Spirit, moves people to a biblical worldview and then to obedient action.

I believe it's important for BSF to preserve this core, to keep fulfilling the call God has given us. But I also believe it is important to position ourselves in the twenty-first century so that people understand that we are welcoming them, that this is something they can participate in.

I believe that God has graciously given BSF tools to do this for an increasing number of people. We understand that our lives are not our own, but are His, and anything we are asked to do is not too much to serve Him.

I believe our BSF system of study and our leadership requirements are tools that God will continue using graciously to bring that message to hundreds of thousands more people worldwide in the twenty-first century.[2]


Executive Director Jean Nystrand helped BSF face its twenty-first-century challenges with a commitment to what makes BSF unique and with faith in what God has in store for the future. This may, indeed, have been her greatest contribution to the organization.

But it would be up to others to refine and implement the changes needed.

Jean Nystrand would retire from her position with BSF effective June 1, 2009.

# EPILOGUE

Though Bible Study Fellowship has celebrated its fiftieth anniversary, the roots from which it was transplanted to southern California reach back to China, where Wetherell Johnson nurtured the seeds in the 1930s and 1940s. So, it seems especially fitting that some of BSF's most exciting recent developments, and its greatest promise for future growth, lie in China, the land loved so much by BSF's founder.

## Full Circle

Wetherell Johnson's dream of taking BSF into China became a reality almost fifteen years after her death. The first classes, in Shanghai and Beijing, were limited to expatriate women with foreign passports, and classes could meet only in major hotels patronized primarily by Western travelers. But the success of those initial classes—among Chinese people returning to their homeland and citizens of other countries in China on international business—soon led to Evening Women's and Evening Men's Classes in Shanghai and, later, an Evening Men's Class in Beijing.

According to BSF's Director of International Operations, Chuck Musfeldt, BSF carefully abided by Chinese government restrictions. "We never tried to contact or go to any of the underground house churches," he said. "We never got involved in politics; we never did anything secretive. We always kept our word. We wanted to maintain the same integrity Miss Johnson demonstrated among the Chinese people seventy years earlier."[1]

In 2004, Jean Nystrand and Chuck Musfeldt (along with Area Advisor Shirley Tan and Board member Bob Duggins) attended BSF's Shanghai Day Women's Class, which met in the Regal International East Asia Hotel. That evening, they attended a prayer meeting for people interested in starting a Men's Class in Shanghai.

During that trip to China, the BSF team hoped to trace Miss Johnson's steps in and around Shanghai, where she had been a missionary for fourteen years. Chuck brought with him Wetherell's autobiography, *Created for Commitment,* to use as their "tour guide."

### ⟶ FROM THE DIRECTOR
*Jean Nystrand:*

We easily found one of the places where Miss Johnson had lived. And when we walked into that apartment building, we noticed one of the first-floor apartments had been taken out and the space remodeled to make *a government-approved Christian bookstore!* Bibles were being sold, along with other Christian books and materials, in the very building where Miss Johnson once lived.

We also visited the location where she taught the Bible to Chinese people while she served with China Inland Mission. Looking at the photo in her book, we identified the building, which is now a pediatric hospital.[2]

They also wanted to see the Longhua internment camp where Miss Johnson had been a prisoner.

## ⟶ In Others' Words

*Dr. Chuck Musfeldt:*

I explained to our driver that I realized any buildings from a World War II prison camp were probably gone, but we really hoped to find the plot of land where it had been, to stand on the spot that had been so important in the life of Wetherell Johnson.

Our driver assured us, "I can take you to the Longhua prison site, but another building now sits on that land—the Regal International East Asia Hotel."

The very place of Miss Johnson's imprisonment, where, despite her own hardship, she had prayed on her knees for the Chinese people during World War II, was now the site of the first BSF class in Shanghai! That gives me goose bumps every time I think of it.[3]

Miss Johnson's loving legacy of ministry had come full circle.

## Classes for the Chinese

Much has happened with BSF in China since that 2004 pilgrimage to Shanghai. During a 2006 trip to Beijing, Chuck Musfeldt made significant progress in the organization's relationship with the Chinese government. He talked with communist officials about expanding BSF's presence and ministry in their country.

Chuck's first meeting with the head of China's Religious Affairs Committee took place over dinner. After formal introductions were made, Chuck gave the official a copy of Wetherell Johnson's autobiography. He explained that she had been a Christian missionary to China in the 1930s and imprisoned in the Longhua internment camp for three years during World War II. Chuck explained that after the war Miss Johnson continued to serve and love the Chinese people. He said that when she had to depart China she was very sad, but she continued to care for its people.

The Religious Affairs official remained quiet for a couple of minutes. When he responded to Chuck in Chinese, it was translated, "If Miss Johnson is not in too frail of health, we would like for her to be our honored guest to speak to our seminary students in Beijing."

Chuck replied, "The good news is that Miss Johnson is in wonderful health. She's with Jesus in heaven. But I know that she would consider it a tremendous honor to have been invited to speak to the seminary students in Beijing."

After a while, the official offered, "Then *you* can speak to the seminary students in Beijing."

Chuck asked, "What would you like the topic of my talk to be?"

The official replied, "I'd like your topic to be 'Why would a physician work for a Bible study?'"

So Chuck shared his personal testimony with the seminary students in Beijing as he also explained what Bible Study Fellowship was all about.

Later, Jean Nystrand returned to China and spoke to those seminarians.

### ✎ FROM THE DIRECTOR
*Jean Nystrand:*

God used Chuck's meeting with that Religious Affairs official. That contact led to permission for a demonstration class in October 2006, where we offered the five-week *Philippians* pilot study to about thirty pastors from the official, government-regulated Three-Self Church and a group of Yancheng seminary students. Those students had been hand-selected by Religious Affairs officials to participate in our *Philippians* study, in order to see how they might be more effectively trained to teach God's Word and help the people in their churches.

The success of that pilot study subsequently led to an invitation from the government's Religious Affairs Bureau for BSF to offer classes for the very first time to Chinese citizens in an Evening Men's and an Evening Women's Class, to be held in a Beijing Three-Self church. The government even granted permission for us to bring in experienced Asian BSF teaching leaders to lead the two Beijing pilot classes in the spring of 2008. Both of those classes graduated to full classes, which were ready to begin the fall of 2008. However, in the wake of the Beijing Olympics, procedural difficulties delayed the opening of those classes until September of 2009, when the Beijing YMCA opened its doors to host the 2009–2010 classes for Chinese nationals in the capital city. Two months later, a top Chinese official for religious affairs reiterated his government's invitation to BSF leadership for the organization to start as many classes as they wished. Almost immediately, BSF began receiving requests from various Three-Self pastors to launch classes in their churches.

We pray that the people in those classes will learn what they need to be of help to their pastors in Beijing's Three-Self churches. Those churches are full and the pastors don't have enough assistant pastors, so they need lay leaders who have trained to assist them in their work. That is what BSF provides, which is why the government graciously allows us to do this.[4]

Because so many Chinese pastors have requested training for themselves, as this book goes to press, BSF has begun consulting with seminary administrators and theologians about special classes just for Chinese pastors. And, BSF International's Board of Directors is considering a joint venture with a newly formed BSF China to provide services for a growing number of classes in China and to translate the BSF program into Mandarin.

### ⁓ IN OTHERS' WORDS
*Dr. Chuck Musfeldt:*

So far, the government officials that I have met with are not only pleased with the new classes, but they are also extremely appreciative of our legacy, going back to Miss Johnson. They see this as a continuous program of integrity going back seventy years, not just the recent years we've had classes in Hong Kong,

Shanghai, and Beijing.

Which reminds me of that chapter in Miss Johnson's book where she talked about the "bewilderment of the good work spoiled" when she had to leave China. She ended her chapter quoting a poem from Amy Carmichael that talks about the "mystery that baffles" and the "sense that hushes the heart," but "far, far hence," there's a field "thick with golden grain" that only God can see and, in the end, God will explain it. When I sat for my first dinner with that Religious Affairs official, then again when I attended the demonstration class at the Three-Self church in Beijing, and every time I've returned to China since, I have looked around in amazement and thought, *This is the field thick with grain that Miss Johnson knew God could see in the future.*[5]

## Bible • Study • Fellowship • International

Even Wetherell Johnson might have marveled at all that has come about through Bible Study Fellowship's first fifty years. But she would not have been surprised. For she, like the organization she founded, always had a high view of God.

### ⟶ IN OTHERS' WORDS
*Dr. Garth Bolinder:*

What makes BSF so unique is its unwavering commitment both to the Word of God and to the teaching and the learning of that Word, experienced and practiced in community. That's the organization's profound taproot. And that taproot is still focused in clarity from the Board, through the administration, on to the staff, and out into the classes.

The simple, almost generic name Wetherell Johnson gave the organization really defines it. It's *Bible*—first, foremost, and central. It's *study*—not just seeing or listening, but the study of the Bible. Done in *fellowship*—not just individually or in isolation. And it's now very much international. It's all four of those things combined.[6]

And so it has been through fifty years of ministry, as BSF has remained faithful to God's call and true to His Word.

To God be the glory!

# AFTERWORD

by Susie Rowan

As its fourth-generation leader, BSF chose Susan C. Rowan (Susie), a woman long involved with the organization domestically and internationally. Here is her story.

 ## FROM THE DIRECTOR

*Susie Rowan:*

When I was in my early thirties, with an infant and a toddler, I became very aware of my own sin. But I wasn't sure what to do about it. Then, sitting in church next to my husband, Roger, I finally grasped what I had been taught as a youth: Jesus Christ died, not just for the world's sins, but for *mine*. He alone could carry the guilt weighing me down. I turned my life over to Jesus and He released me from my burden.

A year or two later, I was invited to Bible Study Fellowship. I had never studied the Bible. But God made it clear that this was something He wanted me to do. In a class of more than three hundred people, I knew only one other person. But I felt as if I had come home.

Six months into my study, Roger said to me, "You're a

Susie Rowan

different woman than the one I married. I love what I'm seeing. I'm going to that Bible study to find out what it's all about." He began attending BSF.

The following year I was invited into leadership, first as Discussion Leader, then as Substitute Teaching Leader. It was around this time I realized that my commitment to serve God through the ministry of BSF was a life calling. Not long after, God began to make it clear that He was calling our family to serve internationally with BSF. When I asked Roger to pray about the opportunity, he looked at me as if I were crazy. After all, I'd once told a friend who'd felt a similar call, "I'm glad it's you—and not me!"

A week later, though, I asked Roger what he was thinking. He took a couple of cards out of his wallet and said, "Since you asked me to pray, I haven't been able to get away from these two verses." One was from Psalm 40. In my Bible, next to the exact verse, I had written, "God's call on my life."

That's when we began to get nervous.

We were the most unlikely people in the world to go. We'd lived in Kansas City all our lives. We'd never even been on a short-term mission trip. Moving just twenty minutes south of where I'd grown up had been a major trauma for me. Were we insane? Some friends thought so. But we *knew* God had asked us. It was the only thing we could do.

I called BSF headquarters and asked Susy Harbick if they'd be interested in someone willing to go abroad for only two years—no longer.

Suzy replied, "Let me send you an application, and let's see what God is doing."

Clearly, He was doing something. In 1995 Roger and I packed up our two children and our dog and headed to São Paulo, Brazil, to work with The World Outreach and, later, Rafiki. We launched evening classes and nurtured them along until local leaders were able to take over. Then we came home—six years later.

We quickly settled back into our Kansas City routine. Roger reestablished his real estate career. I began working with him. Our son joined the business. Roger started teaching a Men's Class. I started back at BSF as a Children's Leader, then a Teaching Leader. God restored our bank account. We were enjoying our teaching ministry. We were surrounded by family. We were nearby to support ailing parents. Life was good.

Then, in 2004, God began to stir things up again.

Roger and I were in the office together when an email arrived from Linda Hunt, inviting us back to Latin America and suggesting we meet the new BSF Director of International Operations, Dr. Chuck Musfeldt. As we were reading the email, we got a phone call. It was Dr. Chuck Musfeldt asking if we'd be willing to go abroad once again.

Maybe someday, we said, but not right now. Now was not a good time.

Next morning, preparing my BSF lesson on Hebrews, there it was—a reference to Psalm 40. I shut my Bible so fast!

That night Roger was working on his BSF lesson and was confronted by the reference to Psalm 40. He came to me. "Susie, have you done your lesson?"

"Yes," I told him, "but I don't want to talk about it."

At a citywide prayer gathering the following day, I broke into tears, overwhelmed by the Lord's call. I phoned Roger and said, "I am struggling. But I am beginning to believe that I would be in great disobedience if I did not at least admit that God is calling us back overseas."

"Good," Roger said. "I've been waiting for you to get ready."

It was an incredible test of faith. I wanted one thing. God clearly wanted another. Faced with a decision to reject God's will in favor of fulfilling my own selfish desires, I knew I could not deny my Lord. So I held tight to God and called Chuck Musfeldt. By 2006, we were back in the field, this time in India, teaching BSF classes as Foreign Resident Ambassadors.

Our time in India also marked twenty years of studying the Bible through the BSF methods. God began to speak to my heart about the life change He had wrought in me over these twenty years. It was as if my Lord continually reminded me to consider who I would have become if left to my own devices. I realized that serious commitment to study God's Word and obey it had kept me from a life of sin and destruction of not only myself but also others. My gratitude to God for His life-saving work in me translates to a passion for others to know Him as I know Him and to find real joy and satisfaction in Him alone. Sin is such a deceiver, but life lived for God's praise, pleasure, and proclamation is good and right—and it is also rich and full. I had learned that living for and walking with God was the greatest privilege, purpose, and pleasure of life. That is something I long to share with others.

Fast-forward to April 2008. Another phone rings. Another call is made, this one perhaps the most challenging yet. It's Ron Rogg on the line. He asks if I'd be willing to be considered for the Executive Director position at BSF, replacing the retiring Jean Nystrand. One long talk and a lot of questions later, I said yes—to going through the process, at least.

After I hung up, I was pretty shaken. I couldn't even pray. But I am a trained BSFer: I could read my Bible. I went to the next passage in my reading schedule. It was Deuteronomy 31, God's call to Joshua. As I read, I began to sense that this was what God had in store for me and that I was to trust Him, not myself.

That May, Roger and I came home for a furlough. Members of the BSF search committee interviewed us. I remember a delightful conversation with them and the joy of hearing Roger say, "There is not a single reason why my wife should not be the next Executive Director of BSF."

We returned to India. Months went by. In August, Ron Rogg called again. The search committee, he said, had decided to present one candidate to the Board for consideration: I was the one.

The next step was a telephone interview with the full Board. Routine, right? Not in India, where our spotty phone service made dropped calls the norm. We were prepared to make numerous attempts, but the line held for a full hour-and-a-half interview. As I fielded question after question, Roger knelt in the next room, praying.

For every question asked, the answer was on my tongue. Except one. It was a technical question that I didn't even understand. But the next moment I found myself answering, with full knowledge. The Lord enabled His servant.

A day or so later, Ron called again. Once again the line held, enabling me to hear his words: "The Board of Directors of BSF has unanimously voted to extend to you the call to be the next Executive Director of BSF."

By March 2009, we were in San Antonio. Jean Nystrand graciously invited me to be at headquarters on a daily basis, to ramp up. She retired on May 31. On June 1—welcomed by BSF headquarters staffers wearing running shoes and carrying signs saying, "Team BSF! We're ready to run with you!"—I took the reins.

BSF staff in 2010

The early days with the Headquarters staff were spent in examination, repentance, and prayer. This process continues to this day. Soon ideas started to flow unrestrained. By August, a strategic plan was ready for Board consideration and planning for a fiftieth anniversary gala was underway.

On November 14, 2009, we hosted a great celebration of God's faithfulness. And what a party! Seventeen hundred BSFers from around the world gathered in San Antonio to commemorate the fiftieth anniversary of BSF! The people who attended that party represented every decade of BSF (1959–2009), eighteen different nations (Australia, Brazil, Canada, Germany, Ghana, India, Kenya, South Korea, New Zealand, Nigeria, Peru, Singapore, South Africa, Switzerland, Tanzania, Uganda, United Kingdom, and the United States), and forty-five states in the United States.

The evening overflowed with joy as we gave glory to God for fifty years of His blessings of changed lives through the study of the Bible in BSF. We prayed for the Lord's hand in the current and future work of BSF. And we looked ahead to how God is directing our future.

Back in July 2009, as we began planning that fiftieth anniversary party, God gave us this verse from Isaiah:

> O Lord, you are my God;
> I will exalt you and praise your name,
> for in perfect faithfulness
> you have done marvelous things,
> things planned long ago. (Isaiah 25:1)

The week before the fiftieth anniversary gala, just when I needed the Lord's strength and encouragement for that big event, I opened my BSF study of Isaiah (the staff is doing the new Isaiah study in preparation for its introduction in fall 2010), and God brought that verse to me again. I had the joy of reading the Isaiah notes about this very passage, "The Song of the Redeemed."

God is perfectly faithful! And He is perfectly faithful in such a way that when He is faithful to you, He never betrays His faithfulness to me or to anyone else. What a great God we serve!

God has been perfectly faithful to the ministry of BSF. At the same time, He has been perfectly faithful to every person who has ever studied in BSF and perfectly faithful to the ministry of every church and every other Christian ministry and Bible study that God wrote into His sovereign plan of history.

Can you grasp how big is the faithfulness of God?

Because God has proved His faithfulness and power through BSF for the last fifty years, I have utmost confidence and full assurance that our faithful God has marvelous things—things planned by Him long ago—that He intends to accomplish in the next fifty years of BSF.

But the future for BSF is not without challenges. There is a famine of the Word of God in many parts of the world. People in the United States and other Western nations, especially young people, are increasingly becoming biblically illiterate. And still many people in the world do not know the name of Jesus.

Never have BSF and other good Bible-teaching ministries been needed more.

But our fast-paced, technology-packed world requires new approaches. We must look to God as our Wisdom and Provider and believe that He is faithful and will do marvelous things— things planned long ago.

Several times the Lord has given me 1 Chronicles 12:32 about the "men of Issachar, who understood the times and knew what Israel should do." How often I have prayed to understand what BSF must do to effectively minister the Word of God in the nations.

If we go in our own strength, we are in trouble. As we look to God, we trust that day by day He will show us the way to minister His never-changing truth in an ever-changing world.

So, what does the future look like for BSF? Carefully and prayerfully, the BSF Board of Directors, in a meeting at the end of August 2009, adopted the four strategies listed below. These were shared with the seventeen hundred BSFers who came to the anniversary party and with BSF classes in January 2010.

Susie Rowan with the Board in 2009

# Strategy 1: Reverse the decline in U.S. enrollment, resulting in thriving, growing North American BSF classes.

- BSF is about passion for Jesus Christ and compassion for every single person whom God brings to a BSF class. We have wonderful procedures and structures in BSF. But some cultures of the world are more relaxed than they used to be.

- So BSF classes are being encouraged to take a more compassionate, flexible, and contextual approach toward people while continuing the faithful, expository, Christ-centered teaching of Scripture.

- We will continue to teach the whole counsel of God. So we are launching a new study on Isaiah—a challenging book, one that many describe as the Romans of the Old Testament. It has thirty-nine chapters before we get to

"Comfort, comfort my people." But I cannot tell you how much bigger my God is because of what the prophet Isaiah has taught me. We will introduce that new thirty-week study in 2010.

- In 2010 we will launch a Men's Division to strengthen the Men's Classes. We are doing this, not because the Men's Classes are weakening, but because they are becoming stronger.

## Strategy 2: Increase worldwide the number of participants under forty years of age.

Have you ever experienced the fright of thinking a child in your care had been abducted? Once I lost one of my children in a department store. My response was to do everything in my power to bring that child back safely. I called in all the help I could get. I prayed without ceasing, until with great joy that child was returned to my arms.

Today young adults, youth, and children are being spiritually abducted at alarming rates. We could lose our children to the world with its glamour and its technology and its relativism.

How will we at BSF stand against the assault on our children? We are executing plans to extend the reach of BSF's Bible teaching and leadership training ministry to the young. We are finding ways to attract more adults in their twenties and thirties to our BSF classes.

- Eight pilot classes worldwide have paved the way for all Day Women's Classes to offer an under-two-year-old program. We want to encourage women to attend BSF with their infants and toddlers. Children can come as newborns and begin to be taught the Bible. That includes leaders praying Scripture over babies, singing hymns over eighteen-month-olds, and telling very short Bible stories with pictures.

- Some new methods are being introduced to our Young Adult Classes. In BSF we love our old hymns. But young adults don't know those hymns and were not

singing in the opening. We have asked the Young Adult
Teaching Leaders to introduce contemporary music.
We are hearing that the young people are warming
up, singing the more contemporary songs, and then
learning to sing the hymns. Music and technology are
key to reaching young adults. We want to use both in
ways that honor God and minister to the hearts of the
young.

- We have established an Information Technology
  Division and are making better use of the Web, moving
  forward as technology changes. Class members may
  already download the BSF questions, answer them on
  their computers, and print a copy. We plan to make
  Home Discussion pages and Home Training Lessons
  available on the Web. And we are making our "Find a
  Class" feature user-friendlier. It is likely that BSF will
  have a new "look" in days to come while maintaining its
  core purpose and values.

## Strategy 3: Increase the global impact of BSF.

God is opening the global gates wide. He is asking BSF to
walk through those gates with Him to teach His Word.

- We are expanding rapidly in certain parts of the world.
  In fall 2009, we trained eighty-seven Teaching Leaders,
  many for new classes. Malawi and Ethiopia, which
  have not had BSF before, will have pilot classes soon.
  In Nairobi, we have fifteen classes in the city, many
  at capacity with 400 or more members and with 150
  people on some waiting lists. We have two pilots about
  to launch and need six more.

- Over the years, many seeds have been planted for BSF
  in China. Classes for expatriates were established in
  Shanghai and Beijing several years ago. As long as
  someone had a foreign passport, he or she could attend
  BSF. But Chinese citizens were not allowed to come.
  Just before the Olympics, in a real breakthrough, a

pilot class was held for Chinese pastors, and two pilot classes began for Chinese citizens in Beijing with the approval of the government. Then progress stopped and the FRAs were brought home. The door for classes for Chinese citizens seemed to have closed.

In July 2009 God began to open doors again. That August, classes were established for citizens, a class for men and one for women, meeting at a YMCA. In November 2009, we met with

the Minister of the State Administration for Religious Affairs. We thought it would be an introductory meeting. Instead, he told us, "BSF is welcome to have many classes in China on the basis of mutual respect."

Now pastors are be-ginning to ask for BSF classes as soon as we can provide leaders. And pastors are requesting training. Since it had been beyond the mission of BSF to train pastors,

School in Malawi

we are in touch with a seminary, to collaborate with us to meet that need for Chinese pastors. And we are calling on people of Chinese descent, in BSF classes, to return to China to help us as BSF leaders.

- A new initiative has been launched by our Board of Directors—translation! BSF will begin to translate materials into Chinese. Next will come Spanish. A Translation Fund has been established in the BSF International Fund to receive gifts toward this important project.

## Strategy 4: Strengthen the pool of resources needed to expand the global reach of BSF.

- In September 2009 the BSF International Board of Directors authorized the formation of a new arm of ministry to be known as the BSF Alumni Connection. The BSF Alumni Connection will allow for the ongoing participation of all who have benefited from a BSF class.

  The Alumni Connection will provide prayer support for the ministry of BSF from an even wider circle of BSFers and friends. And through the Connection, we will share needs and information about the current ministry of BSF, our international work, volunteer opportunities at BSF headquarters, and enrichment, travel, and fellowship opportunities for BSF alumni.

After these four strategies were shared with the seventeen hundred people at the fiftieth anniversary gala, we divided into groups of two or three for prayer. A chorus of prayer rose up across the auditorium as together we sought the will of our Father for BSF. What a precious time of oneness in prayer!

In my twenty-five years of involvement in BSF I have never been more excited about the future of our organization. God has set before us an open door in the twenty-first century, to involve many nations and places in the world. We are praying that as we walk through that door God will use the ministry of BSF so that the name and the fame of the Lord Jesus Christ will be renowned in all the earth.

# APPENDIX

## Chronology of Key Events in the History of Bible Study Fellowship

1950     Wetherell Johnson leaves China. She speaks at a prayer meeting in Altadena, California, where she meets Alverda Hertzler.

1952     Five women ask Miss Johnson to teach them Colossians. She insists that she will not "spoon-feed" them.

1953–54     The study outgrows Miss Hertzler's house, moves first to the home of Horton and Edna Voss and then to a church. The group takes the name Bible Study Fellowship, begins offering a nursery, and divides into discussion groups. Wetherell Johnson establishes the policy that one cannot share in class without having a written answer.

1957     Kay Gudnason meets Wetherell Johnson at Mount Hermon.

1958     Billy Graham holds a crusade in the Bay Area, with Ernest Hastings as co-chair of the follow-up committee. Miss Johnson moves to Oakland and establishes the first BSF class in the Bay Area, at Melrose Baptist Church.

1959    Miss Hertzler moves to the Bay Area to help Miss Johnson. BSF applies for incorporation.

1960    BSF is granted incorporation. Wetherell Johnson begins the first Couples Class.

1961    A class begins in Indiana—the first outside California.

1962    BSF purchases its first headquarters, on Foothill Boulevard in Oakland. This year, 13 classes are in operation, including those in Indiana and Arkansas.

1963    The Children's Program begins. Miss Johnson and Miss Hertzler build a home on Snake Road in Oakland.

1964    The ministry adds an addition to the basement of the Foothill headquarters. This year 23 classes are in operation, with 3,000 members.

1965    This year 35 classes are in operation in 5 states.

1966    This year 48 classes are in operation in 8 states. Dr. Robert Stevens is hired to head up "the men's work."

1967    Miss Hertzler suffers a heart attack.

1968    This year 70 classes are in operation in 12 states.

1969    The ministry purchases a new headquarters at Skymount and its first orientation house. This year more than 100 classes are in operation, with 20,000 members. BSF holds its first Biennial Seminar.

1970    This year 110 BSF classes are in operation. BSF begins in Australia. The leadership decides to accept no children under two years of age into the Children's Program.

1971    This year 131 classes are in operation, with 30,000 members. Dr. Francis Schaeffer speaks at a Teaching Leader seminar. The ministry holds its first pilot class on Colossians. BSF begins in Liverpool, England.

1972    To expand the headquarters, the ministry purchases Lower Skymount.

1973     BSF holds its first Young Adult Class. Classes are limited to 450 members. The first class is held in Canada. Rosemary Jensen becomes a Teaching Leader. A second printing addition is built at headquarters.

1977     BSF constructs a new production building adjacent to Upper Skymount. Wetherell Johnson suffers a recurrence of cancer. There are now classes in 40 states, including Hawaii.

1979     Miss Johnson retires. Rosemary Jensen begins her tenure as Director of BSF. The Board decides to move the organization to San Antonio. "Mass meetings" are held in Anaheim and Oakland, California. This year there are 50,000 class members in 280 classes.

1980     Rosemary Jensen begins as Executive Director. The new roles of Area Class Administrator and Children's Area Coordinator are created to form three-member area teams with Area Advisors. The ministry gets its first computer.

1981     The staff relocate to San Antonio and are reorganized. The new headquarters is dedicated. The first Ambassador is appointed. The first Summer Institute is held. There are now 316 classes in operation.

1982     Graduate Seminars begin. There are now 350 classes in operation.

1983     The first class is held in New Zealand. Four Teaching Leader Institutes are held. This year 385 classes are in operation, with 77,222 adult members and 12,566 children.

1984     The Home Discussion page is created. Rosemary Jensen visits Africa. Wetherell Johnson dies. There are 449 classes and 13,808 children in the Children's Program.

1985     The children begin studying the same passage the adults study. The House of Heroes is built at headquarters. BSF establishes its African division office.

This year 512 classes are in operation, with 91,570 members and 25 new Evening Women's classes.

1986     BSF holds its first classes in Africa, Asia, and continental Europe. There are 548 classes in operation, with 25,181 children in the Children's Program.

1987     Memorial Auditorium is dedicated. For the first time, the same BSF series is studied worldwide. BSF establishes the Rafiki Foundation. This year 596 classes are in operation in 12 nations, and 25,608 children are enrolled in the Children's Program.

1988     BSF leaders begin praying for BSF classes in capital cities of the world. The BSF Board clarifies the organization's mission statement. BSF holds its first leaders retreat in Africa. This year 650 classes are in operation, with more than 100,000 members. Classes are started in two new states: Nevada and West Virginia.

1989     This year 720 classes are in operation. The first class in the state of New York begins.

1990     The Board changes the organization's name to BSF International and chooses a new logo. A Hertzler Press is installed at headquarters. BSFI establishes its TWO (Third World Outreach) Division. This year 768 classes are in operation, with 118,210 members.

1991     This year 825 classes are in operation in 21 countries. New classes begin in Maine and New York City.

1992     Obadiah, housing for volunteers, is built at headquarters. The Board of Directors visits Africa. The first May magazine comes off the presses. This year 857 classes are in operation, with 122,094 members. Meanwhile, 23 classes are closed to meet new enrollment guidelines.

1993     The first class is held in South America. There are 866 classes in operation, comprising 134,362 members.

1994     BSF launches a new study called *The Life of Moses*. There are 882 classes in operation, with more than 200,000 adult members and 32,809 children.

1995    The first BSF classes are held in India. Worldwide, 885 classes are in operation, with 259,746 members.

1996    The School Program begins. There are 903 classes in operation, with 176,017 members and 50,650 children.

1997    A new study is launched: *The Acts of the Apostles*, revised from *The Life and Letters of Paul*. There are 914 classes in operation.

1998    Level 4 is added to the School Program. There are 945 classes, with 194,029 members, 57,853 children, and 20,000 young people in the School Program.

1999    BSF launches another new study: *Romans*. A Romans Institute is held for all Teaching Leaders.

2000    Rosemary Jensen retires, and Jean Nystrand begins her tenure as BSF's third Executive Director. The ministry begins classes for expatriates in Shanghai, China. It constructs new cottages and buildings for Rafiki. The Senior Level is added to the School Program. The Harris 1500 press is renovated and just-in-time shipping is implemented. This year 971 classes are in operation, with 218,428 adult members and 64,565 children.

2001    The International Fund is established. Classes for expatriates begin in Beijing.

2003    The Foreign Resident Ambassador Program begins. Leaders undertake a SWOT analysis of the ministry's strengths and weaknesses.

2004    Jean Nystrand adds a new level of administration, with Directors of Domestic and International Operations. She and Chuck Musfeldt visit China.

2006    A demonstration class for nationals begins in Beijing.

2007    BSFI conducts a worldwide survey of every leader and class member in the organization. This year more than

1,000 classes are in operation in more than 30 countries, with 200,000 members and 60,000 volunteers.

2008    This is the first year that a high school senior could graduate from BSF, having started as a two-year-old and progressed through the School Program.

2009    Jean Nystrand retires. Susie Rowan begins her tenure as BSF's fourth Executive Director. BSFers from 18 nations and 45 states gather in San Antonio to celebrate the fiftieth anniversary of BSF. The first classes are started in Malawi and Ethiopia. The BSF Alumni Connection is formed to allow the ongoing participation of all who have benefited from a BSF class. Doors are opened again for BSF classes for nationals in China.

2010    BSF launches its new study on *Isaiah*. It creates a Men's Division, an Information Technology Division, and an under-two-year-old program. The organization introduces contemporary music into Young Adult classes. For the first time, BSF questions, Home Discussion pages, and Home Training Lessons are made available on the Web. The board also approves the translation of BSF materials into Chinese in order to more effectively reach the people of China. And in partnership with the publishing arm of Biblica, BSF tells the story of its first 50 years of ministry by publishing *True to His Word*.

# NOTES

**Chapter 1** At Life's Crossroads
1. Wetherell Johnson, speech at the Oakland Coliseum, Oakland, California, December 1, 1979.
2. Ibid.
3. Wetherell Johnson, *Created for Commitment* (Wheaton, IL: Tyndale, 1982), 184.
4. Ibid., 189.

**Chapter 2** No Spoon-Feeding
1. Alverda Hertzler, speech at the Oakland Coliseum, Oakland, California, December 1, 1979.
2. Wetherell Johnson, *Created for Commitment* (Wheaton, IL: Tyndale, 1982), 197.
3. Wetherell Johnson, speech at the Oakland Coliseum, Oakland, California, December 1, 1979.
4. Johnson, *Created for Commitment,* 200.
5. Ibid., 203.
6. Wetherell Johnson, speech at the Oakland Coliseum.
7. Ibid.
8. Vergene Lewis, interview by the authors, 2004.

**Chapter 3** Bible Study Fellowship in the Bay Area
1. Kay Gudnason, speech at dedication of the Bible Study Fellowship headquarters, San Antonio, Texas, September 12, 1981.
2. Myrl Glockner, interview by the authors, 2006.
3. Ernest Hastings, interview by the authors, 2004.
4. Vergene Lewis, interview by the authors, 2004.

**Chapter 4** Ideal Partners
1. Kay Gudnason, speech at dedication of the new Bible Study Fellowship headquarters, San Antonio, Texas, September 12, 1981.
2. Wetherell Johnson, *Created for Commitment* (Wheaton, IL: Tyndale, 1982), 215.
3. Alverda Hertzler, farewell letter, December 1979.
4. Wetherell Johnson, speech at the Oakland Coliseum, Oakland, California, December 1, 1979.
5. Ernest Hastings, interview by the authors, 2004.
6. Betty Hunter, interview by the authors, 2007.
7. Jan Myers, interview by the authors, 2005.
8. Ruth Stagner, interview by the authors, 2005.
9. Jean Werum, interview by the authors, 2005.
10. Ernest Hastings, interview by the authors, 2004.

**Chapter 5** God's Plan for Expansion
1. Ernest Hastings, interview by the authors, 2004.
2. Wetherell Johnson, *Created for Commitment* (Wheaton, IL: Tyndale, 1982), 226.
3. Mary Nell Schaap, interview by the authors, 2007.
4. Vergene Lewis, interview by the authors, 2004.
5. Myrl Glockner, interview by the authors, 2006.

**Chapter 6** The Youngest BSFers
1. Ernest Hastings, interview by the authors, 2004.
2. Marcella Altmann, interview by the authors, 2006.
3. Marcella Altmann, handwritten letter to the authors, 2006.
4. Marcella Altmann, *BSF Newsletter,* fall 1972.
5. Janice Pinckney, interview by the authors, 2003.
6. *BSF Newsletter,* fall 1970.
7. Wetherell Johnson, *BSF Newsletter,* fall 1970.
8. Marion Mann, interview by the authors, 2005.
9. Marguerite Carter, *BSF Newsletter,* fall 1972; Marcella Altmann, *BSF Newsletter,* fall 1972; Lynn Murphy and Audrey King, *BSF Newsletter,* fall 1974.

**Chapter 7** Adding Bass Notes to the Harmony
1. Bob Stevens, interview by the authors, 2005.
2. Wetherell Johnson, *Created for Commitment* (Wheaton, IL: Tyndale, 1982), 248.
3. Larry Heppes, interview by the authors, 2005.
4. Bob Stevens, interview by the authors, 2005.
5. Ibid.
6. Rollin Mann, interview by the authors, 2005.
7. Myrl Glockner, interview by the authors, 2006.

8. Larry Heppes, interview by the authors, 2005.

9. Mary Nell Schaap, interview by the authors, 2007.

10. Carolyn Edwards, interview by the authors, 2007.

11. Johnson, *Created for Commitment,* 250–51.

12. Norm McBride, interview by the authors, 2005.

13. Johnson, *Created for Commitment,* 251–52.

14. Bill Knopsis, interview by the authors, 2004.

**Chapter 8** From Foothill to Skymount

1. Wetherell Johnson, *Created for Commitment* (Wheaton, IL: Tyndale, 1982), 231.

2. Ibid., 237.

3. Quoted in ibid., 238.

4. Ernest Hastings, interview by the authors, 2004.

5. *BSF Newsletter,* November 1967.

6. Anna Kingsbury, interview by the authors, 2004.

7. *BSF Newsletter,* November 1967.

8. Wetherell Johnson, *The Story of Skymount* (Oakland, CA: Bible Study Fellowship, September 11, 1969).

9. Bill Knopsis, interview by the authors, 2004.

10. Johnson, *The Story of Skymount.*

11. Marguerite Carter, *BSF Newsletter,* fall 1972.

12. Alverda Hertzler, *BSF Newsletter,* fall 1972.

13. Johnson, *Created for Commitment,* 232.

14. Anna Kingsbury, interview by the authors, 2004.

15. Ernest Hastings, interview by the authors, 2004.

**Chapter 9** A Youth Movement

1. Wetherell Johnson, *BSF Newsletter,* fall 1972.

2. Anna Kingsbury, interview by the authors, 2004.

3. Wetherell Johnson, *Created for Commitment* (Wheaton, IL: Tyndale, 1982), 272.

4. Ibid., 275.

5. Ibid., 276.

6. Ibid., 277.

7. Anna Kingsbury, interview by the authors, 2004.

8. Johnson, *Created for Commitment,* 277.

9. Susy Harbick, interview by the authors, 2005.

10. *BSF Newsletter,* spring 1973.

11. Karen Dable, interview by the authors, 2005.

12. Pearl Hamilton, *BSF Newsletter,* spring 1973.

13. Karen Dable, interview by the authors, 2005.

14. Skip Brey, interview by the authors, 2005.

15. *BSF Newsletter,* fall 1974; *BSF Newsletter,* summer 1975; Alverda

Hertzler, *BSF Newsletter,* Christmas 1975; *BSF Newsletter,* Christmas 1976.

16. Karen Dable, interview by the authors, 2005.

17. Johnson, *Created for Commitment,* 278.

18. Karen Dable, interview by the authors, 2005.

19. *BSF Newsletter,* May 1990.

**Chapter 10** Repeating the Pattern, Part 1

1. Wetherell Johnson, *Created for Commitment* (Wheaton, IL: Tyndale, 1982), 240–41.

2. Ibid., 228.

3. Ibid., 258–59.

4. Skip Brey, interview by the authors, 2005.

5. Ibid.

6. Jeanette Tompkins, interview by the authors, 2004.

7. Johnson, *Created for Commitment,* 254.

8. Ruth Larson, interview by the authors, 2005.

9. Johnson, *Created for Commitment,* 253–56.

10. Marion Mann, interview by the authors, 2005.

11. Johnson, *Created for Commitment,* 257.

12. Mary Nell Schaap, interview by the authors, 2007.

**Chapter 11** Repeating the Pattern, Part 2

1. Wetherell Johnson, *Created for Commitment* (Wheaton, IL: Tyndale, 1982), 257–58.

2. *BSF Newsletter,* December 1967.

3. Jan Myers, interview by the authors, 2005.

4. Mary Nell Schaap, interview by the authors, 2007.

5. Ruth Larson, interview by the authors, 2005.

6. Lorrie Kemp, interview by the authors, 2005.

7. Mary Nell Schaap, interview by the authors, 2007.

8. Jan Myers, interview by the authors, 2005.

9. Lorrie Kemp, interview by the authors, 2005.

10. Lois McCall, interview by the authors, 2007.

11. Jan Myers, interview by the authors, 2005.

**Chapter 12** An Arm of the Church

1. Ernest Hastings, interview by the authors, 2004.

2. Wetherell Johnson, *Created for Commitment* (Wheaton, IL: Tyndale, 1982), 212.

3. Ibid., 223.

4. Jan Heal, interview by the authors, 2003.

5. Barb Watson, interview by Anna Kingsbury, 2003.

6. Anita Newton, interview by Anna Kingsbury, 2003.

7. Rollin and Marion Mann, interview by the authors, 2005.

8. Chuck Musfeldt, interview by the authors, 2007.

9. Jerry Prenzlow, interview by the authors, 2006.

10. Lois McCall, interview by the authors, 2007.

11. Vergene Lewis, interview by the authors, 2004.

12. Skip Brey, interview by the authors, 2005.

13. Mary Nell Schaap, interview by the authors, 2007.

14. Myrl Glockner, interview by the authors, 2006.

15. Lorrie Kemp, interview by the authors, 2005.

**Chapter 13** Retreats and Seminars

1. Skip Brey, interview by the authors, 2005.

2. *BSF Newsletter,* fall 1962.

3. Wetherell Johnson, *Created for Commitment* (Wheaton, IL: Tyndale, 1982), 259–60.

4. Ibid., 261.

5. *BSF Newsletter,* spring 1971.

6. Pearl Hamilton, *BSF Newsletter,* summer 1974.

7. Vergene Lewis, interview by the authors, 2004.

8. Mary Nell Schaap, interview by the authors, 2007.

9. Marion Mann, interview by the authors, 2005.

10. Jan Myers, interview by the authors, 2005.

11. Jeanette Tompkins, interview by the authors, 2004.

12. Anne Graham Lotz, interview by the authors, 2006; Dottie McKissick, interview by the authors, 2005.

13. Anna Kingsbury, interview by the authors, 2004.

14. *BSF Newsletter,* fall 1971.

15. Jan Myers, interview by the authors, 2005.

16. Pearl Hamilton, *BSF Newletter,* fall 1972.

17. *BSF Newsletter,* summer 1974.

18. Wetherell Johnson, *BSF Newsletter,* May 1979.

19. Johnson, *Created for Commitment,* 265.

**Chapter 14** New Leaders, New Classes, New Cities

1. *BSF Newsletter,* October 1970.

2. Anne Graham Lotz, interview by the authors, 2006.

3. Mary Heppes, interview by the authors, 2005.

4. Lorrie Kemp, interview by the authors, 2005.

5. Lois McCall, interview by the authors, 2007.

6. Shirley Mills, interview by the authors, 2003.

7. Wetherell Johnson, speech at the Oakland Coliseum, Oakland, California, December 1, 1979.

**Chapter 15** Heading Overseas

1. *BSF Newsletter,* summer 1970.

2. *BSF Newsletter,* spring 1971.

3. *BSF Newsletter,* fall 1972.

4. Marguerite Carter, *BSF Newsletter,* summer 1974.

5. Ann Cook, interview by Anna Kingsbury, 2003.

6. Alverda Hertzler, *BSF Newsletter,* October 1970.

7. Ann Cook, interview by Anna Kingsbury, 2003.

8. *BSF Newsletter,* fall 1971.

9. Ann Cook, interview by Anna Kingsbury, 2003.

10. Gwyneth MacKenzie, interview by Anna Kingsbury, 2003.

11. Ann Colmer, interview by Anna Kingsbury, 2003.

12. Gwyneth MacKenzie, interview by Anna Kingsbury, 2003.

13. Ann Colmer, interview by Anna Kingsbury, 2003.

14. "New Classes," *BSF Newsletter,* spring 1973.

15. Anita Newton, interview by Anna Kingsbury, 2003.

16. Ann Colmer, interview by Anna Kingsbury, 2003.

17. Barbara Watson, interview by Anna Kingsbury, 2003.

18. Ann Cook, interview by Anna Kingsbury, 2003.

**Chapter 16** A Change of Leadership

1. Wetherell Johnson, *Created for Commitment* (Wheaton, IL: Tyndale, 1982), 289.

1. Betsy Wray, interview by the authors, 2007.

2. Rosemary Jensen, interview by the authors, 2005.

4. Johnson, *Created for Commitment,* 290.

5. Betsy Wray, interview by the authors, 2007.

6. Jane Roach, interview by the authors, 2005.

7. Johnson, *Created for Commitment,* 291.

8. Ibid., 291.

9. Ibid., 292.

10. Karen Dable, interview by the authors, 2005.

11. Johnson, *Created for Commitment,* 293.

12. Rosemary Jensen, remarks at the BSF staff Day of Prayer, May 2000.

13. Ibid.

14. Wetherell Johnson, speech at the Oakland Coliseum, Oakland, California, December 1, 1979.

15. Rosemary Jensen, speech at Romans Institute, San Antonio, Texas, 1999.

**Chapter 17** The Texas Transition

1. Rosemary Jensen, interview by the authors, 2005.

2. Alverda Hertzler, *BSF Newsletter,* Christmas 1978.

3. Wetherell Johnson, *Created for Commitment* (Wheaton, IL: Tyndale, 1982), 294.

4. Dottie McKissick, interview by the authors, 2005.

5. Jan Myers, interview by the authors, 2005.
6. Pearl Hamilton, *BSF Newsletter,* Christmas 1980.
7. Mary Siemens and Anna Kingsbury, *BSF Newsletter,* Christmas 1980.
8. Steve Gately, interview by the authors, 2003.

**Chapter 18** Signs of God's Blessing
1. Rosemary Jensen, remarks at the BSF staff Day of Prayer, May 2000.
2. Betsy Wray, interview by the authors, 2007.
3. Richard Walenta, remarks at the BSF staff Day of Prayer, May 2000.
4. Rosemary Jensen, *BSF Newsletter,* Christmas 1980.
5. Rosemary Jensen, speech at Romans Institute, San Antonio, Texas, 1999.
6. Tony Zepeda, interview by the authors, 2003.

**Chapter 19** Putting on the Finishing Touches
1. Rosemary Jensen, speech at Romans Institute, San Antonio, Texas, 1999.
2. Rosemary Jensen, remarks at the BSF staff Day of Prayer, May 2000.
3. Ibid.
4. Ernest Hastings, Kay Gudnason, Paul Hesson, and Dr. Grant Whipple, speeches at the dedication of the San Antonio BSF headquarters, September 12, 1981.
5. Wetherell Johnson, dedicatory prayer at ibid.
6. Ernest Hastings, speech at ibid.
7. Francis Schaeffer, speech at ibid.

**Chapter 20** Settling In
1. Rosemary Jensen, speech at Romans Institute, San Antonio, Texas, 1999.
2. Rosemary Jensen, remarks at the BSF staff Day of Prayer, May 2000.
3. Susy Harbick, interview by the authors, 2005.
4. Rosemary Jensen, interview by the authors, 2005.
5. Rosemary Jensen, speech at Romans Institute, 1999.
6. Rosemary Jensen, remarks at the BSF staff Day of Prayer, May 2000.
7. Ibid.
8. Ibid.
9. Ibid.
10. Ibid.
11. Ernest Hastings, interview by the authors, 2004.
12. Jane Roach, interview by the authors, 2005.
13. Ibid.

**Chapter 21** God Closes a Chapter
1. Wetherell Johnson, *Created for Commitment* (Wheaton, IL: Tyndale, 1982), 311.

2. Jerry Prenzlow, interview by the authors, 2006.

3. Jane Roach, interview by the authors, 2005.

4. *BSF Newsletter,* May 1983.

5. *BSF Newsletter,* May 1984.

6. Ibid.

7. Anne Graham Lotz, *My Heart's Cry* (Nashville: Thomas Nelson, 2002), 109–10.

8. Larry Heppes, interview by the authors, 2005.

**Chapter 22** On the Same Page

1. Jan Myers, interview by the authors, 2005.

2. "Home Discussion Pages Added," *BSF Newsletter,* December 1984.

3. *BSF Newsletter,* May 1986.

4. Rosemary Jensen, speech at Romans Institute, San Antonio, Texas, 1999.

5. Kitty Magee, *BSF Newsletter,* Christmas 1984.

6. Janice Pinckney, interview by the authors, 2003.

7. Anna Kingsbury, interview by the authors, 2004.

8. Jane Roach, interview by the authors, 2005.

9. Anna Kingsbury, interview by the authors, 2004.

**Chapter 23** Making More Room

1. Rosemary Jensen, remarks at the BSF staff Day of Prayer, May 2000.

2. Rosemary Jensen, "Remarks from Rosemary," *BSF Newsletter,* May 1983.

3. Anna Kingsbury, interview by the authors, 2004.

4. Wetherell Johnson, speech at the Oakland Coliseum, Oakland, California, December 1, 1979.

5. Ernest Hastings, interview by the authors, 2004.

6. Rosemary Jensen, remarks at the BSF staff Day of Prayer, May 2000.

7. Carolyn Edwards, interview by the authors, 2007.

8. Jeanette Tompkins, interview by the authors, 2004.

9. *BSF Newsletter,* October 1970; *BSF Newsletter,* Christmas 1978; *BSF Newsletter,* Christmas 1990; *BSF Magazine,* May 1996; *BSF Magazine,* May 2001.

10. Rosemary Jensen, remarks at the BSF staff Day of Prayer, May 2000.

11. Rosemary Jensen, "Remarks from Rosemary," *BSF Newsletter,* Christmas 1987.

12. Jane Roach, interview by the authors, 2005.

**Chapter 24** A Universal Body

1. Rosemary Jensen, remarks at the BSF staff Day of Prayer, May 2000.

2. Kitty and Bob Magee, *BSF Newsletter,* May 1985.

3. Rosemary Jensen, "Remarks from Rosemary," *BSF Newsletter,* May

1985.

4. Pearl Hamilton, *BSF Newsletter,* May 1986.

5. Cheryl Hutchinson and Pat Edwards, interview by the authors, 2003.

6. Shirley Tan, interview by the authors, 2003.

7. Susy Harbick, interview by the authors, 2005.

8. Ann Colmer, interview by Anna Kingsbury, 2003.

9. Holly Holmquist, interview by the authors, 2003.

10. Anita Newton, Ann Colmer, interview by Anna Kingsbury, 2003.

11. Ernest Hastings, interview by the authors, 2004.

12. Rosemary Jensen, "Remarks from Rosemary," *BSF Newsletter,* May 1987.

13. Linda Hunt, interview by the authors, 2003.

14. Barb Watson, interview with Anna Kingsbury, 2003.

**Chapter 25** Person to Person

1. Rosemary Jensen, speech at Romans Institute, San Antonio, Texas, 1999.

2. Gwyneth MacKenzie, interview by Anna Kingsbury, 2003.

3. Candy Staggs, interview by the authors, 2008.

4. Holly Holmquist, interview by the authors, 2003.

5. Gordon Ziegler, interview by the authors, 2003.

6. Linda Hunt, interview by the authors, 2003.

7. Donna Read, interview by the authors, 2003.

8. Jan Heal, interview by the authors, 2003.

9. Barbara Chrouser, interview by the authors, 2003.

10. Carolyn Edwards, interview by the authors, 2007.

11. Chris Morris, interview by the authors, 2003.

12. Val Atkinson, interview by Anna Kingsbury, 2003.

13. *BSF Newsletter,* May 1989.

**Chapter 26** Growing a Different Way

1. Jane Roach, interview by the authors, 2005.

2. Ibid.

3. Chuck Musfeldt, interview by the authors, 2007.

4. Barb Watson, interview by Anna Kingsbury, 2003.

5. Dottie McKissick, interview by the authors, 2005.

6. Rosemary Jensen, "Remarks from Rosemary," *BSF Newsletter,* Christmas 1984.

**Chapter 27** Mission to Developing Nations

1. Rosemary Jensen, speech at Romans Institute, San Antonio, Texas, 1999.

2. Chris Morris, interview by the authors, 2003.

3. Rosemary Jensen, speech at Romans Institute, San Antonio, Texas, 1999.

4. Susy Harbick, interview by the authors, 2005.

5. Rosemary Jensen, interview by the authors, 2005.

6. Barbara Chrouser, interview by the authors, 2003.

7. *BSF Newsletter,* May 1993.

8. Genelle and David Pipes, interview by the authors, 2003.

9. Rosemary Jensen, *BSF Newsletter,* April 1998.

10.  *BSF Newsletter,* April 1998.

**Chapter 28** Welcoming the Next Generation

1. Susy Harbick, interview by the authors, 2005.

2. Rosemary Jensen, speech at Romans Institute, San Antonio, Texas, 1999.

3. Rosemary Jensen, "Remarks from Rosemary," *BSF Newsletter,* Christmas 1995.

4. Janice Pinckney, interview by the authors, 2003.

5. Susy Harbick, *BSF Magazine,* May 1997.

6. Anna Kingsbury and Eileen Smith, *BSF Newsletter,* May 1997.

7. Janice Pinckney, interview by the authors, 2003.

8. Norm McBride, interview by the authors, 2005.

9. Carolyn Edwards, interview by the authors, 2007.

10.  Shirley Mills, interview by the authors, 2003.

11.  Rollin and Marion Mann, interview by the authors, 2005.

12.  Susan Crawford, *BSF Magazine,* May 1997.

13.  Ann Colmer, interview by Anna Kingsbury, 2003.

14.  Rosemary Jensen, "Remarks from Rosemary," *BSF Magazine,* May 1997.

**Chapter 29** New in the Cycle

1. Rosemary Jensen, speech at Romans Institute, San Antonio, Texas, 1999.

2. Rosemary Jensen, *BSF Newsletter,* May 1994.

3. Jane Roach, interview by the authors, 2005.

4. Rosemary Jensen, *BSF Newsletter,* May 1995.

5. Jane Roach, interview by the authors, 2005.

6. Rosemary Jensen, speech at Romans Institute, 1999.

**Chapter 30** A Farewell

1. Rosemary Jensen, *BSF Magazine,* May 2000.

2. Susy Harbick, interview by the authors, 2005.

3. Chuck Musfeldt, interview by the authors, 2007.

4. Ernest Hastings, interview by the authors, 2004.

5. Shirley Mills, interview by the authors, 2003.

6. Rosemary Jensen, remarks at the BSF staff Day of Prayer, May 2000.

## Chapter 31 Another Change of Leadership
1. *BSF Magazine,* May 2000.
2. Carolyn Edwards, interview by the authors, 2007.
3. Jean Nystrand, interviews by the authors, 2003, 2007.
4. Suzanne Sloan, interview by the authors, 2008.
5. Ernest Hastings, interview by the authors, 2004.

## Chapter 32 Third-Generation Vision
1. Jean Nystrand, Teaching Leader Institute, San Antonio, Texas, summer 2000.
2. Ron Rogg, interview by the authors, 2008.
3. Garth Bolinder, interview by the authors, 2008.
4. Jean Nystrand, Teaching Leader Institute, San Antonio, Texas, summer 2000.
5. Garth Bolinder, interview by the authors, 2008.
6. Jean Nystrand, Area Advisors meeting, San Antonio, Texas, November 2002.

## Chapter 33 Growing Separate Ways
1. Susy Harbick, interview by the authors, 2005.
2. Jean Nystrand, Teaching Leader Institute, San Antonio, Texas, summer 2000.
3. Suzanne Sloan, interview by the authors, 2008.
4. Barbara Reoach, interview by the authors, 2008.
5. Chuck Musfeldt, interview by the authors, 2007.
6. Jean Nystrand, interview by the authors, 2007.
7. Garth Bolinder, interview by the authors, 2008.
8. Ernest Hastings, interview by the authors, 2004.

## Chapter 34 One Thousand Classes
1. Ron Rogg, interview by the authors, 2008.
2. Candy Staggs, interview by the authors, 2008.
3. Chuck Musfeldt, interview by the authors, 2007.
4. Ron Rogg, interview by the authors, 2008.
5. Nick Sennert, interview by the authors, 2008.
6. Gary Liaboe, interview by the authors, 2008.
7. Barbara Reoach, interview by the authors, 2008.

## Chapter 35 Looking to the Future
1. Garth Bolinder, interview by the authors, 2008.
2. Jean Nystrand, Teaching Leader Institute, San Antonio, Texas, summer 2000.

## Epilogue
1. Chuck Musfeldt, interview by the authors, 2008.

2. Jean Nystrand, interview by the authors, 2008.

3. Chuck Musfeldt, interview by the authors, 2008.

4. Jean Nystrand, interview by the authors, 2008.

5. Chuck Musfeldt, interview by the authors, 2008; see Wetherell Johnson, *Created for Commitment* (Wheaton, IL: Tyndale, 1982), 186.

6. Garth Bolinder, interview by the authors, 2008.